# Self-Control

Good self-control is a crucial factor in the distribution of life outcomes, ranging from success at school and work, to good mental and physical health, and to satisfying romantic relationships. While in the last decades psychologists have learned much about this all-important trait, both social theory and politics have not caught up. Many academics and policymakers still seem to believe that everybody has unlimited capacity for self-control and that maintaining discipline is purely a matter of volition. This book shows that such beliefs are fundamentally mistaken. It presents the state-of-the-art in research on self-control, explains why this trait has been largely overlooked, and sets out the profound implications of this psychological research for moral responsibility, distributive justice and public policy. It shows that the growing emphasis in politics on "personal responsibility" is deeply problematic, and outlines alternatives more in accord with human psychology.

W. L. TIEMEIJER is Professor of Behavioural Science and Public Policy at Erasmus University Rotterdam and a Senior Research Fellow at the Netherlands Scientific Council for Government Policy, The Hague.

# Self-Control

Individual Differences and
What They Mean for Personal
Responsibility and Public Policy

W. L. TIEMEIJER

CAMBRIDGE
UNIVERSITY PRESS

# CAMBRIDGE
## UNIVERSITY PRESS

University Printing House, Cambridge CB2 8BS, United Kingdom

One Liberty Plaza, 20th Floor, New York, NY 10006, USA

477 Williamstown Road, Port Melbourne, VIC 3207, Australia

314–321, 3rd Floor, Plot 3, Splendor Forum, Jasola District Centre, New Delhi – 110025, India

103 Penang Road, #05–06/07, Visioncrest Commercial, Singapore 238467

Cambridge University Press is part of the University of Cambridge.

It furthers the University's mission by disseminating knowledge in the pursuit of education, learning, and research at the highest international levels of excellence.

www.cambridge.org
Information on this title: www.cambridge.org/9781009098564
DOI: 10.1017/9781009089678

© W. L. Tiemeijer 2022

First published 2022

Printed in the United Kingdom by TJ Books Limited, Padstow Cornwall

*A catalogue record for this publication is available from the British Library.*

ISBN 978-1-009-09856-4 Hardback

*To Alice*

*The qualities most useful to ourselves are, first of all, superior reason and understanding, by which we are capable of discerning the remote consequences of all our actions, and of foreseeing the advantage or detriment which is likely to result from them: and secondly, self-command, by which we are enabled to abstain from present pleasure or to endure present pain, in order to obtain a greater pleasure or to avoid a greater pain in some future time. In the union of those qualities consists the virtue of prudence, of all the virtues that which is most useful to the individual.*

Adam Smith, *The Theory of Moral Sentiments*, Part IV, chapter 2

# Contents

# Figures

# Tables

# Acknowledgments

The intellectual foundation for this book was laid during a fellowship year at the Center for Advanced Study in the Behavioral Sciences (CASBS) at Stanford University. I want to thank all the wonderful people at CASBS for the unique opportunity they gave me to study at this endlessly inspiring and stimulating place.

Many people have helped me with valuable comments, criticisms, and other forms of support. They include Mark Bovens, Frans Brom, Ruth Chang, Phylicia Codrington, Godfried Engbersen, Paul Jargowsky, Anton Hemerijck, Annemarie Kalis, Anne-Greet Keizer, Terry Maroney, Batja Mesquita, Corien Prins, Denise de Ridder, Maureen Sie, Yayouk Willems, and Cas Wouters. A heartfelt thank you! I want to mention and thank two people in particular: Joel Anderson and Owen Flanagan. Without your warm friendship and invaluable help in the various stages of the project, this book would simply never have seen the light of day.

# 1 Introduction

This book is about self-control. I nevertheless begin with a few words on cognitive ability – or what in everyday life is often referred to as "intelligence."

To say that people differ in cognitive ability is stating the obvious. It is a basic fact of life. A well-ordered society accommodates these differences, for instance by providing different educational tracks and employment opportunities, some cognitively more demanding than others. It would be absurd to require all children to attain the highest educational level and obtain a PhD. It would be equally absurd to expect all adults to be able to do the intellectually most difficult work.

This is reflected in our morality. Nobody blames people of only modest cognitive ability for not reaching the top of the educational or labor market ladder. This capacity is not a matter of volition, but largely determined by genes and early upbringing. Since both genetic inheritance and childhood family environment are beyond our control, it would be unfair to hold anyone fully responsible if, as a result, they do less well in life than others – just as it would be unfair to blame a five-foot-tall youth for not being a top basketball player.

All this seems self-evident.

*Why then are things so different for self-control?* Some people are clearly better at maintaining self-control than others – at focusing their attention, inhibiting their urges and impulses, and thus achieving their long-term goals. Others make lofty resolutions but fail to realize them time and again because they do not persist and easily succumb to temptation. Their lives are marked by an endless string of self-control failures.

But in stark contrast to differences in cognitive ability, differences in self-control are *not* mirrored in how society is organized. The educational system caters to children with different levels of cognitive talent, but not to children with varying levels of self-control. Schools may offer remedial teaching or special education for children with extremely poor self-control, but that is it. The same goes for the labor market. Some jobs require only limited cognitive skills and are mostly taken by the lower educated, whereas other positions require elaborate cognitive qualities and are mostly filled by the higher educated. But differences in self-control never seem to play a role. Job advertisements never ask for "good self-control." Employers apparently think it is not so important, or simply assume that everybody has it.

Again, this is reflected in our morality. No reasonable human being would blame a fellow citizen of only modest cognitive ability for not obtaining a university degree, for being unable to do cognitively demanding work, or for failing to understand abstruse regulations. Most of us carefully avoid being judgmental about differences in intelligence. In contrast, many people have no qualms about blaming their fellow citizens for poor self-control. If someone fails to muster the discipline to study hard, get a job, live healthy, and pay the bills on time, the consequences are for her alone to shoulder. After all, everyone *knows* these behaviors are important. People who lack self-control only have themselves to blame. Next time, try harder!

The message of this book, however, is that self-control is not just a matter of volition. Self-control strength is a personality trait that, like cognitive ability, is largely determined by genes and early upbringing, and it remains relatively stable over the course of adult life. And like cognitive ability, self-control is limited. Some of us do better than others, but even champions of willpower cannot control themselves indefinitely. Sooner or later, they give in. Sooner or later, there comes a point when saying "just try harder!" is as absurd as saying "just be more intelligent!"

These psychological realities have profound implications for what a just and well-ordered society looks like. Such a society should not only accommodate differences in cognitive ability but also take into account that self-control capacity is limited, with some having less of it than others. Unfortunately, most Western societies are far removed from that situation. In fact, more or less unwittingly, we have constructed an "iron cage" that poorly befits the realities of the human mind. As a result, all of us are increasingly at risk of falling into a trap we have set for ourselves.

## *Keeping Up with Change*

Numerous studies have revealed that good self-control contributes to a broad range of desirable life outcomes: better school achievement and work performance, better physical and mental health, more satisfying relationships, less financial struggle and fewer setbacks, and less deviant and delinquent behavior. Differences in self-control thus have a major impact on the distribution of life chances. Although this should be more than enough to warrant serious attention, interest in self-control – in both social theory and everyday politics – has always been tenuous. Those who call the tune in these areas do not seem to view differences in self-control as a phenomenon of great importance in matters of justice and government.

What explains this relative neglect? One reason may be that much of the psychological understanding of self-control is fairly recent. It is only in the last decades that scientists have come to better understand the sources of self-control and the detrimental effects of, for instance, chronic stress and sleep deprivation. And it is only in the last decades that it became possible to peek inside the brain and see how neurological processes affect self-control. Another reason may be that, until not long ago, there simply was less cause to study the role of self-control in our lives. Several centuries ago, the average person, to make a living, needed muscle power and the stamina to work long hours on the land or the assembly line, not the ability to keep smiling to irate customers complaining about the service. Paths in life were relatively fixed, social control was strong, and modern-day problems such as impulse buying and overeating had yet to be invented.

All this has changed. Work today requires very different aptitudes, such as the ability to concentrate and sustain attention, meet strict deadlines, and work in teams, while rude and uncontrolled behavior may get you fired. Willpower has become more important than muscle power. The traditional institutional and social structures, moreover, have lost much of their sway. Not straying off course has become one's own responsibility, and social benefits have become conditional on proper conduct. Perhaps most visibly, in almost every domain of life, the number of options and temptations has virtually exploded. Without ever leaving the couch, you can buy almost anything, day and night. And thanks to social media, a single flash of impulsiveness – a careless tweet, a juicy picture – can suffice to ruin your life.[1]

In sum, good self-control has become a crucial factor in the distribution of life outcomes – at times even more important than cognitive ability. The good news is that psychology in the intervening decades has learned a lot about this trait, placing us in a much better position to recognize and negotiate this reality. The bad news is that the worlds of social theory and politics have not caught up. Many of the theories and policies that define contemporary society were developed decades ago, when much less was known about the psychology of self-control, and good self-control was not that important anyway. But as the world keeps evolving and our knowledge keeps growing, these theories and policies seem increasingly out of date, no longer suited to the demands of modern society.

Hence this book. Its goal is to set out the state-of-the-art in our knowledge of self-control and to explore the implications of this knowledge for some prominent ideas about society and policy in general, and for the current heavy emphasis on personal responsibility in particular. The book consists of two parts:

- Part I discusses the relevant psychology. To what degree is self-control correlated with various individual and social outcomes? What factors undermine self-control and why? Can self-control be improved? And why are some people more motivated to exercise self-control than others?
- Part II explores the broader implications of these psychological findings. Why has self-control become increasingly important for navigating life? What do the research findings mean for moral responsibility? And what are the consequences for distributive justice?

The final chapter addresses the crucial question "What is to be done?" What does all this mean for society and policy? It results in three conclusions that partly transcend the subject of self-control, applying to politics and government more generally.

So that is the overall structure of the book. In the rest of this introductory chapter, I provide an overview of the main concepts, findings, and arguments, including my conclusions and resulting recommendations.

## 1.1 Individual Differences in Self-Control

Self-control challenges are ubiquitous and woven into the very fabric of life. They begin when the alarm clock sounds in the morning, as it requires willpower to get out of bed on time. They keep coming until it is time to sleep again, when one must resist the urge to stay up late and keep watching TV. In between these two moments, the day is packed with self-control challenges – remaining friendly to colleagues, retaining focus during tedious meetings, tackling long-overdue paperwork, making that difficult phone call, refraining from eating and drinking too much. One study found that we spend almost a quarter of our day in some way inhibiting our impulses and urges.[2]

But what exactly is "self-control"? The psychologist Denise de Ridder and her colleagues provide a useful definition: Self-control is "the capacity to alter or override dominant response tendencies and to regulate behavior, thoughts, and emotions."[3] Self-control involves situations of conflict, often between responses that lead to immediate reward versus responses that promote some desirable future goal. One should read a boring report that will be discussed in tomorrow's meeting, but surfing the net and checking social media beckons. One should save money for next month's rent, but the new flat-screen TV is on sale now. Self-control is roughly equivalent to willpower: It is the power to delay gratification.

Self-control not only involves *inhibiting* behavior but also *initiating* behavior, such as going to the gym or starting to study for an exam. This is sometimes overlooked as most self-control research focuses on the inhibition of some impulse or urge. In everyday language, moreover, the term usually refers to instances of *not* doing something rather than starting something. But self-control as defined above encompasses both. It also means "altering or overriding" the "response tendency" to remain passive. Inhibition and initiation are, in fact, two sides of the same coin. They both concern the *regulation* of behavior toward some desired goal, just like a car's brake and accelerator serve the same purpose: to get to one's destination quickly and safely.

### Bridging the Gap

In functional terms, self-control can be viewed as the capacity to act on one's intentions – to bridge the gap between "choice-making" and "choice-following."[4] This gap is one of the perennial problems of life. We all *know* that we should pay attention, eat healthy, stop procrastinating, and so forth. Then why do we so often fail to *act* accordingly? Aristotle was already puzzled by this question. "How does it happen that thinking is sometimes followed by action and sometimes not, sometimes by motion, sometimes not?".[5]

"Self-control failure" can thus be defined as a failure to act on one's intentions. Here it is useful to distinguish between two types of self-control failure. The first encompasses instances of "bypassing of the will" – the classic example being the attention lapse. I am doing my best to follow the lecture when I suddenly realize that my mind has been wandering. This is not something one chooses to do; it just happens. Such moments of inattention are more likely when one has already grown tired after listening attentively for some time. The second type of self-control failure encompasses instances of "weakness of will" – the classic example being the breaking of New Year's resolutions.[6] I fail to live up to my earlier intentions because at some point the desire for the forbidden fruit has become so overwhelming that I am no longer able to resist. Although I know perfectly well that it would be better to stick to my resolutions, I cave in anyway.

The distinction between these two types of failure in self-control is mostly analytical. In practice, the boundary is far from clear-cut. Both mechanisms will often be in play simultaneously, making it hard to determine which one tipped the scale. But either way, the result is the same: a disconnect between intention and behavior.

## *Perfectly Self-Controlled People?*

Classical economic theory assumes that people are perfectly rational. When making choices, they use all of the information at their disposal, process this information in a logical and statistically sound manner, and unfailingly select the option that yields the highest utility. By now, it is widely accepted that this assumption is incorrect. Psychological research – in particular the work of Amos Tversky and Daniel Kahneman – has shown that real people make all kinds of "mistakes," basing their choices on incomplete information, making logical and statistical errors, relying on gut feelings, and so forth. Perfectly rational people do not exist.

How about their close siblings, perfectly *self controlled* people? Do such people exist? And what would they look like? In classical economic theory, there is no such thing as limited willpower. Economists therefore have no reason to contemplate such questions. In psychology, there is no such thing as *un*limited willpower. Psychologists therefore have no reason to contemplate such questions either. For an answer we must resort to philosophy. According to Alfred Mele, a perfectly self-controlled person is someone who:

- exercises self-control in all domains of life. Someone who is very disciplined at work but shows weakness of will in drinking and eating is not perfectly self-controlled;
- never exercises self-control errantly but only in support of his or her better judgments, values, principles, and the like;
- exercises self-control whenever he or she reflectively deems it appropriate to do so;
- and whose self-control is perfectly effective. His or her exertions of self-control always succeed in supporting what they are aiming to support.[7]

Obviously, perfectly self-controlled people are just as imaginary as perfectly rational people. Even the most disciplined person will not meet these criteria. There are two reasons why people fall short of the ideal – and some more than others. The first has to do with *trait* self-control, the second with *state* self-control.

## Trait Self-Control

An individual's baseline level of self-control strength is part of her personality and is therefore called *trait* self-control. As is often the case with personality traits, the distribution of this capacity follows a normal distribution. At one end, we find what the philosopher Joseph Heath has dubbed "the self-control aristocracy" – a small group of lucky dogs who are exceptionally good at delaying gratification and therefore likely to do well in life.[8] At the other end, we find their antipodes: people who act on every impulse and seem incapable of controlling themselves, stumbling from one hapless incident to another. Most of us are somewhere in between – not very good at self-control but not very bad either.

What factors determine where one is situated in this distribution? It partly depends on early upbringing. Some children grow up in warm, responsive, and supportive families that foster self-control. Their parents value this trait, set a good example, teach them self-control techniques ("First count to ten") and reward them for not acting on every impulse. Other children grow up in less conducive circumstances. Their parents have poor self-control themselves, lack the skills for teaching their offspring how to do any better, and family life revolves around immediate gratification. But the capacity for self-control is also a matter of nature. Just as some people are genetically endowed with more talent for intellectual achievement, some are genetically endowed with more talent for self-control. About 60 percent of individual differences in self-control can be attributed to differences in genes. So when it comes to this other important quality, some people have a better starting position in life than others *by nature*.

## State Self-Control

But readers with good trait self-control should not conclude that this book is not about them, because one rule applies to all: Self-control is limited. The longer we have to exert self-control, the harder it gets. Sooner or later, even the most strong-willed people will be overcome by mental fatigue; their minds will begin to wander, and their impulses and urges will gain the upper hand. This phenomenon is, of course, all too familiar. We all know how, after a long day at work requiring continuous focus, placating demanding costumers, foregoing drinks at the office party, and keeping one's cool with the children causing a ruckus – we all know how, after all these challenges to our self-control, we may find ourselves raiding the fridge late in the evening, gorging ourselves on unhealthy snacks.

It is not only the prior exertion of self-control that can undermine self-control; other conditions, such as stress, can have the same effect. It is much harder to control yourself when pressure is mounting. This is particularly evident in people who get into financial trouble. Chances are that some readers of this book, at some point in their lives, have experienced a period of indebtedness or poverty.[9] If so, they may have discovered that, perhaps to their surprise, this precarious situation undermined their mental functioning. Chances are that their behavior became less controlled and more erratic. It became harder to stay focused, keep urges and impulses in check, and stay calm and clear-headed, while it also became harder not to lapse into passivity, but keep doing whatever was necessary to fend off further financial trouble.

Another condition that undermines self-control is insufficient sleep. The shortage of sleep alters the balance in neurobiological processes responsible for self-control, thus making failure more likely. Feeling tired is also a major cause of negative mood. As a strategy to alleviate this negative mood, people tend to succumb to temptation – chocolate, alcohol, new shoes! – in the hope that this will make them feel better. Moreover, reduced self-control can make it harder to get to bed in time, thus potentially setting off a downward spiral. The solution to all this misery is obvious – get enough sleep! – but unfortunately, people tend to do the very opposite. In much of the world, the average amount of sleep is declining. Precisely in this day and age when self-control has become so important, people are cutting down on one of its main wellsprings.

The message is that self-control capacity not only depends on genes and early upbringing but also on the particulars of the situation. Psychologists speak of *state* self-control: one's *operational* capacity for self-control in a *specific* situation at a *specific* moment in time. Even those fortunate people who normally have tremendous discipline – Joseph Heath's "self-control aristocrats" – may find themselves in tough situations that markedly impair their capabilities, resulting in behaviors they would otherwise never exhibit, and would probably denounce as "utterly irrational."

## Improving Self-Control?

Is it possible to improve self-control through training, education, or some other type of intervention? It depends. In their first years of life, children are quite susceptible to interventions as their capacity for self-control is still developing. But once this capacity begins to crystallize, things become harder. In popular psychology, it is sometimes claimed that "willpower is like a muscle" that can be strengthened through regular exercise. As more research findings come in, however, the conclusion seems to be that exercise hardly makes a difference. The muscle metaphor does not hold.

There may yet be alternatives. Several techniques can help people to utilize their limited capacities more cleverly and efficiently, and thus to better deal with the ongoing stream of self-control challenges that cross their path. In Chapter 4, I recount the most common tips and tricks found in the self-help literature. These range from devising little "if-then" plans and nutritional advice to strategies such as avoiding temptation all together. For readers eager to work on their own self-control, this summary may serve as a one-stop shop for the techniques currently on the market. Unfortunately, there is a catch. If everyone were taught these techniques, the net result would be that individual differences in self-control would actually widen. Those who already did poorly would only fall further behind.

## Self-Control Motivation

If self-control is limited, an important question is how best to spend one's available "budget" for self-control. What is the optimal allocation of this scarce resource?

This brings us to the role of motivation. The mere fact that some people are blessed with excellent self-control does not necessarily mean that they will always *utilize* this capacity. It is like the difference between having a tool and using it. Whether you will use this tool or not depends on your preferences. People will be highly motivated to exert self-control for goals they consider important – say, being successful at school or work – but less motivated to use this capacity for goals they do not care about – say, becoming a chess grandmaster. Unhealthy behaviors such as smoking, therefore, do not necessarily indicate poor self-control. An inveterate smoker may simply value his daily dose of nicotine more than his future health and exhibit great powers of self-control in other domains of life, such as work.

So what determines a person's goals? It could be almost anything, of course. The spectrum runs from needs and desires, norms and values, social or cultural pressures, to cues and incentives in the environment. In this book, however, I discuss one factor in particular, namely a personality trait called "time orientation." Some people are, *in general*, more oriented toward the future and the long-term goals they have set themselves, whereas others are, *in general*, more oriented toward the here-and-now and opportunities for immediate gratification. This across-the-board tendency is part of their character and may affect their overall motivation to exert self-control: the more oriented toward the future, the stronger this motivation.

The distinction between self-control *motivation* and self-control *capacity* is extremely important. One of the principal arguments of this book is that confounding them can result in serious injustices.

Yet unfortunately the distinction is not always made – neither in the scholarly literature nor in everyday life. To some degree this is understandable as the two often go together. People who score low on self-control capacity tend to score low on self-control motivation and vice versa. This is hardly surprising since most of us derive little pleasure from activities we are not good at.[10]

But again, these are fundamentally different concepts. Being *unable* to control behavior is not the same as being *unwilling* to control behavior. In many places in this book, I therefore speak of "self-control *capacity*" rather than just "self-control." By using this – strictly speaking, tautological – term, I hope to avoid any misunderstanding about what is being discussed, and to ensure that capacity and motivation are not confused. This will give us a better view of psychological reality – a view that may have far-reaching consequences for society and public policy.

## 1.2 The End of Personal Responsibility?

Which brings me to the second part of this book. Those who govern society may be tempted to shrug their shoulders over the above psychological findings. Their job is to make laws and institutions, not to fathom the intricacies of whatever goes on inside the black box of people's minds. But they would be mistaken. These findings on self-control have profound implications for a concept that lies at the very heart of contemporary political discourse: personal responsibility.

Let me explain. Suppose it were true that people are perfectly self-controlled. Then, barring external obstacles or mental delusions, all behavior must be seen as voluntary and intentional. So, if someone knows he should consume fewer calories but nonetheless goes for fast food time and again, then apparently this is what he wants. He may pretend otherwise, but when push comes to shove, he prefers hamburgers and cheesecake over good health. Of course, he is entirely free to make this choice. But if later in life he is struck by some lifestyle disease, he should not complain as he only has himself to blame. Society is under no moral obligation to cover his costs.

Or suppose two people have equal talents and opportunities, but one becomes rich and successful whereas the other ends up destitute. This unequal outcome can only be explained by a difference in *choices*.

Perhaps the first person chose to study and work hard because she wanted to be successful later in life, whereas the second person preferred to take it easy and have a good time now. Again, both are entirely free to make those choices, but they must shoulder the consequences themselves. Society is under no moral obligation to lift the burden of those who take no responsibility for their own future. In fact, people who are lazy *deserve* to be poor.

This line of reasoning may sound familiar – perhaps all too familiar for some readers. Over the past decades, the "personal responsibility" discourse has been trumpeted everywhere in the Western world, and has become the bedrock of many public policies and social practices. In our day and age, people are expected to invest in their education and labor market prospects, live healthy and care for the environment, save for a rainy day and arrange proper insurance, and so forth. If, despite all the policies and incentives promoting these behaviors, people act otherwise, there can only be one conclusion: that is what they *prefer*. They have *chosen* to behave irresponsibly.

Or have they? What if something else was going on? What if the individuals above did not end up miserably because they were *unwilling* to do the responsible thing, but because they were *unable* to do the responsible thing? What if they lacked the *capacity* to resist high-calorie foods or work hard every day? Perhaps they had the bad fortune of being endowed with poor trait self-control. Or perhaps their life circumstances were so precarious that their self-control capacity was chronically exhausted. These are not matters of volition. We do not get to choose our parents and how they raise us, nor do we have complete control over our life circumstances. Yet these factors determine self-control. It may thus be unfair to insist that these people only have themselves to blame. Of course, it could well be that their fate is entirely of their own making. But we should at least acknowledge the *possibility* of the alternative explanation: They really did their utmost best but lacked the required capacity for self-control.

In short, self-control research casts doubt on a fundamental assumption underlying current policies. This is the assumption that – except for a tiny minority of extreme outliers or clinical cases – all adults possess the mental capacities necessary for being a responsible agent, *including* the capacity for self-control. But, as the previous section suggested, this assumption may be unwarranted. Poor self control is not a rare condition but is actually quite common. Even those who under normal circumstances do pretty well may encounter such difficult circumstances that their self-control is seriously compromised. So what does this mean for policies that implicitly assume that all of us have perfect self-control? Are such policies fair? We do not blame people for the consequences of their poor intelligence because IQ is not something one gets to choose. Why then should things be different for the consequences of (bouts of) poor self-control?

These are important questions. But they are also dangerous questions as they lead us straight into a quagmire. The moment we allow for the possibility that, *in some instances*, poor self-control may be a valid reason for mitigating responsibility, two formidable problems arise: one metaphysical and one epistemological. In Chapters 8 and 9 I attempt to defuse these challenges. To give a taste of the argument of these more philosophical chapters, let me briefly sketch both problems and summarize my proposed solutions.

## Is Anyone Ever Responsible?

The metaphysical problem is that once we begin searching for the *real* causes of one's behavior, the floodgates are open. The closer we look, the more behaviors that were assumed to be free and voluntary turn out to be caused by circumstances beyond our control, such as genetic inheritance, early upbringing, and social background. This is a classic slippery slope. Before we know it, we are forced to conclude that no one is ever responsible for anything. Everything people say and do is the inevitable result of a long chain of cause and effect, set in motion even before they were born. It may feel as if we have freedom of choice, but this is an illusion as things could not have gone otherwise. This means that no one ever "deserves" to be blamed or praised for anything, and that no one ever "deserves" to be punished or rewarded. The whole idea that we can distinguish between responsible and irresponsible conduct is a "piece of metaphysical nonsense".[11]

If this is true, we have a massive problem. This conclusion goes against our deepest intuitions and provides no basis for social coordination. How could people ever successfully live together in a world in which no one ever is to be blamed or praised for anything?[12] So, the million-dollar question is this: Can we be more responsive to the self-control findings of psychology on the one hand, *without* having to entirely abandon the idea of moral responsibility on the other?

*Rescuing Moral Responsibility*

As I will show, the answer is yes. It is indeed possible to be more responsive to these findings while preserving the concept of moral responsibility. The key is to remember that we are exploring the implications of the limited nature of self-control *for society and policy*. This means that the perspective of science is not the only relevant perspective. We must also engage the perspective of the *subjects* who make up society and the perspective of the *policymakers* who must determine what will work best for society. In other words, we must ask not only what ascriptions of responsibility most accord with the objective facts but also what ascriptions of responsibility people *feel and believe* to be fair and what *ascriptions* of responsibility *work best* to achieve collective goals. I will call these three disparate perspectives the objective standpoint, the subjective standpoint, and the instrumental standpoint. The key is to recognize that judgments of responsibility *must be informed by all three standpoints*.

In many cases the imperative to consider all three standpoints will create few problems, because in many cases they point in the same direction. If someone fell down the stairs and had to be rushed to the hospital, thereby failing to do his chores, meet his deadline, or apply for a job, there would be little debate. Each standpoint leads to the same conclusion: this person should be excused. But in other cases, these standpoints may pull in different directions. There may be situations where someone can plausibly argue that, given his tough and stressful circumstances, he could not possibly muster the self-control to do his chores, meet the deadline, or apply for the job, and therefore should be excused from responsibility. In such cases, we might go along with his defense or we might decide that, *despite* his difficult circumstances, he should be held responsible *anyway* – for instance because we want to uphold and communicate certain social norms, or because letting him off the hook "just does not feel right." In other words, even if a person not really *is* responsible, we may have good reasons to nonetheless *hold* him responsible.

This is the heart of the solution. By introducing two extra standpoints, moral responsibility is no longer exclusively determined by what caused the behavior, and thus can be preserved. Unfortunately, the solution comes at a price. The consequence of this tripartite approach is that no single and unambiguous answer can be given to the question of to what extent poor self-control mitigates responsibility. Sometimes the conclusion will be that, all things considered, the facts and considerations for upholding responsibility are more compelling. At other times, the conclusion will be that, all things considered, the facts and considerations against assigning responsibility are more compelling. It all depends on the circumstances.

This is highly impractical. By adopting the tripartite approach, we may have rescued the concept of moral responsibility but we get another, hardly less vexing problem in return. For society to function properly, we cannot go with "it all depends on the circumstances." To build a robust social order, we need clarity and guidance. We need rules to go by in matters of self-control and responsibility.

At this point, I return to the empirical research. Based on this research, I argue that it is best to take as the *default assumption* that all people have sufficient capacity for exerting self-control and can therefore be held responsible for their conduct. So long as it is not proven otherwise, this is the rule to go by. At the same time, we should be open to the possibility that in *specific* instances, people's self-control may be so poor that it is only fair to excuse them from (full) responsibility. Whether this is indeed the case is a matter of good judgment that must be informed by the answers to three questions that correspond to the three standpoints: What are the facts, what feels right, and what works?

This, in a nutshell, is my answer to the question about the proper relationship between self-control and responsibility. It does not definitively settle all matters regarding self-control and responsibility as it provides only rough guidelines and allows for exceptions. Although some may lament this lack of closure, I argue that this is actually a strength. It guarantees that the conversation will always continue and that, when exceptions accumulate, the question will arise whether the rules are in need of revision. And here we get to the heart of the matter: *The time for revision has come.* More on that later.

## Disentangling Capacity from Motivation

But first the epistemological problem: How we can *know* the causes behind failures of self-control? How can we determine whether one's current life circumstances derived from a lack of self-control *motivation* or from a lack of self-control *capacity*? Take the person with the lifestyle disease. How can we know whether his illness is due to a free and voluntary choice to smoke, drink, and overeat, or to aggressive marketing, social pressure, and addictive ingredients that are just too overwhelming for someone with little self-control? Or take the person who ended up in poverty. How can we know whether her financial hardship is due to a genuine preference for having a good time now over studying and working hard for later, or to a combination of bad genes, poor upbringing, and adverse circumstances that undermined her capacity to delay gratification?

In classical economic theory, solving the epistemological problem is easy. Barring external obstacles, what someone *does* reveals what he *wants* – end of story. If someone lights up another cigarette, thereby ending his attempt to quit, or if someone keeps showing up late for work, thereby risking her job, we must conclude that, apparently, this is what they prefer. Lack of self-control, by definition, stems from lack of motivation. But the research on self-control drives a wedge between the two: What people *do* does not necessarily equal what people *want*. Choice-making does not necessarily mean choice-following. Overt behavior, therefore, is no reliable guide for establishing to what degree someone's behavior is the result of voluntary choice or circumstances beyond their control.

But then what? How can we disentangle what caused what? If we cannot resolve this issue, we have yet another massive problem, especially regarding the distribution of scarce resources like income and social benefits. It is generally maintained that the distribution of these resources should track personal responsibility. If people suffer poverty or financial setbacks due to circumstances beyond their control, they are the victims of bad luck and should get some form of help or relief. But if people suffer poverty or financial setbacks due to their own irresponsible behavior, their misery is of their own making and they have to carry the consequences themselves. These are deeply held intuitions that lie at the heart of many public policies. Giving up on them would not be easy. So here is another million-dollar question: Can we uphold these policies if overt behavior is no reliable guide for deciding whether someone was *unwilling* or *unable* to behave responsibly?

## Giving Up on the Responsibility Approach

As I will argue, the answer is no. Rescue missions for the epistemological problem are doomed to collapse. First, the research on self-control makes clear that we need to look into people's minds to determine to what extent someone's current *behavior* is the result of voluntary choice or circumstances beyond their control. We need to lift their skulls, as it were, to uncover the respective contributions of capacity and motivation. This is anything but easy. But, second, to determine to what extent their current *life situation* is the product of voluntary choice or circumstances beyond their control, we *also* have to trace back what happened in their minds *at earlier moments* in their life, when the behaviors occurred that brought about their current life situation. This is simply impossible.

The inevitable conclusion is that policies seeking to attune the distribution of scarce goods to responsible conduct are built on quicksand. The intuition that the distribution of these goods should track "deservingness" is not necessarily wrong and may be an interesting topic for academic debate or cocktail conversation. But it is impossible to translate this intuition into concrete policies that are going to work in the real world.

Okay, then what? Whether we like it or not, we need to make *some* choice on how scarce goods – income, social benefits, or whatever outcome is deemed valuable – should be distributed. We must decide whether we are fine with the current state of affairs or whether some other distribution is preferable. If personal responsibility is not a viable criterion, what else could be the yardstick? Well, maybe we should stop looking for one. Several scholars have come up with a radical solution to the problem: simply abandon the quest for an optimal distribution. Some people have more than others, some people are luckier than others, and that is just how it is. Nobody ever said that life is fair! The only thing that matters is that no one becomes so poor that they are unable to lead a minimally decent life and that no one becomes so rich that the integrity and cohesion of society is threatened. But within these limits, material inequality is not a problem.

This may indeed sound like a radical solution – the operation was a success, but the patient has died. Whether one subscribes to it or not is ultimately a matter of political taste, so I leave the choice to the reader.

However, I argue that this solution has one major advantage that cannot be ignored: It sits much more comfortably with the research findings on self-control than the current "personal responsibility" approach.

## 1.3 So What Is to Be Done?

The final chapter addresses the question "What is to be done?" What do all these findings and insights mean for the government of society? This chapter results in three recommendations that partly transcend the issue of self-control, applying to politics and policymaking more generally. Let me summarize them briefly.

### More Psychology at the Policy Table

My first recommendation concerns the knowledge base of politics and public policies. When considering the question "What is to be done?" all three standpoints must be taken into account: the objective, the subjective, and the instrumental. Politicians who ignore one or more of these standpoints and their respective truths do so at their own peril. In fact, a well-ordered state contains *built-in guarantees* that all three are given due consideration, as part of its checks and balances. Perhaps we should not only have a *trias politica* but also a *trias epistemologica*.

Within this general framework, more attention should be given to everything psychology has learned about human behavior. Traditionally, the world of policymaking is dominated by lawyers and economists; psychologists have always been a rare species in government circles. The good news is that since the 2010s, this has begun to change, triggered by influential publications such as *Nudge* by Richard Thaler and Cass Sunstein. Since then, "Behavioral Insight Teams" (BITs) have mushroomed around the world. But the bad news is that this development goes nowhere near far enough. The problem is that (at the time of writing) behavioral expertise is only mobilized in the policy *implementation* phase. But we also need behavioral expertise in the policy *making* phase. Or even further upstream, in the larger debate about the ideologies and paradigms that, sometimes for decades, set the overall policy parameters. In fact, the current narrow focus on the implementation phase could even make things worse by extending the lifecycle of public policies fundamentally at odds with the empirical reality of limited self-control.

## More Epieikeia

My second recommendation follows from various findings and insights that fall under the heading of "brokenness" and "imperfection." Psychology makes abundantly clear that people maintain contradictory beliefs and desires. In fact, the brokenness in our mental states is why self-control problems arise in the first place. And since none of us has perfect self-control, we all experience moments of weakness. There is nothing unusual or remarkable about this. It is simply part of "the human condition."

But when it comes to governing society, we need to consider a second type of imperfection: no rule or regulation can cover all cases. Earlier in this chapter, I wrote that we should accept a certain lack of closure in the rules regarding self-control and responsibility. But this point applies more generally. In *every* domain of public policy, closure is beyond reach. Even the most ingenious and sophisticated rules are merely heuristics that will sometimes get it wrong, because all rules and regulations are based on an incomplete and inconsistent representation of the reality they seek to regulate. Normally we do not see the broken character of this epistemological foundation, but once we take a closer look, the cracks and fissures become visible again. Perhaps we should call this imperfect state of affairs "the regulatory condition."

Both conditions – the brokenness and imperfection of both people and rules – imply that it is impossible to make laws and regulations that will always produce fair and just outcomes. There will always be special cases in which following the rules yield judgments and decisions that do not feel right. We should thus create space for what Aristotle called *epieikeia*: the rectification of the law as an expression of the highest form of justice. And one of the reasons for *epieikeia* may be limited self-control. This also means that, sooner or later, there may come a moment when institutional arrangements, social practices, or public policies need to be reconsidered and realigned with our growing knowledge of the workings of the world.

## Paradigm Relaxation

My third and final recommendation is that the time for such reconsideration and realignment has arrived. Over time, self-control demands have become higher and higher, partly due to autonomous

## Box 1.1 Important Remarks on Terminology

A brief note about terminology before we dive in. Psychology is plagued by what some have dubbed the "jingle fallacy" and the "jangle fallacy." The former refers to the incorrect assumption that two different things are the same because they bear the same name. The latter refers to the incorrect assumption that two identical things are different because they bear different names.[13]

In studying self-control, the risk of encountering one or both fallacies is close to 100 percent. "Self-control" is just one member of an extended family of concepts all closely related in meaning. Many psychologists speak of "self-regulation" rather than "self-control," or consider the terms synonymous. Other terms in use are "impulsiveness," "executive control," and "executive functioning." Despite their subtle differences in meaning, all share the idea of deliberate *self-government* in order to attain a *future goal* (or, in the case of impulsiveness, the lack of such self-government). To keep things simple, I stick to the term "self-control," even when the research I cite uses one of the alternatives.[14]

Another issue is that, although many psychologists define "self-control" as a *capacity*,[15] the term in everyday usage also frequently refers to a *type of behavior*. It is perfectly normal to say that people *exercise* great self-control. And it is perfectly normal to compliment people we know to *have* poor self-control (a capacity) when they manage to *maintain* self-control in a particularly challenging situation (a type of behavior). In practice, these dual meanings never give rise to misunderstandings as the context clarifies what is meant. It will be the same here. For ease of reading, I will use what works best in the particular context, alternatively referring to "self-control capacity," "self-control strength," "self-control resources," "exerting self-control," and sometimes simply "self-control." But in all likelihood, the reader will barely notice these variations, as the context will make clear what is meant.

There is one thing about which I wish to be absolutely clear: When I talk of people with poor self-control, I only mean to say something about their psychological condition. In some parts of the world, terms such as "poor self-control" or "lack of self-control" have acquired an extra layer of meaning, and implicitly refer to certain racial or ethnic segments of the population. That is certainly not my intention here. When I use these or similar terms, I am simply referring to some psychological reality – one that can be measured with the appropriate instruments, and the distribution of which is entirely unrelated to racial or ethnic background.

A last point about terminology: When I talk of "intelligence," I refer to the traditional meaning of intelligence as general cognitive ability. In psychology, this ability is known as *g* and usually assessed with IQ tests, which measure cognitive skills believed to be indicative of *g*. Since the late twentieth century, however, it is not uncommon to distinguish between multiple types of intelligence, including (but not limited to) musical, bodily, social, practical, and emotional intelligence. I do not deny the reality or importance of these other types of intelligence, but it should be noted that their exact status and nature are not beyond scientific dispute. And perhaps more relevant here, they are *not* the subject of this book. When I speak of intelligence, I mean the cognitive understanding of the concept.

### WESTERN CULTURES
This book has been written with the societies I am most familiar with in mind: advanced Western liberal democracies (sometimes referred to as WEIRD societies: Western, Industrialized, Educated, Rich, and Democratic).[16]

Not everything I discuss is equally applicable to every culture around the world. To be sure, I would not be surprised if the findings with regard to self-control *capacity* turn out to be pretty universal, as they seem to be rooted in human (neuro)biology. But I am less certain whether the findings with regard to self-control *motivation* are similarly universal, as motivation is at least partly a function of the incentives, norms, and values of the culture one lives in. And certainly *not* universal are the public policies I discuss in Part II of this book. The strong emphasis on "personal responsibility" is a relatively recent phenomenon that has spread to many corners of the world, but certainly not all of them.

developments such as ever-denser networks of interdependency and partly due to deliberate interventions such as the growing emphasis on "personal responsibility." As a result, poor self-control has more and more become a liability. At least for some groups, we may be reaching the limits of what they can handle. Simply pushing them to try harder by further raising the stakes may no longer work, or even be counter-productive – not only for these people but also for society at large.

The most important conclusion of this book is that many of the prevailing political views and policies are based on beliefs about self-control that are simply false. As stated at the beginning of this chapter, we as a society may have constructed an "iron cage" that poorly befits the realities of the human mind. We are therefore increasingly at risk of falling into a trap that we have set for ourselves. Perhaps the time has come to loosen the reins. We do not need a full paradigm *shift*, but the time seems ripe for a paradigm *relaxation*. This may benefit everyone. The message of self-control research is that *no one* is immune to the self-control-undermining effects of an overly stressful and demanding life. Poor self-control is not a problem confined to the fringes of society. At the end of the day, a well-measured relaxing of demands could make life more pleasant and productive for all of us.

# PART I

# Self-Control

# 2 | *A Gift for Life*

By far the most famous study on self-control is the so-called marshmallow study, conducted by psychologist Walter Mischel and colleagues in the early 1970s. Readers may already be familiar with this study, but as a reminder, let me give a brief summary. Mischel's participants were children of about four years old, who were faced with the following challenge. The child was seated at a table with a marshmallow on it, literally within reach. The experimenter then told them she briefly had to leave the room. The child was allowed to eat the marshmallow now, but if they managed to wait until the experimenter returned, they would be rewarded with *two* marshmallows. This experiment thus tested the child's ability to delay gratification. Were they capable of resisting a small reward now in favor of a larger reward later?

It turned out that most children gave in before the experimenter returned. Some ate the marshmallow almost immediately, others were able to control themselves for longer, but only a handful managed to wait until the experimenter finally returned (usually after about fifteen minutes). Why did this simple experiment become so famous? Because about a decade later, Mischel contacted the parents and questioned them about how their children – by now adolescents – were doing. The results were remarkable. The children who had been able to wait longer at age four had developed into adolescents whose parents rated them as more academically and socially competent, and as better able to handle stress and frustration. They also scored higher on the Scholastic Aptitude Test (SAT).[1] In short, childhood self-control turned out to be a significant predictor of success later in life.

The marshmallow test measures what psychologists call *trait* self-control. This is one's average or baseline capacity for self-control. Some people tend to be very good at controlling their impulses and urges, while others easily succumb to temptation. This chapter discusses the causes and consequences of this aspect of personality. More specifically, the main questions are *what determines a person's level of trait self-control, and to what extent is trait self-control correlated with various individual and social outcomes.*

## 2.1 The Many Benefits of Self-Control

Mischel's experiments have garnered so much attention that one might easily get the impression it is the only study on self-control around – which is anything but true. Numerous surveys and experiments have studied the relationship between trait self-control and life outcomes, and they all point in the same direction. A meta-analysis by psychologist Denise de Ridder and colleagues revealed that self-control is related with a wide range of beneficial life outcomes. She found the largest effects for school and work achievement, but self-control is also associated with many other behaviors, including eating and weight-related behavior, and planning and decision-making.

### *Individual Outcomes*

To give a better idea of the findings, I briefly describe three studies. The first was by psychologist June Tangney and colleagues, who assessed the self-control strength of about 600 undergraduate students using the Self-Control Scale. (The brief version of this scale has become the most-used scale for measuring trait self-control. Box 2.1 presents its thirteen items). The researchers correlated students' scores on this scale with their grade point average, and with a whole battery of scales gauging numerous aspects of behavior and personality.

The results showed that better self-control is associated with higher grades, fewer impulse control problems, including binge eating and alcohol abuse, and fewer self-reported psychopathological symptoms. High self-control students also reported greater self-esteem, more empathy, and better relationships and interpersonal skills (as indicated by better family cohesion and less family conflict). In addition, they more often reported a secure attachment style, less anger, and better anger management. Tangney concluded that "it seems safe to regard high self-control as a marker of good adjustment. Indeed, given the breadth of positive outcomes it predicts, self-control may well be at the core of psychological adjustment."[2]

---

**Box 2.1 Brief Self Control Scale³**

1. I am good at resisting temptation.
2. I have a hard time breaking bad habits.
3. I am lazy.
4. I say inappropriate things.
5. I do certain things that are bad for me, if they are fun.
6. I refuse things that are bad for me.
7. I wish I had more self-discipline.
8. People would say that I have iron self-discipline.
9. Pleasure and fun sometimes keep me from getting work done.
10. I have trouble concentrating.
11. I am able to work effectively toward long-term goals.
12. Sometimes I can't stop myself from doing something, even if I know it is wrong.
13. I often act without thinking through all the alternatives.

---

The second example is a study by Angela Duckworth and Martin Seligman. These psychologists examined the correlation between self-control and academic achievement among eighth grade students. The study assessed students' self-control capacity during the fall and then measured their school achievements in the following spring.[4] Self-control was assessed not only by self-report but also through other measures: The children had to perform a delayed gratification test,[5] and parents and teachers were asked to rate the self-control strength of each child. Duckworth and Seligman found that, compared to their more impulsive peers, highly self-controlled eighth graders began their homework earlier, spent more time on it, watched less television, and had fewer absences. Their discipline seemed to pay off as they earned higher grade point averages and achievement-test scores, and were more likely to gain admission to a competitive high school program. In fact, self-control seemed more critical for school success than intelligence, accounting for more variance in grade point average and, unlike intelligence, predicting gains in academic performance over the school year. Duckworth and Seligman concluded that "programs that build self-discipline may be the royal road to building academic achievement."[6]

The third – and most impressive – example is a study by psychologist Terrie Moffitt and colleagues, based on data from a long-running study of 1,000 New Zealand children who were born between April 1972 and March 1973, and who have been followed since. The study compared self-control scores during childhood with life outcomes at age thirty-two. As an index of self-control, Moffitt used researcher, teacher, and parent reports of self-control at ages three, five, seven, nine, and eleven, combined into a single measure. Life outcomes at age thirty-two were assessed through health, wealth, and criminal record. Health was measured by physical exams and clinical interviews to assess depression and substance dependence, the latter verified by people whom subjects had nominated as informants. Wealth was assessed by socioeconomic status, income, parental situation, self-reported financial planfulness and struggles, as well as informant reports on financial problems. Criminal record was assessed by searching the computer systems of the New Zealand police and court records in New Zealand and Australia.

Moffitt found a significant correlation between childhood self-control and adult physical health, substance dependence, personal finances, and criminal offenses (see Figure 2.1). Importantly, these correlations held when she controlled for childhood socioeconomic status and intelligence. Self-control, socioeconomic status, and intelligence each had about the same predictive power.[7]

These three studies raise the question what the exact relationship is between self-control and intelligence. As Adam Smith noted, these qualities are not the same. But are they entirely unrelated? Judging by these three studies, they are somehow connected. Mischel found that childhood self-control predicted later SAT scores, Duckworth and Seligman found that eighth graders' self-control predicted their grade point averages, and Moffitt and colleagues found a correlation between childhood intelligence and childhood self-control. The latter finding is particularly significant as it suggests a direct link. What might this link be? Discussion of this question must wait until Chapter 5. For now, it is important to note that, even though there may be a connection between self-control and intelligence, the research clearly shows these are disparate mental capacities. After controlling for intelligence, self-control remains a powerful predictor of a wide range of life outcomes.

Before moving on, one seemingly minor detail deserves our attention: These studies suggest that one cannot have *too much* self-control. Although this may seem obvious, not everyone would agree. Sometimes it is claimed that too much self-control is harmful as it makes people rigid. Too much self-control may invite suppression of emotions or needs, and induce people to keep going on, thus pushing

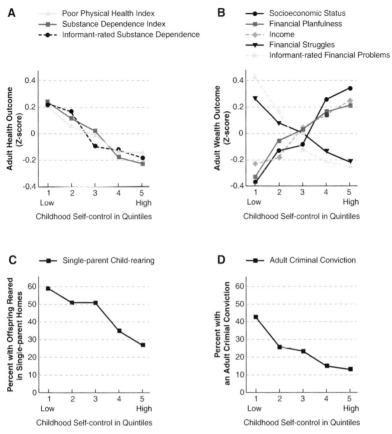

**Figure 2.1** Childhood self-control and life outcomes at age thirty-two, Dunedin study. Children with low self-control had poorer health (A), more wealth problems (B), more single-parent child-rearing (C), and more criminal convictions (D) than those with high self-control. Reproduced with permission from: Moffitt, T. E., Arseneault, L., Belsky, D., Dickson, N., Hancox, R. J., Harrington, H., ... & Sears, M. R. (2011). A gradient of childhood self-control predicts health, wealth, and public safety. *Proceedings of the National Academy of Sciences, 108*(7), 2693–2698.

themselves over the edge. The above research, however, provides no evidence for any potential downsides to high self-control. Tangney explicitly tested for this possibility, but found no nonlinear effects, not even for indicators of eating disorders or obsessive-compulsive behavior.[8] The same holds for the Moffitt study: The highest self-control quintile consistently had the best outcomes.[9]

This is not to say that "overcontrolled behavior" cannot exist. It is certainly true that some people stubbornly persist in inhibiting their urges, and keep chasing their goals in situations where it might be wiser to let go, or at least to slow down. Such extremely disciplined behavior, however, does not indicate an excess of self-control *capacity* but an excess of self-control *motivation*. Sometimes the desire to attain future rewards is so overwhelming that short-term needs are neglected, with potentially dire consequences. It is not unlike the athlete who wants to win so badly that she goes beyond what her body can endure, physically harming herself. But the true cause of this destructive behavior lies not in her physiology but in her mind.[10]

## Social Outcomes

Good self-control is not only beneficial for the individual but also for the community as a whole. The harder people work and the healthier they live, the more they will be able to contribute to society.[11] And the more prudent their financial conduct, the less likely they will default on their obligations and saddle society with the costs. But these are not the only wider benefits. Self-control is also linked with two phenomena of vital concern to social cohesion and public safety: prejudice and crime.

Several studies have suggested that people with poor self-control are more likely to express negative attitudes about (members of) outgroups – not because they are more prejudiced, but because they possess fewer resources to regulate cultural stereotypes.[12] Due to our lifelong immersion in culture, these stereotypes are deeply inscribed in our brains, and spring up automatically the moment we encounter a member of an outgroup. Of course, you need not endorse these stereotypes, and can attempt to suppress or ignore them. One might expect, therefore, that people with good self-control are better able to respond in an unprejudiced manner.

Support for this hypothesis comes from an experiment by psychologist Keith Payne, who asked white participants about their impression of "John," an African-American man about whom somewhat ambiguous information was provided, that could be interpreted either positively or negatively. The results showed that John was rated most negatively by participants who both scored high on implicit racial bias and had poor cognitive control. Payne concluded that cognitive control served "as a sort of gatekeeper between automatic activation and overt discrimination."[13] Another study found a correlation between self-control and the negative rating of outgroup members, but only for participants who were *motivated* to control prejudice.[14]

It should be noted, however, that only a handful of studies have explored the link between self-control and prejudice, so we should be cautious about drawing far-reaching conclusions. Many more studies have addressed the relationship between self-control and crime. According to criminologists Michael Gottfredson and Travis Hirschi, low self-control is the single most important cause of criminal behavior. In their highly influential 1990 book *A General Theory of Crime*, Gottfredson and Hirschi argued that, in contrast to what many believe, crime is *not* caused by social factors such as weak social bonds, having the wrong friends, educational or occupation failure, or living in a bad neighborhood. The *real* cause of crime is low self-control. Insofar as social factors correlate with criminal behavior, these are spurious correlations as both sides of the equation are ultimately determined by low self-control.

These are strong claims – perhaps too strong. Subsequent research has made clear that Gottfredson and Hirschi were too dismissive of social causes of crime, which definitively play a role. But they are certainly right that self-control is of major importance. Moffitt's study is far from the only one to find a link between low self-control and criminal behavior, other studies found similar results. An example is a survey by David Evans and colleagues, who asked nearly 500 white Americans how often they had committed each of 17 criminal acts in the past year, ranging from not paying for bus rides, breaking into buildings or vehicles in order to steal, to attacking people with the intention of seriously hurting or killing them. The survey further asked how often the respondents had engaged in behaviors that were "analogous" to criminal activity as they were "deviant" and provided for easy and immediate gratification. The list included behaviors such as being drunk or urinating in public spaces, possession of marijuana or hash, or driving a car more than fifteen miles above the speed limit. Evans found that self-control predicted both criminal and deviant behaviors – apparently part of a single cluster of interrelated behaviors that all stem from low self-control.[15]

### Box 2.2  Self-Control and COVID-19

As I write these lines, the world is in the midst of the fight against
COVID-19. People everywhere are trying to deal with this disruption
of their lives as best they can.

Again, this is a domain where good self-control seems highly beneficial. All of a sudden, people had to inhibit the impulse to shake hands,
hug or kiss when greeting others, or touch surfaces that might carry
the virus. And of all a sudden, they had to develop new, sometimes
unpleasant, habits such as wearing a face mask and keeping physical
distance. Unsurprisingly, studies found that people with good self-
control did better than people with poor trait self-control. They more
often complied with social distancing guidelines, more often wore face
masks, more often stayed at home when experiencing symptoms, and
so on.[16]

A telling example is a survey conducted by sociologist Amy Nivette
and her colleagues. During the first wave of the pandemic, she inter-
viewed participants in a cohort study of young adults who had entered
primary schools in Zürich in 2004, and who had been followed ever
since. By the time the pandemic struck, they were twenty-two years old.
In April 2020, when the country was in lockdown, Nivette contacted
the participants and asked them to what extent they complied with
various social distancing rules. She then linked their responses with
data about risk factors of each participant that had been collected in
earlier waves of the study, and calculated to what extent these risk
factors predicted compliance with social distancing rules. Figure 2.2
presents the results. Low self-control clearly stands out as the strongest
predictor of noncompliance.[17]

Good self-control is not only important for reducing the spread
of the virus. It also helps to meet the many challenges of life during
lockdown. People suddenly had to find new ways to organize their
daily activities, such as study or work, and to keep their households
running – particularly demanding for those with young children.
Again, those with good self-control seem to have the advantage. One
study found that homeschoolers with higher self-control more reliably
worked on the tasks the teacher had given them.[18] Another found that
students with higher self-control were more successful in pursuing their
pre-pandemic goals, partly because they were better able to form new
habits for staying on track.[19] And importantly, studies also suggest that
good self-control buffered against potential mental distress resulting
from the pandemic.[20]

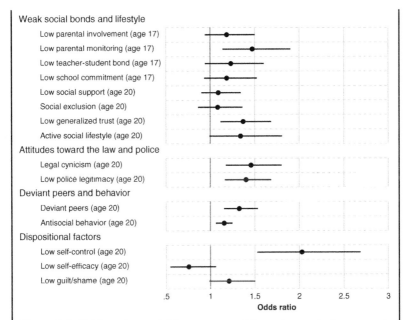

Figure 2.2 Odds ratios and 95 percent confidence intervals for antecedent risk factors for social distancing noncompliance at age twenty-two
(controlling for sex, socioeconomic status, education level, and migrant
background). *Source:* Nivette et al. (2021)

These are only initial findings, collected during the first months of
the pandemic. Without doubt, by the time this book reaches the reader,
much more research will be available.

Ten years after the publication of Gottfredson and Hirschi's seminal
book, a meta-analysis concluded that low self-control ranks as "one
of the strongest known correlates of crime".[21]

## 2.2 Origins of Self-Control

What determines a person's level of trait self-control? As with all
human traits and characteristics, it is a combination of genes and
social influences, especially during the first years of life. That one's
self-control capacity is partly determined by genetic inheritance is in

itself not a remarkable claim, since *all* human traits and characteristics are partly heritable.[22] The more relevant question is *to what extent* self-control is determined by genetic inheritance.

The relative contribution of genes and social environment to human traits is usually established through twin or adoption studies and expressed in heritability estimates. Unfortunately, although there has been ample research on the heritability of intelligence and on the heritability of the "Big Five" personality dimensions, few studies have looked into the heritability of trait self-control. Only recently, psychologist Yayouk Willems and her colleagues published the first meta-analysis. Based on a total sample of more than 30,000 twins (mostly older children and adolescents), they found a heritability of about 60 percent.[23] This means that 60 percent of individual differences in self-control capacity in the population can be attributed to differences in genetic endowment, and the remaining 40 percent to differences in social environment. Comparatively speaking, this is quite a lot.[24] On the one hand, it is somewhat *lower* than the heritability of intelligence (less than 50 percent in children, but increasing to about 80 percent in older adults), but on the other, it is *higher* than the heritability of the Big Five dimensions (about 40 to 50 percent). Willems emphasizes that more research is needed, especially among (older) adults, but for now the conclusion must be that differences in self-control capacity are, for a substantial part, a matter of genes.[25]

### Nurture

What are the effects of early upbringing on the development of trait self-control?[26] Although few studies have examined the effects of early childhood experience on later self-control *as defined in this book*, numerous studies have explored the relationship between early childhood experience and constructs *related* to self-control, such as attentional control or emotion regulation.[27] In general, these studies find that two factors are of crucial importance: stress and the quality of parenting.

Stress arises when environmental demands tax or exceed a person's resources. This triggers a range of physiological responses, most prominently a temporal increase in the level of stress hormones, such as cortisol, preparing the body to deal with these demands. Stress is a natural part of everyday life and not necessarily negative. On the contrary, moderate and brief periods of stress can actually support the development of good self-regulation. Of critical importance here is the availability of a caring and responsive adult who helps the child cope with the stressor. According to pediatrician Jack Shonkoff and colleagues, if a child is buffered by an environment of stable and supportive relationships, "positive stress responses are a growth-promoting element of normal development. As such, they provide important opportunities to observe, learn, and practice healthy, adaptive responses to adverse experiences."[28] In line with this, a review of more than 100 studies concluded that parental warmth, responsiveness, and sensitivity predict the development of self-regulation.[29]

But trouble looms when the intensity, frequency, or duration of stressful stimuli become too high – especially when caregiver support is lacking. In fact, parental abuse, neglect, and harshness are major stressors themselves. Without the buffering protection of a supportive adult relationship, the prolonged activation of the stress system and chronically elevated levels of stress hormones have a detrimental impact on brain development and functioning, often in ways that last a lifetime. Shonkoff and colleagues call this "toxic stress." Among other things, toxic stress impairs the development of the prefrontal cortex – a part of the brain responsible for the controlling of thoughts, feelings, and behavior – and undermines the development of the stress response system, resulting in higher sensitivity and quicker and more intense responses to stress. These neurobiological and biophysical changes are permanent, and increase the likelihood of self-regulation issues in adulthood.

In conclusion, although few studies have specifically addressed the effects of early childhood environment on trait self-control in later life, it seems safe to conclude that the combination of chronic stress and harsh and unresponsive parenting harms the development of this capacity. Conversely, the combination of moderate stress and warm and supportive parenting, with caregivers helping to cope with stress, may promote the development of good trait self-control.

## Stability

Personality traits, by definition, show a certain degree of stability over the life course. At the same time, they are not set in stone, as personality keeps evolving into old age. Is this also true for self-control? Do people grow more disciplined (or impulsive) as they mature? Again, the problem is that few studies have specifically addressed the development of self-control over the life span. But again, we can get a fairly good idea by looking at two closely related constructs: effortful control and conscientiousness.

"Effortful control" is a concept from developmental psychology. It largely overlaps with trait self-control, as it refers to the ability to inhibit a dominant response in order to perform a less dominant response, to detect errors, and to engage in planning.[30] This ability starts to form during the second year of life, then rapidly develops between the ages of two and seven, especially during the preschool years, and keeps maturing until young adulthood.[31] "Conscientiousness" is a concept from personality psychology and is one of the dimensions of the Big Five model. The "adult version" of effortful control, it encompasses facets such as self-discipline, orderliness, and achievement striving. Conscientiousness remains pretty stable during adolescence, but then makes remarkable gains in young adulthood and midlife. After age forty, this personality dimension continues to develop but at a slower pace.[32]

Given the similarities between self-control on the one hand and effortful control and conscientiousness on the other,[33] it is plausible that self-control follows a roughly similar trajectory: rapid development in the preschool years, followed by a period of little change until young adulthood, significant gains between the ages of twenty and forty, followed by another period of slow change. (By the way, as many parents will attest, the adolescent years can be especially turbulent. Changes in the adolescent brain induce increased risk seeking and heightened emotional reactivity, but these tendencies are not yet countervailed by an equal increase in self-control.[34] Only in young adulthood does self-control "catch up" and is balance restored.)

In conclusion, people's capacity for self-control is never completely set but keeps evolving into old age. Nonetheless, radical shifts are unlikely. When children are merely three years old, predictions can already be made about their personality at age twenty-six.[35] Moreover, as discussed in the previous section, there is a clear correlation between self-control at a young age and later behaviors that require self-control, such as financial planfulness. Those who were good at self-control as children tend to be good at self-control as adults as well.[36]

## 2.3 Conclusion

The evidence for the beneficial effects of good self-control is overwhelming. The research discussed in this chapter suggests that self-control is a significant predictor of school and work achievement, income and socioeconomic status, financial planfulness and struggle, physical health, eating and weight-related behavior, substance abuse, planning and decision-making, relationships and interpersonal skills, ability to deal with anger, frustration, and stress, and – last but not least – run-ins with the law. For all these cases, higher self-control is associated with the more desirable outcome. The correlations are considerable, often similar in size to the correlation with intelligence, sometimes even larger. So, good self-control truly is "the other important quality!"[37]

Self-control capacity is partly determined by genes. Based on the currently available evidence, the heritability of this trait is about 60 percent. This means that 60 percent of individual differences in self-control can be explained by differences in genetic inheritance, and the rest by differences in social environment. The early childhood years are particularly important. A combination of too much stress and harsh and unresponsive parenting during those first years can have negative effects that last a lifetime. After the first childhood years, self-control capacity keeps evolving, but at a slower pace, and one's position in the self-control hierarchy may be set. Those who had poor self-control as children may gain in self-control as they grow older but, in all likelihood, they will remain at the bottom of the ladder as their peers will also gain in self-control.

# 3 | *How Situation Undermines Self-Control*

We all have good and bad self-control days. On some days, maintaining self-control comes naturally and easily, or at least does not require vast amounts of willpower. Other days are worse. Even someone who is pretty self-controlled under normal circumstances, will find it difficult to stick to his diet or remain calm and constructive after three consecutive nights of poor sleep, a morning fight with his partner, bullying by his boss, and now a mountain of work due before the weekend. In other words, there is a difference between *trait* self-control and *state* self-control.

As discussed in Chapter 2, *trait* self-control refers to people's baseline capacity for self-control. Trait self-control is, by definition, fairly stable. It is part of our personality, and once people have reached adulthood, trait self-control changes only very gradually. However, *state* self-control refers to our capacity for self-control *in a specific situation at a specific moment in time,* for instance, at the supermarket this evening at 6 p.m., facing the choice between fresh vegetables or a bag of chips. State self-control can vary from day to day, or even from hour to hour, depending on a wide range of factors. People usually have better self-control in the morning when they are not yet tired from a hard day's work, and they usually have better self-control when they feel good and calm, without too many troubles on their mind. In short, state self-control strength can be seen as situationally determined fluctuations around the baseline level of trait self-control (see Figure 3.1).

This chapter asks: *What factors reduce state self-control? And why do these factors have this effect?* I discuss, in turn, the role of negative affect, cognitive load, the prior exertion of self-control, acute stress, and sleep deprivation. Along the way, it will become clear why self-control is limited. Two constraints turn out to be relevant: limited working memory capacity and limited energy resources

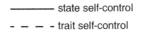

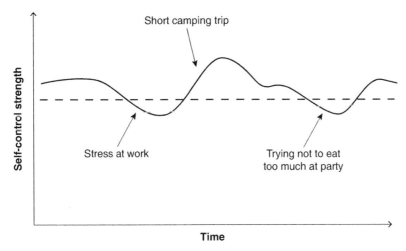

**Figure 3.1** State self-control fluctuating over time.

Let me concede at the outset that the second constraint is controversial. Until not too long ago, most psychologists believed that self-control is fueled by some limited resource, the depletion of which increases the chances of self-control failure. But this theory has recently come under fierce attack. According to its critics, the idea that self-control wanes over time is an artifact of publication bias, while the idea that self-control feeds on some limited resource is just plain wrong, for the simple reason that this resource does not exist. Whether one persists in self-control, is purely a matter of volition. In this chapter, I argue that these critics are, at best, only half-right.

The last part of this chapter tackles what is – for the purposes of this book – a crucial question: Do the factors and constraints undermining self-control make it *impossible* to resist temptation? Or do they only make it *harder*, and can you still maintain self-control provided you put in the effort? This section is more philosophical in character. I explain how – somewhat paradoxically – both answers are correct.

## 3.1 Negative Affect and Cognitive Load: The Role of Working Memory

"Negative affect may very well be the most potent disinhibitor of restrained behavior," write psychologists Dylan Wagner and Todd Heatherton. "When people feel worthless, depressed, or rejected, they are more likely to engage in a variety of self-defeating behaviors."[1] Negative mood can prompt people to eat more than they usually would, break their diets, consume alcohol, have unprotected sex, spend too much money, and procrastinate when faced with tedious tasks. Negative mood also increases the craving for alcohol in alcoholics, for cigarettes in smokers, and for drugs in drug abusers. Relapses among former smokers, substance abusers, and sex offenders, are typically preceded by periods of negative emotion.[2]

Why does negative affect diminish the exertion of self-control? What are the psychological mechanisms at play? One possibility is that people, when they are upset, assign more priority to feeling better immediately. Support for this hypothesis comes from experiments by psychologist Dianne Tice and colleagues, who found that participants in distress will normally try to improve their mood, for example by indulging in immediate gratification, *unless* they are led to believe that their mood is temporarily "frozen," and gratifying some immediate desire will provide no emotional relief.[3] Another possibility is that negative affect absorbs all attention. Feeling bad is often linked to worrying, ruminating, and unwanted thoughts that can overtake the mind, leaving fewer attentional resources available for successfully exercising self-control.[4]

### Cognitive Load

This brings us to a second threat to self-control: cognitive load. This refers to the total cognitive demand placed on an individual at any given time. Resisting temptation requires focus and attention. Any distraction can therefore undermine self-control. If people must spend their scarce cognitive resources on other, more salient or pressing demands, they may simply "forget" to monitor their behavior and resist temptation.

Although the literature on cognitive load is extensive, only a few studies have focused on its effects on self-control. Most of these studies concern eating behavior. An experiment conducted by psychologists Andrew Ward and Traci Mann, for example, investigated the effects of cognitive load on the eating behavior of chronic dieters and nondieters. Ward and Mann told participants they were investigating the impact of mood on memory. Participants were presented with foods that induce positive moods (nacho chips, M&Ms, and chocolate chip cookies) and instructed to eat as much as they wanted during the experiment. The experiment itself consisted of a simple and easy reaction time task. During this task, the experimental group *also* had to watch a series of slides which they had to memorize for a later recognition task. This additional task imposed a huge cognitive load on working memory. Now, Ward and Mann were not interested in how well participants did on the reaction or memory task, but in how much they ate. Cognitive load, it turned out, had an *opposite* effect on dieters and nondieters: The dieters ate *more* and the nondieters ate *less* than the control group.[5]

What explains these opposite effects? Ward and Mann argue that dieters feel an inhibitory pressure. Because they have to control their craving for high-calorie foods, they must monitor their behavior. When cognitive load reduces available mental resources for monitoring behavior, their impulses are no longer checked, leading to greater levels of food intake. In contrast, nondieters are unlikely to feel this inhibitory pressure, so they do not need to monitor their behavior. Cognitive load will therefore make no difference, or may even serve as a distraction from these tempting foods, thus reducing food intake.[6]

Psychologist Malte Friese and colleagues also found that cognitive load can undermine self-control, but they furnish a slightly different explanation.[7] They argue that the impairing effects of cognitive load are rooted in the dual nature of brain processes. In normal, nontaxing circumstances, the reflective brain system controls the impulsive brain system, thus determining behavior.[8] But cognitive load may change the "balance of power" and tax the reflective system to such an extent that not enough mental resources remain for controlling the impulsive system. Due to this shift, the second system will take over behavior.

## Memory Working Capacity

Although these explanations differ, the critical variable in both is "working memory capacity."[9] Since this is an important concept that will frequently return in what lies ahead, it is necessary to delve a little deeper into this topic. Unfortunately, there is no generally agreed upon definition of what working memory entails: Some psychologists use a narrow definition, others a broader one.

In the narrow definition, working memory capacity is the capacity to hold information actively in mind and work with it.[10] This is a prerequisite for self-control. It is impossible to exercise self-control without at least a minimum of available working memory space, as self-control requires the active representation of some goal in mind. Without this active representation, it would be unclear what behavioral impulses must be inhibited or overridden, and self-control would be directionless. The question is, therefore, what this capacity's limits are. How much information can people hold actively in mind? As it turns out, no more than four to seven chunks of information.[11] A shopping list is easy to remember if it contains just three items, but hard to remember if it contains eight. Some people may do slightly better than others, but working memory capacity is severely limited for all of us.

But the capacity to hold information actively in mind is – in itself – not enough for successful self-control, because not any information will do: The *right* information must be kept in mind and *irrelevant* information kept out. You need to *regulate* what information is brought online and what information is kept offline. Otherwise, the content of working memory at any point in time would merely be the volatile reflection of the external stimuli that are most salient, plus whatever thoughts spontaneously spring to mind. This would result in purely impulsive behavior.

This is one of the reasons why some researchers take a broader view of working memory.[12] In the broader definition, working memory is not only the capacity to hold chunks of information actively in mind and work with them. It *also* encompasses the capacity to regulate *which* chunks of information are kept in mind, by selecting goal-relevant information and inhibiting or blocking out interfering information. This part of working memory is often referred to as

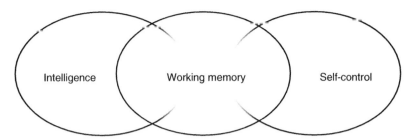

**Figure 3.2** Relation between intelligence, working memory, and self-control.

"attention control."[13] Again, although some people are better at controlling their attention than others, there are clear limits. It is not only the number of items that can be kept actively in mind that is finite, so is the capacity for controlling our attention. This is confirmed by both psychological research and everyday experience. No one can stay focused indefinitely.

Working memory capacity in general and attention control in particular might well be the *linking pin* between self-control and intelligence. As mentioned in Chapter 2, studies have found a moderate correlation between self-control and IQ. At that point of the book, it was unclear what might explain this relation, but now we can get some idea. The relation is as follows. On the one side, working memory capacity is closely related to general intelligence, with studies reporting a considerable correlation between these two mental concepts. This is hardly surprising, since both concern the manipulation of information.[14] On the other side, working memory is also closely related to self-control. The exact nature of this relationship depends on which view of working memory you subscribe to. In the narrow view, working memory and self-control are separate concepts, but one requires the other. In the broader view, working memory and self-control partly overlap, because working memory capacity *includes* the inhibition or blocking out of distracting information. This is a form of self-control since – in this book – self-control is defined as "the capacity to alter or override dominant response tendencies and to regulate behavior, *thoughts*, and emotions."[15] In the broader view, the relationship is as represented in Figure 3.2, with intelligence and self-control being distinct but moderately related concepts.[16]

## Conclusion

Negative affect and cognitive load reduce the likelihood of successful self-control. Sometimes what seems to be a failure of self-control may simply be a shift in priorities, a conscious choice for immediate gratification, perhaps to alleviate feelings of sadness. But in other instances, it is a genuine failure of self-control. The crucial psychological mechanism is the allocation and control of attention. People must keep their eyes on the ball. They must actively keep in mind the future goal – the two marshmallows, the job promotion, the trip to Paris – and monitor their behavior in light of that goal, inhibiting or blocking out any distracting feelings or thoughts. This requires working memory capacity. Because this capacity is limited, everything else that taxes the mind potentially impairs self-control. Negative affect and cognitive load may result in "attentional myopia"[17] or "transcendence failure"[18] – a loss of capacity to transcend the immediate stimulus environment and to focus on more distant goals. Negative affect and cognitive load shrink the world to the here and now.

## 3.2 Prior Self-Control: The Role of "Energy"

A third factor that may undermine self-control is the prior exertion of self-control. When people must maintain self-control for sustained periods – say studying for hours on end while ignoring their phone – sooner or later their self-control will start to wane. This has nothing to do with feeling sad or being distracted, for it also happens to people who feel perfectly happy, focused, and calm. Even in ideal circumstances, self-control cannot be maintained indefinitely. Apparently, working memory capacity is not the only limit to self-control. What else might cause self-control to wane over time?

This brings us to the hotly debated work of psychologists Roy Baumeister, Kathleen Vohs, and their collaborators. Self-control, they argue, is fueled by a limited energy resource, and the more of this resource is used up, the harder it becomes to sustain self-control.[19] Only a period of rest – a good night's sleep, for example – will replenish it. The gradual exhaustion of this limited resource has been dubbed "ego depletion," and is one of those psychological findings that has escaped the world of academia to permeate popular discourse. Baumeister has often invoked the metaphor of a muscle to illustrate the mechanism, so today it is not uncommon to read in the popular science literature that "willpower is like a muscle" that grows tired after intensive use, requiring a resting period to recover.[20]

The standard design for investigating ego depletion is the so-called dual-task paradigm. In this setup, participants in the experimental group must perform two consecutive tasks that both require self-control. For example, in the first task they must refrain from eating delicious-smelling, freshly baked chocolate cookies placed right under their noses. Then, in a seemingly unrelated experiment, they must do a second task that requires self-control. For example, they will be asked to solve difficult and frustrating puzzles, for which they can take as long as they want. After they are finished, their performance on the second task is compared to that of a control group, which only had to perform the second task but not the first. If the experimental group gave up more quickly on the puzzles than the control group, this is deemed proof of ego depletion.[21] Working on the first task has, apparently, consumed mental resources, leaving less available for working on the second task. Since the 1990s, the ego-depletion effect has been found in hundreds of experiments along these lines.[22,23]

However, while Baumeister's theory on the limits to self-control has gained quite some notoriety, since the 2010s it has come under fierce attack. Two controversies are central: Does ego depletion really exist? And if so, is this phenomenon really caused by some limited resource? I will discuss both controversies.

## Controversy 1: Does Ego Depletion Really Exist?

Until about 2010, no one doubted the empirical reality of the ego depletion effect. It was part of the scientific consensus. But today, psychologists are no longer so sure. The effect appears to be much smaller than initially believed, while some have even argued that it does not exist altogether and that the psychological community was led astray by publication bias. In the hope of putting an end to these growing doubts, in 2015, a high-powered multilab replication study was set up, but – to the surprise of many of the participating labs – this study found no ego depletion effect at all.[24] How could this happen? Almost instantly, the replication effort itself became the target of debate and was followed by new research and two other, hardly less ambitious replication efforts. One *did* find significant results, but only very modest in size, the other yielded more ambiguous results, casting further doubt on the reality of the effect.[25]

So what to believe? Is ego depletion real or not? The debate on this matter can get very technical, and readers interested in the details are referred to the literature.[26] Yet, as I write these lines in early 2021, my overall conclusion is that although the ego depletion effect is probably smaller than initially believed,[27] there is no reason to deny its existence altogether.[28] An important argument in support of this conclusion is that the effect was not only found in many of the dual-task experiments but also in several field studies. Let me describe two of them.[29]

The first study was conducted by psychologist Wilhelm Hofmann and colleagues. They asked 205 volunteers – mostly students – to report about their desires during the day for a one-week period. Each participant was provided a Blackberry PDA that would send a signal at seven moments randomly picked over the course of the day, at which the participants had to report on their current desires. In each instance, they were asked whether they felt a desire right now or had felt one in the past thirty minutes. If so, they were asked what the desire was about, how strong it was, to what extent it conflicted with other personal goals, and the nature of these conflicting goals. In addition, participants were asked whether they had tried to resist the desire and whether they had (partly) enacted the desire. The study furnished a total of nearly 8,000 desire reports. Analysis of these reports showed that "the more frequently and recently participants had resisted any earlier desire, the less successful they were at resisting any other subsequent desire"[30] (see Figure 3.3).

The second study was conducted by Hengchen Dai and colleagues, who investigated how frequently nurses washed their hands in-between patients. It is an important rule in healthcare that medical staff always wash their hands before seeing the next patient. But although well aware of this rule, nurses often skip handwashing. Why is this? Dai hypothesized that compliance with handwashing standards calls on resources for self-control, and that noncompliance is (partly) caused by ego depletion due to the exacting demands of the job. Nurses have to pursue multiple and sometimes competing goals, often in conditions

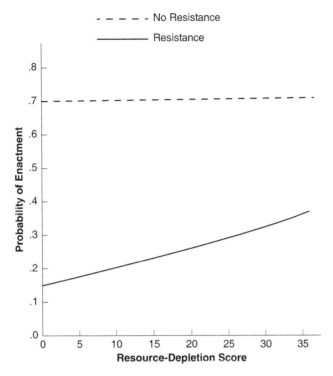

**Figure 3.3** Enacting desires and ego depletion. Probability with which participants enacted a given desire as a function of resource-depletion score, separately
for occasions on which people did and did not attempt to resist the desire. The
resource-depletion score reflects the number of previous resistance attempts
(regardless of desire content) on the same day. *Source:* Hofmann et al. (2012)

of high workload, fast-paced assignments, and time pressure. If this
hypothesis is correct, compliance with handwashing requirements
should decrease as nurses advance through their shifts. To test this
hypothesis, Dai analyzed the handwashing behavior of more than
4,000 nurses in 35 hospitals, as collected by an electronic hand
hygiene monitoring system. This furnished a total of nearly 14 million
potential handwashing moments. As predicted, she found that handwashing discipline decreased as shifts progressed, especially for nurses
experiencing high work intensity. At the end of a typical twelve-hour
shift, the likelihood of nurses washing their hands in-between patients
had decreased by a third (see Figure 3.4). Further supporting the ego

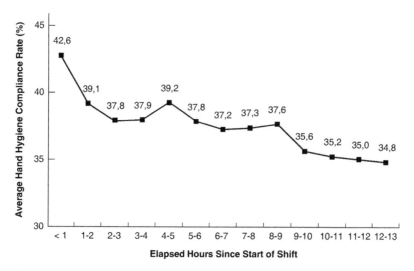

**Figure 3.4** Relationship between elapsed hours since start of shift and hand hygiene compliance. Copyright © 2015, American Psychological Association. Reproduced with permission from: Dai, H., Milkman, K. L., Hofmann, D. A., & Staats, B. R. (2015). The impact of time at work and time off from work on rule compliance: The case of hand hygiene in health care. *Journal of Applied Psychology, 100*(3), 846.

depletion hypothesis, resting periods led to the recovery of handwashing discipline, with longer breaks leading to stronger recovery.[31]

## Controversy 2: A Limited Resource?

The second controversy concerns the *cause* of self-control failure. Baumeister and Vohs claim that self-control depends on a limited energy resource. The more of this resource is consumed, the more likely self-control failure happens. This model is often referred to as the "strength model" or "resource model" of self-control. Importantly, it posits that this limited resource fuels not only self-control but also other top-down mental functions, such as logical reasoning, decision-making, and active planning. For instance, one study found that students who had to make a series of decisions on how their class would be taught, gave up faster on a subsequent task requiring self-control.[32] Another study found that participants who had to suppress their emotions while watching a distressing video performed

worse on a subsequent task that required elaborate information processing.[33] Yet another study found that, after a strenuous self-control
task, participants were less willing to make a plan for how to pursue
their goals in the upcoming weeks.[34] According to Baumeister and
colleagues, all these mental functions and behavioral tendencies rely
on the same shared but limited resource.[35]

But there is one pressing question: *What exactly is this scarce
resource?* Where in the body can it be found? And is it really some
form of energy? Nobody knows. As I write these lines, no one has
yet managed to identify this elusive resource.[36] Baumeister's critics do
not deny that after the prolonged exertion of self-control, people can
feel "as if" they have run out of energy and need to refuel. However,
this is but a metaphor. We should not take this figure of speech literally. Furthermore, is this resource really *limited*? Research shows that
when rewards are increased, people tend to maintain self-control for
longer. Apparently, they have some reserve of this "limited" resource
they can appeal to when the situation calls for it.[37] But if this is true,
the crucial variable is not resource *availability* but resource *allocation*.
Self-control failure would indicate not a lack of capacity but a lack of
motivation.

So can the resource model be sustained? No, not according to psychologists Michael Inzlicht and Brandon Schmeichel, who reject the
very idea of a depletable resource, and have proposed an alternative
model. They do not deny that self-control wanes over time and people start feeling fatigued after a while. They claim, however, that this
has nothing to do with limited resources, but is caused by gradual
changes in motivation. Self-control wanes over time "not because
people have no energy but because people experience a shift in motivation away from 'have-to' goals, which are carried out through
a sense of obligation and duty, and instead come to prefer 'want-
to' goals, which are fun, personally enjoyable, and meaningful."[38]
In other words, after prolonged self-control, people simply want to
engage in more pleasurable activities. Inzlicht and Schmeichel call
their theory the "shifting priorities model."[39]

So who is right? All things considered, I think that Inzlicht and Schmeichel are right to draw attention to the often overlooked role of
motivation, but wrong in their sweeping claim that limited resources
play no role *at all*, and that the dynamics of self-control failure can
be explained by shifts in motivation *alone*.[40] After all, is it really true

that people, after hours, days, or weeks of assiduously maintaining self-control, suddenly come to *prefer* to break their diet, light up that cigarette, and yell at their boss? That they have come to the conclusion that, from now on, this is what they really want? Such a reversal of judgment would be unlikely. Most people describe such episodes as moments of weakness, wayward behaviors they often regret almost instantly (which, incidentally, would mean an equally swift *re*-reversal of judgment, rendering these behaviors even more incomprehensible). If resources played no role at all, it would make more sense to simply not let such moments of weakness happen. And another thing: If resources truly played no role, why do people start feeling *fatigued* after sustained exertions of self-control? Where does this feeling come from? That remains unclear. Inzlicht and Schmeichel have advanced an alternative explanation for these growing feelings of fatigue – an explanation also proffered by critics such as Robert Kurzban and his colleagues – but as I argue in the appendix, this explanation is unconvincing.

### Pushing the Limits

But perhaps the best way to find out whether self-control really depends on some limited resource is to put it to the test, to see what happens when people are pushed to the very limits of their powers. Athletes in extreme sports such as ultra-triathlon, push themselves so far that some have literally dropped dead. Could something similar happen in cases of "extreme self-control"?

Of course, conducting an experiment to find out would be unethical, but several studies suggest that exerting self-control may indeed have detrimental health effects, as it triggers the body to direct resources away from other functions such as the immune system.[41] An experiment by psychologist Suzanne Segerstrom and colleagues, for example, sought to determine whether active regulatory effort has an effect on participants' responses to a delayed-type hypersensitivity (DTH) skin test, a measure of cellular immunity. Participants had to perform a mental arithmetic task before this DTH test was administered. As an indicator of how much effort participants were likely to put into the task, Segerstrom measured participants' level of "conscientiousness" (a personality dimension that overlaps with trait self-control).[42] She found that participants high in conscientiousness had a significantly weaker immune response to the DTH test than participants low in conscientiousness. Apparently, active and persistent regulatory effort consumes physiological resources that otherwise would have been available to the immune system.

Another study found that the frequent exercise of self-control can actually take a physiological toll. Psychologist Gregory Miller and colleagues found that among young African Americans from low socioeconomic backgrounds, high self-control is associated with less depression, substance use, aggressive behavior, fewer internalizing problems, and greater educational attainment *but also* with higher allostatic load (a marker of physiological wear and tear)[43], faster epigenetic aging of immune cells (a marker of biological age)[44], greater likelihood of becoming ill after inoculation with a rhinovirus (cause of the common cold)[45], and greater susceptibility to metabolic syndrome and insulin resistance (which increases the risk of heart disease, stroke, and type 2 diabetes).[46] So for these young African Americans, exercising self-control appears to result in better life outcomes, *but this comes at a biological cost.*

Of course, these findings do not *prove* the existence of the limited energy resource that Baumeister and Vohs postulate. So long as no one has actually *seen* this resource and its connection with the inhibition or overriding of impulses, it cannot be ruled out that other biological mechanisms explain these negative health outcomes, for example stress responses.[47] But these findings are certainly suggestive. They support the claim that self-control comes at a biophysical price. The costs of maintaining self-control are more than just foregone opportunities for leisure and pleasure. As mentioned in Chapter 2, there is no such thing as too much self-control *capacity*, but the above research clearly suggests one can have too much self-control *motivation.*[48]

## The Gray Zone

To summarize, it is not only negative affect and cognitive load that may undermine self-control, the same goes for prior self-control exertion and other top-down mental processes such as decision-making. This cannot be explained by limited working memory, because the effect builds up only gradually and lasts after working memory is no longer being taxed. A second constraint thus has been postulated: self-control

## Box 3.1 Self-Control Boosting Situations?

Although scientists doubt whether self-control (and higher executive functioning in general) really feeds on some limited energy resource, it certainly feels "as if" this were the case. People routinely talk about how much energy it takes to exercise restraint in tempting situations, and after a long day of hard mental work, it is not unusual to say your battery is empty. But interestingly, alongside reporting that certain activities feel depleting, people also claim that certain activities feel *reinvigorating*. Pursuing a hobby, going out with friends, or doing sports "gives them energy."

This raises the intriguing question of whether we can improve state self-control by providing people with more opportunities for doing whatever "gives them energy." Research by Richard Ryan, Edward Deci, and colleagues suggests this might well be the case. Unlike many of their peers, these psychologists have no qualms talking about energy. "The feeling of having energy is one of the most familiar and salient phenomenal experiences people have and one about which they readily and reliably can report."[49] Ryan and Deci, however, prefer the term "vitality." This is a feeling of enthusiasm, aliveness, and energy one can harness for purposive action. "It is the energy that allows people to decide how to behave, to hold other appealing behaviors in abeyance, and to maintain a positive attitude toward the activities in which the individuals decide to engage."[50]

Vitality depends not only on somatic factors such as diet, exercise, and sleep but also on the satisfaction of fundamental psychological needs. Three psychological needs lie at the heart of Deci and Ryan's work:

- The need for autonomy. This is the need to self-regulate experiences and feel ownership with respect to one's actions, as opposed to being controlled by external forces. It is satisfied when you can act in congruence with your authentic interests and values.
- The need for competence. This is the need to feel effectance and mastery in interactions with the environment, as opposed to feeling helpless or incompetent. It is satisfied when you experience feelings of efficacy and achievement, for instance in your work.
- The need for relatedness. This is the need to feel connected and involved with others and having a sense of belonging. It is satisfied when you feel cared for, related to others, or when giving and contributing to others.

According to Deci and Ryan, satisfying these psychological needs "can engender energy and, in interaction with physical influences on the individual, determine the overall energy to the self."[51] This means that resting is not the only way to refuel. The same effect can be achieved by doing what you really want, by performing activities that make you feel competent, and by interacting and connecting with people you care for. These activities might thus improve self-control capacity!

Or at least in theory. To date, the research base for the claim that satisfying these fundamental needs enhances vitality, thus increasing the likelihood of self-control, remains limited. But if Deci and Ryan are correct, we would have yet another set of circumstances which affect self-control capacity – and this time circumstances which *boost* this capacity. If Deci and Ryan are correct, some people are lucky. They have interesting and challenging jobs that match their talents and skills and offer plenty of possibilities for achievement and personal growth. If they are even luckier, they are also well connected with colleagues, family, and friends. These lucky dogs have plenty of opportunities for satisfying their needs for autonomy, competency, and relatedness. This will maximize their energy, thereby making it easier to maintain self-control, which, in turn, further increases their life chances. Other people are less fortunate. They are condemned to mind-numbing jobs that offer anything but a challenge. Outside of work, they may lead lives of loneliness and isolation. For them, there is little opportunity for satisfying basic psychological needs and thus boosting their energy.

"runs" on some limited resource. It remains unclear, however, what this resource might be, whether it is truly some kind of energy, or perhaps something else in the body or brain. It will take much more research to obtain an answer – if we ever get one. But as the scientific adage goes: Absence of evidence is not evidence of absence.

That being said, Baumeister and Vohs concede that their initial theory on the limits of self-control was too strongly stated. People have more leeway to invest extra resources in self-control when the circumstances so require than initially believed. They have therefore renamed their "resource model" the "conservation model."[52] People probably never completely run out of energy, since that would be fatal. Human neurobiology and physiology are designed to protect resources and conserve enough energy for other bodily functions and for unforeseen needs and emergencies. This implies that the crucial question is how many resources one is *willing* to expend on self-control. Self-control effort is thus not determined by one but two variables: motivation *and* capacity. Self-control failure happens when either one or both fall below the critical threshold.

This leads to an important point: When people give in, the culprit cannot always be determined. There is a "gray zone" between the state of having ample resources for self-control on the one hand, and the state of being completely drained on the other. In this gray zone, maintaining self-control is still feasible, and raising the stakes may induce people to commit extra resources. But keeping up self-control becomes more and more strenuous and imposes higher and higher demands on one's reserves, perhaps to the detriment of other goals, such as good immune system functioning. In this zone, the distinction between capacity and motivation becomes blurry – where the one ends and the other begins is unclear. When people eventually succumb, it is hard to say whether this happens due to a lack of capacity or a lack of motivation. We simply do not have the knowledge and instruments to make that assessment.[53]

## 3.3 Acute Stress and Insufficient Sleep

Self-control may also be reduced by conditions that directly impact the functioning of the body or brain. These negative effects are not caused by mental activity – sad feelings, distracting thoughts – but by biophysical processes. The classic example is alcohol intake. Everyone knows that the copious consumption of booze is a major cause of self-control failure. Fortunately, for those eager to prevent this from happening, there is an easy solution: don't drink. In this section I discuss two threats to self-control that are more difficult to avoid: stress and insufficient sleep.

### Acute Stress

Psychologists distinguish between acute and chronic stress. *Acute* stress occurs when someone faces a particular and immediate stressor, for example, having to give a presentation in front of 500 people in 10 minutes. This activates the stress system, elevating stress hormone levels. When the stressor is no longer present, things gradually return to normal. *Chronic* stress occurs when exposure to stressors is so frequent and intense that the system is continuously activated and stress hormones remain at elevated levels. In this section I only discuss the effects of acute stress.

Although much research has been done on the effects of acute stress on health and mental functioning, very few studies have focused on the effects of acute stress on self-control. One of the rare exceptions is an experiment by psychologists Lars Schwabe and Oliver Wolf, who investigated the impact of acute stress on the ability to switch between goal-directed and habitual behavior. The first type of behavior is governed by goals and adjusted or corrected to the extent that the goal is achieved. The second type of behavior is an automated reaction to stimuli, not governed by goals, and hence not subject to adjustment or correction while being executed. Schwabe and Wolf found that when acute stress was induced, participants persisted longer in habitual behavior that was no longer productive for the purpose at hand. They concluded that stress favors habitual performance at the expense of goal-directed performance: "Stress seems to shift us from 'thinking' to 'doing'."[54]

What mechanisms are responsible for the detrimental effects of acute stress? Partially, the limitations discussed earlier. Almost by definition, stress taxes working memory and consumes mental resources. Stress is often a cause of negative affect, rumination, and other intrusive thoughts, while coping with stress requires top-down mental effort, such as suppressing anxiety and cognitive restructuring.[55]

But this is not the only route through which stress can undermine self-control. Stress also affects the interplay between brain regions implicated in impulsive behavior and self-control. According to Dylan Wagner and Todd Heatherton, maintaining self-control is like a balancing act. During successful self-control, "there is a balance between prefrontal regions involved in self-control and subcortical regions involved in representing reward incentives, emotions or attitudes."[56] On one side of the balance is top-down control from the prefrontal cortex (PFC). Three regions in particular are important: the ventromedial PFC (vmPFC), the lateral PFC (lPFC), and the anterior cingulate cortex (ACC). The first area is critical for regulating behavior in social, affective, and appetitive domains, the second area is necessary for planning behavior and maintaining regulatory goals, while the third area monitors performance and signals the need for recruiting control systems to regulate

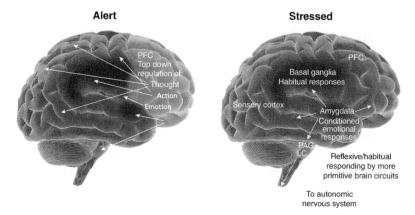

**Figure 3.5** Changes in brain systems controlling behavior under conditions of alert safety versus uncontrollable stress. Reprinted by permission from Springer Nature, *Nature Neuroscience 18*(10), 1376, Stress weakens prefrontal networks: Molecular insults to higher cognition, Arnsten, A. F. Copyright 2015.

behavior.[57] On the other side of the balance are the subcortical regions whose neural responses the PFC needs to downregulate. The relevant subcortical regions vary depending on the stimulus. When people try to keep emotions in check, regulation targets the amygdala, a region sensitive to emotionally arousing stimuli. When people try to resist stimuli like food or drugs, regulation targets the nucleus accumbens, part of the brain's reward system.[58]

Stress alters this delicate balance (see Figure 3.5). It triggers the release of high levels of noradrenaline and dopamine, which take the PFC "offline" and strengthen the functions of more primitive brain circuits. Attention regulation switches from thoughtful "top-down" control by the PFC to "bottom-up" control by the sensory cortices, giving salient stimuli a stronger hold on attention. As a result, orchestration of the brain's response patterns switches from slow, thoughtful PFC regulation to the reflexive and rapid emotional responses of subcortical regions.[59] All this accords with Schwabe and Wolf's conclusion that "stress seems to shift us from 'thinking' to 'doing'."

## Insufficient Sleep

An often overlooked but all too common cause of self-control failure is lack of sleep. Research shows that sleep deprivation impairs various mental functions, such as sustained attention, (working) memory,

**Figure 3.6** Squeezing a handgrip.

and – most relevant for our purposes – response inhibition.[60] A recent meta-analysis found that inhibitory control, as measured by computerized tasks such as the so-called Stroop task, is "particularly sensitive" to restricted sleep.[61] Given these experimental findings, it would not be surprising if sleep deprivation also impairs self-control in everyday life.

And indeed, this appears to be the case. Several studies have found an association between sleep deprivation and behaviors commonly associated with poor self-control, such as smoking and snacking,[62] while a couple of studies have also directly tested the relationship between sleep and self-control. An example is a study by psychologists Larissa Barber and David Munz, who surveyed undergraduate students on a broad range of sleep-relevant traits and behaviors, and asked them to keep a daily log of their sleeping behavior for five consecutive days (from Monday to Friday). Both at the beginning and end of this five-day period, Barber and Munz assessed the students' stress and self-control. For measuring stress, they used a standard ten-item scale with questions such as "How often have you found that you could not cope with all the things you had to do?" and "How often have you felt difficulties were piling up so high that you could not overcome them?" For measuring self-control, they used a physical endurance task in which participants must squeeze a handgrip for as long as they can (see Figure 3.6). This task is often used to measure behavioral self-control strength.

Barber and Munz found that at the end of the five-day period, participants who slept better over the course of the week reported less stress and persevered longer on the handgrip task. The findings held even when controlling for a wide range of factors, including trait self-control, psychological well-being, health behavior, and experience of stressors during this period. Interestingly, the positive results were *only* found among participants who slept both sufficiently *and* consistently. It was not enough to sleep seven or eight hours a day *on average*. It was also important to have a *consistent* sleeping pattern, that is, to sleep about the same number of hours each night. Apparently, the detrimental effects of sleeping five hours one night cannot be offset by sleeping ten hours the next night.[63]

Why does insufficient sleep make self-control harder? As with stress, part of the explanation lies in the earlier discussed limitations. Among the most robust consequences of sleep disruption are increased feelings of negative affect,[64] and since these feelings may cause cognitive load, this is a potential pathway for diminishing self-control capacity. Lack of sleep may also increase the need for impulse control. The more tired you are, the more effort it takes to stay focused, and the harder you must fight the desire to close your eyes and doze off. This continuous mental effort consumes precious resources – of which you will have fewer in the first place, since less sleep means less replenishment.

In addition, as with stress, lack of sleep alters brain processes implicated in self-control. Lack of sleep has effects on both sides of the neural "self-control balance." On the one side, it leads to stronger subcortical responses to emotionally charged stimuli. One study found that skipping a single night of sleep led to 60 percent amplification in reactivity of the amygdala in response to emotionally negative stimuli.[65] On the other side, lack of sleep reduces the top-down regulatory control of the PFC over these subcortical responses, either due to impoverished activity or impoverished connectivity with the relevant subcortical regions. The net effect is an increased chance of self-control failure.[66]

While sleep deprivation leads to poor self-control, the reverse is true as well: Poor self-control leads to sleep deprivation. Two mechanisms are relevant here. First, poor self-control may be linked to behaviors that impair a good night's sleep, such as drinking too much coffee or alcohol late at night, or playing exciting videogames right until bedtime.[67] Second, people with poor self-control may go to bed too late, because they cannot bring themselves to turn off the TV, put away their phone, or just stop doing whatever it is they are doing. Support for this second mechanism comes from a study by psychologist Floor Kroese and colleagues on "bedtime procrastination." Kroese surveyed Dutch adults on their sleeping habits and asked them to keep a sleep diary for one week. As part of the survey, she measured trait self-control with the Brief Self-Control Scale, and bedtime procrastination with a scale containing items such as "I easily get distracted by things when I actually would like to go to bed" and "I have a regular bedtime which I keep." Kroese found that self-control and insufficient sleep are indeed correlated, and that this relationship is mediated by bedtime procrastination. This may then fuel a vicious circle: Insufficient sleep undermines self-control, making it harder to behave in ways that promote a good night's sleep, which leads to further impairment of self-control, and so on.[68]

## Conclusion

Acute stress and insufficient sleep can undermine self-control in two ways. First, they tax the mind. Stress generates thoughts and feelings that take up working memory space, thus increasing the likelihood of "attentional myopia" and "transcendence failure," whereas coping with stress requires top-down mental effort, thus increasing the likelihood of ego depletion. More or less the same goes for lack of sleep, a well-known source of negative affect. Second, stress and insufficient sleep set off a chain of biophysical processes that upset the balance between top-down brain control and bottom-up reflexive responses. As a result, behavior becomes more governed by external stimuli, impulses, and habits.

## 3.4 Unable or Unwilling?

Before concluding this chapter, I wish to raise a crucial question. As we have seen, self-control can be undermined by negative affect, cognitive load, the prior exercise of self-control, acute stress, and insufficient sleep. But how strong are their effects? Do they make it *impossible* to maintain self-control and resist temptation? Or do they just make it *more difficult*, and can you always control your impulses and urges as long as you try hard enough? Does self-control failure happen because you *choose* to no longer resist temptation?

How we answer this question has profound consequences for our view on responsibility and deservingness – two concepts at the heart of Part II of this book. But as the discussion of "the gray zone" between capacity and motivation has already suggested, the answer is far from straightforward. As I argue in what follows, it ultimately depends on which temporal perspective one takes. This section differs in character from the previous ones, as it does not introduce yet another body of empirical research but sets out a theoretical argument.

## *Weakness of Will*

Let me begin with a philosophical question: Is genuine self-control failure *at all possible*? Self-control failure means that you act against your preferences. But how could such a thing ever happen? Can you act in a manner that you want and not want *at the same time*? I am, of course, not the first to raise this question. The puzzle was already discussed by Socrates and Aristotle. It is called the problem of "akrasia" or "weakness of will" and revolves around this question: Can a person *freely and intentionally* act against his better judgment? This seems logically impossible. In cases where such behavior seems to occur, there are only two possibilities:

- This person is *not* acting freely and intentionally. Something or someone is forcing him to act in this manner.
- Though *he may claim otherwise*, this course of action is what he actually *prefers*. Otherwise he would not do it!

Either way, it would be incorrect to call this weakness of will. Some philosophers have therefore concluded that weakness of will – or in my terms, self-control failure – is conceptually impossible. This class of events simply cannot exist.[69]

This is a very counterintuitive conclusion, one that deeply conflicts with our everyday experience in which the phenomena of poor willpower and self-control failure seem all too common and real. To insist that weakness of will cannot exist seems an instance of philosophy gone awry. Fortunately, we do not need to accept this counterintuitive conclusion, as the psychological findings discussed in this chapter provide a framework for a more productive approach to this age-old puzzle. This approach is a combination of proposals advanced by the philosophers Richard Holton and Chandra Sripada, and conceptualizes self-control as the struggle between two separate mental realities: intentions and desires.[70] Let me explain.

On the one side are intentions: mental commitments to some future course of action.[71] Intentions often align with one's better judgment, but not necessarily. What matters is the *commitment*: You have reached the conclusion that this is what you want to do. You identify with this course of action and plan to stick to it. This implies that intentions have a certain degree of stability; they are not changed or revised at every whim. Put differently, intentions have a transcendent quality. They are detached from the immediate here and now, in that they represent a more general plan or policy regarding a set of potential future behaviors. The prototypical example is the New Year's resolution.

On the other side are desires: Emotions, drives, and cravings – the more visceral states that constitute the impulses and urges that are the object of self-control. Desires are *dispositions* or *inclinations* to act in a certain manner, but unlike intentions, they do not imply a *commitment* to act in that way.[72] Moreover, whereas intentions have a certain stability and transcendence, desires are more connected to the here and now, and thus more volatile. For instance, the intention or resolution to diet is, by definition, relatively stable, but the desire to gorge on unhealthy food changes from moment to moment and from situation to situation. This desire may grow stronger when you are hungry, or when you walk through the food court of a shopping mall, only to recede as you leave the mall and other things capture your attention.

The crux is that intentions and desires are fundamentally different in nature, both conceptually and empirically. Conceptually, because they cannot be reduced to each other. Intentions are the outcome of a process of deliberation and judgment, of a *monologue intérieur* on what to do, whereas desires are merely (one of) the inputs to this process of deliberation and judgment, one of the voices seeking to be heard. Empirically, because they are associated with different regions of the brain. Intentions are associated with the PFC, whereas desires are associated with subcortical areas, such as the amygdala and the nucleus accumbens. While these areas are connected, the connection may grow weaker due to stress or sleep deprivation.

Once we accept this portrayal, it becomes clear that self-control failure is perfectly possible. Self-control failure is simply what happens

---

**Box 3.2 Once Again: Limited Resources?**

As discussed in Section 3.2, until recently it was believed that exercising self-control consumes some depletable resource, thereby limiting the capacity for self-control. But this theory has been challenged. Critics argue that self-control failure is not caused by depletion of some elusive resource that no one has ever managed to identify, but by shifting motivations. Are they right? As discussed, I have my doubts.

But suppose I am wrong. Suppose future research convincingly shows that this resource really does not exist, and that ego depletion effects can be entirely explained by gradual changes in motivation. Would that mean that genuine self-control failure cannot occur, because people always have the freedom and choice to put in more effort? And that giving in to temptation must therefore always be understood and explained as a revision of intentions?

No. All the fuss about ego depletion and the role of motivation should not make us forget that self-control *also* requires working memory capacity. And it is beyond doubt that working memory capacity is strictly limited. Everything that takes up working memory space potentially undermines self-control. In fact, I would argue that limited working memory is even *more* of a bottleneck than limited energy. Everyday life is replete with competing demands on our attention, but we can concentrate on only one thing at a time. So even if willpower were unlimited, self-control failure could still occur because attention is limited. In other words, many self-control failures may stem not from "weakness of will" but from "bypassing the will." In addition, stress and insufficient sleep can undermine self-control, as they alter the balance and functional connectivity between the relevant brain areas. Again, this has nothing to do with limited resources, but nevertheless hinders the neural machinery to function properly.

So even if self-control does not (co)depend on some limited energy resource, it can still be undermined by situational factors, resulting in desires taking over from intentions. For perfect self-control to become a practical possibility, life would have to be entirely devoid of distractions, negative feelings, stressful circumstances, noisy neighbors, and cats keeping you awake at night.

---

when the balance of power is tipped in favor of desires. Sripada calls this the "divided mind" account of self-control. This is certainly a fitting label.[73] After all, the essence of self-control is that humans are not all of a piece, but simultaneously hold opposing response tendencies.

More generally, the human condition is one of inner conflict – between desires, beliefs, intentions, values, and so forth.[74] Which side prevails in any given situation depends on many factors, one of them being self-control capacity.

## Time Slice Failure versus Cumulative Failure

A further question is to what degree temptations are truly *irresistible*. People who give in to desire often say they simply could not help themselves. They really tried as hard as they could, but the temptation was just too strong.

Does the excuse hold? If someone held you at gunpoint, would you still be unable to resist the dessert or another beer? If there was a policeman at your elbow, would you still be incapable of controlling the urge to steal the item from the grocery? Of course not. If only the stakes are high enough, almost everyone is able to control their urges and impulses. This is even true for highly addictive behavior such as smoking. When diagnosed with a life-threatening disease, many inveterate smokers suddenly turn out to be capable of quitting after all. In other words, what we commonly believe to be a lack of *capacity* almost invariably boils down to a lack of *motivation* – an unwillingness to allocate sufficient resources to the self-control goal at hand. Does this not prove that, except maybe in the most extreme circumstances, there is no such thing as genuine self-control failure?

Yes and no. It is true that people have considerable leeway in how they allocate their mental resources, and if your life is in immediate danger, it makes sense to throw in everything you have. But the thing is that self-control challenges are not isolated events that occur only sporadically. To the contrary, life is an ongoing barrage of self-control challenges. In many domains of life, such as study and work, health, or personal finances, the challenge is not to maintain control during just one single moment of critical importance, but almost continuously, because the self-control challenges just keep coming. As mentioned in Chapter 1, one study estimated that people spend almost a quarter of their day on some form of controlling desire.

The question is, therefore, how you would do if someone held you at gunpoint *all day*? How would you do if the policeman did not stay in the grocery store but followed you around, and was at your elbow every waking moment? Would you *never* fail to maintain self-control? Never fall prey to even the briefest moment of inattention or weakness? Even when stress keeps mounting and you are close to exhaustion? The point is that, as Sripada argues, we should not focus on "time slice failure" but on "cumulative failure" – the likelihood of self-control failure over an *extended period of time*.[75]

Let me explain. Suppose you are able to maintain self-control in 99 of every 100 cases. Only in 1 of every 100 cases you fail, either due to weakness or bypassing of the will (or because, as Sripada suggests, a random error occurs in the complicated mental machinery responsible for exerting self-control). This certainly sounds like a good score. To give some context, recall the study by Hofmann and colleagues, in which over 200 students were asked 7 times a day to report on their desires. Hofmann found that, on average, the students managed to resist desires that conflicted with their personal goals in 83 of every 100 cases. So if you are able to maintain self-control in 99 of 100 cases, that would make you a true champion of self-control.

Unfortunately, even this excellent score may not be enough to quit smoking. It usually takes weeks before the physical (not to mention psychological) craving for a cigarette begins to wane. Hence, if during the first two weeks you feel this craving on average 10 times a day, it is very likely that you will cave in at least once during this period, since these two weeks comprise a total of 140 moments that you must resist the urge to light up a cigarette. And as every (former) smoker knows, just a single moment of weakness may suffice to derail the attempt. This logic not only applies to addictive behavior but also to other domains of life. In work settings, you have to keep your temper in front of difficult customers or abusive managers not just once or twice, but all day and every day. Even a single moment of impulsiveness may get you into serious trouble. Or take financial behavior. If you live on a shoestring budget, it is not enough to have only average or even good self-control. Your self-control must be next to perfect, as a single moment of irresponsible spending can trigger a downward spiral of ever-growing debt.

In conclusion, it is true that in isolated high-stakes moments, people can choose to spend all their energies on maintaining self-control – and perhaps even can rise above themselves. But we should not restrict our view to such isolated moments. We need to consider the total volume of self-control challenges that cross people's paths over an extended period of time, and ask how likely it is that, as the challenges keep coming, people will succumb at least once. In the words of Sripada, "exceptionally high probabilities of self-control success at each instant can co-exist with substantial probabilities of self-control failure in the aggregate."[76]

## Conclusion

What the issues discussed in this section have in common, is that they all concern the potential objection that self-control failure is not a genuine failure, but simply an instance of not trying hard enough. Maybe the conditions discussed in this chapter – negative affect, cognitive load, prior exertion of self-control, acute stress, lack of sleep – make it *harder* to maintain self-control, so the objection goes, but they do not make it *impossible*. Hence, when people give in to temptation, it is because they *choose* to give in to temptation. It is not a matter of being *unable*, but of being *unwilling*.

I have argued against this position. Of course we should not be naïve, and must acknowledge that sometimes – or even quite often – people take the road of least resistance and freely and intentionally give in. But not always, and not by definition. Genuine self-control failure is a real possibility, both conceptually and empirically. Moreover, although people usually have ample reserves to call upon in high-stakes moments, instances of failure are likely to occur for behaviors that require good self-control on a more or less continuous basis. In everyday situations, we should focus not on the "point probability" but on the "cumulative probability" of self-control failure.

## 3.5 Conclusion

Time to wrap up. The chapter has sought to answer the question *what* situational factors reduce state self-control, and *why* do they have this effect. I have discussed the influence of negative affect, cognitive load, the prior exertion of self-control (and other forms of top-down mental effort), acute stress, and insufficient sleep. All of these factors are potential threats to self-control. Along the way, it became clear that the dynamics of self-control are governed by two constraints:

- *Limited working memory capacity.* Situational influences may undermine *current* self-control capacity if they tax working memory. Negative feelings, ruminations, and other intrusive thoughts make it harder to stay focused on the self-control goal at hand and monitor progress toward that goal, thus increasing the likelihood of impulsive behavior.
- *Limited resources.* Situational influences may undermine *later* self-control capacity by consuming the scarce resource that "fuels" top-down mental effort. The longer one has to concentrate and maintain self-control, the more resources are used up, and the harder it gets. Other forms of top-down cognitive labor, such as decision-making, have the same effect.

On top of this, acute stress and sleep deprivation may also undermine self-control. This can happen in two ways. First, stress and sleep deprivation often give rise to negative affect and cognitive load, while coping with stress and fighting sleep requires mental effort. Both conditions take up working memory space and deplete available resources. Second, stress and sleep deprivation trigger biophysical processes that may impair self-control because they weaken top-down regulation by the PFC and strengthen responses from subcortical brain regions.

The overall message of this chapter is that situation matters. One's self-control capacity in a specific situation at a specific moment in time is not only a function of genetic inheritance and early upbringing but also of the current situation. In principle, every stimulus in the environment has the potential to undermine self-control, because everything that people perceive and experience evokes thoughts, feelings, and behaviors. Therefore, everything they perceive and experience impacts available working memory space, available energy resources, and stress levels. Of course, most stimuli provoke only mild or moderate responses, and will barely make a difference. An unfriendly remark by a passing stranger may be unpleasant, but is probably quickly forgotten, and will hardly undermine self-control. But other situational influences may be hugely consequential. A growing body of research, for instance, suggests that poverty is a major cause of cognitive load, negative affect, ego depletion, severe stress, and lack of sleep, and therefore seriously hampers self-control. I discuss the effects of poverty in Chapter 6.

A crucial question is whether situational influences make exercising self-control *impossible* or just *more difficult*. The answer depends – at least partly – on the time frame. If we consider isolated events, it is nearly always possible for people to walk the extra mile and reduce the likelihood of self-control failure to practically zero. But if we consider longer periods, a different picture emerges. Many small chances of failure at specific points in time add up to a near-certain chance of failure over the long haul.

As time passes, it may indeed be impossible to keep self-control failure from happening *at least once.*

## Appendix

Why do people sooner or later stop exerting self-control? Is that because of depletion of some limited resource, as Baumeister and Vohs maintain? The problem is that – as yet – no one has identified that elusive resource. Therefore, several psychologists have proffered alternative explanations. More specifically, since about 2010, self-control theory has witnessed a "motivational turn." A new family of models has emerged that, although different in various ways, all share the basic assumption that motivation rather than limited resources is the critical factor. If people stop exerting self-control, this is not an effect of depleted resources but of shifts in motivation. It means that the perceived costs and benefits of self-control have evolved in such a way that sustaining self-control is no longer deemed the option that yields the highest utility.

In this appendix I focus on the "shifting priorities model" proposed by Michael Inzlicht and Brandon Schmeichel, as they are perhaps the most outspoken in their rejection of the existence of an (allegedly) limited resource. Their model "dispenses with the resource concept altogether."[77] Yet other models within this new family of self-control models are similar in their emphasis on the decisive role of motivation (such as the "opportunity cost model" developed by Robert Kurzban and colleagues, and the "motivated effort-allocation model" developed by Daniel Molden and colleagues.[78]

### Shifting Motivations

Inzlicht and Schmeichel do not deny that self-control wanes over time and that people begin to feel fatigued. They claim, however, that this has nothing to do with limited resources, but is caused by changes in motivation. Self-control wanes over time "not because people have no energy but because people experience a shift in motivation away from 'have-to' goals, which are carried out through a sense of obligation and duty, and instead come to prefer 'want-to' goals, which are fun, personally enjoyable, and meaningful."[79] In other words, after prolonged self-control, people simply want to engage in more pleasurable activities.

But why would people make this shift? Why not continue pursuing "have to" goals? Sure, it may not be "fun, personally enjoyable, and meaningful" to study all evening instead of going out, to stay friendly with obnoxious consumers, to not drink before driving, and to forego that high-calorie dessert, but the benefits of these behaviors are obvious. In the long run, you will be better off. So why give in? According to Inzlicht and Schmeichel, this has to do with costs and benefits. All cognitive effort is inherently aversive and costly. People will therefore only maintain self-control so long as the benefits of this course of action outweigh the costs. But sooner or later, there comes a tipping point. Sooner or later, the further delay of gratification no longer outweighs the (increasing) costs, and this will mean the end of exerting self-control.

So far so good. Baumeister and Vohs would probably not disagree. But the million-dollar question is *why* cognitive control feels aversive and costly. What causes these feelings? In Baumeister and Vohs' strength model, the answer is straightforward: Self-control is costly because it consumes scarce resources. In the shifting priorities model, however, an alternative explanation is needed because, *even though* Inzlicht and Schmeichel acknowledge that self-control is costly and generates feelings of fatigue, and *even though* they acknowledge these feelings grow stronger over time, they deny the existence of a limited resource. So it must be something else that makes engaging in self-control aversive and costly. What might that be?

Before going into their solution, it should be noted that *all* models within this new strand of thinking struggle with this question. What is beyond dispute, is that all cognitive effort is aversive and costly. We know this from our own experience, and it is supported by psychological research. If people are free to choose between a cognitively more and a cognitively less demanding task, most choose the latter. Most people prefer cognitive leisure to cognitive labor.[80]

But what remains fiercely debated, is how to *explain* this preference for the road of least cognitive resistance. Psychologists who deny that limited resources have anything to do with it, must offer an alternative answer.

Inzlicht and Schmeichel's explanation is that self-control is costly because of its *opportunity costs*: Time spent on engaging in self-control cannot be spent on leisure activities.[81] The feeling of fatigue is *not* a signal indicating that some scarce resource is getting depleted, but a signal indicating that the costs and benefits of the current self-control effort are shifting in such a way that pursuing another course of action would yield higher utility. Inzlicht and Schmeichel argue that a motivational system that generates such stopping signals would be evolutionary adaptive, because it prevents human beings from continuing a course of action that is no longer the most beneficial. "[N]atural selection would have favored adaptations that minimize opportunity cost caused by a poor decision about whether to engage or disengage from a task [...] One such adaptation is making effortful control aversive, so that it has inherent disutility."[82]

However, this explanation is deeply problematic.

## Shifting Benefits?

Let us first look at the benefit side of the equation. Do the perceived benefits of the immediate reward remain stable, or do they change over time? Obviously, the latter is the case. One reason may be changes in external circumstances. Life is an ongoing barrage of external cues and influences affecting the strength of competing desires. As you walk through a shopping center, for instance, the desire to spend your hard-earned money or to have unhealthy foods is constantly primed, which may boost the perceived benefits of giving in. Fortunately, leaving the shopping center and getting in your car may have the opposite effect. But interestingly, not only (changes in) external circumstances are of relevance. The activity of exerting self-control itself may also influence desire. As mentioned in this chapter, a handful of studies found that after having exercised self-control for a certain amount of time, people report and display greater sensitivity to immediately rewarding stimuli, such as food, money, and drugs.[83]

Fair enough. But what difference does it make if self-control capacity does not depend on some finite resource? If resources are unlimited, a gradual increase in perceived rewards will hardly make a difference, because one will always have abundant resources to resist this (gradually more tempting) reward. In other words, if resources are unlimited, an increase in the perceived benefits of the immediate reward is in itself no reason to stop exerting self-control.

If we take a functional perspective, it is also unclear why, at some point in time, giving in to desires would become the most beneficial course of action. After a few minutes, hours, or days have passed, it still remains a bad idea to break your diet, light up a cigarette, or start shouting at customers. Indulging in sweets or starting to smoke again are still bad for your health, and shouting at costumers may still get you fired. Of course, things would be different if you were told by your doctor that you only have three more months to live. In that unfortunate case, refraining from these behaviors may indeed no longer be the most beneficial course of action. But otherwise, these behaviors are as wise and sensible as they were last week, last month, or last year. In other words, contrary to what Inzlicht and Schmeichel suggest, there is no "diminishing marginal utility" on the benefit side of the self-control equation, because the utility of maintaining self-control does not derive from the value of the activity itself, but from the value of the goal this activity will bring about.[84]

## Shifting Costs

This brings us to the cost side of the equation. Do the costs of prolonged self-control remain constant, or do they change over time? Inzlicht and Schmeichel claim that these costs gradually increase, because the more time is spent on exerting self-control, the more aversive it gets. However, it remains hard to explain this gradual increase if there are no internal costs to self-control, and the only cost would be opportunity costs: foregone opportunities to pursue other, more enjoyable or rewarding courses of action. It is certainly true that engaging in self-control has opportunity costs, which must be weighed before the decision to exercise self-control (or not) is made. But it is *not* true that, after one has decided to exercise self-control and is in the process of doing so, these opportunity costs gradually increase. If people continuously monitor and update the (perceived) costs and benefits of the behavioral options open them, leisure and pleasure activities that were forgone in the past minutes, hours, or days are *irrelevant*. They are *sunk* costs, which by definition have no bearing on the costs of future courses of action. Opportunity costs do not accumulate over time.

In fact, it would be more logical to argue the opposite: As the process of maintaining self-control goes on, opportunity costs gradually *de*crease, because the moment that the delayed reward will materialize comes closer and closer. The longer one stays at the office party, the less time remains before the party ends, and therefore the lower the opportunity costs of not drinking before driving home. The longer one studies for tomorrow's exam, the less time remains for hanging out with friends, and the fewer opportunities for having fun and partying before the exam begins. Opportunity costs are the highest at the *start* of any self-control attempt.

Expected future opportunity costs can only increase if, while in the process of exerting self-control, one acquires new information or beliefs about the costs and benefits of persevering. For example, one may come to realize that it will take much longer to achieve the future reward than initially expected – who knew that learning to play the violin could be so hard! – or one may learn that the future reward is much less certain than initially believed. When inflation skyrockets, saving for later loses much of its attractiveness. Such new beliefs or changing circumstances may be reason for a recalculation of costs and benefits. What at first seemed to be a good decision – to go for the delayed reward – may turn out to be not such a great idea after all.

However, such instances of changing beliefs or circumstances do not seem very relevant for most everyday self-control challenges, such as doing one's chores, studying and working hard, dieting and exercising, refraining from drinking and smoking, and so forth. People usually have a fairly good idea of the stakes and the – sometimes very long – delay periods they must endure. In most everyday cases, there is little reason to assume that self-control failure is the result of unforeseen new information or insights, which brought about a "game-changing" reappraisal of the costs and benefits.

## Where Are the "Need to" Goals?

Inzlicht and Schmeichel explicitly refer to the work of fatigue researcher Robert Hockey. Interestingly, Hockey discerns not two but *three* types of motivational goals that must be weighed when people feel subjective fatigue and must engage in a cost-benefit analysis of alternative courses of action. In addition to "want to" and "have to" goals, Hockey also discerns "need to" goals. These pertain to the maintenance of equilibrium and optimal states of bodily functions. "They may be referred to as need to goals, since they are driven by seemingly urgent motivational or emotional demands – for eating, drinking, sex, waste elimination – but also, perhaps, by milder need, such as for change or rest or sleep, or an urge to sit in the sun."[85]

Inzlicht and Schmeichel, however, only distinguish between "want to" and "have to" goals. They do not mention Hockey's third type of goals. In their dichotomy, we are thus forced to conclude that someone who is fasting, feels increasingly hungry, and therefore at some point caves in and has a big meal, is *not* driven by a desire to restore bodily equilibrium, but by a desire for leisure – for engaging in what is "fun, personally enjoyable, and meaningful." This is quite a stretch. By restricting themselves to "want to" and "have to" goals, Inzlicht and Schmeichel obfuscate the role of bodily and emotional needs. By excluding "need to" goals, they reconceptualize "resting" from a need into a want, from the equivalent of sleep to the equivalent of leisure and fun. This is highly dubious. In any case, had Inzlicht and Schmeichel allowed for "need to" goals, it would have been much easier to conceptually accommodate the idea of "limited resources" as a potential cause of self-control failure.

## Conclusion

The role of motivation in self-control is almost certainly greater than was initially assumed in the strength model. The extent to which people are inclined to exercise self-control cannot be explained by limited resources *only*. But attempts to explain the dynamics of self-control through motivation *only* remain unconvincing. Opportunity costs alone are not enough to do the trick. The conclusion is that self-control depends on (at least) two factors: motivation and some limited resource. Unfortunately, as I write these lines, what exactly this limited resource might be remains a mystery.[86]

# 4 | *Building Self-Control?*

Can you get better at maintaining self-control through regular exercise? Are there strategies or techniques for keeping your impulses in check and circumventing the traps of temptation? Can poor self-control be remedied?

It may be true that some people have less talent for self-control than others. And it may be true that every stimulus has the potential to undermine self-control. But if people can improve their self-control, either through deliberate training or by deploying the right mental techniques, the problem can be fixed. Then keeping self-control, even in stressful circumstances, is basically a skill almost anyone can learn. Health, wealth, and happiness would then be within reach for all, including those who, as a child, were unable to resist the marshmallow. However, if self-control is *not* susceptible to training or technique, things look different. Then we must accept that some people just have more discipline than others, and that no intervention can change this state of affairs.

This chapter therefore asks: *To what extent is it possible to improve self-control?* There is no shortage of tips or tricks to boost the "other important quality." Box 4.1 contains fifteen tips I have distilled from one popular self-help book and a host of webpages with titles such as "The six secrets of self-control" and "Ten simple exercises that will strengthen your willpower." For readers keen to improve their own self-control, this box may serve as a one-stop shop, offering a representative sample of the most common tips and tricks currently on the market.

But do these tips and tricks really work? Some of the recommendations are better supported by evidence than others. For instance, the efficacy of "if-then plans" (tip # 3) is well established, while few would doubt the importance of getting proper sleep (tip # 10). Other tips are more dubious. As I write these lines, many websites still make strong claims about strict limits to self-control resources (see tip # 13), often explicitly referring Baumeister's work. But as we saw in Chapter 3, psychologists today doubt whether these limits are set in stone.

**Box 4.1  Working on Self-Control**[1]

### TIP # 1: HAVE A SPECIFIC, CONCRETE, AND REALISTIC GOAL

Vague and abstract self-control goals such as "work harder" or "exercise more" are bound to fail. Better are concrete goals such as "start each workday with answering all new emails" or "run at least two miles on every other weekday for the coming four weeks." Goals must also be realistic. If you want to reduce calorie intake, it is not feasible to switch all at once from your present high-fat lifestyle to a diet of only fruits and vegetables. Break up the behavior change in small steps toward the desired goal. And set priorities. You cannot do everything at the same time – quit smoking, eat healthy, work harder, control your temper, and save money. Start with the behavior you most want to change.

### TIP # 2: KNOW THYSELF

Better self-control begins with self-awareness. What situations induce the behavior you want to control? How do you react to stress? Do you tend to indulge in drinks or food when feeling sad? Make a list of cues that trigger the unwanted behavior, and identify the need behind these temptations. If binge eating is your reaction to sadness, call a friend instead of indulging in chocolate. Be mindful of your habits. Why do you always put two sugar cubes in your coffee? Why do your never answer emails right away? Raising these behavioral patterns to the level of consciousness is the beginning of changing them.

### TIP # 3: MAKE IF-THEN PLANS

Make little "if-then" plans for how to respond when facing temptation you want to resist. Be as specific as possible. If you will be attending a party tonight, say to yourself: "If someone offers me an alcoholic drink tonight, then I will ask for club soda with lime." When you expect your boss to be her usual offensive self at the next meeting, say to yourself: "If she provokes me, I will take a deep breath, count to ten, and then change the subject." Rehearsal of such if-then plans strengthens the association between the situational cues and the intended response, thus increasing the likelihood that you will act as intended.

### TIP # 4: MOTIVATE YOURSELF

Keep your goal clearly in mind, and do not get lost in detail. Remind yourself regularly of the "why" behind your behavior. Focus your mind on the long-term favorable consequences of an action. Write down the reasons for what you want to achieve, hang them on the door of the fridge, or carry them in your wallet. If you want to quit smoking, write down the costs of smoking, such as the effects on your health and the ashtray breath, and write down the benefits of quitting, such as saving money and whiter teeth. And reward yourself for successful self-control. For instance, with the money not spent on cigarettes you can treat yourself to a massage.

### TIP # 5: KEEP BELIEVING IN YOURSELF

Maintain that "can do" attitude. The more firmly you believe that you can achieve the goals you have set for yourself, the greater the chances you will succeed and persist in the face of setbacks and difficulties. Use self-affirmations by saying things to yourself such as "I am the master of my life" and "I am fully in control of myself." And rather than saying "I can't resist x," say "I don't want x." In this way, you are reminding yourself of what you want instead of telling yourself you are forcing yourself to do something you do not want.

### TIP # 6: AVOID TEMPTATIONS

Remove the candy bowl from your desk, put your phone away, and keep your home free of unhealthy snacks. If you are trying to cut down on spending, do not go for stroll through the shopping mall but pick a park instead. If you are trying to quit drinking, do not hang around with your drinking buddies and avoid the local bar. If it is impossible to avoid temptations, prepare yourself by making if-then plans, or make the temptations less attractive. If you are trying to quit smoking, think of the potential harm, such as lung cancer. Or distract yourself. Immerse yourself in something that consumes your attention, perhaps doing something with your hands, such as folding origami. Or use your imagination to mentally travel somewhere else, perhaps your last holiday destination.

### TIP # 7: FORM NEW HABITS

One of the secrets of self-control is to develop the right habits. People who seem particularly good at self-control have organized their daily lives in such a way that they are not overwhelmed by temptation. So make it a habit to do the groceries after meals rather than before, to go to work by bike rather than by car, to do your hard reading in the morning, and so forth. Forming these habits may take willpower, but once they are set, your willpower will no longer be called upon. The deeper these habits are ingrained, the more likely they will rescue you in times of stress.

## TIP # 8: MONITOR YOUR BEHAVIOR

If you are trying to save money, make it a habit to write down what you spend. If you are trying to lose weight, weigh yourself daily. Monitoring progress helps you to become an expert on your own behavior and identify what works. Apps and websites can help you to keep track. Write down on what moments or days your self-control fell short, and see if there is a pattern. Perhaps you will learn that some situations or periods are particularly stressful, say the holidays. Knowing this, you can better prepare, for example by forming if-then plans tailored to these situations or periods.

## TIP # 9: EXERCISE AND EAT REGULARLY

Even short periods of moderate exercise increase the blood and oxygen flow to the brain and release neurotransmitters which help your brain to control impulses. "Exercise turns out to be the closest thing to a wonder drug that self-control scientists have discovered."[2] Eat regularly and healthily. Exerting self-control is hard when you are starving. Do not skip meals as this can make your blood sugar level drop. For a quick boost to your self-control, sip some lemonade. This signals to the brain that there is plenty of energy for exerting self-control. But be careful as this only provides a quick boost. As a rule, it is better to maintain a consistent level of glucose by eating small meals rich in protein and fiber at regular intervals.

## TIP # 10: GET PROPER SLEEP

Lack of sleep impairs your judgment and undermines your self-control. When you are tired, your brain cells' ability to absorb glucose is diminished. The prefrontal cortex is especially hard hit and loses control over the regions of the brain that create cravings and the stress response. If you want to improve your self-control, getting a good night's sleep – every night – is one of the best moves you can make.

## TIP # 11: MANAGE STRESS AND MEDITATE

Stress is your worst enemy. High levels of stress consume energy resources that cannot be invested in self-control, and increase the likelihood of impulsive behavior and decisions based on short-term outcomes. One particularly good way to counter the effects of stress and improve self-control is meditation, which will help you control your thoughts and feelings. Significant result can be obtained after only eight weeks of brief daily meditation training. Techniques like mindfulness, which involves focusing on your breathing and your senses, will improve your ability to resist impulses.

---

### TIP # 12: TRAIN YOUR WILLPOWER MUSCLE

Exercise your "willpower muscle" regularly so it will grow stronger. Even simple exercises for only a few weeks will help. For example, work on your posture or use your opposite hand for one hour per day, create and meet self-imposed deadlines, or squeeze a handgrip for as long as you can each day. An advanced exercise is to carry around something tempting all day, say a chocolate bar, but refrain from consuming it.

### TIP # 13: BEWARE OF MENTAL FATIGUE

Avoid ego depletion. Although exercising self-control is a good way to build willpower, you should not overdo it. You only have a finite amount of resources. If you consume too much of it, too little is left for other self-control challenges. Therefore, limit the number of goals you try to attain. Do not try to quit smoking, adopt a healthy diet, and start a new exercise plan all at once.

### TIP # 14: ORGANIZE SUPPORT

Let your friends and family know that you are attempting to change your behavior, ask them to remind you of your goals, and to support you if you need help. They may give you pep talks, listen when you need it, and help to reinforce your decisions. There is an abundance of apps to assist you.

### TIP # 15: DON'T PUSH YOURSELF

Last but not least: Do not be too harsh on yourself. Take small steps and break the goal down into manageable pieces. If you want to stop yourself from getting distracted while studying, do not begin with locking yourself in for a whole day, but start small by studying for at least an hour without checking your email. And when your attempt at self-control fails, do not give up in despair, but forgive yourself and move on. Focus on how you will do better next time. Just try again.

---

Overall, the research on "what works" for improving self-control is rather scarce. Given this state of affairs, I do not delve into the details of each and every recommendation, but confine myself to some general findings, conclusions, and musings. In Section 4.1, I discuss interventions to improve self-control *strength*. Is it possible to build stronger "self-control muscles" through regular exercise? Section 4.2 addresses self-control *techniques* such as cognitive reframing or changing habits. Here we will also meet Odysseus, an early pioneer of self-control technique. In Section 4.3, I will introduce an increasingly popular alternative for helping people with less than perfect self-control: nudging.

## 4.1 Self-Control Training

Since the early twenty-first century, the idea that "self-control training" can build stronger "self-control muscles" has become a staple of the self-help literature. Just as lifting weights every day builds *physical power*, exercising self-control each day is believed to build *willpower*. According to tip # 12, even simple exercises for only a few weeks will help. "For example, work on your posture or use your opposite hand for one hour per day, create and meet self-imposed deadlines, or squeeze a handgrip for as long as you can each day."

Only recently have psychologists begun investigating whether this is actually true and self-control training really works. The research often has the following design: First, participants' self-control strength on one particular task is measured, then they have to practice a *different* task or skill that requires self-control for a couple of weeks, and then, at the end of this practice period, participants' self-control strength on the *original* task is measured again, to see if there is any improvement.

One of the better studies was done by psychologist Mark Muraven.[3] His participants were people who wanted to quit smoking. In a preparatory phase, prior to their actual quitting attempt, they had to do daily exercises for two weeks. Participants were told that these exercises might boost their self-control, thus increasing chances of success. However, only the two experimental groups were given exercises that actually targeted self-control. One group had to not eat sweets for two weeks, the other group had to squeeze a handgrip for as long as possible each day. The two control groups were given exercises that required effort but did *not* target self-control. One group had to keep a diary on how they dealt with temptation, the other had to solve math problems twice a day. After the two-week exercise period was over, the actual quitting attempt began. Muraven monitored how his participants were doing over the next four weeks. He found that participants in both experimental groups persevered significantly longer in not smoking than those in both control groups, and that, following this four-week period, significantly fewer had relapsed.

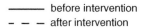

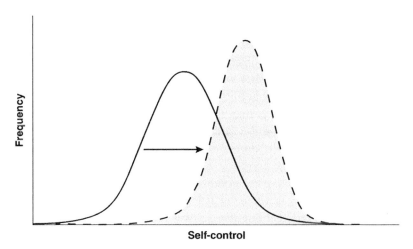

**Self-control**

**Figure 4.1** Hypothetical effect of the training of self-control strength. If everyone receives training of their "self-control muscle," the average level of self-control capacity shifts to the right, and the distribution in self-control capacity becomes less wide.

This is good news! Apparently, self-control muscles can indeed be strengthened. If such quick and easy exercises already suffice, training programs could be developed to boost self-control, thus preparing people for the numerous self-control challenges of modern life. If everyone received this training, the distribution of self-control capacity among the population would shift, as depicted in Figure 4.1. On average, everyone would gain, but those at the lower end of the distribution would gain more, as they have more room for improvement. Individual differences in self-control strength would not be entirely eliminated but would at least be reduced.

Unfortunately, Muraven's positive results are not very representative. Psychologists were initially quite optimistic about the prospects for self-control training, perhaps because one early set of studies found huge improvements.[4] But after doubts arose about this particular set of studies, and after more experimental results came in, expectations had to be tempered. As I write these lines, a few dozen studies have been done. Several found no training effect at all, while recent meta-analyses suggest only small average effect sizes.[5] It also remains unclear how long improvements last. Even if training *does* boost self-control, the effect may be short-lived, a mere fluctuation caused by a temporary change of incentive structure that does not really alter one's baseline level of self-control. In addition, it is unclear what psychological mechanism is responsible for the temporary improvements. It cannot be ruled out that they were nothing but placebo effects.

On reflection, these sobering results should come as no surprise. After all, how likely is it that trait self-control – a personality trait largely determined by genes and early upbringing – can be significantly and permanently altered by just a few quick exercises, such as using your opposite hand for an hour per day during a couple of weeks? That sounds just too good to be true. As stated in Chapter 2, self-control capacity is not set in stone but keeps evolving into adulthood, even into old age. But *change* over the life span does not imply *malleability* over the life span. After all, the human brain and body go through massive changes over the life course – witness the complete overhaul during adolescence – but these are mostly autonomous processes determined by our biological programming, hardly open to outside tinkering. The same may be true of self-control. It seems that the development of trait self-control over the life course is mostly biologically determined.

## Medication?

This raises the question whether we can perhaps intervene in people's biology. More specifically, can self-control be improved through medication? Although controversial, we should not exclude this possibility if we want to have a full overview of the possible avenues for boosting self-control.

The idea is that extremely poor self-control may be an indication of ADHD.[6] Although these two conditions should not be equated, there is a tight connection. Children and adults with ADHD cannot focus their attention for more than a few minutes on anything they do not find interesting or immediately rewarding. Their behavior seems to be completely governed by impulses. As adults, they lead chaotic lives marked by an endless series of ill-considered and reckless choices. Increasingly, lack of inhibition is seen as the core deficit underlying

ADHD. According to Russel Barkley, one of the most prominent experts in the field, ADHD is "primarily a problem of poor inhibition of behavior specifically and poor executive functioning more generally."[7]

The good news is that many children and adults with ADHD respond well to medication such as Ritalin or Concerta. Almost the instant they take these drugs, they become more composed, and are better able to concentrate and control their impulses. The bad news is that once the effects of these stimulants begin to wane, they relapse into their old behavior. It is therefore important to keep taking the medication on a daily basis, perhaps for the rest of their lives. Despite this drawback, for many ADHD patients and their families, such medication is a godsend that has vastly improved their quality of life.

Could medication be the solution? Should we simply distribute pills to people with less than excellent self-control? This conclusion seems premature. First, it is far from clear that *all* self-control problems can be solved this way. Medication may help ADHD patients, but these are individuals who by definition have severe problems in staying focused and controlling impulses. They are at the extreme end of the distribution. It does not follow that these drugs will be equally effective for the vast majority of people who are closer to the middle of the curve, and experience self-control failure only every now and then. Second, the debate continues about the possible side effects of these drugs. Although it is clear that many ADHD patients respond well to medication, less is known about the long-term effects. As long as these remain unclear, it is better not to take risks, and only give these drugs to people who really cannot do without them.

And there is a further issue: Should we medicalize a mental phenomenon that is so widespread and common that it seems to be part of the human condition? Medication may be a godsend for the small percentage of people who, often from an early age, suffer such a dramatic and persistent lack of self-control that it makes normal functioning next to impossible. But if taking medication becomes a prerequisite for successful participation in society for large parts of the population, perhaps something is wrong with society. Fortunately, we need not agonize over these issues here. Maybe someday in the future poor self-control will be a condition that can quickly and easily be cured with cheap and harmless pills – the self-control equivalent of aspirin. When that day arrives, these thorny questions will need to be addressed. But for now, they are of purely theoretical concern.

## 4.2 Self-Control Techniques

So the prospects for improving self-control *strength* are not too bright. This section, therefore, discusses a second and perhaps more promising approach: improve people's self-control *technique*. Try to modify their thoughts, emotions, and behaviors in such a manner that they are able to utilize their limited self-control resources more efficiently and effectively. Just as athletes with less than superior muscle power can still excel by developing superior technique, people with less than superior self-control strength can still achieve their goals by developing outstanding self-control technique.[8]

### Cognitive Techniques

A first technique is distraction. Tip #6 advises us to "[i]mmerse yourself in something that consumes your attention, perhaps doing something with your hands, such as folding origami. Or use your imagination to mentally travel somewhere else, perhaps your last holiday destination." This advice harks back to the original marshmallow studies, where Mischel found that some children facilitated their waiting by not looking at the treats, covering their eyes, or generating diversions, such as talking to themselves or inventing games with their hands and feet (adorable examples of how children desperately tried to ignore the marshmallow can easily be found online). Children also performed better if the experimenter suggested that they think of something fun while waiting, such as singing a song or playing with toys.[9] Mischel concluded that "learning *not* to think about what one is awaiting may enhance delay of gratification."[10]

A related strategy is to think *differently* about the object of desire. In one of the most interesting variants of the experiment, Mischel and his colleague Nancy Baker manipulated how the children *thought* about the marshmallows. The experimenter either emphasized the arousing and motivating "consummatory" qualities of the marshmallow, such as their taste, or the "nonconsummatory" qualities of the marshmallow, neutral properties without motivating potential, such as their shape. More specifically, before the waiting period began, children were taught a game called "think about." It was suggested that they could perhaps play this game while waiting. The experimenter explained this game in two variants:[11]

Look at the marshmallows. They are sweet and chewy and soft. When you look at marshmallows, think about how sweet they are when you eat them. When you look at marshmallows, think about how sweet they taste. Or you can think about how soft they are. When you look at marshmallows, think about how soft and sticky they are in your mouth when you eat them. Or you can think about how chewy they are. When you look at marshmallows, think about how chewy and fun they are to eat. Now, why don't you try playing "think about"? When you look at the marshmallows, what can you think about?

Or alternatively:

Look at the marshmallows; they are round and white and puffy. When you look at marshmallows, think about how white and puffy they are. Clouds are white and puffy too – when you look at marshmallows, think about clouds. Or you can think about how round and white a marshmallow is. The moon is round and white. When you look at marshmallows, think about the moon. Or you can think about how round a marshmallow is on top. A ball is round. When you look at marshmallows, think about playing ball. Now, you try playing "think about." When you look at marshmallows, what can you think about?

The children were able to wait more than twice as long after hearing the second variant. Overall, the secret to successfully delaying gratification seems to lie in the cognitive ability to transform one's mental representation of a stimulus from "hot" into "cool" – from a representation that triggers our reflexive and affective system into a representation that triggers our reflective and cognitive system.[12] Such "cooling down" reduces the arousing, motivating, and behavior-inducing potential of the stimulus, thus making it easier to resist.[13]

But there is a caveat. Before we grow overly optimistic about the prospects of "fixing" poor self-control through distraction or cognitive reappraisal, we need to realize that these strategies require exactly what they aim to achieve: effective self-control. By definition, these techniques involve the ignoring or overriding of certain cognitions and replacing them with others, and by definition, this directly calls on the capacity and motivation for self-control. The only difference is that the object of control has been shifted from the behavior *itself* toward thoughts and emotions that could trigger this behavior. Perhaps we should speak of "second-order self-control."

## Changing Habits

Another strategy is to simply *avoid* situations in which your self-control will be tested. In the supermarket, shoppers who need to watch their diet could, of course, try really, really hard to control their urges while walking through the aisle with the sweets. Or they could try really, really hard to convince themselves that these are just cartons with items full of dubious chemicals, produced by stainless steel machines in large factory halls. But alternatively, they could decide to avoid this aisle all together, and not expose themselves to temptation in the first place. This might be a lot easier. Or when planning to study, people who are easily distracted could make it a habit not to study at home but in a library, where distractions are minimal. Studies suggest that the secret of people who seem to have very good self-control lies in routines such as these. True paragons of discipline have adopted habits that shield them from temptations to begin with.[14] They avoid the aisle with the sweets more or less automatically and pick the library as their preferred study place by default.

So perhaps interventions should not target raw willpower or techniques for distraction and cognitive reappraisal, but teach people strategies for changing their behavior and developing habits that impose fewer demands on their self-control. Ideally, these should be applicable to all domains of life. Teaching people to "never walk through the aisle with the sweets" may help to reduce calorie intake, but would be useless for studying or getting control over one's personal finances. What we need are "general-purpose techniques": rules and strategies that can be deployed in a wide range of domains. A primitive example would be the well-known "first count to ten" rule. This simple rule can prevent people from acting rashly in almost any situation.

What are the prospects for such an approach? Psychologist Gabriele Oettingen and colleagues did some promising experiments. As part of a twenty-one-week vocational training program for low-income women, she taught participants two general techniques for behavior change: mental contrasting[15] and forming implementation intentions.[16] The first technique motivates people to take action by asking them to mentally contrast the future goal they want to achieve with their present situation, and then reflect on the obstacles that must be overcome to attain that future goal. The second technique helps them to resist temptation in some target situation by asking them to think up beforehand what specific action they will take if that situation does indeed occur (see tip #3). Over the course of five sessions, Oettingen trained participants in the use of these techniques for several areas of life, such as academic performance and impersonal relationships. Crucially, after the program was over, Oettingen also measured whether participants had improved in an area that had *not been touched* in the program: time management, as indicated by program attendance. She found a significant effect. Apparently, participants had spontaneously used their newly acquired techniques for goals that were not part of the program. Oettingen concluded that the combination of mental contrasting and forming implementation intentions "can be effectively taught as metacognitive strategy that people can use on their own to successfully change their behavior".[17]

So it seems possible to teach people "general purpose techniques" to change their behavior, thus enabling them to develop habits that shield them from self-control challenges. But again, there is a caveat. Building new habits is hard work that requires exactly what it seeks to render obsolete: self-control. You must inhibit the impulse to do as you have always done, and initiate the new behavior you hope to make a habit instead. And not just once, but numerous times. It may take weeks or months before the new behavior settles in and becomes automatic. Up to that point, executing the intended behavior requires effort and discipline. This means that, other things being equal, people who already have good self-control have better chances at successfully developing new habits than people with poor self-control.[18] As depicted in Figure 4.2, if everyone were taught these techniques, the self-control distribution would not be shifted but stretched. On average, everyone would gain, but those who already have pretty good self-control would gain more.

The same applies to many of the tips and tricks mentioned in the box, such as the advice to exercise regularly, to eat healthy, and to get enough sleep (tips # 9 and # 10). These behaviors can be considered "techniques" to increase the likelihood that you will have sufficient resources at your disposal in moments of temptation. Although they are surely good advice, they also have a circular quality. Exerting

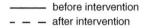

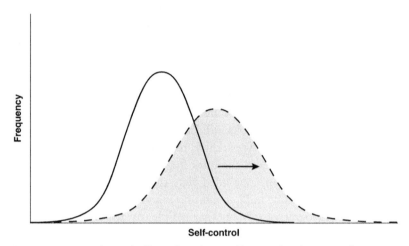

**Figure 4.2** Hypothetical effect of teaching self-control techniques. If everyone were taught self-control techniques, the distribution of self-control may be stretched to the right and flattened.

these behaviors typically requires discipline, and therefore these tips and tricks will only work for those who already have a basis of self-control they can build on. Or take the suggestion to manage stress, for example through regular meditation (tip # 11)? Yet another excellent idea, but easier said than done, especially when the problem you are trying to overcome is poor self-control. On closer examination, nearly *all* of the tips and tricks in the box require at least a modicum of self-control to stand a chance. They are all recommendations to *inhibit* the normal flow of thoughts, feelings, and actions, and *initiate* alternative and more productive thoughts, emotions, or actions. It thus remains uncertain whether they are of much use to those people who need them the most.

## Self-Binding and Commitment

No work on avoiding self-control failure is complete without a reference to Odysseus, the hero of Homer's eponymous work. As the story goes, Odysseus, sailing home from Troy, had to pass the Island of the

Sirens. Sailors who hear the Sirens' beautiful song are bewitched by its sweetness and face certain death as they are drawn to the island and their ship splinters on the rocks. Odysseus, well aware of the danger, wants to hear the singing nonetheless. Before reaching the island, he orders his crew to tie him to the mast and to plug their ears with wax so they cannot hear the singing. He instructs them to continue rowing as they pass the island, and not untie him no matter how hard he prays otherwise. And so it happens. When the ship passes the island, Odysseus hears the mesmerizing singing and begs to be untied so he can swim toward the island. But his men do as instructed and even tighten the ropes, releasing him only after the Sirens are no longer within earshot and Odysseus and his men are safe.

This story is the canonical example of "self-binding": the deliberate decision to curb your freedom in order to protect yourself against the risk of self-control failure. Popular as this story may be, however, it is hard to come up with contemporary examples of self-binding. Freedom is so deeply ingrained in Western law that it is virtually impossible to authorize others to rein in your personal freedom against your later will. In today's world, self-binding usually takes a milder form, not unlike the suggestions given in tip # 14. For instance, you can tell friends and family about your resolutions and ask them to actively discourage you from breaking them in future moments of weakness. But they cannot *force* you to stick to your resolutions. And you can order your bank to automatically transfer part of your monthly salary to a savings account, thus reducing the temptation to spend it right away. But you can still access your savings if you really need the money now (although it may incur a fine).

Perhaps what comes closest to Odysseus' self-binding are apps that temporarily block your access to YouTube, Facebook, Instagram, or whatever digital temptation you wish to resist. Once you have programmed into these apps how long you want access to be blocked, there is no way to undo it. Only after the blocked period has expired will you have access again. In some apps, you can also schedule blocks in advance. If you know, for example, that you tend to begin the working day by endlessly checking social media, you can set the app to automatically block access to these sites during the morning hours. Apps such as these are examples of "commitment devices": arrangements for disciplining yourself by making future self-control failure more costly (sometimes literally, for instance by obliging yourself to

**Box 4.2 Early Childhood Intervention**

What are the prospects of early childhood intervention to improve self-control? There is an enormous literature on the effects of early childhood interventions on all kinds of cognitive and noncognitive outcomes, too much to summarize here. But let me make a few general points.

First, most studies on the effects of early childhood intervention have been set in the United States, many of them targeting children from low-income/high-risk families, or children with socio-emotional or behavioral problems. This means that, regardless of the specifics of these interventions, these studies may find larger effects than interventions targeting "normal" children, for the simple reason that there is more room for improvement.

Second, these studies vary widely in the type of intervention being evaluated and the type of outcome the researchers were interested in, thus making it hard to draw general conclusions. Several reviews have been published that seek to answer the extent to which early childhood interventions can improve "noncognitive skills" or "self-regulation" or "executive function,"[19] but since these are broad categories, these reviews tend to lump together interventions directed at very diverse outcome variables, such as working memory, planning, social skills, emotion regulation, coping strategies, or conflict resolution. Given this wide array of variables, it is not surprising that these reviews often find that results vary greatly. Some interventions show substantial effects, but many others do not.

For self-control as defined in this book, it is hard to draw robust conclusions. Criminologist Alex Piquero and colleagues reviewed forty-one studies on the effects of early self-control improvement programs and found a significant average effect size. But they used a much broader definition of self-control, one including social skills and coping strategies.[20] Developmental scientists Adele Diamond and Kathleen Lee reviewed interventions for enhancing executive functions. Some programs resulted in better attentional control and response inhibition "but none report improvement in the inhibitory control needed to delay gratification."[21]

All in all, it seems plausible that children, to some degree, can be taught to better control their impulses and urges, but it remains an open question *what* exactly gets better. Do these interventions improve self-control *strength* or self-control *technique*? As argued in this chapter, which of the two is improved is far from trivial.

donate money to a charity if you break your resolution).[22] Several studies have found that commitment devices may help to maintain self-control.[23]

What would happen if these self-binding strategies were taught to everyone? Again, I suspect that it would benefit some more than others. First, as with the techniques mentioned, those who already have pretty good self-control may benefit more as it requires at least a modicum of self-control to not only have the intention to commit yourself, but to actually take action, to ask friends and family to keep you on track, to arrange for that monthly bank transferal, or to install that app and set it properly. Second, and perhaps more so than with the techniques mentioned, you need *foresight*. Like Odysseus, you must be willing and able to think ahead, envision what situations might come up the next hours, days, weeks, or even years, and foresee how you might react in those future situations. As I explain in Chapter 5, some people have more talent for such "mental time travel" than others.

## 4.3 A "Third Way": Nudging

Thus far, we have not found the silver bullet. But maybe there is an alternative. Maybe "nudging" is the solution. This new instrument for influencing people's behavior, introduced by behavioral economist Richard Thaler and legal scholar Cass Sunstein, has rapidly gained in popularity. The hallmark of nudging is that this instrument explicitly acknowledges human limits to rationality and willpower, but does not seek to *remedy* these shortcomings. Instead, it *exploits* these shortcomings to move people toward the behavioral option that, in all likelihood, will best serve their interests.[24] In other words, nudging capitalizes on human imperfection. If nudging really works, perhaps we can end our hitherto not very successful search for interventions to improve people's self-control. We can simply "nudge" them to do the right thing.

So what exactly are nudges? Thaler and Sunstein describe nudges as "any aspect of the choice architecture that alters people's behavior in a predictable way without forbidding any options or significantly changing their economic incentives. To count as a mere nudge, the intervention must be easy and cheap to avoid. Nudges are not mandates. Putting the fruit at eye level counts as a nudge. Banning junk food does not."[25] The crucial concept here is "choice architecture."

Choice architecture pertains to all aspects of design, presentation, or context that influence choice or behavior. Examples include the presentation and layout of options in questionnaires and forms, how products are displayed in supermarkets, and aspects of the physical environment, such as the location of stairs and escalators.

The textbook example of a successful nudge is automatic enrollment in 401(k) pension plans in the United States. Normally, new employees who want to enroll in their employer's 401(k) pension plan have to actively sign up. If you do not "opt in," you do not participate. The problem is that many new employees, while certainly having the intention to sign up, never actually do so. They are too preoccupied with other things, such as settling into their new job, or cannot find the time to do all the paperwork, or keep postponing, or simply forget. As a result, they end up with no or only meager pensions. To solve this problem, Thaler and his colleague Shlomo Benartzi proposed switching the default choice from "opt out" to "opt in." In this reverse choice architecture, all new employees are automatically enrolled in their employer's 401(k) plan. If you would rather not participate, no problem, but then you must actively sign out. Everyone who does not sign out is automatically enrolled. Research has shown that this change in default vastly increases the number of enrollments.[26]

Nudges such as these are sometimes called "inertia-nudges," since they target the widespread tendency to procrastinate or forget. To recall, self-control is not only about *inhibiting* certain behaviors but also *initiating* certain behaviors. Self-control failure, thus, comes in two varieties: failure of inhibition and failure of initiation. Inertia-nudges target the second variety and – as several studies found – can be highly effective.[27]

### Partial Solution at Best

Does this mean that nudging is the cure for all self-control problems, as some enthusiastic observers appear to believe? Unsurprisingly, the answer is no. Two problems force us to, yet again, temper expectations.[28]

The first problem is that although nudges may be well suited for countering failures of initiation, they seem less useful for countering failures of inhibition, such as unhealthy lifestyle behavior or impulse buying. Nudges to prevent the latter behaviors might be called "contra-nudges," as they seek to interrupt the ordinary flow of one's impulses and behaviors. There are important differences between inertia-nudges and contra-nudges. For instance, inertia-nudges usually involve infrequent choice situations – arranging for a pension plan is not an everyday occurrence – whereas contra-nudges usually involve highly frequent choice situations. Life is replete with temptations to consume calories, spend money, check social media, or what have you. As a consequence, even if nudges such as placing fatty foods at the back of the cafeteria work for the first couple of days or weeks, customers may quickly find out how they are being manipulated and adjust their behavior accordingly. All it takes is reaching a little further. Another difference is that inertia-nudges *build on* already existing urges – that is, the tendency to procrastinate and favor more enjoyable pastimes – whereas contra-nudges *go against* already existing urges, such as the craving for certain foods, alcohol, or luxuries. These impulses are often deeply rooted in habits, which are notoriously hard to change. In short, inertia-nudges go *with* the grain, whereas contra-nudges go *against* the grain. It is thus not surprising that contra-nudges typically show much weaker effects, and sometimes have no effect at all.[29]

The second problem is that nudging presupposes a physical choice architecture that can be manipulated, such as an online form or a cafeteria. But many situations in which people with poor self-control could surely use a helping hand are not embedded in a physical choice architecture. Life is an endless stream of self-control challenges that emerge from the ongoing flow of events. People must get up from the couch, do their best at school and work, behave correctly toward significant others – situations in which it is difficult to see how nudging could be of any help. Of the innumerable choice situations that make up life, nudging can only address the small subset of choices that are anchored in a tangible choice architecture amenable to manipulation.

## 4.4 Conclusion

This chapter has asked: To what extent can self-control be improved? Unfortunately, the conclusion appears to be that poor trait self-control is not something that can easily be remedied. It is not a skill like reading or writing that almost anyone can learn. Trait self-control is more like intelligence, a capacity that is largely determined by genes and early upbringing. It is therefore not surprising that many studies on training programs to boost self-control have found no or only modest effects. Moreover, these modest effects may not last for long. Medication may help in certain cases of extreme inhibitory problems, but it is unclear what it does for milder, more everyday instances of self-control failure, while little is known about the long-term effects. It is also questionable whether poor self-control should be considered a "disorder" that must be treated with drugs.

Alternatively, one might attempt to improve self-control by teaching people self-control techniques. People can be taught strategies to reduce the "hot" properties of seductive stimuli or strategies for changing behavior and developing habits that reduce the need for self-control altogether. Several studies suggest this might actually work. But there is a catch: Successfully deploying techniques such as cognitive reframing or changing habits requires at least a modicum of self-control capacity, since these strategies are all recommendations to inhibit the normal flow of thoughts, feelings, and actions, and to focus on alternative thoughts, emotions, and actions. "Lessons in self-control technique" may therefore benefit people who already have reasonable self-control and allow them to do even better, but they will hardly make a difference for people at the bottom of the self-control ladder. These lessons amplify what is already there, and if there is little to amplify, the gain will be close to zero. The net effect may be that social inequalities will only grow bigger. And to add insult to injury, it would only become easier to blame people with low self-control for their sorry fate. After all, if they are taught techniques to improve self-control, but nevertheless persist in their irresponsible conduct, it must be of their own choosing, right?[30]

One final observation. In Chapter 3, I explained that every stimulus has the potential to undermine self-control. This means that self-control capacity is partly a function of situation. The tips and tricks presented in this chapter, however, ignore these situational influences. In terms of the so-called agency-structure debate, they only target the first half of the equation. (Granted, tip #6 recommends removing temptations from the environment, and tip #14 recommends asking for social support, but it remains the individual who has to take action.) This singular focus on the individual is characteristic of what sociologist Heidi Rimke calls "self-help ideology." In self-help literature, the social dimension of problems is denied or obscured, and subjects are constructed as possessing an inner reservoir of power that with the right technique can be developed at will. "Self-help ideology" relies upon the principles of personal responsibility and reinforces a world-view which postulates that people can exercise control and mastery of themselves and their lives.[31] A similar focus on the individual can be found in the scholarly literature. Most studies on preventing self-control failure concern interventions that target individuals rather than the wider environment. A review by Angela Duckworth and colleagues, for example, describes more than twenty strategies to reduce food-related self-control failure. Most of these strategies are directed at the individual and her intentions, for instance the use of commitment devices, engaging in mindfulness, or the provision of choice-relevant information. None seeks to boost self-control through altering the environment.[32]

I will return to these issues later in the book. For now, I restrict myself to the general conclusion that individual differences in self-control are here to stay. There is little support for the claim that exercise builds stronger "self-control muscles," while teaching people self-control techniques may be least effective for precisely those who would benefit most. Nudging can help to prevent some types of self-control failure, but will definitely not solve all problems. At the end of the day, the fact remains that some people simply have more talent for self-control than others, and thus better prospects for achieving health, wealth, and happiness than others. We may have no choice but to accept this reality.

# 5 | The Value of the Future

What determines how many resources people are willing to spend on maintaining self-control? Since resources are limited, this is an important question. The answer depends – at least in part – on how much they care about the future. Why live healthily if you do not care about getting old and prefer to enjoy the good life now? It also depends on whether people believe the effort will pay off. Why forego pleasure and work hard to get a diploma if you expect to be unemployed anyway? Or save money for later when inflation is in the double digits? In such cases, one may be perfectly *capable* of exerting self-control but nonetheless unwilling to actually *use* that capacity. This brings us – once again – to the role of motivation.

The extent to which people are motivated to exercise self-control hinges on many factors, including external cues that activate certain desires or intentions, the value of the various behavioral options available, the expectations of significant others, social and cultural norms, and so forth. These are all aspects of situation and, therefore, when circumstances change, the motivation for self-control may change as well. If you wish to manipulate motivation, these are the levers to pull. Much of the behavioral change literature focuses on interventions that target these situational factors.

This chapter, however, examines an influence on self-control motivation that does not reside in the environment but within the person: *time orientation*. The essence of self-control challenges is that you must choose between a smaller reward now and a larger reward later. People differ in their overall pattern of preferences vis-à-vis such intertemporal choices. Some people are strongly moved and motivated by the future. They are guided by the goals they have set for themselves for the coming weeks, months, or even years, and try to resist all derailing temptations and distractions. Others are more strongly moved by the here and now, with all its temptations, opportunities, and gratifications. They seize the day without fretting too much about tomorrow or next week, let alone next year. Put differently, some people have a more future-oriented personality, others a more present-oriented personality. Some people, therefore, tend to be more motivated to exercise self-control than others.

Against this background, this chapter asks: *What factors determine time orientation? And why do these factors have this effect?* Armed with some answers, we will be better placed to understand why some people seem more inclined to delay gratification than others. In Sections 5.1 to 5.3, I review the well-established research on "delay discounting," and explain that time orientation is dependent on a factor we met earlier: working memory capacity. This capacity enables us to envision the future situations that are the wellspring of self-control motivation. In Sections 5.4 and 5.5, I switch to a relatively new body of research called "life history theory." This theory suggests that time orientation is partly determined by certain aspects of childhood environment: people who grew up in a harsh and unpredictable environment tend to be more present-oriented and thus less motivated to restrain their behavior. But before delving in, there is a practical problem we must solve.

## 5.1 How to Measure Time Orientation

Before we can get to the main question, we first need a valid and reliable measure of time orientation. How can we assess whether someone has a more present or a more future-oriented personality?

This is anything but straightforward. Our first inclination might be to look at overt behavior. Some people tend to act in ways that are rewarding in the short term but harmful in the longer term, while others are the mirror opposite. From this pattern of behaviors, one might conclude that the first group is more present-oriented, and the latter more future-oriented. But is this conclusion correct? Not necessarily. The first group's behavior could also stem from a lack of willpower. It is possible that someone is strongly oriented toward the future and highly motivated to pursue future goals, but nonetheless lacks the self-control capacity to achieve these goals, either because he is not endowed with much talent for self-control to begin with, or because his life circumstances are so stressful that his self-control capacity is chronically exhausted. Overt behavior, therefore, is not a suitable indicator of time orientation.

Our second inclination might be to consult psychology and look for some well-established instrument to assess time orientation. The literature suggests two potential candidates: the Consideration of Future Consequences Scale (CFC)[1] and the Zimbardo Time Perspective Inventory (ZTPI).[2] Unfortunately, both scales suffer from the same problem as overt behavior: It is rather unclear what they measure. Consider four statements taken from these scales:

- "Often I engage in a particular behavior in order to achieve outcomes that may not result for many years"(CFC);
- "My behavior is only influenced by the immediate (i.e., a matter of days or weeks) outcomes of my actions" (CFC);
- "I do things impulsively" (ZPTI);
- "I am able to resist temptations when I know there is work to be done" (ZPTI).

Do these statements measure a *general orientation* toward immediate or future rewards? Or do they measure the *capacity* to resist immediate rewards and wait for future reward? Particularly the last item seems a pure measure of capacity, as it explicitly mentions "being able" to resist temptation. What does it mean if someone disagrees with this statement? It only says that this person has *trouble* delaying gratification, not that he *does not care* about the work getting done.[3] Many statements in these scales are merely descriptions of behavior that – on closer inspection – tell us nothing about the relevant motivations or preferences. They are not valid measures of time orientation.[4] What we need, instead, is an indicator that gives a clear assessment of how people *value* future outcomes compared to present ones, *regardless* of their actual capacity to achieve these outcomes.

The indicator that comes closest is the "delay discounting rate." Delay discounting is the tendency to assign less value to outcomes that are remote in time than to outcomes that are immediate. For instance, given the choice, most people would prefer getting $95 today over $100 a year from today. This is not necessarily irrational. After all, who knows what will happen in the intervening period? One bird in hand is worth two in the bush and there is inflation to consider. But interestingly, many people are willing to forego more than just $5 to get the reward now. They will also prefer less than $95 today – say $85 – over $100 a year from today. Some will settle for even less – say just $50 – so long as they can have the cash right now. The more someone is willing to give up in order to get something earlier rather than later, the steeper his delay discounting rate. I take this rate as an indicator of time orientation.

Delay discounting has been studied extensively. The most widely used procedure for assessing a person's delay discounting rate is to ask him to make a series of (hypothetical) choices between a monetary reward now and a larger monetary reward later. By varying the amounts of money and the delay periods, it is possible to calculate an individual's discount rate: a coefficient reflecting how much value this person assigns to rewards that come about only later. Box 5.1 contains an often used series of intertemporal choices to assess a person's discount rate: the so-called "Monetary Choice Questionnaire." In this series, the delay period varies from one week to six months, and the delayed reward runs up to nearly thrice the immediate reward. Other questionnaires, with longer periods and larger sums, have been used as well.

Note that the capacity for self-control is in no way mentioned or implicated in this questionnaire: It is simply a series of questions about preferences. Many behavioral scientists nevertheless talk of delay discounting and self-control (or impulsivity) as if these were merely different names for the same thing.[5] This is confusing. Delay discounting refers to a pattern of preferences, self-control to a pattern of behaviors. Granted, from a distance they may look the same, as steep discount rates and behaviors commonly associated with poor self-control often go together. People who have steeper discount rates are, for instance, more likely to be obese and exhibit addictive behaviors.[6] Moreover, one's discount rate may partly derive from self-control capacity. As people grow older, they may learn from experience how good or bad they actually are at self-control, and adjust their temporal preferences to these lessons of life. But again: Both are not the same. It is entirely possible for someone to prefer a delayed larger reward but *nonetheless* fail to obtain that reward due to poor self-control capacity. As anyone who has ever made a New Year's resolution knows, it is one thing to *make* a choice but quite another to *sustain* that choice.[7]

All things considered, measures of delay discounting, such as the Monetary Choice Questionnaire, are the best instruments for gauging time orientation currently available on the psychological market.[8] To be sure, they remain far from ideal. Life is about more than just

---

**Box 5.1  Monetary Choice Questionnaire[9]**

For each of the next twenty-seven choices, please indicate which reward you would prefer: The smaller reward today, or the larger reward in the specified number of days?

  1. Would you prefer $54 today, or $55 in 117 days?
  2. Would you prefer $55 today, or $75 in 61 days?
  3. Would you prefer $19 today, or $25 in 53 days?
  4. Would you prefer $31 today, or $85 in 7 days?
  5. Would you prefer $14 today, or $25 in 19 days?
  6. Would you prefer $47 today, or $50 in 160 days?
  7. Would you prefer $15 today, or $35 in 13 days?
  8. Would you prefer $25 today, or $60 in 14 days?
  9. Would you prefer $78 today, or $80 in 162 days?
 10. Would you prefer $40 today, or $55 in 62 days?
 11. Would you prefer $11 today, or $30 in 7 days?
 12. Would you prefer $67 today, or $75 in 119 days?
 13. Would you prefer $34 today, or $35 in 186 days?
 14. Would you prefer $27 today, or $50 in 21 days?
 15. Would you prefer $69 today, or $85 in 91 days?
 16. Would you prefer $49 today, or $60 in 89 days?
 17. Would you prefer $80 today, or $85 in 157 days?
 18. Would you prefer $24 today, or $35 in 29 days?
 19. Would you prefer $33 today, or $80 in 14 days?
 20. Would you prefer $28 today, or $30 in 179 days?
 21. Would you prefer $34 today, or $50 in 30 days?
 22. Would you prefer $25 today, or $30 in 80 days?
 23. Would you prefer $41 today, or $75 in 20 days?
 24. Would you prefer $54 today, or $60 in 111 days?
 25. Would you prefer $54 today, or $80 in 30 days?
 26. Would you prefer $22 today, or $25 in 136 days?
 27. Would you prefer $20 today, or $55 in 7 days?

---

money. A more sophisticated instrument might include other question formats and a broader array of choices, for instance between taking a short trip this weekend versus a two-week vacation in six months, or between eating whatever you like today versus being healthy after retirement. But then again, money can buy many of the things people most value, so the delay discounting rate may be a pretty good "summary indicator" for time orientation after all.

## 5.2 Individual Differences in Delay Discounting

Research suggests that, like self-control capacity, delay discounting may be considered a personality trait.[10] An individual's baseline discount rate is partly determined by genetic inheritance and remains relatively stable over time. It does not change from one day, week, or month to another.[11] But like self-control, delay discounting is influenced by situational variables. Psychologist Jennifer Lerner and colleagues found that people who had just watched a sad film clip were more inclined to favor the immediate reward over the larger delayed reward. They conclude that, apparently, "sadness makes one myopic".[12] Another study found the exact mirror image: Participants who had just viewed a funny film clip were more inclined to favor the delayed reward over the immediate reward.[13] Positive feelings, apparently, make people more farsighted. Stress also makes a difference. A meta-analysis found that stress prompts stronger preferences for immediate rewards.[14]

Delay discounting is associated with various sociodemographic variables. Table 5.1 presents the results of a survey among 43,000 respondents in the United Kingdom aged twenty-one to sixty-five who were asked to make a hypothetical choice between receiving £45 in three days or £70 in three months.[15]

Preference for the earlier reward is significantly associated with female gender, lower education, lower income, younger age of first sexual intercourse, sexual infidelity, smoking, and higher Body Mass Index (BMI). Although this survey used only a single question, the findings are consistent with other studies using more elaborate measures.[16]

### *Intelligence and Working Memory*

Interestingly, delay discounting is also associated with intelligence. Psychologist Harriet de Wit and colleagues surveyed over 600 middle-aged adults, and found that IQ predicts the delay discounting rate *even after controlling* for potentially confounding factors such as education and income.[17] At first sight, this may seem rather puzzling. Why would less smart people be more oriented toward the present? That makes little sense. Don't we all have dreams and goals for the future? Don't we all want to be healthy and happy, find a good job, live in a nice place, and – perhaps – start a family? Why would IQ make a difference here? The explanation probably lies in differences in working memory

Table 5.1 *Delay discounting as a function of demographics and behaviors.*

|                          | £45 in three days | £70 in three months |
|--------------------------|-------------------|---------------------|
| *Gender*                 |                   |                     |
| Female                   | 51.8%             | 48.2%               |
| Male                     | 46.9%             | 53.1%               |
| *Education*              |                   |                     |
| Secondary                | 59.3%             | 40.7%               |
| Sixth form               | 55.4%             | 44.6%               |
| University               | 46.1%             | 53.9%               |
| Postgraduate             | 40.1%             | 59.9%               |
| *Income*                 |                   |                     |
| £0–10K                   | 52.7%             | 47.3%               |
| £10–25K                  | 53.1%             | 46.9%               |
| £25–50K                  | 45.0%             | 55.0%               |
| Over £50K                | 39.1%             | 60.9%               |
| *Sexual behavior*        |                   |                     |
| Had sex before age 16    | 55.5%             | 45.5%               |
| Had sex after age 16     | 47.7%             | 52.3%               |
| Been unfaithful          | 54.9%             | 45.1%               |
| Not been unfaithful      | 47.3%             | 52.7%               |
| *Substance use*          |                   |                     |
| Coffee drinkers          | 48.9%             | 51.2%               |
| Smokers                  | 59.5%             | 40.5%               |
| Regular drinkers         | 48.5%             | 51.5%               |
| Drug users               | 56.6%             | 43.4%               |
| *BMI*                    |                   |                     |
| Normal                   | 47.2%             | 52.8%               |
| Overweight               | 49.8%             | 50.2%               |
| Obese                    | 54.2%             | 45.8%               |

Reprinted from: *Personality and Individual Differences*, 47(8), 973–978, Reimers, S., Maylor, E. A., Stewart, N., & Chater, N., Associations between a one-shot delay discounting measure and age, income, education and real-world impulsive behavior, Copyright 2009, with permission from Elsevier.

capacity. This explanation is not very straightforward, though, so let me break it down into three steps.[18]

The first step is to recognize that monetary choices require working memory. As discussed in Section 3.1, working memory refers to the capacity to actively hold information in mind and work with it.

In other words, working memory refers to the capacity to work with information *that is not perceptually present.*[19] The monetary rewards in delay discounting tasks clearly fall within this category. A comparison with the marshmallow test will help to clarify the point. In the marshmallow test, the immediate reward is perceptually present. It is right there, on the plate in front of you, where it can be seen, touched, and smelled, giving it all its arousing and motivating qualities. The same goes for the delayed reward: It is simply that thing in front of you times two. In cognitive terms, therefore, the marshmallow test is easy, because it involves options that are part of the here and now. Both the immediate and delayed reward are easy to envision, all it takes is to keep your eyes open. In contrast, the delay discounting task is cognitively more demanding, because it is exclusively set in the symbolic world. Both options are not physically present but must be imagined, which by definition requires working memory. Moreover, to determine the subjective value of both options, additional cognitive work must be done. After all, these options are just numbers ("x dollars") without intrinsic value. They derive their value from the stuff you can buy with that money, and from what that stuff means to you. So determining the subjective value of both options requires further information processing and additional working memory capacity.

The second step in the argument is to recognize that the competition between the two monetary options is an unequal struggle, because it is probably easier to determine the subjective value of the *immediate* option than the subjective value of the *delayed* option. It is easier to assess what a financial gift you receive today will mean to you – perhaps you can buy that new TV set you always wanted or finally pay off your debts – than to assess what a gift you will receive sometime in the future will mean to you. In the latter case, you *also* have to consider how your life and the world may have changed during the intervening period, you *also* have to consider what your wants and needs may then be, and you *also* have to take inflation into account. All this requires more cognitive processing and thus more working memory. (If you are not convinced, try it for yourself. See what comes easier to mind: What you will do with $1,000 I give you today, or what you will do with $ 3,000 I will give you five years from now.) This asymmetry means that when working memory capacity is scarce, the immediate option probably has stronger motivating force because it is easier to envision and connect with. People with limited working

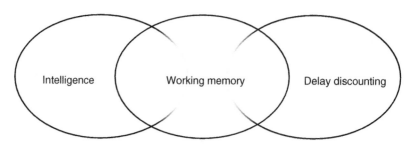

**Figure 5.1** Relation between intelligence, working memory, and delay discounting.

memory capacity may thus prefer immediate over delayed rewards for the simple reason that it is easier to know *what you want now* than to know *what you want in x years*.

If this explanation is correct, cognitive load should lead to (temporarily) steeper discount rates, as cognitive load taxes working memory. And indeed, this is exactly what was found in a study by psychologist John Hinson and colleagues. In one of their experiments, participants had to make decisions in a series of delayed discounting choices while *at the same time* keeping a string of letters or digits in memory. Results showed that these participants discounted more steeply than participants in a control group, who were not given the memory task. In another experiment, Hinson taxed working memory by making the choices more complex. Instead of the usual two options, each choice consisted of three or four options that had to be evaluated. This also led to steeper discounting.[20] Both experiments confirm that reduced working memory causes a stronger preference for immediate rewards.

The third and final step in the argument is to make the connection to intelligence. After all, what must be explained is not the correlation between delay discounting and *working memory*, but the correlation between delay discounting and *intelligence*. This last step is easy. As discussed in Chapter 3, working memory capacity is strongly correlated with general intelligence. It logically follows that discount rate is *also* correlated with general intelligence. In other words, working memory is the *linking pin* between intelligence and discount rate. Figure 5.1 represents this relationship.[21] As the observant reader will notice, this is the same type of relationship as was found in Chapter 3 between intelligence and self-control capacity.

## 5.3 Mental Time Travel

If time machines existed, chances are people would more often choose the delayed rather than the immediate reward, because they would no longer have to construct a mental image of the delayed reward and the situation in which it would be received. They could simply take a trip to the future to see and feel what it would be like. This direct experience of the delayed reward might have much more motivating power than the vague and incomplete images in their mind. The time machine would have created a "level playing field" for the competing options.

Needless to say, time machines do not exist. The decade of the 2010s, however, has seen a rapid growth in research on "mental time travel."[22] This is the capacity to project oneself into the future by *mentally simulating* future events and situations.[23] As the word "simulating" suggests, mental time travel is not just *knowing* what might happen, but *pre-experiencing* future events by using your imagination. It is the active act of envisioning a future situation in which you really have become that healthy and attractive person you always wanted to be, wearing that beautiful dress or smart suit that was always too tight, receiving compliments from your friends (and secret admirers) – or in which you, after all those years of saving, really are lying on the beach of that tropical island, hearing the ocean waves, feeling the sun on your skin and enjoying a Margarita. In a sense, mental time travel is the exact opposite of "attentional myopia" or "transcendental failure" – concepts discussed in previous chapters that refer to the inability to see beyond the here and now.[24]

Mental time travel, therefore, may alter intertemporal preferences by allowing people to create detailed and vivid simulations of future rewards and the contexts in which they are enjoyed.[25] Of critical importance are the affective consequences of these simulations. Although mental time travel is primarily a cognitive activity rooted in working memory,[26] visual and auditory imagery combine with activation of emotional circuitry.[27] In the words of psychologists Daniel Gilbert and Timothy Wilson, when thinking about the future "the cortex generates simulations, briefly tricking subcortical systems into believing that those events are unfolding in the present and then taking note of the feelings these systems produce".[28] This "preview" of the hedonic consequences of future events can influence current decision-making by altering the balance of subjective values, thus motivating people to forego immediate pleasures in favor of later rewards.[29] Simply put, mental time travel provides a "motivational brake" on impulsive and myopic behavior.[30]

## Making Time Travel Easier

This suggests that the more lively, detailed, and vivid the mental simulation of the future reward and its context, the greater the likelihood of tipping the balance in the unequal struggle between immediate and future rewards toward the latter. Empirical support comes from a spectacular experiment by Hal Hershfield and colleagues.[31] In this experiment, participants were primed to envision the future as clear and vividly as possible by setting up an "encounter" with their future selves. More specifically, participants entered a virtual reality environment in which they could see a digitally created avatar representing a seventy-year-old version of themselves (see Figure 5.2). The avatar was projected onto a virtual mirror in front of the participants. As with a real mirror, the avatar moved in perfect synchrony with the participants. Participants in the control group entered the same virtual reality environment, but saw an avatar of their current selves, like in a normal mirror. The participants were then given a hypothetical monetary allocation task. How would they divide an unexpected windfall of $1,000 over several options? Hershfield found that participants who had been exposed to their future selves allocated more than twice as much money to a retirement fund than participants who had seen their current selves. In a variant of this experiment, after being exposed to their future selves, participants were given a series of delay discounting choices. Compared to the control group, they were more likely to prefer later over immediate ones.[32]

But we don't need to set up flashy virtual reality environments to establish the effect of mental time travel on time orientation. Less elaborate manipulations may also do the trick. In one study, for example, psychologists Adam Bulley and Matthew Gullo asked participants what future events they were looking forward to, such as a birthday or a trip to Paris, and then presented them with a series of delay discounting choices. While making these choices, participants were reminded of future events which, as they had reported earlier, would take place at about the same time as the moment of receiving the delayed reward

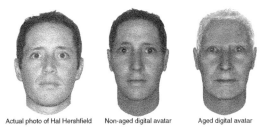

Actual photo of Hal Hershfield    Non-aged digital avatar    Aged digital avatar

**Figure 5.2** Example of age progression. *Source:* Hershfield et al. (2011)

in question. For example, if a participant had mentioned he was going to Paris in six months, he was reminded of this future trip when he had to choose between x dollars now and y dollars in six months. Bulley and Gullo found that these reminders made people more inclined to prefer the delayed reward.[33]

Other studies show similar results.[34] The more vividly participants imagined the upcoming events, and the greater the emotional intensity participants felt while imagining these events, the stronger the shift toward delayed rewards.[35] The effect is also stronger if events are tied to personally relevant goals.[36] However, reminding people of future events only increases the preference for delayed rewards if these events are positive in emotional valence. If they are negative, such as getting ill or failing an exam, the effect is the opposite: steeper discounting.[37] Bulley and colleagues conclude that mental time travel "enables humans to flexibly respond to anticipated contingencies, which can also include an increased tendency to indulge in immediate temptations when the content of prospective images is grim".[38]

## Conclusion

In a sense, mental time travel is the supplement to the cognitive techniques for delaying gratification that Walter Mischel discovered in the 1970s. His young participants were better able to resist the marshmallows if they managed to get them "out of their mind," for instance by distracting themselves or looking away, or if they managed to reduce the marshmallows' arousing qualities by focusing on their "cool" aspects such as their shape and color. Mental time travel is the exact reverse. The delayed reward, by definition, is not perceptually present, and the challenge is to get this reward "into the mind" by generating visual and auditory imagery. The more vivid and detailed the simulation, the "hotter" the delayed option can become, and the greater the likelihood it will overpower the lure of the present.

What both techniques have in common is that they rely on working memory. This implies that cognitive load may undermine self-control not in one but *two* ways. In Chapter 3, we saw that cognitive load can impair the *capacity* for self-control by making it harder to keep the future goal actively in mind and to monitor progress toward this goal. People simply "forget" to control their behavior, and the impulsive system gets the upper hand. Now we can add that cognitive load can also undermine the *motivation* for self-control by making it harder to mentally simulate future states that are sufficiently vivid and detailed to provide a "motivational brake" on immediate gratification. Although the difference is subtle and the two mechanisms partly overlap – after all, both involve working memory – they are analytically distinct. In the first case, it is a matter of keeping a future goal in mind and not getting distracted, in the second, it is about having a future goal with motivating power *in the first place*.

## 5.4 Living Fast and Slow

We now turn to a slightly different subject. As reported in Section 5.2, research has found that delay discounting correlates with (indicators of) socioeconomic class. What explains this association? No doubt the correlation will partly be spurious, as both socioeconomic class and delay discounting are related to intelligence. But this cannot be the whole story. After all, the lower socioeconomic classes also more frequently exhibit behaviors that suggest steep discounting rates but which have little to do with cognitive abilities, such as eating unhealthy foods or smoking. It is implausible that the lower classes would lack the cognitive abilities to grasp how these behaviors could harm their future selves. Moreover, everyday life is replete with vivid reminders of what can happen to you if you persist in unhealthy habits. Just go outside and have a look at some of your compatriots, or buy one of those cigarette boxes with graphic pictures of blackened lungs and gruesome tumors.

This section, therefore, provides an alternative explanation: The stronger present orientation of the lower socioeconomic classes is – at least partly – the result of their particular life situation. The argument leading up to this conclusion is quite complicated, though, and requires a detour through evolutionary biology.

## Unreliable Experimenters

Let me begin with the observation that delaying gratification only makes sense when it is reasonably certain that the future reward will actually materialize. This may not always be the case. The longer the delay period, the more likely that something will come in between, that things will not go as expected or predicted, or that for some other reason the reward will not eventuate. Who knows what might happen between now and a month, a year, ten years? People will only be motivated to exercise self-control if they have reason to believe that the goods will be delivered. If this is uncertain, it may be more rational to take the immediate reward.

This principle is nicely illustrated in a study by psychologist Celeste Kidd and colleagues. Once again, it involves marshmallows. Kidd replicated the classic marshmallow experiment, but with a twist: She manipulated the reliability of the experimenter. In half of the cases, children were led to believe that the experimenter was reliable, while, in the other half, they were led to believe that she was *un*reliable. Specifically, before the marshmallow experiment began, all children participated in an "art project" to "decorate-your-own-cup." At its outset, the experimenter told the children they could either use a set of well-used crayons now, or if they were able to wait for a few minutes, could use a big set of cool art supplies the experimenter had to fetch from another room. "The big set has markers, pens, colored pencils – a lot of cool stuff."[39] In the reliable condition, the experimenter returned with the promised art supplies after 2.5 minutes, but in the unreliable condition, the experimenter returned empty-handed, told the children she did not have the supplies after all, and suggested they use the well-used crayons instead. Next, after the children had drawn for some minutes, the procedure was repeated, this time with a choice between a small sticker now or a larger collection of better stickers later, which the experimenter had to fetch from another room. Again, in the reliable condition the experimenter returned with the promised articles, whereas in the unreliable condition she returned empty-handed.

The actual marshmallow experiment took place immediately after this art project. The children were told that, as a reward for finishing in time, they could have one marshmallow now or two marshmallows later if they were able to wait until the experimenter returned. Kidd found big differences between the groups. Children in the reliable group waited about twelve minutes on average before eating the marshmallow, and most waited the full fifteen minutes before the experimenter returned. Children in the unreliable group, however, waited only three minutes on average, while hardly any of them waited the full fifteen minutes. In conclusion, it is not only self-control capacity that determines how long children will delay gratification. No less important is the perceived probability that the delayed reward will actually materialize.

## Life History Theory

This experiment illustrates a more general point: In a harsh and unpredictable environment, it may be rational to take whatever is available now, and not bet on any future rewards, which may never arrive. In fact, if children grow up in a harsh and unpredictable environment, a strong orientation toward the present may become part of their character – a personality trait that persists well into adulthood, even if their later life conditions improve. Or at least, this is one of the claims of a branch of evolutionary biology called "life history theory." This still young theory provides an ambitious framework for understanding and explaining differences in time orientation between those at the bottom of the socioeconomic ladder and those higher up.

Like all theories in evolutionary biology, life history theory revolves around the question of what traits and behavioral strategies are most *adaptive*. The theory starts from the premise that time and energy are limited, and that organisms therefore tend to allocate these limited resources in a way that optimizes their chances to reproduce. Crucially, this requires trade-offs. At the most basic level, organisms must choose between investing in growth, health, and development (developing strength, skills, and knowledge), or investing in reproduction (mating and caring for their offspring). It is either the one or the other. Now here is the dilemma: On the one hand, if organisms delay reproduction and first invest in growth, health, and development, their offspring will be of better quality, thus increasing their chances of reproduction. But due to this delay, they run a serious risk of dying before they actually start to reproduce, so their genes will not be transferred to the next generation. On the other hand, if organisms start reproducing soon after birth, they may be successful in transferring their genes but their offspring may be of such poor quality that they, in turn, have little chance of reproducing themselves. Their genes will not be transferred either.

How to solve this dilemma? At first sight, the obvious solution is to find some middle ground: find the best compromise between these two competing strategies for survival and reproduction.

But there is a complicating factor. Which strategy is most adaptive *depends* on one's environment. Some environments are harsh and unpredictable.[40] Chances of early death by disease or violence are high, and making long-term plans or commitments is risky, because tomorrow's world might be totally different from today's. In the words of Hobbes, life is nasty, brutish, and short. According to life history theory, in such an environment a "fast life strategy" provides the best chance of reproduction. This fast strategy is characterized by the early onset of puberty and first sexual activity, prioritization of reproduction, focus on a great number of offspring, and little parental investment in each. People who grow up in such a harsh and unpredictable environment will have a short time horizon. They look for opportunities in the here and now and are willing to take risks, even if these are costly to their health. In such an environment, it is most adaptive to take the metaphorical one marshmallow now.

In a more secure and stable environment, however, it is more adaptive to take your time. As the chances of disease and early death are smaller, and as one can be pretty sure that the foreseeable future will not be radically different from the present, it may pay off to follow a "slow life strategy," and invest in quality instead of quantity. The slow strategy is characterized by the later onset of puberty and first sexual activity, greater longevity, and a focus on producing a smaller number of offspring and investing heavily in them. People who grow up in such an environment will have a longer time horizon and are less willing to take risks. In such an environment, it is most adaptive to wait for the two marshmallows.

The two strategies are summarized in Figure 5.3. (The columns should be understood as the ends of a continuum. Life strategy is not a binary choice between fast or slow.)

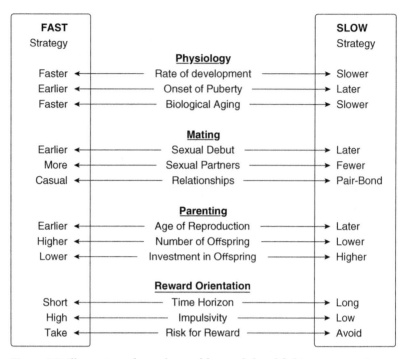

**Figure 5.3** Illustration of correlates of fast and slow life history strategies. *Source:* Griskevicius et al. (2013)

Obviously, human beings do not know beforehand in what type of environment they will enter the world. Through gene expression, developing children can therefore adjust their – not yet fixed – pattern of time and energy allocation to the environment they are born and grow up in. The first five to seven years are critical. During these years, children deduce to what type of environment they must adapt, based on cues like the warmth and stability of their family, and the prevalence of death and disease in their wider environment. During those first years, the parameters are set, and the tendency toward a slower or faster life strategy becomes part of personality. This means that people's overall time orientation is not only dependent on their current life circumstances but also on the circumstances of their early childhood years.[41]

Or so the theory goes. How about the empirical evidence? There is a growing body of research consistent with the claim that (indicators of) harshness and unpredictability during childhood predict human development, time orientation, and behavior.[42] Reviewing the literature, evolutionary psychologist Bruce Ellis and collaborators conclude that "reliable associations" exist between *harshness* and life strategy. Lower socioeconomic position, low local life expectancy, exposure to violence, neighborhood hazards, and low parental investment are all linked with a faster strategy.[43] A handful of studies show that *unpredictability* is also associated with life strategy. The number of changes in parental figures during childhood (for instance, because of divorce, cohabitation, or placement in foster care) predicts a faster life strategy, as does frequency of residential change during childhood.

But these findings must be interpreted with caution, as most of them are correlational. Causality cannot be determined and spurious correlations cannot be ruled out. This is why a series of studies by Vladas Griskevicius and colleagues is of particular interest. These behavioral scientists used an experimental design to determine the effects of a harsh and unpredictable childhood environment on various indicators falling within the "reward orientation" cluster of life history theory (see the lower cluster in Figure 5.3). With these studies, we also return to delay discounting, since this was one of Griskevicius' dependent variables.

In one set of experiments, Griskevicius examined the effects of mortality threat on delay discounting. Participants in the experimental group first had to read an article from the *New York Times* entitled "Dangerous Times Ahead: Life and Death in the 21st Century."[44] The article described recent trends toward violence and death in the United States, and concluded that the future would be treacherous. Next, participants were presented with a series of monetary delay discounting choices. As a proxy for harshness and unpredictability of childhood environment, Griskevicius used childhood socioeconomic status (SES). This was measured by asking participants to indicate their agreement with statements such as "My family usually had enough money for things when I was growing up" and "I grew up in a relatively wealthy neighborhood." Griskevicius found a significant effect for childhood SES. Among participants from low-SES backgrounds, the mortality threat led to a stronger preference for the *immediate* reward, whereas among participants from high-SES backgrounds, mortality threat led to the opposite: a stronger preference for the *delayed* reward. Mortality cues, in other words, made low childhood-SES participants more *present*-oriented and high childhood-SES participants more *future*-oriented.[45]

In another set of experiments, Griskevicius examined how feelings of economic insecurity affected delay discounting. These feelings were primed by showing participants images indicative of economic recession, such as home foreclosure signs, unemployment lines, and recently emptied office spaces. Next, participants were asked to make a series of delay discounting choices. Figure 5.4 shows the results, revealing the same pattern: When insecurity is primed, low childhood-SES participants become more present-oriented, whereas high childhood-SES participants become more future-oriented. Griskevicius found this pattern for other dependent variables as well: Recession cues led low childhood-SES participants to make riskier choices and to approach luxury brands such as Rolex and Porsches more quickly, but had the opposite effect among high childhood-SES participants, who made fewer risky choices and approached luxury goods more slowly.[46]

What is particularly interesting is that, apparently, these diverging tendencies only surface when circumstances are harsh or unpredictable. In normal circumstances, they lie dormant. In normal conditions, people from lower and higher SES backgrounds react in similar ways. But when the going gets tough ("Dangerous times ahead ...") their reactions realign with the disparate "programs" installed in their minds during early childhood. Threat and insecurity make people who grew up in harsh and unstable circumstances more present-oriented, and those who grew up in secure and stable circumstances more future-oriented. This means that – other things being equal – the first group will be *less motivated* to exert self-control when faced with threat and insecurity, whereas the second group will be *more motivated* to exert self-control.

### Conclusion

Life history theory is a relatively new and ambitious theory. Many of its predictions have yet to be empirically tested. This is scientific work in progress, so we would be well advised not to jump to hasty conclusions. That said, the theory surely resonates with everyday experience. Many readers will remember that, during their high school years, there were "cool kids" and "serious kids," who were opposites in almost every respect. The cool kids seemed to mature quickly, were sexually active, and had first intercourse early. They did not care too

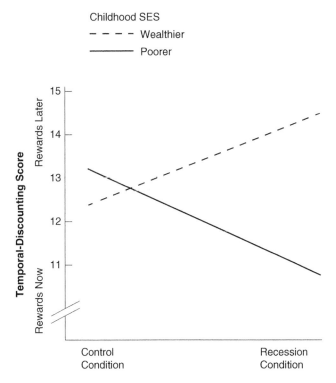

**Figure 5.4** Mean temporal discounting score (as a function of condition and childhood socioeconomic status). *Source:* Griskevicius et al. (2013)

much about studying, often acted impulsively, and lived exciting and somewhat dangerous lives. The serious kids were more diffident, cautious, and perhaps somewhat timid. They always worked hard, took no risks, caused no trouble, and perhaps were still virgins at eighteen.

One of the ironies of life is that the tables can turn by the time we reach adulthood. More than once, the cool kids end up badly, in low-paying and precarious jobs, with unstable relationships and children out of wedlock, or even land in prison. And more than once, the serious kids, after their unremarkable childhoods and adolescent years, end up well. They get good jobs, have stable relationships with kind and reliable partners, have nice kids, and live long and happily ever after. The moral of the story: A fast life strategy is – ultimately – not very adaptive for societies in which the ability to delay gratification is crucial for achieving health, wealth, and happiness.

## 5.5 Conclusion

How motivated people are to exercise self-control is influenced by their overall time orientation. This chapter asked *what* factors determine time orientation, and *why* these factors do so. Two conclusions can be drawn.

First, some people may be less inclined to exert self-control because they are less capable of mentally simulating future situations and events. All self-control decisions require some form of mental time travel, and the more vivid and detailed the representations that arise from these trips into the future, the greater the likelihood that these representations will induce emotions that serve as a "motivational brake" on immediate gratification. Working memory capacity is quite plausibly the critical factor here, since working memory is by definition about holding information in mind that is perceptually not present. It may therefore be harder for people with only modest working memory capacity to motivate themselves to pursue future goals that are abstract in nature, and that only with considerable cognitive effort can be brought to mental life and translated into appealing imagery. These will often be goals that are marked by long delay periods, such as achieving academic or professional milestones, and goals that have to do with money, such as saving for retirement.

Perhaps we could place self-control challenges on a spectrum running from cognitively simple to cognitively complex (see Figure 5.5). Simple challenges such as not drinking too much or not losing your temper in front of your boss require willpower but not much else. The goal is perfectly clear. All you need to do is keep your eyes on the ball and persevere. Complex self-control challenges, however, require more cognitive effort, especially if the waiting period is long. They demand not only willpower but also quite elaborate processing of information: One must think up all potential outcomes, calculate or estimate their respective probabilities and values, factor in contingencies, and translate these data into a feasible goal that is sufficiently "hot" to keep you from immediate gratification.

Granted, this distinction between simple and complex self-control challenges is speculative, but a 2015 experiment lends some support. Economists Cary Deck and Salar Jahedi measured delay discounting under cognitive load, but with a twist: Participants were not only given the usual monetary choices ("x dollars now versus y dollars in one

**Cognitively simple**  **Cognitively complex**

**Figure 5.5** Simple and complex self-control challenges.

week") but also choices between different snack servings (e.g. a 12 oz. package of M&Ms now versus a 19 oz. package of M&Ms in one week). They found that cognitive load led to steeper discounting in the monetary choices – which is consistent with earlier findings – but made *no difference* for the snack choices.[47] Apparently, choosing between easy-to-grasp alternatives such as less candy now versus more candy later requires little working memory capacity.

Second, some people may be less inclined to exercise self-control because they do not expect the delayed reward to ever materialize. To be sure, sometimes they will be right. When circumstances are highly volatile and unpredictable, it may be rational to take no risks, and go for the one bird in hand now. In other cases, however, the preference for the immediate reward is not due to the careful analysis of current circumstances but an echo from early childhood experiences and events. Life history theory posits that humans calibrate their overall time orientation to the (perceived) harshness and unpredictability of the environment during their first years of life, thus setting their mental software for intertemporal choice. Some people, therefore, grow up to have a more present-oriented personality than others.

I suspect that many readers of this book are experienced mental time travelers, who do not need to be convinced of the substantial benefits of looking and planning ahead. They know the importance of controlling their impulses and urges in favor of future goals. I also suspect that many readers will have the basic confidence that if they manage to restrain themselves, the rewards, sooner or later, will come. If we keep our part of the bargain, life will do the same and deliver the goods. These attitudes and expectations are more or less automatically imprinted in those who grow up in (upper) middle-class environments in Western countries.

But things are different when you grow up in a harsh and unpredictable environment. In such an environment, the recurrent message is that it is smarter to take the one marshmallow now. Research suggests that these early lessons of life tend to stick and, through gene expression, become ingrained in personality. Interestingly, this suggests new and perhaps unexpected answers to one of the great mysteries of modern life: Why do people at the bottom of the socioeconomic ladder, on average, exhibit less self-control than people higher up? This mystery is the subject of the next chapter.

# 6 | The Self-Control Effects of Poverty

As we near the end of Part I of this book, I wish to show that all of these psychological findings are not merely of academic interest but highly relevant for real-world affairs. More specifically, these findings shed new light on one of the perennial questions of modern societies: Why do people at the bottom of the social ladder tend to display less self-control than people higher up? Why do so many seem to prefer immediate gratification over delayed reward?

A recurrent theme in debates on the ills of the lower classes is their (allegedly) poor discipline. In the 1960s, political scientist Edward Banfield claimed that the lower class was "radically present-oriented" in lifestyle and outlook. The lower-class individual "lives from moment to moment [...] Impulse governs his behavior, either because he cannot discipline himself to sacrifice a present for a future satisfaction or because he has no sense of the future. He is therefore radically improvident: whatever he cannot consume immediately he considers valueless".[1] After Banfield, other observers have made similar claims (although most were more diplomatic in their wording).[2]

But is it true? Are people at the bottom of society really less predisposed toward self-control? In general, the answer seems to be yes. The studies described in Chapter 2 found that *childhood* self-control correlates with adult socioeconomic status, and since self-control capacity does not radically change after childhood, it logically follows that *adult* self-control is also correlated with adult socioeconomic status (SES). More direct evidence comes from a survey of more than 3,000 people living throughout the United States, who answered an 8-item version of the Brief Self-Control Scale. The results confirmed that self-control is somewhat lower at the bottom of the socioeconomic ladder.[3] Furthermore, as discussed in Chapter 5, people with less education or income tend to have steeper discount rates. This means that, other things being equal, they will be less motivated to exercise self-control.[4]

To avoid any misunderstanding: These are merely statistical tendencies. In everyday life, there are numerous exceptions. People at the bottom of the socioeconomic ladder can show amazing levels of discipline, and people at the top a complete lack thereof. It is just as with height. The statistical fact that, on average, men are taller than women, does not mean that *all* men are taller than *all* women. That said, the overall pattern in research findings is hard to dispute.

The million-dollar question is *why* lower SES is correlated with lower self-control and stronger present orientation. At first glance, this makes no sense. If anything, one would expect the reverse – at least regarding motivation. After all, poor people have every reason not to acquiesce in their predicament but to look ahead, to set goals for a better future, and to work hard to get there. For the poor, there is much to be gained if they manage to keep their urges in check. Moreover, since they have meager financial buffers, the poor have every reason not to succumb to temptation, as even a brief moment of weakness can lead to serious financial trouble. In contrast, people who are well-off can take things easy. They may comfort themselves in the knowledge that they have sufficient means to buffer for financial setbacks arising from self-control failure. They can afford the luxury of celebrating the here and now, without fretting too much about tomorrow.

Then why is reality the opposite? First, this pattern might simply be due to sorting. People with a strong present orientation will probably not study or work very hard, will not save money for a rainy day, are prone to potentially harmful behaviors such as alcohol abuse or unwanted pregnancies, and so forth. This increases the chances that they will end up in the lowest strata of society. Second, this pattern might be caused by the sheer urgency of the problems that come with poverty. For those who have very little, making ends meet and keeping heads above water is a daily challenge that may absorb all their attention. They simply have no mental resources left for looking further ahead. Third, social and cultural influences may play a role. Some observers have argued that a strong present orientation is part of a specific lower-class culture, into which members of this class are socialized.

While all these explanations may be part of the answer, in this chapter I want to focus on a fourth possible explanation: Poverty may undermine both the capacity and the motivation for self-control.

Poverty, in other words, is not only a consequence but also a *cause* of poor self-control. In this chapter, I set forth this argument by showing how poverty is related to the various determinants of self-control capacity and motivation identified in the previous chapters.

## 6.1 Poverty and Trait Self-Control

We begin with the impact of early upbringing and childhood environment on the development of trait self-control. It is not entirely clear what the effects of these circumstances are, but it seems that the development of good self-control is fostered by a combination of moderate stress and warm and supportive parenting, with parents helping their children to cope with stressors. In contrast, the combination of chronic stress and harsh and unresponsive parenting impedes this development.

Unfortunately, poverty is often associated with the latter combination. Reviewing the literature, psychologist Gary Evans concludes that compared to middle- and high-income children, "low-income children are disproportionately exposed to more adverse social and physical environmental conditions. They suffer greater family turmoil, violence, and separation from their parents. Their parents are more nonresponsive and harsh, and they live in more chaotic households, with fewer routines, less structure, and greater instability".[5] This does not exactly sound like the warm and supportive environment with only moderate stress that fosters good trait self-control. (To be clear, poor parenting does not necessary indicate a lack of parental capabilities, but may simply be the consequence of financial hardship. Poverty puts parents at risk of emotional distress, behavior problems, and marital conflict – circumstances that are not conducive to involved and supportive parenting).[6]

But I do not wish to dwell too long on differences in parenting. The link between poverty and a harsh and unresponsive parenting style is well established.[7] Instead, I wish to focus on the second part of the harmful combination: stress. To recall, prolonged exposure to stressors during childhood can have toxic effects. It may lead to a chronically activated stress system and permanently elevated stress hormone levels, which affect brain development and increase stress reactivity, thus compromising self-regulation well into adulthood.

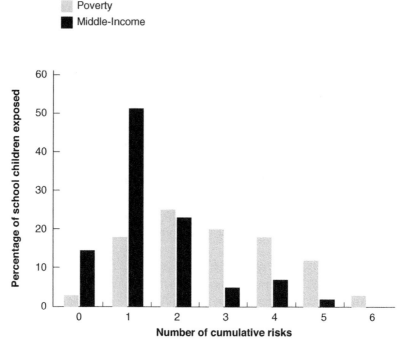

Figure 6.1 Cumulative exposure among low- and middle-income rural nine-year-olds. Copyright © 2004, American Psychological Association. Reproduced with permission from: Evans, G.W., The environment of childhood poverty. *American Psychologist, 59*(2), 77–92.

Research has found that these processes occur more frequently in low-income families. An example is a series of studies by psychologist Gary Evans and colleagues, who examined the effects of childhood stress on predominantly white children from low- and middle-income families in rural upstate New York. These children (and their mothers) were first surveyed at age nine, and then again at ages thirteen, seventeen, and twenty-four.[8] In the first wave of the study, Evans measured the extent to which these children were exposed to six potential stressors: substandard housing, noise, crowding, family turmoil, separation from family, and exposure to violence. He found clear differences between income groups. On average, children living in middle-income families were exposed to 1.5 stressors, whereas children living in low income families were exposed to almost three stressors (see Figure 6.1).[9]

Given these differences, it is hardly surprising that family income was related to chronic stress. Evans assessed how long the children had lived in poverty from birth until age nine, and measured in each study wave how they scored on markers of chronic stress, such as level of stress hormones. The results showed that childhood poverty was correlated with higher scores on these stress markers not only at age nine, but also at ages seventeen and twenty-four. Furthermore, the poorer the subjects were during childhood, the more these scores had increased between ages nine and twenty-four. This shows that childhood poverty can have a lasting effect on the stress system, thus potentially compromising later self-control capacity.[10]

Which brings us back to the subject of self-control. In the study's first wave, Evans and colleagues had children take the classic marshmallow test. They could have a smaller plate of candy now, or a larger plate of candy later if they managed to wait until the experimenter returned. The results clearly showed that the lower the family income, the greater the difficulty children had in delaying gratification.[11] Evans also assessed self-control at ages nine and twenty-four by measuring how long subjects persisted in solving a puzzle that, unbeknownst to them, was unsolvable – a task often used as an indicator of self-control. Evans found that the poorer the household of origin, the less time subjects persisted on the puzzle, at both age nine and twenty-four. Even after controlling for self-control at age nine, childhood poverty was associated with lower persistence at age twenty-four. This means that the difference in self-control between subjects from lower- and middle-income backgrounds had actually *increased* in the fifteen years since the first wave of the study.[12]

In sum, childhood poverty is related with less supportive parenting and a higher incidence of chronic stress, thereby increasing the likelihood of low trait self-control. This means that children from poor families who manage to escape poverty, will nevertheless carry the mental traces of their adverse childhood experiences. Childhood poverty gets under the skin, as it were, and may hamper self-control later in life, leaving such people vulnerable in the face of adversity. In contrast, those who grow up in affluence but happen to fall into poverty later in life are more likely to be endowed with good trait self-control. Compared to their counterparts who grew up in poverty, they are therefore better equipped to recover from financial setbacks.

## 6.2 Poverty and State Self-Control

This does not mean that those of us who had the good fortune of growing up in affluence are immune to self-control failure. This is emphatically not the case. *State* self-control – the capacity for self-control right here and right now – can be seriously compromised by *current* poverty. People who are perfectly capable of restraint under normal circumstances may, perhaps to their own surprise, become much more impulsive and myopic when hit by financial distress. As discussed in Chapter 3, five situational conditions tend to undermine self-control. In this section, I show that poverty is correlated with a higher incidence of these conditions.

### Negative Affect

The first threat to self-control is negative affect. It is highly plausible that poor people will experience more negative feelings than people who are well-off. After all, being poor may in itself be a reason for sadness, while struggling to make ends meet may require activities that are far from uplifting, such as having to do dirty, degrading, or mind-numbing work. Poor people also lack the financial means to do things that might improve their mood, such as buying nice clothes or having an enjoyable night out.

Surprisingly little research has directly tested the link between SES and negative affect.[13] The best evidence to date comes from a study by two Nobel laureates, Daniel Kahneman and Angus Deaton, who analyzed the results of long series of daily surveys conducted among US residents. These surveys asked respondents whether they had smiled or laughed a lot on the previous day, and whether they had experienced feelings such as happiness, enjoyment, worry, and sadness during much of the previous day. Kahneman and Deaton combined the answers for smiling, laughter, happiness, and enjoyment into an index for "positive affect," and the answers for sadness and worry into an index for "blue affect." Figure 6.2 shows how the frequency of these feelings was related to income level.

It turns out that higher annual income is correlated with more positive affect and fewer blue feelings *up to about $75,000.*[14] Emotional well-being rises with income, but beyond this amount there is no further progress. Kahneman and Deaton also found that the pain of some of life's misfortunes is exacerbated by poverty. For instance, low-income

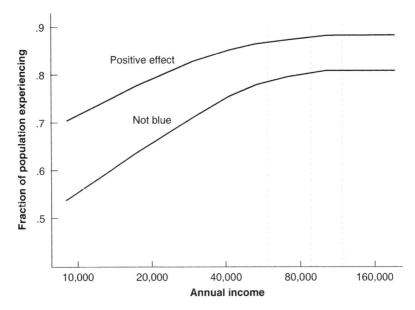

**Figure 6.2** Affect and income. Positive affect is the average of the fractions of the population reporting happiness, smiling, and enjoyment. "Not blue" is 1 minus the average of the fractions of the population reporting worry and sadness. (Note that the horizontal axis is not linear; income doubles with each step.) Reproduced with permission from: Kahneman, D., & Deaton, A. (2010), High income improves evaluation of life but not emotional well-being, *Proceedings of the National Academy of Sciences, 107*(38), 16489–16493.

people who are alone or divorced report feelings of sadness and worry far more often than high-income people in the same situation.

## Cognitive Load

A second threat to self-control is cognitive load. In their 2013 best-seller *Scarcity: Why Having Too Little Means So Much*, behavioral economists Sendhil Mullainathan and Eldar Shafir argue that financial worries will be top of mind for those who have little money, thus crowding out all other thoughts or considerations. "The very lack of available [financial] resources makes each expense more insistent and more pressing. A trip to the grocery store looms larger, and this month's rent constantly seizes our attention".[15] Acute financial problems, in other words, are a major cause of cognitive load.

Empirical evidence comes from a study by Anandi Mani and colleagues.[16] They examined the psychological consequences of scarcity by presenting shoppers in an American mall with a set of financial dilemmas. For example, suppose their car broke down, would they have it repaired or not? And if so, how would they pay for that? The question was asked in two versions: a cheap and an expensive version. In the cheap version, the repair would cost $150, an amount most Americans can pay without too much trouble. In the expensive version, the repair would cost $1,500, an amount not everyone can pay and that may trigger financial worries. Participants were then told they could reflect on the issue for a few minutes, while in the meantime taking two short tests – one measuring intelligence and the other cognitive control. After participants had finished the tests, the experimenter asked them to make a decision on the financial dilemma. To round off, some income data were collected. Now, Mani was not interested in the participants' answers to the dilemma but in their scores on both tests. It turned out that in the cheap version ($150), low- and high-income participants performed equally well, but that in the expensive version ($ 1,500), low-income participants *did significantly worse*. Apparently, the expensive version had provoked financial worries that impaired the latter's cognitive performance and cognitive control. The magnitude of the effect was equivalent to a thirteen-point decrease in IQ.

Mani and colleagues obtained similar results in a field experiment among sugarcane farmers in India. Before harvest, the financial situation of these farmers is usually more precarious than after harvest. They have more trouble paying bills and often have to borrow money. Mani gave these farmers intelligence and cognitive control tests similar to the ones in the experiment described above. The farmers took both tests twice, once before harvest and once after. It turned out that they scored significantly better the second time. Apparently, before the harvest their minds had been more preoccupied by financial worries than after, reducing their available cognitive resources.[17]

### Prior Top-Down Mental Effort

The third item on the list is prior top-down mental effort. Does poverty lead to ego depletion? This is not easy to determine because ego depletion – a decline in some as yet unidentified physiological resource – can only be assessed indirectly, by measuring performance on tasks believed to consume this resource, such as exerting self-control and decision-making.

To my knowledge, only one study – by economist Dean Spears – has tested the potentially depleting effects of financial scarcity.[18] In one experiment, residents of poor and wealthy villages in India were visited at home and offered luxury soap for 60 percent below the retail price. They were entirely free to buy the soap or not. For the wealthy residents, this was not a difficult choice because they could easily spare the money. For the poor residents, however, this was quite a dilemma: On the one hand, it was a luxury they could not afford, but on the other, such a bargain was hard to turn down. The experimenter also asked the participants to squeeze a handgrip for as long as they could, a task often used for to measure self-control strength. Crucially, some participants were asked to squeeze the handgrip *before* the soap offer was made, others *after*. The results showed that when the handgrip task preceded the offer, participants from the poor and wealthy villages performed equally well. But when the handgrip task followed the offer, participants in the poor villages did worse. Apparently, mulling over this difficult choice had diminished their available resources.[19]

## Stress

Poverty is also related to stress. For instance, studies have found a clear correlation between Americans' income and their score on the Perceived Stress Scale as well as between SES and stress hormone levels.[20] This is hardly surprising. It is easy to get worked up if you have to look twice at every penny. Interestingly, "stress" was also one of the items in the Kahneman and Deaton study already described. Figure 6.3 shows their results again, but now with a third line added, representing the fraction of respondents who answered "no" to the question whether they had experienced stress during much of the previous day. The same pattern is visible: Higher income is correlated with less stress, but only up to a point.

Further evidence for the link between poverty and stress comes from studies on the effects of sudden income changes. One example is an experiment by Johannes Haushofer and Jeremy Shapiro, who studied the reaction of poor households in rural Kenya to financial windfall. They found that, compared to a control group, households who received a gift of $1,500 showed significantly lower cortisol

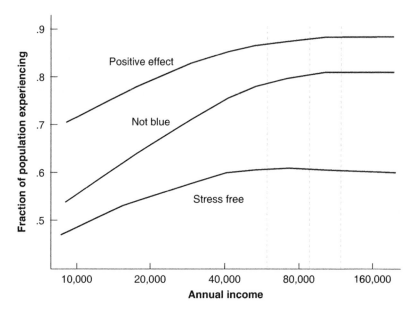

**Figure 6.3** Stress, affect, and income. "Stress free" is the fraction of the population who did not report stress for the previous day. (Note that the horizontal axis is not linear; income doubles with each step.) Reproduced with permission from: Kahneman, D., & Deaton, A. (2010), High income improves evaluation of life but not emotional well-being, *Proceedings of the National Academy of Sciences, 107*(38), 16489–16493.

levels a few months after having received this gift.[21] Another example is a study by Matthieu Chemin and colleagues, who investigated the relationship between rainfall and the cortisol levels of farmers and metal workers in Kenya. Lack of rain means a sharp decline in income for farmers but not for metal workers. Chemin found that the amount of rainfall in the preceding year predicted self-reported stress and cortisol among farmers but not among metal workers.[22] Both studies suggest that the link between income and stress is not merely correlational but causal.[23]

## Sleep

The last pathway through which poverty may impact self-control is lack of sleep. Several studies have found that lower SES is associated with shorter sleep duration, worse sleep quality, and higher rates of sleep complaints.[24] An example is a longitudinal survey by Katherine

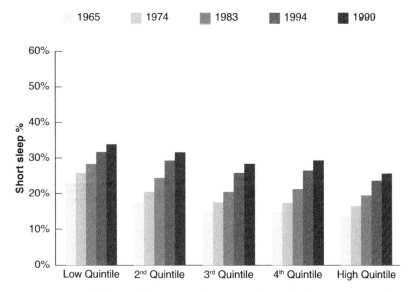

**Figure 6.4** Probability of short sleep duration by household income quintile. Reprinted from *Annals of Epidemiology*, *17*(12), Stamatakis, K. A., Kaplan, G. A., & Roberts, R. E., Short sleep duration across income, education, and race/ethnic groups: Population prevalence and growing disparities during 34 years of follow-up. Copyright 2007, with permission from Elsevier.

Stamatakis and colleagues among residents of Alameda County in California.[25] In each of the five waves of this study, respondents were asked to indicate the number of hours of sleep they usually got. Sleep durations of six hours or less were coded as "short sleep." Figure 6.4 shows the likelihood that people in each income quintile are short sleepers.

The figure clearly shows that the lower the income, the greater the likelihood of short sleep (and that, for all income levels, the likelihood of short sleep has been steadily rising over recent decades).[26] Importantly, according to sleep researcher Michael Grandner, it is not poverty *as such* that makes the difference, but the consequences of poverty. "[M]oney may not buy sleep, but many of the benefits of income may contribute to healthy sleep".[27] One of the things money can buy is a decent house in a safe and quiet neighborhood. Research shows that neighborhoods that are crime-ridden, not socially cohesive, and dirty, are associated with worse sleep quality. Light and environmental noise can also disrupt sleep, so neighborhoods that are active at night can have detrimental effects as well. Last but not least, crowded homes are more likely to foster insufficient sleep.[28]

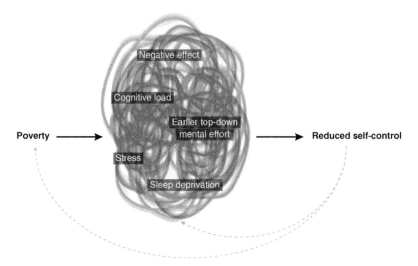

**Figure 6.5** The effect of poverty on self-control.

## Conclusion

Poverty and feelings of scarcity are significantly correlated to negative affect, cognitive load, self-control strength, frequent stress, and sleep deprivation. Note that several of the studies mentioned are not correlational but experimental. They suggest that poverty and feelings of scarcity are indeed the *causes* of these self-control-undermining conditions. These various threats to self-control frequently evoke one another, developing into an inextricable knot of harmful influences (see Figure 6.5). When people are faced with major financial troubles, they may start worrying and lie awake at night, which requires fears to be suppressed and tough decisions to be made, thus depleting self-control resources. This may lead to impulsive purchases, perhaps to alleviate a depressed mood, but such careless spending only makes things worse, leading to more intense worrying, sad feelings, sleepless nights, and elevated stress hormone levels, which makes exerting self-control even harder, and so forth.

## 6.3 Poverty and Uncertain Outcomes

As discussed in Chapter 5, whether someone will exercise self-control partly depends on the perceived likelihood that this course of action will pay off. Studying hard, working long hours, refraining from unhealthy behavior, saving for later – these actions only make sense if you have reason to believe that one day you will reap the benefits. If the future is highly uncertain, though, the rewards may never materialize. And if life is nasty, brutish, and short, you may not even *live* to see that happy day. In such circumstances, it may be more rational to take the one bird in hand than to wait for two in the bush. In a harsh and unpredictable environment, present-oriented behavior may be "the contextually appropriate response".[29]

This raises the question whether poverty is associated with harsher and more unpredictable environments. If so, we would have identified yet another piece of the puzzle: Poor people tend to be more present-oriented because they face more uncertainty over whether they will ever enjoy the rewards of delayed gratification. Moreover, if they grew up in a tough and precarious environment, an overall tendency to favor the immediate reward may be ingrained in their personality.

The answer to this question is affirmative. Poor people are, almost by definition, more likely to face harshness and unpredictability. As discussed in Section 6.1, Gary Evans found that low-income children suffer greater family turmoil and violence, and live in more chaotic households, with fewer routines, less structure, and greater instability. For the poor, life *beyond* the confines of the family is more insecure as well. In this section, I focus on two key indicators of harshness and unpredictability: mortality and economic insecurity.

## Mortality

Death and disease are part of life, but more so for people in low-SES environments. Time and again, research has found that mortality is substantially higher among low-income groups. Health psychologist Nancy Adler and colleagues concluded that, in the United States, "the risk of dying before the age of 65 is more than three times greater for those at the bottom than for those at the top"[30] (see Figure 6.6). Economist Raj Chetty and colleagues analyzed a dataset containing millions of Americans and calculated life expectancy at age forty. They found a significant association between longevity and income: The gap in life expectancy between the richest 1 percent and the poorest 1 percent of forty-year-olds was 14.6 years for men and 10.1 years for women.[31]

The United States is far from unique. A study of twenty-two European countries revealed that lower SES is correlated with higher

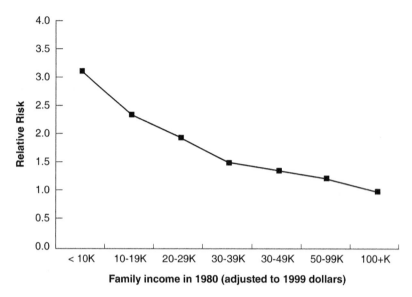

**Figure 6.6** Relative risk of premature death and family income. Reproduced with permission from: Adler, N. E., & Stewart, J., Health disparities across the lifespan: Meaning, methods, and mechanisms. *Annals of the New York Academy of Sciences, 1186*(1), 5–23. © 2010, New York Academy of Sciences.

mortality in all of them.[32] Moreover, a 2017 meta-analysis covering seven high-income countries found an association between higher mortality rate and lower SES as indexed by occupational position. This association remained significant after the results were adjusted for six risk factors that are more prevalent among low-income people (i.e. high alcohol intake, physical inactivity, current smoking, hypertension, diabetes, and obesity).[33] This leads to a related point: Lower SES is consistently associated with poorer health. For almost every disease and health condition, people at the bottom score worse than people higher up. This problem is known as the "social gradient in health" and has proven to be remarkably stubborn.[34] For decades, governments and health professionals around the world have sought to fight this health disparity but, thus far, to little avail.[35]

Another aspect of harshness is crime. Again, those who live in poverty get the short end of the stick. Reviewing mostly American literature, criminologist Robert Sampson and Janet Lauritsen concluded that "[a]lmost without exception, studies of violence find a positive and usually large correlation between some measure of area poverty and violence – especially homicide".[36] There is some debate on whether *absolute* or *relative* poverty is the best predictor of homicide, but either way, those living in poor areas are worse off.[37] Poor people are also more frequently victims of nonfatal violent crimes, such as rape, robbery, and aggravated assault. In 2019, for example, Americans with a household income below \$25,000 were twice as likely to become victims of such crimes as Americans with a household income above \$25,000.[38]

In sum, poverty is related to higher mortality, higher incidence of serious health problems, and a higher chance of being victimized.[39] Such people are thus more likely to be exposed to cues that suggest a harsh environment. The message of these cues is that taking the immediate reward may be the most rational choice, and that a fast life strategy may be the most adaptive.

## Economic Insecurity

Another cue that may impact intertemporal decisions is economic insecurity. This can be defined as the risk of economic loss faced by individuals and households as they encounter the unpredictable events of modern life.[40] A major cause of economic insecurity is income *instability* – a concept that should be clearly distinguished from income *level*. People can earn a modest income but nonetheless be economically secure if their income is likely to remain stable or gradually increase along predictable lines. Conversely, people may be doing financially well now, but nonetheless be economically insecure if their income fluctuates, and it is uncertain whether they will be making enough money next month or year.

Almost all research on economic insecurity has been done in the United States, perhaps because it is the only country that has undertaken the long-running panel surveys required for this type of research.[41] The general picture emerging from most of these surveys is that earnings instability among men rose sharply from the late 1970s until the mid-1980s, then flattened out at this higher level, and has since been fluctuating, depending on the state of the economy (and depending on the dataset).[42] Other studies have examined household incomes rather than individual earnings. Most found that household income instability increased from the 1970s to the 2000s.[43]

What matters for us, however, is not the precise timing and direction of these trends but the differences in economic insecurity between low- and high-SES individuals. Here the results are unequivocal: Each and every study reveals that people with lower incomes face greater economic insecurity than people with higher incomes. For example, economists Peter Gottschalk and Robert Moffitt found that the earnings instability of the 25 percent lowest earners was "much higher" than the earnings instability of the other 75 percent.[44] Moreover, over the past several decades the gap in economic insecurity between groups has *widened*, because the increase in income instability since the 1970s is concentrated in the lower-skilled portion of the population.[45] In another study, based on data running up to 2011, economists Michael Carr and Emily Wiemers concluded that "since the 1990s, the entire increase in earnings variability has been driven by increases among workers with less than a college degree while college-educated workers have seen flat or declining earnings variability".[46]

In sum, income instability in the United States has increased, especially for the poor. Sociologist Bruce Western concludes that whereas "rising economic *inequality*, at least since the late 1980s, is a story about increasing incomes at the top of the distribution, rising *insecurity* appears to be a story about increasing risks to households at the bottom".[47] People who live in poverty are thus more likely to be exposed to cues that signal unpredictability. This may affect their intertemporal decisions and, if they grow up in such unpredictable circumstances, their overall time orientation.

(To be clear, these data only concern the United States. The gap may be narrower in other countries, due to differences in national labor markets and social policies. It is certainly *plausible* that low-SES individuals in other countries also face more economic insecurity – after all, neoliberal policies have been implemented in many parts of the Western world – but we do not know for sure, as we lack solid data.)

## 6.4 Conclusion

Why do people on the lowest rungs of the socioeconomic ladder display – on average – less self-control than people higher up? Why do many of them appear to prefer immediate gratification over delayed reward? Psychology suggests some new answers. To briefly summarize:

- children who are born and grow up in poor families are more likely to experience harsh and unresponsive parenting and chronic stress. This unfortunate combination may impede the development of adequate self-control;
- people facing financial hardship are more likely to experience negative affect, cognitive load, ego depletion, frequent stress, and sleep deprivation. These conditions may (temporarily) reduce self-control capacity and increase present orientation;
- the life environment of the poor is more likely to be harsh and unpredictable. This may diminish their expectation that self-control will pay off, thus undermining self-control motivation. Moreover, children who grow up in such an environment are more likely to develop a general orientation toward short-term opportunities and rewards.

Two circumstances lend further significance to these findings. First, the poor, by definition, have no or scant financial buffers to cushion the monetary effects of self-control failure. Even a single moment of inattention or weakness of will may therefore suffice to thwart attempts at escaping poverty – or worse, set off a downward spiral of accumulating debt. Second, as discussed in Chapter 3, for many behaviors we should not restrict our view to single and isolated moments, but consider the total volume of self-control challenges that cross people's paths within the relevant time frame, and ask how likely it is that, as these challenges keep coming, people will drop the ball at least once. Sooner or later, this single but potentially fatal moment of inattention or weakness of will is almost certain to happen.

These findings shed new light on the – on average – stronger present orientation and weaker self-control of the lower classes. This new light is certainly welcome. Over recent decades, much ink has been spilled on the alleged existence of a "culture of poverty" – a distinct set of values and beliefs characteristic of the poor, with a strong present orientation being one of its defining features. Through socialization, this present-oriented culture is said to be transmitted from one generation to the next. However, the "culture of poverty" hypothesis is unconvincing. Of course, immersion in any group culture will affect people's values and beliefs, but this is not much of an explanation, as it begs the question where this group culture came from. This "explanation" merely shifts the focus of attention from the individual to the group level. To make matters worse, many scholars doubt whether this "culture of poverty" exists at all. It is often decried as nothing but a myth.[48]

This chapter, however, firmly suggests the existence of a "psychology of poverty." I am not the first to make this claim. Since 2010, scholarly interest in the psychological consequences of poverty and scarcity has grown rapidly.[49] Much of the research in this newly emerging field stems from the United States or developing countries such as India and Kenya, yet the findings have wider significance. There is no reason to believe they would only apply to the inhabitants of these countries, because – ultimately – these effects are rooted in people's psychological and biological makeup. Self-control capacity is limited for *all* human beings, and situational variables, such as severe stress or lack of sleep, undermine mental functioning in *all* human beings.

What does this mean for our judgment of people who seem to lack the discipline to do whatever is necessary to lift themselves out of poverty? Are they merely the victims of an unfortunate combination of bad genes, poor upbringing, and the control-undermining effects of their life circumstances? Should we therefore absolve them from any responsibility for their misfortunes? Part II of this book is about normative questions like these.

# Implications for Society and Politics

What have we learned thus far? Three main findings:

- Good self-control predicts many life outcomes, ranging from school and work achievement, income and socioeconomic status, physical health, to substance dependence and criminal conviction. In all of them, better self-control is associated with the more desirable outcome.
- Self-control capacity is limited and is further reduced by situational factors such as cognitive load, acute stress, and sleep deprivation. Although increasing the stakes may induce people to invest more effort, even champions of self-control cannot indefinitely restrain their impulses and urges. Attempts to improve self-control strength through regular exercise have not been very successful.
- People differ in their self-control capacity. Teaching people techniques to use their limited capacity more cleverly and efficiently will probably not reduce these differences and could even make them larger, as these techniques will probably most benefit those who are already doing relatively well.

Part II explores the implications of these findings for some key ideas and beliefs underlying the current institutional and social order. More specifically, I address two questions.

First, what do these findings mean for *moral responsibility*? When is someone to blame for his or her actions? A tenet of both scholarly theory and everyday intuition is that people should only be held accountable for behavior *that was under their control*. However, the findings from psychology make clear that, even barring external obstacles, not everything people do accords with their intentions. Sometimes, people really *want* to do what is right but, due to circumstances beyond their control, lack the required self-control capacity to follow through on their intentions. In other words, they are not *unwilling* but *unable* to do the right thing. Does this mean that, in such cases, people cannot be held morally responsible for their actions? Is poor self-control a valid excuse?

135

Second, what do these findings mean for *distributive justice*? Who deserves to get what? The consensus is that people should be rewarded for effort and hard work, and that society has no moral obligation to relieve people from hardship or adversity that stem from laziness, poor choices, or imprudent behavior. But many people feel that society *does* have a moral obligation to help or compensate people when they are the victims of "bad luck" – that is, when their hardship or adversity derive from circumstances beyond their control, such as being born with a physical disability. Now, suppose that someone tries really hard to live responsibly and make her own living, but nonetheless falls into abject poverty, *not* for lack of effort or some physical disability, but because she is endowed with exceedingly poor self-control. Does this condition also count as a case of "bad luck" that merits help or compensation?

In sum, the findings recounted in Part I suggest the possibility of a gap between, on the one hand, the standards for self-control capacity that are implicit to the current institutional and social order and, on the other hand, the amount of self-control people *actually have*. At least part of the population may, at least part of the time, have trouble meeting these standards. If this is true, what does it imply for our moral and social practices? I address these questions in Chapters 8 and 9.

But first, in Chapter 7, I make the case that self-control has, over the course of history, grown increasingly important for negotiating life. It has not always been like this. Several centuries or even just decades ago, life chances were less dependent on this personality trait. Being endowed with poor self-control was less of an obstacle than it is today. Perhaps this explains why social theory to date has paid scant attention to the broader implications of the limits to self-control. Many of the theories about responsibility and deservingness that I discuss in Chapters 8 and 9 were advanced several decades or even longer ago – at a time when poor self-control had less of an impact on individual and collective outcomes than it has today.

So actually, there are *two* compelling reasons to address these normative questions. The first is that the findings of recent psychological research suggest that established ideas and theories about responsibility and deservingness are at odds with the facts. The second is that this discrepancy is becoming increasingly problematic, because good self-control is getting more and more important. In a sense, psychological insights have been moving in one direction, whereas society and public policies have been moving in the other, thus widening the gap. What began as a minor crack has become a major rift. The net result is that, more so than in the past, incorrect assumptions about the nature of self-control may be leading to injustice.

# 7 | *The Ever-Growing Importance of Self-Control*

Has good self-control become more important for achieving wealth, health, and happiness? Has society evolved in such a way that, more than in earlier times, the ability to delay gratification is critical for staying out of trouble?

The answer is yes: Self-control has indeed become more important. More than ever before, having good discipline is a gift for life. But why? One could perhaps argue that this development is caused by changes in domains such as work and consumption. In agrarian and industrial societies, what mattered most were physical strength and endurance, not the capacity to control your emotions, to finish your homework in time, or to stay polite to rude customers. People also had less money to spend, and there were far fewer products to buy. For the average John and Jane, resisting the urge to waste their precious earnings on luxury goods was not an everyday challenge.

But does this explanation hold? One could equally well argue that good self-control has *always* been important. Although labor used to be more physical, it not only required bodily strength, but also willpower and discipline, not least because working days were much longer. And it has always been imperative to control your anger and stay friendly toward others, perhaps even more so in the hierarchical world of the past when there was little to protect us from the whims of the powerful. Granted, dieting was probably less of a challenge, since high-calorie foods were not as abundantly available as today, but alcohol and substance abuse have always been with us.

So things are not that straightforward. We must dig deeper. This chapter therefore asks: *Why has the ability for self-control become more important?* Obviously, this question cannot be answered by means of psychological experiments. We need to turn to sociohistorical scholarship, which is why this chapter is more narrative in character then the previous ones. Section 7.1 covers the *longue durée*. Central to this section is the "civilization thesis" advanced by the German

139

sociologist Norbert Elias. This thesis holds that since the late Middle Ages self-control and foresight have grown more important as a consequence of two large-scale social transformations: the monopolization of violence and the lengthening of the chains of human interdependence. Section 7.2 focuses on policy developments since the late twentieth century, especially the "new punitiveness" in fighting crime and the turn toward "conditionality" in welfare provision. These developments have significantly raised the costs of self-control failure.

## 7.1 The Civilization Process: Ever-Growing Interdependency

I begin with Norbert Elias. In his book *The Civilizing Process*, published in 1939, Elias argues that during the European Middle Ages people lived out their emotions and urges more directly and openly than today, without much calculation or thought of the future consequences. People lived from moment to moment, their emotions and behaviors could swing abruptly from one extreme to the other, and they experienced life with an immediacy and intensity that was almost childlike. Violence and cruelty were part and parcel of everyday life as knights, warriors, and armed bands roamed the country, creating havoc at whim, while towns were rife with wars between families and cliques. Control came not from within, but from outside forces, such as public humiliation, priestly condemnation, and neighborhood surveillance.[1]

All this changed from the fifteenth century onward. From that period on, human conduct in northern Western societies has undergone a "civilizing process" – a gradual change in the locus of control from external constraint (*Fremdzwang*) to self-restraint (*Selbtszwang*). It gradually became more important for people to suppress their violent tendencies, to regulate their emotions, and to attune their behavior to the long-term requirements of increasingly complex networks of social interaction. Among the main sources Elias used to support this claim, were books and guides on etiquette and manners that were published between the fifteenth and late nineteenth centuries. These publications display a slow but steady development toward ever more sophisticated and strict advice on issues such as table manners, bedroom behavior, and relations between men and women.

Two major developments were responsible for this civilizing process. The first was the monopolization of violence. Arms and armed troops became concentrated under one authority, and violence became

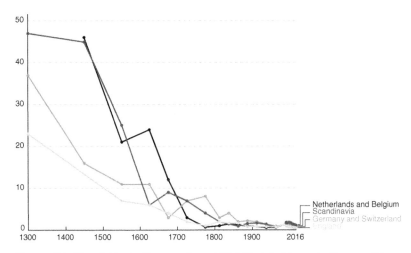

**Figure 7.1** Homicide in Europe (per 100,000 inhabitants). *Source:* Eisner (2003), Institute of Health Metrics and Evaluation (IHME), published online at OurWorldInData.org

the monopoly of ever-larger and more powerful states. The everyday reality of sudden and unforeseeable violence was gradually replaced by the more calculable threat of punishment for those who broke the law. As a result, people no longer had to live in a permanent state of physical insecurity. But obviously, this also meant that they had to control their *own* behavior. The individual "is largely protected from sudden attack, the irruption of physical violence into his or her life. But at the same time he is himself forced to suppress in himself or herself any passionate impulse urging him or her to attack another physically".[2]

Support for this account comes from research on homicide. Criminologists have gathered data going all the way back to the Middle Ages. Figure 7.1 presents a rough summary of the numbers for Western Europe. Although these historical data should be handled with care, most scholars agree on the general trend: Since the late Middle Ages, the incidence of homicide has declined dramatically.[3]

The second major development was the differentiation of society. In the medieval world, ordinary people were dependent on few others as they largely lived off the produce of their own land. A strong and continuous moderation of drives and affects was therefore neither necessary nor useful. However, population growth, urbanization, and especially the pressure of economic competition, led to a previously unknown range, diversity, and interdependence of competing social positions and functions. The more differentiated these became, the larger grew the network of people on whom the individual was somehow dependent. In modern societies, countless others are – directly or indirectly – involved in ensuring that you will eat dinner tonight. Relations also became more ambivalent than in the black-and-white, friend-or-villain society of the Middle Ages. People could be friends, allies, or partners in one context but opponents, competitors, or enemies in another. This "fundamental ambivalence of interests" is "one of the most important structural characteristics of highly developed societies, and a chief factor moulding civilized conduct".[4]

Thus, it became increasingly important for people to consider the future consequences of their actions. Although it is often argued that free markets foster selfishness, the need to attract and retain customers *also* fosters empathy, trustworthiness, and good manners. As the economist Samuel Ricard wrote over two centuries ago, through commerce "man learns to deliberate, to be honest, to acquire manners, to be prudent and reserved in both talk and action".[5] According to Elias, the larger and denser the networks of interdependence become, "the more threatened is the social existence of the individual who gives way to spontaneous impulses and emotions [and] the greater is the social advantage of those able to moderate their affects".[6]

### Automatic Self-Control

Interestingly, Elias does not only argue that these transformations led to a change in behavior. He makes the more radical claim that they induced a change in *personality* – or in his terms, a change in "habitus." Self-restraint became *second nature*. "The web of actions grows so complex and extensive, the effort required to behave 'correctly' within it becomes so great, that beside the individual's conscious self-control an automatic, blindly functioning apparatus of self-control is firmly established".[7] This habitus, instilled in children from an early age, becomes part of the self.

From earliest youth individuals are trained in the constant restraint and foresight that they need for adult functions. This self-restraint is ingrained so deeply from an early age that, like a kind of relay-station of social standards, an automatic self-supervision of their drives, a more differentiated and more stable "super-ego" develops within them, and a part of the forgotten drive impulses and affect inclinations is no longer directly within reach of the level of consciousness at all.[8]

One might say that Elias projected the Freudian developmental story of the individual onto the historical process in which the childlike directness and impulsiveness of medieval man slowly develops into the more reflected, tempered, and controlled style of the bourgeois adults of his era. The social is transformed into the psychological.[9]

The growing self-restraint began in the upper strata of society. They lived on the frontlines of these social developments and were the first to feel the need for more self-control and foresight. But it gradually spread to the lower strata, whose members grew "more accustomed to restraining momentary affects, and disciplining their whole conduct from a wider understanding of the total society and their position within it".[10] According to Elias, the civilizing process is a comprehensive movement, expanding in ever wider circles through the Western world. Writing nearly a century ago, however, he notes that "even though the moulding of drives and affects, the forms of conduct, the whole habitus of the lower classes is increasingly approaching that of other groups, *we have not yet reached the theoretical endpoint*, in which *all* classes are equal in this respect".[11]

## Civilizing Offensives

*The Civilizing Process* is among the most influential books ever published in sociology, but it has also garnered criticism on several fronts. For instance, although in contemporary Western societies the risk of violent death is incomparably lower than during the Middle Ages, those times were probably not as violent and normless as Elias depicts them to be.[12] And although most historians accept the claim of a gradual shift from external to internal restraint, precisely what caused this shift remains a matter of debate. According to sociologist Robert van Krieken, for example, Elias overlooked the development of bureaucracy. Inherent to the bureaucratic form of organization is a specific logic that defines people as distinct individuals with rights, duties, and responsibilities, to which they have no choice but to adapt.[13]

But I want to focus on another point: the extent to which the civilizing process is an *autonomous* process. According to Elias, the gradual shift from external to self-restraint is not the result of some preconceived plan or policy devised and implemented by identifiable actors. The civilizing process simply "happened" due to the social and economic developments sketched out. So long as these developments do not stop or reverse, the process will keep unfolding until it has reached all corners of society.

This picture seems inaccurate, though. It ignores the many deliberate attempts to "civilize" the lower strata that history has seen. Van Krieken agrees that while self-discipline may have emerged "from within" as a strategy of self-advancement among ruling social groups such as the court aristocracy and the bourgeoisie, things were different for the lower strata. The increasing interdependency between urban elites *in itself* was not enough reason for workers and peasants to develop similar amounts of discipline and foresight. The ruling classes therefore had to intervene and *make* the lower classes more responsive to the social demands of ever-increasing interdependency. For many workers and peasants, change came upon them "from the 'outside,' in the shape of lawyers, judges, police officers, inquisitors, teachers, employers, and so on, all giving their own particular form to 'the civilizing process,' turning it into a civilizing *offensive*".[14]

Viewed from this perspective, social history can be seen as a dialectic of civilizing *processes* and civilizing *offensives*. Table 7.1 presents an overview of five major "civilizing offensives." For our purposes, the last row, covering the period from the 1980s to the present, is particularly relevant. I return to this most recent offensive in Section 7.2.

### Civilization in the United States

Did the civilization process also come to the "New World"? While Elias only analyzed developments in northwestern Europe, sociologist Stephen Mennell has recently applied Elias' framework to the United States. He found that many parts of Elias' theory "fit quite well with the American case," but that within this broad similarity,

Table 7.1 *Schematic overview of major "civilizing offensives,"*
*eleventh to twenty-first centuries.*

| Period | Core Characteristics Selected |
| --- | --- |
| Courtization of warriors (11th–13th centuries) | Disappearance of "free warriors" Increasing dependence of nobility Courtliness (modesty, patience, restraint, and elegance) as new ethic God's peace and king's peace limit private retaliation rights Beginning monopolization over legitimate use of force Criminalization of killing, institutionalized death penalty Beginning of state-run criminal justice based on written procedure |
| Early absolutist state (late 15th–17th centuries) | Limitation of power of feudal aristocracy, fight against feuding Centralized taxation Monopolization of protection business Standing army Centralization of judicial powers State punitiveness focused on suffering and pain |
| Social disciplining revolution (mid-16th–18th centuries) | Police ordinances expand state control over daily behaviors Emphasis on frugality, duty, deference, orderliness Confessionalization and church discipline intensify social control and promote conscience and ethic of inner control Fight against disorderly pastimes and behaviors Reformation of the poor, workhouses, orphanages |
| Bourgeois civilizing offensive (1830–1900) | Disciplining of working classes in factories (time and work discipline) Universal schooling and mass conscription armies Professional national police forces "Temperance movement" emphasizes self-control "Rational recreation" promotes civilized leisure activities Ideal of domesticity and respectability promote inner-directed family harmony |

Table 7.1 (*cont.*)

| Period | Core Characteristics Selected |
| --- | --- |
| Securitization and new culture of control (1980s to present) | Extended use of surveillance technologies<br>More intensive control of antisocial behaviors<br>Enforcement of discipline and propriety<br>Expanding infrastructure of crime prevention and community<br>Initiatives against welfare dependency |

Republished with permission of University of Chicago Press, from: Eisner, M., From swords to words: Does macro-level change in self-control predict long-term variation in levels of homicide? *Crime and Justice*, 43(1), 65–134. Copyright 2014, permission conveyed through Copyright Clearance Center, Inc.

notable differences exist.[15] Two warrant mentioning here. First, in the United States, pressures toward the monopolization of force have been weaker than in European societies.[16] Violence increasingly became a state monopoly as the still young nation matured, but not as completely as in Europe, particularly not in the South. This is reflected in the incidence of violence. Although the United States saw a gradual decline of the homicide rate, the absolute level, especially in the South, remains substantially higher than in Europe.[17] Second, although the United States, like Europe, saw a shift from external to self-restraint, this transformation was probably less driven by status competition among elites, and more by the lengthening chains of interdependence in general, plus the pressures of free markets in particular. According to historian Thomas Haskell, the spread of competitive relationships provided

an immensely powerful educational force, capable of reaching into the depths of personal psychology. The market altered character by heaping tangible reward on people who displayed a certain calculating, moderately assertive style of conduct, while humbling others whose manner was more unbuttoned or who pitched their affairs at a level of aggressiveness either higher or lower than the prevailing standard.[18]

The market taught people two lessons: to keep their promises and to attend to the remote consequences of their actions. The norm of promise-keeping was elevated to a supreme imperative, while anticipation of the consequences of one's actions became an emblem of civilization itself. It was believed to require not only concentrated attention but also "a capacity to delay gratification that the middle class found

## Box 7.1 Max Weber and the Protestant Ethic

The most famous sociological-historical text ever written in relation to self-control is, without doubt, Max Weber's *The Protestant Ethic and the Spirt of Capitalism*, published in two parts in 1904 and 1905. A chapter on the ever-increasing importance of self-control cannot be complete without a reference to this book. In this essay, Weber ventured to explain why the "spirit of capitalism" – the drive to pursue financial profit as an end in itself rather than just a means for living well – emerged and took hold in some parts of the Western world, but not others. His central argument is that the roots of this capitalist spirit lie in ascetic Protestantism as it developed since the sixteenth century, a type of Protestantism that emphasized the value of discipline and hard work.

### THE QUEST FOR SALVATION

Weber's argument is complex and subtle, and not easy to follow for twenty-first-century readers unfamiliar with the intricacies of Protestant doctrine from centuries ago. The starting point is that, according to Calvinist teaching, all people are predestined. They either belong to the tiny minority of the elect, chosen by God for salvation and eternal grace, or to the mass of the nonelect who will face eternal damnation. Nothing people do in this worldly life, whether they confessed their sins, did good works, or gave to charity, would change their fate. Unfortunately, there was no way to know which group one belonged to. Only God, that inscrutable and all-powerful deity far removed from earthly mortals, knew the truth of our individual destinies. This threw people back on themselves, and caused deep feelings of anxiety and inner loneliness.

How could people cope with the "extreme inhumanity" of the Calvinist doctrine? According to Weber, the urgent need for relief of this overwhelming anxiety translated into an organized and controlled, methodological-rational way of life (*Lebensführung*). Although God's motives could not be known, it was obvious that He demanded virtuous conduct, in strict conformity to His commandments and laws. People must therefore overcome the *status naturae*, the impulsive and spontaneous human nature. Ascetic Protestants came to believe that if they proved to be capable of mastering their selfish desires and leading righteous, dignified lives oriented to God's commandments, they must be among the elect. After all, God would have given this capacity only to those He had predestined for salvation.

Weber saw a fundamental difference between the Catholic and Protestant orientations toward daily conduct. The average Catholic had no need for a methodological-rational way of life. Ethically, he could live from day to day. So long as he conscientiously fulfilled his traditional religious duties, he could believe him to be saved. Moreover, the Catholic Church acknowledged human shortcomings, and offered relief through the sacrament of confession. For the Catholic, life was characterized by the cycle of sin, atonement, and forgiveness, and their eternal destiny depended on a calculus of *isolated* actions. The Calvinist, however,

> could not hope that hours of weakness and frivolity could be compensated for with intensified good will during other hours, as could Catholics and Lutherans. The Calvinist God did not demand isolated "good works" from his faithful; rather, if salvation were to occur, He required an intensification of "good works" into a *system*. [...] In Calvinism, the practical-ethical action of the average believer lost its planless and unsystematic character and was molded into a consistent, *methodical* organization of his life as a whole.[19]

In other words, Calvinists could not afford to live ethically day by day, without a plan or system. From this grew a tempered, dispassionate, and restrained disposition that sought to tame the *status naturae*. The goal was "to be able to lead an alert, conscious, and self-aware life. Hence, the destruction of the spontaneity of the instinct-driven enjoyment of life constituted the most urgent task." This "active self-control" constituted Puritanism's "defining practical ideal of life".[20]

But this way of life was fragile. Temptation was lurking around every corner, and even the sincerely faithful might give in to fatalism and despair. According to Weber, a more solid foundation for the methodical-rational way of life was needed. This foundation only crystallized once the pressing question of salvation became connected to *methodical work in a vocation* and to the *systematic pursuit of wealth and profit*. Through worldly work, Protestants could contribute to the creation of His kingdom on earth, a kingdom of wealth, abundance, and the common good, and through worldly work, keep egocentric wishes and creaturely urges in check, and dispel the overwhelming doubt and anxiety induced by the doctrine of predestination. Pastors, moreover, persuaded the faithful that production of great wealth by an individual meant that God favored that individual. Success in worldly work indicated they were among the elect. It was a sign of grace and provided the desperately longed-for *certitudo salutis*.

Thus the Protestant ethic, argues Weber, laid the foundation for the spirit of capitalism. Its doctrines translated into the duty to work hard for the accumulation of goods, while at the same time prohibiting unnecessary consumption of those goods. The only legitimate goal for the fruits of one's labor was reinvestment, in order to obtain even more goods – and hence to be even more certain of grace.

### SELF-CONTROL = GRACE OF GOD

Weber's essay has attracted intense criticism. For a host of reasons, critics deny the hypothesized causal relationship between Protestantism and capitalism. For this chapter, however, it is irrelevant whether the Protestant ethic really favored capitalism or not. The rise of this ethic is interesting in itself, as it suggests another reason why self-control has become increasingly important. This reason is not rooted in social transformations such as the decrease in violence or growing interconnectedness, but in the emergence of a particular belief system – a system in which the successful exercise of self-control was not just a means to achieve material ends, but a sign of the grace of God. For Protestants, exercising self-control was a way to convince themselves (and others!) that they were among the elect. Which is certainly no trivial incentive.

lamentably lacking in criminals, paupers, madmen, children – not excepting their own – and others who became objects of humanitarian concern".[21] Of course, market forces have left an imprint in *all* modern industrial societies but, according to Mennell, the "American Dream" made their impact especially severe in the United States. If people are convinced that every citizen has a fair chance to achieve wealth and social status through hard work, this in itself is a strong incentive for self-discipline.[22]

## Informalization

Readers may be surprised to learn that people, over the course of history, have become more and more self-restrained. After all, did we not live through the 1960s and 1970s? Has the trend since then not been the exact opposite, toward a *loosening* of constraints? During that era, many people freed themselves from straitjacket of strict control and rigid convention. Either with or without the help of psychotherapy, they regained contact with their inner selves and overcame the fear of letting go. Manners became more informal, and naturalness, authenticity, and a confident ease became highly desired qualities. This was a clear break from the past. In the Victorian age, many people were convinced that being open to "dangerous" emotions, for example regarding sexuality, was the first step on a slippery slope that would irrevocably lead to disaster. Today, few believe this. To the contrary, individuals who seem to be perfectly self-controlled are often looked down on as stiff, inhibited, and boring company – in other words, as *over*controlled.

The sociologist Cas Wouters coined the term "informalization" to describe the relaxation of codes of conduct and the emancipation of emotion. In the footsteps of Elias, Wouters analyzed etiquette guides and manners books in four Western countries that were published since the late nineteenth century.[23] He found that, since then, these countries have witnessed several waves of informalization, most prominently during the 1960s and 1970s. Many modes of conduct that had been curbed or forbidden came to be allowed, particularly in matters of sexuality. "[A]ll behaviours, manners and arts, such as the written and spoken language, clothing, music, dancing, and hairstyles, conduct and emotions became less formally restricted and regulated, thus giving way to a widening range of acceptable behavioural and emotional options".[24]

Paradoxically, this informalization did *not* diminish the need for self-control, but imposed even higher demands on self-regulation. People could no longer rely on well-established norms and conventions and automatically follow the fixed habits ingrained in their minds. Instead, they had to consciously negotiate the increasingly various contexts and behavioral options now open to them, and determine what actions, given the particulars of the situation, were appropriate, desirable, and expedient. The new emphasis on naturalness, authenticity, and being at ease, moreover, engendered a new constraint, namely "a constraint to be unconstrained".[25] Self-regulatory demands also increased at the workplace. As Mennell notes, the modern informal office "calls for a far more subtle capacity for emotion management and sensitivity to invisible boundaries than was the case when there were rigid and formal rules and conventions".[26] At the same time, the trend toward informalization came with an egalitarian ethos that spread to all domains of life. More than ever, people are expected to hide or suppress feelings of superiority, whether pertaining to social class, culture, race, age, or gender. Taken together, informalization "involved rising external social constraints towards such self-restraints as being reflexive, showing presence of mind, considerateness, role-taking, and the ability to tolerate and control conflicts, to compromise".[27]

## Reflective Self-Control

Living up to these expectations can be quite a challenge. In some ways, life before the 1960s was easier. According to Elias, before informalization set in, middle- and higher-class individuals were conditioned to *automatically* control their impulses and suppress dangerous emotions. The civilizing process firmly established "an automatic, blindly functioning apparatus of self-control."[28] People did not need to *reflect* on how to react to temptations, the appropriate responses were already "programmed" in their minds. With the advent of the 1960s, however, this blindly functioning apparatus was dismantled. Previously forbidden drives and feelings regained access to consciousness, and developments such as increasing wealth and the contraceptive pill opened new alternatives in progressively heterogeneous networks of social relationships. Negotiating these new realities required a more conscious and flexible self-regulation and management of emotions.

   This gave birth to what Wouters calls the "third nature personality," a successor to the first and second nature personalities that populated Elias' writings. The "first nature personality" is the personality characteristic of the late Middle Ages: the passionate, spontaneous, and unconstrained individual who, without much reflection or foresight, follows his natural impulses and emotions. The "second nature personality" is the constrained individual produced by the civilization process. In this type of personality, impulses and emotions of first nature are controlled via the automatic counter-impulses and counter-emotions of a rigorous conscience. Because seemingly harmless pleasures such as dancing or having a drink were considered the first steps on a slippery slope that would irrevocably lead to personal ruin, any inclination to dissoluteness had to be nipped in the bud.[29] Informalization, however, brought the crucial insight that being open to the emotions of first nature *does not inevitably* lead to disaster. Allowing these emotions access to consciousness, perhaps giving in to them in a controlled, subtle, and playful manner, may even enrich life. The capability to responsibly *manage* emotions rather than lose control could be considered a *next level* in the civilization process. Elias and Wouters call this the "controlled decontrolling of emotional controls."[30]

By definition, "controlled decontrolling" presupposes a high capacity for self-control. Elias already noted this in *The Civilizing Process*. Discussing the increasing body exposure in the female bathing and sports costumes of his day, he argued that only in a society "in which a high degree of restraint is taken for granted, and in which women are, like men, absolutely sure that each individual is curbed by self-control and a strict code of etiquette, can bathing and sporting costumes having this relative degree of freedom develop".[31] Wouters elaborates on this observation by arguing that informalization requires a proficiency in balancing the forces of both "first nature" and "second nature." The locus of self-regulation shifts from conscience to consciousness, from the realm of automaticity to the realm of reflection. In fact, this is the hallmark of the "third nature personality." Rather than simply caving in to impulses and emotions on the one hand, or simply banishing these impulses and emotions to the dark corners of unconsciousness on the other, the third nature personality is capable of *regulating* the – often opposed – forces of first and second nature, and thus capable of carefully attuning his behavior to the particulars of the situation. Informalization, therefore, does not necessarily signal a step backwards from automatic control to child-like spontaneity and lack of restraint, but may signal a step forward, from automatic self-control to *reflective* self-control.

This is a monumental step. As we will see in Chapter 8, several philosophers consider *reflective self-control* to be the essential precondition of moral responsibility. If they are correct, only "third nature personalities" would truly qualify as autonomous agents who may be held fully accountable for their conduct.

## Population Growth

Before concluding, let me highlight another major transformation that both authors mention only in passing, but that, in all likelihood, has been hugely consequential: The world has become much, much more crowded.[32] Since the Middle Ages, the world's population has multiplied tenfold. Figures 7.2 and 7.3 show how population levels

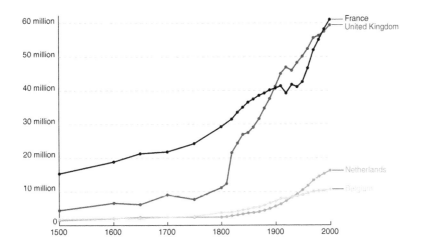

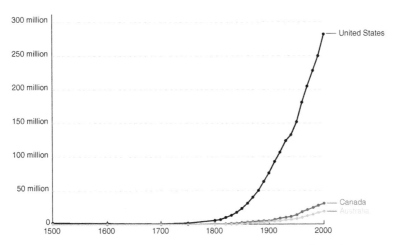

**Figure 7.2** Population by country, 1500–2000. *Source:* Clio Infra (2016), published online at OurWorldInData.org

have risen in select West European and Anglosphere countries over the last 500 years.[33] This dramatic growth, moreover, was not evenly distributed but concentrated in urban areas. In many corners of the world, population density has thus increased dramatically. It seems reasonable to assume that the more people live together in limited spaces, the more often they will encounter situations in which they

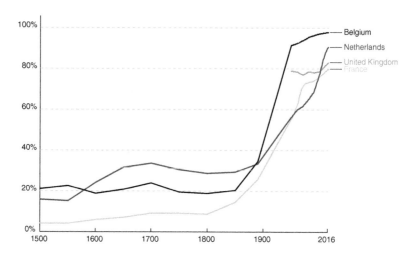

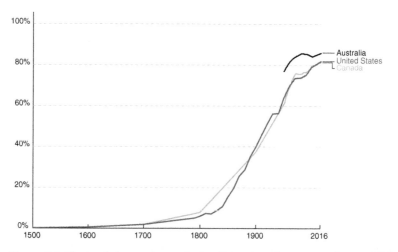

**Figure 7.3** Share of the total population living in urban areas. *Source:* UN World Urbanization Prospects 2018 and others, published online at Our-WorldInData.org

need to restrain themselves and consider other people's thoughts, feelings, and behaviors. Perhaps the most fundamental reason why self-control has become more important is the fact that, there are now so *many* of us and, for better or worse, we must somehow make it together on spaceship earth.

## Conclusion

One need not agree with all that Elias and Wouters assert to subscribe to the general argument that various social transformations have made self-control and foresight ever more important for navigating life.

Can everybody keep up with the rising self-control demands? Elias noted that in some groups the civilizing process had advanced further than in others, and that considerable differences existed between the social classes. He did not, however, pay much attention to the potential consequences of these differences, perhaps because he considered them transitory, merely a phase in a trend that would eventually touch everyone and alter everyone's personality. The implicit assumption behind this vision is that everyone has the *potential* to fully develop the "automatic restraint" that modern life requires. This is supported by Elias' rather Freudian interpretation of the individual development of self-restraint. He seems to consider poor self-control as the result of adverse childhood experiences, unresolved psychological tensions and conflicts, lack of adequate parental guidance, and so forth.[34]

This is clearly at odds with the findings from the psychological research discussed in Part I. These strongly suggest that self-control capacity does not only depend on *nurture* but also on *nature*. Even if all children were raised under perfect conditions by perfect parents, and even if all people lived in exactly the same social circumstances, differences in self-control would still remain, for the simple reason that humans differ in genetic inheritance. These differences may become particularly relevant when informalization sets in. A "controlled decontrolling of control" is only feasible if people have a solid foundation of self-control capacity to build on, in order to counter the downward forces of the slippery slope. But for people who lack this foundation, informalization may turn out to be a mixed blessing. And not only for themselves, but also for their fellow citizens, who may be confronted with the less pleasant consequences of the loosening of constraints. This is the subject of the next section.[35]

## 7.2 A Civilization Offensive: The Age of Responsibility

After the Second World War, the West enjoyed nearly three decades of impressive and uninterrupted economic growth, with governments handing out more and more benefits to the disadvantaged. All citizens were entitled to a fair share of the growing wealth. The latter decades of the twentieth century, however, witnessed a dramatic shift in ideas, beliefs, and public policies regarding, among others, crime and welfare provision. As I explain in this section, these changes placed a further premium on good self-control.

## Crime

In Figure 7.1, which depicts the sharp decline in homicides since the Middle Ages, one can detect a barely noticeable reversal of the trend in the last decades of the twentieth century. Due to the scale of this figure, it may appear to be just a blip, mere noise, but actually it represents a massive change. Among the most significant trends of the second half of the twentieth century was a steep rise in crime from the 1960s to the early 1990s. All across the Western world, homicide and crime rates went up. In the United States, homicide rates more than doubled while the numbers for other violent crimes and property crimes rose even more dramatically (see Figure 7.4). Similar developments occurred in other countries.

But as the figure shows, this increase was only temporary, with the trend reversing again in the 1990s.[36] There is no clear and simple answer to the question what lies behind these dynamics. Likely candidates for the increase in crime since the 1960s are demographic developments, such as the arrival of a large cohort of teenage males, reduced situational and social controls due to urbanization and economies of scale, and cultural developments such as the process of informalization discussed in Section 7.1. Apparently, not everybody is capable of a "controlled decontrolling of control." What is behind the decrease in crime since the 1990s is even more of a mystery. Scholars have ventured a plethora of explanations, some quite curious, such as the nationwide legalization of abortion in the United States in 1973.[37] However, explanations based on circumstances in specific countries do not suffice, since the decrease occurred all over the Western world. We must look for more global explanations.[38]

This brings us to the sea change in ideas about crime that took place in the 1970s. According to sociologist David Garland, in the first decades after the war, academics and criminal justice professionals viewed delinquency and crime as the outcome of personal deficiencies and social deprivation. People became delinquent because they

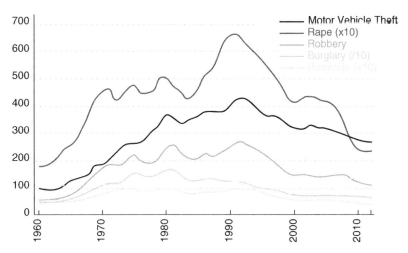

**Figure 7.4** Crime rates per 100,000 population, United States, 1960–2012. Republished with permission of University of Chicago Press from: Tonry, M., Why crime rates are falling throughout the Western world. *Crime and Justice,* 43(1), 1–63. Copyright 2014, permission conveyed through Copyright Clearance Center, Inc.

lacked proper education, family socialization, job opportunities, or treatment for their abnormal psychological dispositions. Penal policies therefore had a strong social engineering bent. "The solution for crime lay in individualized correctional treatment, the support and supervision of families, and in welfare-enhancing measures of social reform – particularly education and job creation".[39] Meanwhile, starting in the early 1960s, crime rates began to skyrocket, confronting criminal justice agencies with a caseload vastly exceeding their capacity. One response to this overflow was to limit the demands placed upon them by "defining deviance down".[40] Minor violations were no longer prosecuted, and offences that previously entailed probation were now dispatched with fines. The threshold for law enforcement was thus raised: Low-level crime and misdemeanors were de facto decriminalized, or responded to with only minimal penalties.

This all changed from the 1970s onward. In just a matter of years, the faith in corrective strategies and the benign effects of welfare provision completely collapsed, partly due to the apparent lack of success, and partly due to ideological changes, notably the rise of neoliberal and neoconservative ideas. Crime was no longer viewed as sign of a deficiency, committed by individuals who are not altogether in control of their behavior, but as "a normal, routine, commonplace aspect of modern society, committed by individuals who are, to all intents and purposes, perfectly normal". And these perfectly normal individuals "will be strongly attracted to self-serving, anti-social, and criminal conduct *unless inhibited from doing so by robust and effective controls*".[41] In other words, criminal acts are calculated, utility-maximizing actions resulting from individual choice. As former British Prime Minister John Major declared, "Crime is a decision, not a disease."[42] This means that preventing criminal behavior is a matter of incentives and pricing. The penal consequences of criminal offending have to be swift, certain, and harsh to function as an effective deterrent.

These new ideas dovetailed remarkably well with the growing call to get "tough on crime." With rising crime and the higher threshold of law enforcement, crime and disorder were no longer anomalies confined to the poor and their neighborhoods, but had spread throughout society, including the suburban neighborhoods where the well-educated middle classes lived. Crime had become part of everyday life. "That this occurred in a period of social and political upheaval in which traditional institutions and forms of authority appeared to many to be close to collapse, only served to exacerbate the felt need to take a tougher line with the control of crime and disorder".[43] New arrangements and partnerships for more intensive control and surveillance were established, and the penal screws were tightened. Garland observes a "punitive turn" exemplified by harsher sentencing, increased use of imprisonment, mandatory minimum sentences, three strikes laws, truth in sentencing, parole release restrictions, no frills prison laws, retribution in juvenile courts, imprisonment of children, boot camps, supermax prisons, multiplication of capital offences, and so forth. The term that perhaps best captured the new spirit was "zero tolerance."

This punitive turn was not a global phenomenon, though. It was most evident in the United States, more moderate in other countries of the Anglosphere, and mild or even absent in most other Western countries.[44] Interestingly, although the crime rate has been falling steadily since the 1990s, this has not led to a relaxation of the penal regime in the most punitive nations. Writing at the turn of the century, Garland concluded that we may be locked in a new "iron cage" – a disciplining structure that has outlived its origins but nonetheless remains in place as it has become self-sustaining. "The new culture of crime control, born of the fears and anxieties of the late twentieth century, could well continue long after its originating conditions have ceased to exist".[45] Thus far, Garland's prediction seems to have come true.

Here I end my nutshell summary of the criminological thought and penal policy of the past half-century. In terms of the core concepts of this book, we can conclude that in the immediate decades after the Second World War, many believed that personal predispositions, such as poor self-control *capacity*, were a principal cause of delinquency and crime. These predispositions, therefore, had to be altered through therapeutic and correctional programs. But since the 1970s, the emphasis has shifted from *capacity* to *motivation*. Delinquency and crime came to be seen as the product of rational calculation. When the rewards of transgression are high, and the risk and price of getting caught are low, people may be insufficiently motivated to control their behavior. The implicit assumption is that potential offenders indeed *do* have the capacity to control themselves. The policy challenge is thus to ensure that they are sufficiently motivated to also *use* this capacity. Hence the need to alter the incentives. In short, since the 1970s, delinquency and crime are no longer viewed as a matter of being *unable* but as a matter of being *unwilling* to abide by the law.

## Welfare Provision

A similar shift in beliefs and ideas occurred in with regard to welfare policies. In many Western countries, the 1950s and 1960s witnessed the rise of ever more comprehensive and generous welfare states. Gradually it became clear, however, that the welfare state was getting too costly and could not be sustained. The elections of Ronald Reagan and Margaret Thatcher in 1980 proved a turning point, setting the stage for a profound restructuring of welfare policies. The shift did not only concern government spending, though. In essence, it was about morality and good citizenship. Margaret Thatcher believed that the welfare state erodes the virtues of hard work and self-reliance, which she considered constituent features of a flourishing life.[46]

The key term here is not "self-control" but "personal responsibility." Since the 1980s, the idea of personal responsibility has become so pervasive in both philosophical and political discourse that, according to political scientist Yascha Mounk, we have entered the "age of responsibility".[47] The strong emphasis on personal responsibility, however, implies that the capacity for self-control has *also* become more important, as it is generally assumed that people should only be held responsible for what is under their control. So although this section may appear to be pursuing another topic, what some have called the "personal responsibility crusade" is central to understanding the ever-rising importance of good self-control.[48]

## Conditionality

The impact of this development was perhaps most dramatically felt in the domain of income security and welfare policy. During the heyday of the welfare state, entitlements came with few strings attached. Everybody with insufficient means was entitled to cash assistance. The only requirement was formal citizenship. But as mentioned, in the 1970s, more and more observers began to doubt the financial sustainability of the welfare state. Moreover, conservative thinkers such as George Gilder and Charles Murray argued that generous welfare provision created a "culture of dependency." In their view, many poor people had simply made the calculation that depending on welfare was an easier and more attractive way of life than to assume the burdens of hard work and self-reliance. Murray's solution was as radical as it was simple: eliminate welfare.[49]

But as the Reagan Administration soon discovered, that was easier said than done. Welfare programs were simply too popular. The political scientist Lawrence Mead, in his 1986 book *Beyond Entitlement*, came up with an alternative plan: Welfare should not be eliminated but made contingent on behavior. The main problem with the welfare state, Mead argued, "is its permissiveness, not its size".[50] Federal welfare programs had set few requirements for how welfare recipients ought to function. In particular, they did not require employable recipients to work in return for support. Welfare provision should therefore be made conditional on meeting work obligations.

This approach clearly broke with the dominant sociological thinking of the time, which had shown little interest in the role of agency.[51] Mead, however, placed the blame for welfare dependency, unemployment, and other forms of poor "functioning," such as criminal behavior, squarely on the poor themselves, and not on the social structure or economic conditions. He conceded that in the first decades after the war obstacles in the environment may have kept the poor from working, but claimed that this argument was no longer plausible after the expansion of civil rights, government aid programs, and economic opportunities in the 1960s. For poor and disadvantaged Americans, "the main barrier to acceptance is no longer unfair social structures but their own difficulties in coping, particularly with work and family life".[52] Hence, if society seriously wants these people to get a job, "it must require them to do so".[53] And if only low-wage and dirty jobs are available, then so be it. Government is under no obligation to make the desired behavior worthwhile.[54]

Mead's message that welfare provision should be made conditional on "responsible conduct" was not only music to the ears of conservatives but also embraced by center-left politicians, notably Bill Clinton, who had campaigned on the pledge to "end welfare as we know it." Acting on this pledge, Clinton signed the Personal Responsibility and Work Opportunity Reconciliation Act into law, and thereby created the Temporary Assistance for Needy Families (TANF) program. In TANF, cash assistance is restricted to a lifetime maximum of five years and made conditional on participation in "work activities," such as job search training, work experience programs, and subsidized employment. Recipients are expected to take any available job that comes around, even low-paying entry-level positions. Noncompliance is sanctioned, usually by cuts in benefits.[55]

The new approach quickly spread to other Western countries, but perhaps no other country has gone further in adopting "active labor market policies" (ALMPs) than the United Kingdom. The introduction of the Jobseeker's Allowance in 1996 proved a turning point. Since then, the British welfare regime has become more and more punitive, with increasingly strict requirements for job search activities and increasingly severe sanctions for not meeting them. In 2012, this culminated in the introduction of the "most punitive welfare" regime ever proposed by a British government.[56] Relatively mild sanctions are given for nonattendance at a Jobcentre appointment or a Work Programme, more severe sanctions are given for failure to be available for work, and the highest sanctions are given for failure to apply for a job or refusal of a Mandatory Work Activity.[57] The United Kingdom also introduced elements of conditionality in other policy domains, for instance social housing. As of 2011, social landlords were allowed to offer new tenants fixed-term renewable tenancies rather than open-ended ones. The British government has encouraged social landlords to give longer tenancies to people who are employed or contribute positively to their neighborhood.[58]

## Social Investment

As the twentieth century drew to a close, however, several European countries seemed to abandon the neoliberal paradigm (at least in its pure and unadulterated form) in favor of a new set of ideas that came to be known as the "social investment perspective." In this new approach, welfare policies were no longer viewed as an *obstacle* but as a *precondition* for economic development. The traditional welfare state was geared toward *compensating* for risks through social insurance, notably the risks of old age, illness, and unemployment. In contrast, the social investment state is geared toward *preventing* risks through investing in human capital. It aims to create a highly educated and skilled workforce, capable of adapting to ever-changing economic circumstances, thus reducing the need for income support and fostering economic growth. "In essence," summarizes political scientist Anton Hemerijck, "social investment is an encompassing strategy of developing, employing, and protecting human capital over the life course for the good of citizens, families, societies, and economies".[59]

The term "social investment state" was coined by the English sociologist Anthony Giddens, perhaps best known for his work on the "third way."[60] Time and again, Giddens emphasizes that in the social investment perspective, people are expected to take responsibility for their own lives. They are expected to invest in their future, keep their knowledge and skills up to date, look after their health, and save for retirement. In this regard, there is no difference to the neoliberal paradigm: no rights without responsibilities. But unlike in the neoliberalism of those days, in the social investment perspective people are not left to their own devices.[61] The state will *enable* them to take this responsibility, for instance by providing subsidized education and childcare, by removing obstacles to participation in the labor market, and through income transfers aimed at preventing marginalization. This type of support is not viewed as merely a cost and a hindrance to economic development, but as an investment that will pay off sooner or later, both for the individual and for society as a whole.

In the late 1990s, the social investment perspective quickly gained traction. It was adopted by several center-left politicians across Europe, including Tony Blair and the German chancellor Gerhard Schröder, and was embraced by the OECD (Organisation for Economic Co-operation and Development) and the European Union. In a comprehensive 2017 volume, Hemerijck concludes that, by and large, European welfare states have moved in the direction of the social investment state. By that time, most countries had universal minimum-income protection programs, coupled with "demanding" activation and "enabling" reintegration measures. In addition, many countries had increased their spending on ALMPs, such as assistance in finding work, incentives to accept jobs, and training and education to improve employability over the life course. This was accompanied by upgrading both the scope and substance of family policies, including subsidized childcare and paid parental leave. Developments on this front have been uneven, though. The Nordic countries continue to be at the forefront, and several other European countries also made steps toward social investment policies, but there have also been backlashes, especially in the wake of the 2008 recession.[62]

Of particular interest for our purposes is the time perspective inherent to the social investment approach. According to political scientists Jane Jenson and Denis Saint-Martin, traditional welfare states are primarily focused on the here and now. They seek to improve people's *present* financial condition by compensating for income loss due to setbacks. Essentially, they are *reactive*. The social investment state, in contrast, is primarily focused on the *future*. The overarching goal is to prevent setbacks from happening in the first place (or if they *do* happen, to remedy them as swiftly and effectively as possible). This more *proactive* stance engenders a strong focus on the "life course." In the social investment perspective, life is not seen as a series of isolated events. Poor jobs, obsolete skills, and unemployment do not arise out of thin air, but are often the result of problems in early life, such as growing up in abject poverty or dropping out of school. The social investment perspective therefore places a heavy emphasis on early childhood care, education, and vocational training. This is where the seeds for future success or failure are planted.[63]

## Conclusion

The upshot of this bit of recent history is that income support has become (more) contingent on behavior. This is a fundamental break from the traditional welfare state of bygone days. Back then, every (male) citizen who fell below a certain income threshold was entitled to cash assistance, regardless of his behavior. It made no difference whether he seriously and scrupulously tried to improve his situation by finding a (better-paying) job, or did nothing but watch TV and drink beer all day. In the traditional welfare state, therefore, neither the motivation nor the capacity for self-control had any bearing on one's right to welfare. Conduct was no criterion. All this changed in the 1990s with the introduction of conditionality in entitlements. This shift in policies spelt trouble for welfare recipients lacking the self-control capacity required for complying with increasingly strict rules and regulations.

Seen more broadly, it can be argued that poor self-control has gradually transformed from a mostly private affair into a collective problem. More so than in the past, poor self-control is considered potentially harmful to society as a whole. Those who engage in deviant or delinquent behavior may not only get in trouble themselves, but also make other people feel unsafe. Those who lead unhealthy lifestyles not only risk their own health but also strain the healthcare system and drive up insurance premiums. Those who do not invest in their employability do not only risk their own life chances, but also potentially burden the public purse. All these behaviors have come under the jurisdiction of Mill's harm principle.

In fact, poor self-control has become an impediment to the effective government of society. Sociologist Nikolas Rose argues that strategies of government differ in the "models of the persons" they assume. Some strategies view people as members of a flock to be shepherded, some view them as children to be nurtured and tutored, other strategies view people as citizens with rights, and yet others view them as rational calculating individuals whose preferences are to be acted on. The 1970s clearly marked a shift toward the latter view, as public policies were rewritten in the key of freedom of choice, autonomization, and responsibilization.[64] According to Rose, in today's society, personal autonomy is no longer the antithesis of political power "but a key term in its exercise".[65] Society *needs* people who are capable of delaying gratification. If people fail to live up to this ideal, they

## Box 7.2 Too Many Calories

Where have all the marshmallows gone? And the sugary drinks and the fatty snacks? Readers may wonder why this chapter had remained silent about health behavior, especially about consuming too many calories – that quintessential instance of self-control failure that figured so prominently in Part I. So let's make up for this omission. In a chapter addressing large-scale social transformations, overweight and obesity deserve special attention, as recent decades have seen a dramatic rise in overweight and obese people. In the United States, for instance, over two-thirds of the adult population are now overweight, while over one-third are obese.[66] Since the 1970s, the number of obese people worldwide has roughly tripled.[67]

What explains this dramatic rise? Does it indicate a decline in people's capacity to control their desires or a decline in their motivation to lead healthy lifestyles? That seems unlikely. Other forms of unhealthy behavior, such as smoking, do not show similar upward trends.[68] The rise is better explained by economic and social developments, such as changes in purchasing power, greater availability of cheap high-calorie foods, larger portion sizes, more intensive and sophisticated marketing, and less time for food preparation. These developments have created a unique new problem. For most of human history, the challenge was to avoid hunger and procure enough calories, but today the challenge is the opposite: resist consuming too many calories. In Elias' terms, the external constraint on overconsumption has gradually weakened, thus making self-restraint more important for those who wish to keep trim and healthy.

But the skeptical reader might question, though, whether these economic and social developments have really led to greater demands on self-control. After all, nobody is *obliged* to live a healthy life. In the realm of crime and welfare, irresponsible conduct has indeed become more costly as sentences have become more severe, and welfare has been made conditional on a host of behavioral requirements. But here things are different: There is no law against overeating. Moreover, few people would consider an unhealthy lifestyle valid grounds for withholding essential care, and in countries with universal healthcare, obese individuals are – as a rule – entitled to the same level of help and treatment as anyone else. In short, people are still free to eat and drink as much as they desire.

### STRONG INCENTIVES

While this may be formally correct, there are nonetheless strong incentives to restrict calorie intake. First and foremost, being overweight or obese poses serious health risks. It may lead to health consequences such as cardiovascular disease (mainly heart disease and stroke), type 2 diabetes, musculoskeletal disorders like osteoarthritis (a highly disabling degenerative disease of the joints), and some cancers (including endometrial, breast, ovarian, prostate, liver, gallbladder, kidney, and colon).

People with serious overweight also face prejudice. They are often stereotyped as lazy, unmotivated, lacking in self-discipline, less competent, noncompliant, and sloppy – not only by the general public but also by health professionals. Hence, it is not surprising that obese patients frequently report unsatisfactory treatment in healthcare, and that obese women are more likely to report delaying or avoiding preventive healthcare.[69] Weight stigma is also common in North American media (or at least, it was until not too long ago). "Whether it be situation comedies, cartoons, movies, advertisements, or news reports, the media is unkind to overweight people," concluded health scientists Rebecca Puhl and Chelsea Heuer in a 2009 review of the research literature.[70] If people internalize these stereotypes – that is, if they apply them to themselves and self-derogate because of their body weight – this can be detrimental to their well-being. A 2018 review found strong relationships between weight bias internalization and outcomes such as depression, anxiety, and poor self-esteem.[71]

Obese people may also suffer discrimination. Puhl and Heuer found that obese employees perceive weight-based disparities in employment and earn lower wages than their normal-weight counterparts, and that obese applicants experience discrimination in job evaluations and hiring decisions. In another review, Lisa Watson and colleagues conclude that obesity discrimination is "common occurrence" in the workplace. It happens in all stages of the employment relationship and at every level, but has the greatest impact in the hiring stage. Even seasoned human relations professionals are not immune to stigmatizing obesity. There is also a clear gender difference: Obese women are more likely to experience weight discrimination in the workplace than obese men.[72] A similar picture emerges from the handful of studies on weight stigma and interpersonal relationships. Being overweight or obese reduces one's prospects on the dating market, especially for women, and reduces sexual attractiveness.

## IN CONCLUSION

Although there is no law against being fat and the provision of healthcare in medical urgencies is not conditional on responsible conduct – or at least, not yet – the pressure to watch your weight is strong.

So here we have yet another social transformation that makes good self-control more important. In the olden days, keeping to a normal weight was easier, not least because there were fewer opportunities to indulge. But nowadays, for many people, high-calorie drinks and foods have become so abundantly available that they pose a continuous challenge to their self-control. Of course, there is nothing wrong with the occasional visit to the proverbial candy store, but when the daily food environment transforms into one giant and omnipresent candy store, a whole new set of problems arises – problems that our ancestors would probably consider a luxury but are very real today.

hinder the achievement of wealth, health, and happiness for all. Citizens who fail at self-control ultimately fail their fellow citizens.

## 7.3 Conclusion

This chapter asked *why the ability for self-control has become more important over the ages.* I discussed two main reasons.

First, over the centuries, good self-control and foresight have become more important due to large-scale social transformations, most notably the monopolization of violence and the lengthening of the chains of interdependence. According to Elias, human conduct in northwestern Europe underwent a "civilizing process": a gradual change in the locus of control from external constraint to self-restraint. Success increasingly depended on "[c]ontinuous reflection, foresight, and calculation, self-control, precise and articulate regulation of one's own affects, knowledge of the whole terrain, human and non-human, in which one acts".[73] The informalization of the 1960s and 1970s only reinforced this trend. It meant that people could rely less on the automatic pilot of habitual restraint, and had to consciously regulate their impulses and emotions.

Although I have not gone into this, it should be noted that since that period, the lengthening of chains of interdependence has continued apace. By the end of the twentieth century, the world had become so interconnected that sociologist Manuel Castells declared the advent of "the network society" – and this was when the Internet was still in its infancy and no one had yet heard of "social media".[74]

Today, a single careless tweet or photo posted on Instagram, one brief moment of impulsivity, may suffice to ruin your life.[75] And there is no end in sight. The rise of the "internet of things" further expands the networks people are embedded in, now including machines and devices that may track behavior. Through personalized advertising, targeting people's weak spots is becoming even easier, and moments of poor self-control may become even more costly (think, for example, of your car sending data about your penchant for speeding to the insurance company).[76]

But the latter is somewhat speculative, as these are only recent developments. It remains to be seen how they play out. However, there is one large-scale social transformation that is anything but recent and is of paramount significance: growing population density. Parts of our planet are getting very, very crowded. The numbers are staggering. World population has grown from less than one billion in the year 1800 to almost eight billion today. Moreover, this growth is heavily concentrated in urban areas. The share of the population living in those areas rose from 7 percent in 1800 to about 55 percent today. One may assume that the more people crowd into limited spaces, the more often they will encounter situations where they need to restrain themselves. Perhaps the most fundamental reason why good self-control has become "the other important quality" is that, nowadays, there are so *many* of us. We must all squeeze in, literally and figuratively.

Second, in recent decades, self-control and foresight have become increasingly important due to changes in ideology and politics. The 1970s marked the beginning of a fundamental shift toward greater emphasis on personal responsibility in general, and increased punitiveness and conditionality in welfare in particular. More than before, self-control failures can lead to harsh sentencing or the loss of entitlements. As a corollary, thinking about tomorrow has become more important too. People are expected to adopt an entrepreneurial attitude, keep investing in their knowledge and skills, and be prepared for whatever lies ahead.

Whereas the civilizing *process* as posited by Elias was largely an autonomous development, rooted in economic, cultural, technological, and demographic changes, the new emphasis on greater personal responsibility is the explicitly intended result of targeted policies. These policies have all the characteristics of a civilizing *offensive*, seeking to mold individuals into the healthy and productive entrepreneurial citizens that contemporary society is believed to need for staying competitive. To a certain extent, this latest civilizing offensive can be seen as a *response* to the problems that arose from the widening gap between, on the one hand, the level of self-control and foresight that became necessary for negotiating modern life and, on the other, the level of self-control and foresight that large segments of the population could muster. In this view, social policies since the 1970s are not the *ultimate* cause of the ever-growing importance of self-control but gave this development an extra push. They were more like hitting the accelerator than hitting the brake.

Which, once again, raises the question: Do people have enough self-control capacity to meet these rising demands? Both Elias and the advocates of personal responsibility seem to believe so. In Elias' analysis, poor self-control is essentially the product of the social environment and poor parenting, whereas in the responsibility approach, poor self-control is essentially the product of the wrong incentives. But as Part I of this book made clear, both assumptions are at best half-true. Whether we like it or not, the empirical fact is that some people are just better at self-control than others. And the empirical fact is that, sooner or later, all of us will hit the limits of our self-control capacity. No intervention in early upbringing, environment, or incentives will ever change this state of affairs. As I argue in Chapters 8 and 9, this has serious ramifications for some key ideas underlying our present institutional and social order.

# 8 | *Self-Control and Moral Responsibility*

Are people who fall into trouble due to poor self-control the innocent victims of circumstances beyond their control? Can someone rightfully claim that it was her bad genes that made her surf social media all day rather than focus on her studies? That his harsh and abusive parents are to be blamed for his inability to resist high-calorie snacks? That she should not be held responsible for failing to save for next month's rent because working two jobs and raising a family on her own puts her in a state of chronic ego depletion?

Not everyone will be persuaded by such excuses. In recent decades, blaming everything that goes wrong in life on a "troubled childhood" or "difficult circumstances" has fallen out of fashion. But is that entirely justified? Do these excuses not contain at least a grain of truth? As we saw in previous chapters, nowadays temptation is everywhere, often just a mouse click away. At the same time, more than a few decades ago, people are expected to delay gratification and to behave prudently and responsibly. They must study and work hard, watch their health, save for retirement, invest in the future of their children, and so on. Self-control demands have become higher and higher. But if it turns out that, more often than we think, poor self-control does not stem from a lack of *motivation* but from a lack of *capacity* caused by genetic inheritance, early upbringing, or adverse life conditions, then also more often than we think, it may be unfair to hold people responsible for the consequences of poor self-control.

Or is it? We are entering dangerous territory here. Is this not the first step on a slippery slope toward excusing everything? How can we, on the one hand, acknowledge that sometimes it is fair to display some leniency toward well-intentioned individuals who have the bad luck of finding themselves in circumstances that undermine their self-control but, on the other hand, prevent that the floodgates are opened, and we are forced to accept nonsensical excuses of the "my genes made me do it" variety?

That is the topic of this chapter. This chapter asks *what the implications are of the psychological findings on self-control for the extent to*

---

**Box 8.1 What This Chapter Is Not About**

This chapter will *not* discuss the potential role of reduced self-control in penal codes or criminal defenses. In several jurisdictions in the Western world, it is possible to excuse a defendant from (full) responsibility if his or her self-control was severely impaired, for instance due to a serious mental defect or insanity. To be sure, this practice is not without problems. For instance, where should we draw the line? As legal scholar Richard Bonnie points out, there is "no objective basis for distinguishing between offenders who were undeterrable and who were merely undeterred, between the impulse that was irresistible and the impulse not resisted, or between substantial impairment of capacity and some lesser impairment".[1] In one of the very few texts on (US) law and the findings of self-control research, legal scholar Rebecca Hollander-Blumoff concludes that "self-control failures in psychology are far more common than the failures of self-control that the law is willing to recognize and allow".[2]

Nevertheless, this chapter does not delve into the intricacies of such penal issues. Our interest is much broader. Although the research findings on self-control are certainly relevant for matters of retributive justice, criminal law is just one of the many, many domains in life where responsibility judgments are made. Schools make decisions about responsibility of pupils if they had a fight, employers make decisions about who is responsible for corporate success or failure, insurance agents make decisions about how far someone is responsible for damages, government caseworkers make decisions about the responsibility of welfare clients for not meeting workfare requirements, and so forth. In short, the psychological insights with regard to self-control have a much wider relevance. I leave it to legal scholars to determine what my overall argument might entail for potential excuses in the criminal domain.

---

*which people should be considered morally responsible for (the consequences of) their poor self-control.* The key concept here is *moral responsibility.* This concept refers to the state or fact of being accountable for some action, of being worthy of praise or blame, reward, or punishment for having performed it.

This will be a lengthy chapter, as moral responsibility is a complicated and contentious issue. To orient the reader, let me explain the global structure of what lies ahead. In this chapter, I approach the main question not from one but from *three perspectives.* This is a break from previous chapters, where I have restricted myself to the perspective of science. It is the job of science to establish the facts and speak "truth to power." However, when considering the implications of scientific findings *for society and policy*, we must also engage the perspective of the *subjects* who make up society, and the perspective of the *policymakers* who have to determine what will probably work best for society. To answer the practical question "What is to be done?" we need to consider all three perspectives. This chapter is, therefore, organized around a *tripartition* in perspectives. I call these the *objective* standpoint, the *subjective* standpoint, and the *instrumental* standpoint.

This will also be an eclectic chapter. Within each standpoint, I will switch back and forth between different fields of scholarship in order to collect a series of building blocks for answering the main question. Two fields are particularly relevant for our purposes. The first concerns what is commonly known as the "free will debate." This infamous debate is not unlike a black hole that sucks up everything that gets too close. Any discussion of "moral responsibility," however, cannot avoid this treacherous area. The second field of scholarship concerns empirical research on moral intuitions in general and intuitions on sentencing in criminal cases in particular. I will discuss several studies on laypeople's judgments on punishment, as these studies provide another set of useful building blocks for determining the implications of the findings on self-control for moral responsibility.

## 8.1 Preliminary Groundwork

Before starting, it is useful to specify what we are talking about. The first thing to note is that we must distinguish between two things:

- The practice of *holding* responsible. In everyday life, we *hold* one another responsible for all kinds of acts and behaviors, such as showing up late for an appointment, damaging another person's property, or not saving for a rainy day. Holding responsible is by definition a social practice, as it always involves a person who blames and a person who is blamed – a "blamer" and a "blamee," so to speak. This practice is rooted in human interaction, and partly governed by formal rules and laws.
- The fact of *being* responsible. This concerns the question whether someone really *is* morally responsible for what happened and really

*deserves* to be blamed. Was it through his own fault that he arrived late, damaged property, failed to save for later? Were these outcomes brought about by his own choices? Or were they caused by circumstances beyond his control, say an emergency with his child, a flipped truck blocking the road, or an economic crisis? This is a question about the nature of reality.

In an ideal world, these two things are in perfect agreement. In an ideal world, people are only *held* responsible in cases where they really *are* morally responsible and *never* in cases where they are *not* morally responsible. Problems arise, however, when there is a gap between the two – that is, when responsibility *judgments* do not match responsibility *facts*. To almost everyone this feels unfair. Unfortunately, in our nonideal world such incongruities are all too common. And to add insult to injury, the message of modern psychology is that this gap between *being* responsible and *holding* responsible may be even wider than most people assume.

Next, some definitions. Moral responsibility refers to the state or fact of being accountable for something. According to the *Stanford Encyclopedia of Philosophy*, to be morally responsible for something, say an action, "is to be worthy of a particular kind of reaction – praise, blame, or something akin to these – for having performed it."[3] Moral responsibility must be distinguished from *causal* responsibility: the mere fact of being the cause of something. If I punch the person next to me due to an epileptic seizure, I am *causally* responsible for his injuries, but most people will not consider me *morally* responsible, as I had no control over my bodily movements.

Moral responsibility, to quote the philosopher Alfred Mele, is a member of the "family of metaphysical freedom concepts."[4] Other well-known members of this illustrious family are "autonomy," "agency," "intention," "free choice," and "free will." You can be quite certain that if one of these concepts enters the conversation, others will soon follow. In this chapter, it will be no different. Since autonomy and agency are often seen as prerequisites for moral responsibility, it is useful to define these terms as well. "Autonomy" is often described as the capacity to govern oneself. To be autonomous is, according to philosopher John Christman, "to be one's own person, to be directed by considerations, desires, conditions, and characteristics that are not simply imposed upon one, but are part of what can somehow be considered one's authentic self."[5] But autonomy alone will not get you very far – you also need "agency." That is usually described as the capacity to *act* in accordance with your intentions. The crucial term here is "intention": the determination to act in a certain way.[6] As these descriptions make clear, autonomy and agency are closely connected concepts that partly overlap and partly complement each other.[7] One could perhaps say that people who fail at self-control due to poor self-control capacity may be autonomous in the sense that they have formed an authentic will, but nonetheless lack agency because they are incapable of translating this authentic will into corresponding actions.

But let me not delve too deeply into definitional issues. The important thing to remember is this: What all members of the "family of metaphysical freedom concepts" have in common, is the idea that *we are the authors of our own lives.* We are subjects who can freely choose to turn left or right, not objects that are merely pushed around, without having any say in where they go. The causes of our choices and actions lie within ourselves and not in external forces. I refer to this type of freedom as "autonomous agency" or just "agency."

## The Other Important Quality

Crucially, autonomous agency and moral responsibility presuppose a basic level of self-control. According to Christman, to be autonomous, certain competency conditions must be met, including "capacities for rational thought, self-control, and freedom from debilitating pathologies," while agency – the capacity to *act* in accordance with one's intentions – entails self-control almost by definition. The same is true for moral responsibility. The philosopher R. Jay Wallace argues that it is fair to hold people morally responsible "if they possess the rational power to grasp and apply moral reasons, and to control their behavior by the light of those reasons."[8] People must be capable of "reflective self-control." Manuel Vargas, a contemporary philosopher whose work I discuss in Section 8.4, makes a similar point: Moral responsibility requires the capacity to detect moral considerations, and the capacity for what he, interchangeably, calls volitional control, self-governance, or self-control.

In sum, people must possess at least a minimum of *both* qualities that Adam Smith found so useful: rational capacities *and* self-command. It is a two-pronged requirement. If one prong is missing, a person cannot be considered morally responsible for his conduct. Self-control truly is "the other important quality" – not only for health, wealth, and happiness but also for moral responsibility.

## 8.2 The Objective Standpoint

Which brings us to the heart of the matter. If we take the scientific findings on the dynamics of self-control seriously, what does this mean for moral responsibility? There are two potential consequences.[9]

First, poor *trait* self-control may be an extra ground for exemption.[10] Due to variations in genetic inheritance and upbringing, people differ in their baseline level of self-control strength. As self-control is an essential ingredient for autonomous agency and moral responsibility, this implies that people will also differ in their "baseline level" of autonomy, agency, and moral responsibility. Empirically speaking, these concepts are not all-or-nothing qualities but *matters of degree*.

Second, poor *state* self-control may be an extra ground for excuse. People may get into situations that are so harmful to their self-control capacity that it would be unfair to hold them (fully) responsible for their actions, at least in that particular situation at that particular moment. We all suffer bouts of poor self-control, due to cognitive load, severe stress, lack of sleep, or whatever drains one's mental resources. Empirically speaking, autonomy, agency, and moral responsibility are not only matters of degree but also *functions of space and time*. The upshot is that, on the spectrum between, on the one side, being *objects* that are merely pushed around and, on the other side, being *subjects* who are the authors of their own lives, all of us hover somewhere in between.

This raises a serious problem. The current institutional order is based on a clear division between just two categories: a very large majority of people who are considered autonomous and responsible agents, versus a small and well-defined minority of people who are not, such as children and the insane. In the world of law, this has always been a grounding assumption and – partly by extension – the same is true for other domains of life that have come under the regime of personal responsibility. This simple black-and-white dichotomy, however, is fundamentally at odds with the many shades of gray that characterize empirical reality.

How can we solve this problem? If the real-world variation in trait self-control within the population follows a normal distribution, but we nonetheless want to uphold this convenient dichotomy, we could introduce some kind of threshold, some minimal capacity for self-control one must have to count as an autonomous and responsible agent. This is not as strange as it sounds. We do exactly the same with age and cognitive capacities. Like self-control, these are continuous variables, but there is a broad consensus on (the need for) thresholds: people must be over eighteen years of age and have minimal cognitive functioning. This approach also aligns with the recognition in many penal codes that an individual must possess at least a modicum of self-control to qualify as a responsible agent. Obviously, if we go for this solution, the critical question is where to set the threshold level for self-control. If the bar is raised too high, many people will not meet the threshold, and will hence be withheld the status of fully responsible citizen. That brings us dangerously close to a society of *un*equals. But if the bar is set too low, many people will be held accountable to standards that exceed their capacities. As a consequence, they may be punished for what was actually beyond their control, which seems unfair.

Alternatively, we could abandon the idea of just two categories, and introduce a third, intermediate level. Perhaps we could place adults who do not suffer a severe mental condition, but who nonetheless score low on trait self-control – say, more than one standard deviation below the population average – in this intermediate category. They would then be treated as people with "diminished" responsibility. Perhaps we could go even further, and introduce *multiple* in-between categories, or even build a whole ladder of gradations in autonomy, agency, and responsibility. Unfortunately, this is not a viable solution either. Even putting aside the practical and normative problems this approach invites, we would still face the second problem: fluctuations in *state* self-control. People can move back and forth between categories. A stressful situation may impair self-control to such an extent that one slips below the threshold for (full) moral responsibility, whereas a good night's sleep or a well-deserved vacation may spur movement in the opposite direction. In other words, the boundaries are highly permeable. The more intermediate levels we introduce, the more transboundary movement there will be.

In sum, the empirical findings on the psychology of self-control challenge the assumption of a clear and simple dichotomy between a large majority of people who may be considered autonomous agents who are (fully) responsible for their conduct, and a small minority who may not. The first group is probably smaller than believed and the second group larger, while the boundary between the two is anything but solid. Therefore, institutional arrangements that hold on to such a strict dichotomy and that, moreover, assume that almost everyone falls within the first category, may be outdated and in need of revision.

## Science Gone Wild?

But this is only the beginning of our troubles. Things get much worse. The fundamental problem is that once we start down the road of empirically testing our assumptions about what determines behavior, the floodgates open. The closer we look, the more exempting or excusing conditions will spring up. In the end, we are forced to conclude that nobody is ever morally responsible for anything.

Let me explain with an example. Suppose someone experiences severe poverty or financial setbacks, and suppose that these circumstances are so stressful and depleting that her self-control capacity is significantly reduced. As a consequence, she starts making mistakes, for instance, she spends more money than necessary because she does not check whether there are cheaper alternatives on the market, or forgets to pay her bills in time, which leads to late payment fees, making her financial problems worse. Is she really to blame for the resulting misery? Does she bear full responsibility? In light of the psychological findings of Part I, it can be argued that this would be unfair, as the adverse circumstances she found herself in may have drained her mental resources for self-control. This is *force majeure*. If you or I were caught up in the same situation, chances are we would fall prey to self-control failure too. Society should therefore offer some kind of help or relief.

At this point, however, the skeptic might object that such adverse circumstances are no valid grounds for excuse, since they do not arise from nowhere. These circumstances resulted from earlier imprudent choices, where this person should have known better. If people are unwilling to work hard, if they refuse to watch their expenses and save for a rainy day, they should not be surprised if sooner or later they get into financial trouble. It is no secret that setbacks are part of life, and responsible people take precautions. One might well agree that poverty and hardship can lead to self-control failure – after all, that is what the psychological research shows – but still hold this person responsible for the resulting misery because the circumstances that induced self-control failure were of her own making. It is like drunk driving: If a driver is no longer able to control his tendency to speed due to consumption of alcohol, we still consider him responsible for any accidents he causes. He should not have chosen to drink before driving in the first place.

But does this objection hold? Not really. All we have done is shift the focus of attention to an earlier moment in the chain of events. Now the question becomes what caused this person to make, at this earlier point in her life, the choices that brought about the later circumstances in which her self-control failed. To arrive at an answer, we must go back even further in time. Perhaps she has always tried to do the right thing but, from early childhood on, has suffered an exceptionally low level of trait self-control, which made it difficult for her to control her impulses. She was therefore unable to finish school, find a decent job, plan for the future, save for later, and so forth. If this were indeed the case, it would be quite a stretch to insist that she has "chosen" her adverse circumstances. Given her personal history, they were inevitable. Or perhaps she grew up in a harsh and unpredictable environment, in which looking ahead more than a few days was a luxury no one could afford. As a consequence, she developed a strong present-orientation that is highly maladaptive for today's society, in which planning for the future has become so crucial. Or perhaps it is simply a lack of knowledge. Perhaps nobody ever taught her how to live on a minimal budget. Who knows.

Whatever the true cause may be, the point is that her unfortunate choices did not arise out of thin air. They were the result of circumstances and mental states that were already there and *caused* her to choose in this way. These circumstances and mental states, however, also did not come from nowhere, but were caused by circumstances and mental states that came before that, which in turn were caused by even earlier circumstances and mental states, and so forth. The search for the "true" cause of an instance of self-control failure sets in an infinite regress, leading all the way back to genetic inheritance and early upbringing – and even further back in time, because this inheritance and upbringing were, in turn, determined by the genes and life circumstances of one's parents, which were determined by situations and events in their pasts, and so on. Once we pursue this line of reasoning, we are forced to conclude that what *really* caused a person's behavior are factors that were already in existence *long before she was even born*, and therefore beyond her control.

## Free Will Skepticism versus Compatibilism

This conclusion fits with a philosophical position called (causal) determinism: the claim that everything that happens in this world is the inevitable result of what came before. Given the antecedent states of the universe and the laws of nature, things could not have gone otherwise. Everything we do is determined by prior mental states and circumstances, which were determined by the mental states and circumstances that came before that, which were determined by even earlier mental states and circumstances, and so forth. It may *feel* as if we are the authors or our lives, but in reality, the book of our lives is already written and we are actors at best.[11]

Many scientists and philosophers are thoroughly convinced that determinism is true, and from this, quite a few have concluded that free will – understood as the capacity for noncaused choice – does not exist.[12] But if this really is the case, it becomes entirely unclear why people who fail at self-control deserve to be blamed, and people who are capable of maintaining self-control deserve to be praised. In either case, their behavior was fully determined, the outcome of a chain of cause and effect that was set in motion long before they were born. So what would justify these dissimilar judgments? In fact, if everything we do is determined, the whole idea of moral responsibility makes no sense.[13] If everything we do is the inevitable result of what came before, freedom concepts such as autonomy, agency, and moral responsibility are mere illusions. They are nothing but "metaphysical nonsense".[14]

This strand of thinking is commonly referred to as "hard incompatibilism" or "free will skepticism."[15] Most philosophers within this strand of thinking argue that because "moral responsibility" cannot exist, the concept should be jettisoned. Determinism and moral responsibility are incompatible, and since the former is true, the latter must go.

However, other philosophers vehemently oppose this conclusion. These so-called "compatibilists" concede that determinism is probably true, yet maintain that people can *nonetheless* be held morally responsible for their actions. In their view, the fact that everything is determined by some antecedent state of affairs is entirely irrelevant. What matters is *not* the causal history of the behavior in question, but whether the behavior is *uncompelled*, and whether the person performing the behavior has the capacity to act on the basis of *reasons*, such as her wants, desires, and beliefs. Could she have done otherwise *if her wants, desires, or beliefs had been different?* This will often be the case. In normal circumstances, nobody is *forcing* me to turn left or right, to eat the unhealthy snack, to not pay my bills, or to punch Bill in the nose – so I must have had my reasons for acting like this. It would be a different story if someone held me at gunpoint and threatened to pull the trigger unless I turned left, ate the snack, tore up the bills, or punched Bill. It also would be a different story if I lacked the cognitive capacity to appreciate the consequences of my behavior, or if I had an epileptic seizure, or was severely hallucinating. But so long as I was not coerced into this behavior, had the rational power to act on the basis of reasons, and was not suffering some agency-undermining condition, I may be held responsible for my conduct. This means that adverse life circumstances or unfavorable character, *including poor self-control*, are not valid grounds for exemption or excuse.[16] In the words of legal scholar Stephen Morse,

we must all take responsibility for our characters, even if we are not causally responsible for what that character may be. Most importantly, we must all learn to manage the consequences of our characters, especially if an agent's personality predisposes the agent to harm others. This is an inevitable feature of human social interaction among flawed creatures such as ourselves.[17]

Does the compatibilist argument hold? Have we rescued moral responsibility from being sucked in the black hole? Many free will skeptics will be entirely unconvinced. Why do compatibilists, on the one hand, consider it critical to what extent the behavior was the product of the person's cognitive capacities and mental states – her reasons, wants, desires, beliefs – but, on the other hand, take these capacities and mental states themselves as givens? Why are they excluded from the causal chain? As mentioned, these do not arise out of thin air. When one acts, claims the philosopher Galen Strawson,

one acts in the way that one does because of the way one is. So to be truly morally responsible for one's actions, one would have to be truly responsible for the way one is: one would have to be *causa sui*, or the cause of oneself, at least in certain crucial mental respects. But nothing can be causa sui – nothing can be the ultimate cause of itself in any respect. So nothing can be truly morally responsible.[18]

## Conclusion

Well, there's another fine mess philosophy has gotten us into! What began as a seemingly innocent inquiry into the possible implications of the limits to self-control, has opened up a Pandora's box of thorny problems.

This is not the first time the box has been opened. In fact, poor self-control, as conceptualized in this book, is only the latest addition to an ever-growing list of potentially excusing or exempting conditions that have been proposed over the ages, and that have fanned the debate on free will and the limits of moral responsibility. In the 1960s and 1970s, social structure and troubled childhood were frequently raised as excuses for (full) responsibility,[19] in the 1990s bad genes and brain defects became popular, while with every new edition of the *Diagnostic and Statistical Manual of Mental Disorders* (*DSM*) we learn of new disorders and syndromes that might be reasons for diminished responsibility. Inherent to the empiricism of science is an endless proliferation of possible excuses and exemptions. As argued, when taken to its logical conclusion, this would obliterate the concept of moral responsibility altogether. However, philosophically consistent as it may be, this conclusion feels deeply counterintuitive. It is also hard to envision how society could ever function properly if the idea of moral responsibility were abandoned altogether. That seems a recipe for alienation and nihilism.

In the remainder of this chapter, I will therefore attempt to reclaim some ground for moral responsibility by carving out a middle way between, on the one hand, more openness and responsiveness to the psychological findings on the limits to self-control while, on the other, preserving the idea of moral responsibility. Obviously, it is beyond my powers to solve the problem of free will. Instead, as mentioned at the outset of this chapter, my strategy will be to broaden the scope of discussion. In thinking through the implications of these findings *for society and policy*, we should not restrict ourselves to the perspective of empirical science, but also engage the perspective of the *subjects* who make up society, and the perspective of the *policymakers* who must determine what will probably work best. This means that we should not only engage the *objective* standpoint of science but also two other standpoints, namely:

- The *subjective* standpoint. Viewed from this standpoint, what matters is not whether beliefs and ideas are objectively true, but whether we *feel and believe* them to be true. In this standpoint, autonomy, agency, and moral responsibility may well exist, because people *experience* autonomy and agency and *ascribe* moral responsibility.
- The *instrumental* standpoint. Viewed from this standpoint, what counts is not whether beliefs and ideas are true, but whether beliefs and ideas are helpful for achieving our goals. In this standpoint, autonomy, agency, and moral responsibility are *assumed*, because doing so yields the highest utility.

In Sections 8.3 and 8.4, I explore the views from these two alternative standpoints. In these sections, I borrow heavily from the literature on free will and the literature on psychology and law. At some points, it may seem as if self-control has completely fallen off the radar. But as mentioned, the question whether poor self-control counts as a valid excuse for moral responsibility is only the latest installment in the broader debate on what role empirical knowledge about the "true" causes of behavior should play in ascriptions of moral responsibility. Therefore, although it may seem as if we are veering off topic, it is worthwhile to consult these literatures, as they will provide us with useful building blocks for answering the chapter's main question.

## 8.3 The Subjective Standpoint

Viewed from the subjective standpoint, what matters is not whether beliefs and ideas are objectively true, but whether we *feel* and *believe* them to be true. Maybe free will skeptics are right that autonomous agency does not "really" exist, but we surely have a *sense* of agency.[20] This sense of agency is not the result of conscious reflection, but an immediate and deeply felt experience, on a par with sensory experiences such as sight and hearing.[21] Free will skeptics may likewise be right that freedom of choice does not "really" exist, but it surely feels *as if* it does. Faced with the competing possibilities of turning left or right, drinking coffee or tea, going out or staying home, having a holiday in Spain or Italy, it definitely feels as if it is *you* who is making the decision. According to Galen Strawson, there is a sense of "radical, absolute, buck-stopping *up-to-me-ness* in choice and action."[22] He often gives this example:

Suppose you set off for a shop on the evening of a national holiday, intending to buy a cake with your last ten pound note. On the steps of the shop someone is shaking an Oxfam tin. You stop, and it seems completely clear to you that it is entirely up to you what you do next. That is, it seems to you that you are truly, radically free to choose, in such a way that you will be ultimately morally responsible for whatever you do choose. Even if you believe that determinism is true, and that you will in five minutes time be able to look back and say that what you did was determined, this does not seem to undermine your sense of the absoluteness and inescapability of your freedom, and of your moral responsibility for your choice.[23]

So viewed from the subjective standpoint, autonomy, agency, and freedom are all too real. And we also automatically project this onto *others*. When a friend drinks coffee rather than tea, stays home instead of going out, and picks Spain as her holiday destination, we assume that this is what she *wants*, and not merely the outcome of an endless chain of events set in motion even before she was born. The default mode for explanation is intentional explanations, not the cause-and-effect chains of science. When explaining the world, we adopt the "intentional stance."[24]

## Reactive Attitudes

The deeply held belief in the reality of freedom concepts is reflected in what are often called moral sentiments or moral intuitions. In a landmark essay, the philosopher Peter Strawson – the father of Galen Strawson – has argued that our (initial) moral judgments do not derive from factual knowledge or general theoretical convictions about the possible causes of someone's behavior, but from so-called reactive attitudes: "essentially natural human reactions to the good or ill will or indifference of others towards us, as displayed in their attitudes and actions."[25] If someone does not live up to our expectations, behaves badly, or breaches the rules, we have a natural tendency to react with anger, resentment, or indignation. These first reactions are an expression of our moral intuitions, and imply that we believe the other acted with intention and thus may be held morally responsible for her behavior. Ascriptions of moral responsibility, therefore, are a product of the emotions that come with everyday human interaction. They are not grounded in knowledge or beliefs on *being* responsible, but in social practices of *holding* responsible.

This does not mean that we are merely slaves to our passions, and that objective facts have no role to play at all. Although we are naturally inclined toward the reactive attitudes, we can switch to what Strawson calls the "objective attitude" (which is equivalent to what I call the objective standpoint). In the objective attitude, we take some distance, and view the wrongdoer in a more objective way, as a person who is posing problems of intellectual understanding, management, treatment, and control. This more detached view may prompt us to revise our initial judgment. We may learn, for instance, that this person was under extreme pressure, or suffering some debilitating mental condition, or that her life was under imminent threat, and she therefore had no choice but to break the rules. If this is the case, our initial feelings of resentment, anger, or indignation may fade, and the person may be acquitted of blame. But crucially, according to Strawson, adopting the objective attitude is not our natural inclination, as it implies a psychological detachment from involvement and participation in everyday human relationships. We are therefore able to adopt the objective attitude for short durations only: "A sustained objectivity of interpersonal attitude, and the human isolation which that would entail, does not seem to be something of which human beings would be capable, even if some general truth were a theoretical ground for it."[26]

Strawson provides no empirical evidence for his assertions, but recent psychological research suggests that he is – at least partially – correct. Based on the available evidence, psychologist Jonathan Haidt concludes that moral judgment is primarily driven by affect. When we perceive an instance of wrongdoing, we immediately and automatically experience "flashes" of negative feeling, such as anger or disgust, which enter consciousness and set the tone for our initial judgment. These first and intuitive reactions can be followed by a slower, less affect-laden, and more reasoned response, in which information about people and their actions is gathered and transformed into a more considered judgment, which may then correct or overturn the initial reaction. Still, this more conscious and controlled process is often biased toward the original flashes of feeling. Moral reasoning "is usually a post-hoc process in which we search for evidence to support our initial intuitive reaction."[27]

## Stubborn Moralists

But what about determinism? If everything is determined, does this not mean that moral responsibility cannot exist? Do people not *see* how mistaken their intuitions are? This is where "experimental philosophers" join the conversation. Since the late 1990s, empirically oriented philosophers have begun to quiz ordinary people – often referred to as "the folk" – about their intuitions on free will and moral responsibility. In our search for building blocks to answer the chapter's main question, it is useful to make a brief stop here.

These philosophical experiments usually have the following design. First, participants are presented with carefully crafted vignettes of some hypothetical situation or world, in which elements that are crucial for the ascription of moral responsibility are varied, for instance, the extent to which everything in this situation or world is causally determined. Then, participants are asked a series of questions, such as whether in this situation or world someone is morally responsible for her behavior.

The overall picture emerging from these experiments is somewhat mixed and incoherent. In one of the better-known studies, for instance, philosophers Shaun Nichols and Joshua Knobe had participants read a description of an imaginary world in which everything that happens is completely determined. "For example, one day John decided to have French Fries at lunch. Like everything else, this decision was completely caused by what happened before it" and therefore it simply "*had to happen* that John would decide to have French Fries."[28] When asked the general question whether murderers in this world are fully morally responsible for their actions, most participants answered no. They tended to agree with philosophers who claim that determinism and moral responsibility are incompatible. Very different results were obtained, however, when participants were told about a specific inhabitant of this world, a man named Bill, who had become attracted to his secretary, and decides that "the only way to be with her is to kill his wife and three children. He knows that it is impossible to escape from his house in the event of a fire. Before he leaves on a business trip, he sets up a device in his basement that burns down the house and kills his family."[29] When asked if Bill is fully morally responsible for killing his family, most participants answered yes. Here they tended to agree with philosophers who claim that it is entirely irrelevant whether the behavior was causally determined or not, and that the only thing that matters is whether the behavior was uncoerced and the agent had the capacity to act on the basis of reasons. So it "appears that people have *both* compatibilist *and* incompatibilist intuitions."[30]

What is going on here? Are the folk schizophrenic? All things considered, I think two conclusions can be drawn from experiments such as these. First, people generally have a strong tendency to view others as free agents who are morally responsible for their actions. This seems to be their "default position." The response in the second scenario ("Yes, Bill is fully morally responsible for killing his family") seems to be the more representative and typical. Experiments such as these show that *in the abstract*, when presented with impersonal cases in a distant world, participants can be "lured" to the incompatibilist conclusion implicated by the information provided. But the closer to home, and the more vivid and emotionally charged the case, the stronger the tendency to neglect this information, and consider wrongdoers as morally responsible. In fact, according to psychologists David Pizarro and Erik Helzer, the evidence suggests that "moralism drives judgments of freedom rather than the other way around."[31] *First* comes the desire to blame or punish the wrongdoer, and *then* beliefs about her freedom to do otherwise are made consistent with this desire. In other words, people are "stubborn moralists."[32]

Second, this general tendency notwithstanding, folk intuitions seem to be characterized by a certain level of dissensus and incoherence. Studies typically find substantial minorities who differ in opinion – in the case just mentioned, people who think Bill is not fully morally responsible for killing his family. Nor are participants very stable in the opinions they report. Psychologist Cory Clark and colleagues found that seemingly minor variations in the order in which information is presented are already enough to change free will and moral responsibility judgments. Moreover, they found indications that participants' answers can be nudged toward the incompatibilist position by reassuring them that free will is *not* an essential requirement for holding people morally responsible.[33] Apparently, if you slightly alter the question, you can get totally different answers.

Now, how weird is that? Actually, not weird at all. This is a familiar pattern in survey research, especially when it concerns complex issues on which people have no fully developed and crystallized opinions.[34] Needless to say, the nature of free will and moral responsibility qualify as complex topics par excellence. Even philosophers profoundly disagree on these matters. The deeper message of these experiments is that, apparently, "the folk" can lead perfectly normal lives *without* being fully consistent in their beliefs on these issues. This is hardly surprising. People generally hold multiple and contradictory beliefs, but usually get by just fine without solving – or even being aware! – of these inconsistencies. One could even argue that most people get by just fine *precisely because* they do not worry too much over potential conflicts in their ideas and beliefs. So long as it does not affect their everyday functioning, there is no urgent need to solve them. And so long as they do not pursue a career as a professional philosopher, they will not be pushed to take a stand on the vexing question of whether determinism and moral responsibility are compatible or not.

In conclusion, it looks as if most people have no well-developed and fully coherent set of beliefs and intuitions regarding the relationship between determinism and moral responsibility. Their default position seems to be that humans are free agents who are morally responsible for their conduct but, in all likelihood, they have not really thought the whole thing through. Beneath the surface lurks an undercurrent of inconsistency and instability. From the philosophical viewpoint, this imperfect state of affairs may be unsatisfying. But there is an important upside: This lack of closure also guarantees a certain level of responsiveness to local features.

## The Objective Attitude

Which brings us back to ordinary life. Whereas very few people have to rack their brains over the philosophical conundrum whether determinism and moral responsibility are compatible *in general*, all of us frequently have to decide if some *particular* individual is morally responsible for her behavior in some *particular* situation. Such local judgments

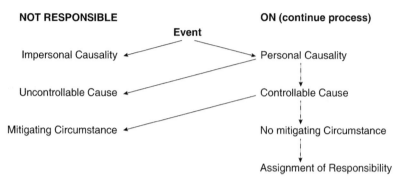

**Figure 8.1** The responsibility process according to Bernard Weiner. A responsibility process is initiated by some event. If there is a judgment of personal causality, then an inference of responsibility may be reached and the process continues. However, if there is impersonal causality, then a judgment of nonresponsibility is rendered and the process stops. The process then proceeds to determine if the cause was controllable or not. Given personal causality, a controllable cause, and no mitigating circumstances, there is an assignment of responsibility. Reprinted from Weiner, B., *Judgments of responsibility: A foundation for a theory of social conduct*. Guilford. Copyright 1995, with permission from Elsevier.

are part and parcel of everyday life. And as said, although the default position is to hold others morally responsible for their conduct, people can – at least temporarily – suspend their initial judgment and switch to the objective attitude. What happens then? If people take this more detached perspective, do they – if only temporarily – transform into free will skeptics who deny moral responsibility after all?

No. They become more like judges who, based on a careful assessment of all the relevant facts, seek to determine *to what extent* someone is morally responsible. They want to know the details of the situation: Did the person really cause the undesired outcome? Did she intend to bring about this outcome? Did she have good reasons for her behavior? Did she have the capacity and possibility to do otherwise? Psychologists have advanced several models summarizing the empirical findings on laypeople's moral reasoning. Figure 8.1 presents the model proposed by psychologist Bernard Weiner.[35] Other models differ slightly, but all emphasize the crucial role of *controllability*: factors that establish personal control over the undesired outcome *intensify* the attribution of blame, whereas factors that constrain personal control *mitigate* the attribution of blame.[36]

At this point, it may no longer come as a surprise that, even when people switch to the objective attitude, their emotions keep seeping through. The initial affective response to the (alleged) transgression may influence the subsequent search for and processing of information. For instance, people tend to notice and accept facts that support their initial judgment more easily than facts that contradict this judgment. This often happens unconsciously. It is just the way the human mind works.[37] So even if we decide to switch to the objective attitude, the echo of the reactive attitudes is heard in the final judgment.[38]

## Proportionality

Before returning to the issue of self-control, I wish to introduce another line of research relevant to the subjective standpoint, namely research on laypeople's judgments regarding punishment for criminal offences. There are some interesting insights to be found here, that not only lend further support to the primacy of moral intuitions but also highlight the importance of proportionality.

In this line of research, participants are usually presented with vignettes describing an instance of lawbreaking, and then asked how severely the wrongdoer should be punished. These experiments generally find that laypeople's judgments are primarily driven by *retributive* principles: Offenders should get what they *deserve*. The severity of the punishment should be *proportional* to the *moral wrongness* of the offence, as indicated by the intentions of the offender, the magnitude of the harm inflicted, the presence or absence of extenuating circumstances, and so forth.[39] By contrast, laypeople tend to ignore *utilitarian* principles. These are principles pertaining to future harms and benefits for society. For instance, the longer the prison sentence, the longer a criminal is taken off the streets, and the stronger the deterrent effect on potential future offenders. (The "punitive turn" described in Chapter 7, seems mostly informed by utilitarian considerations.) Research has found that in their verdicts laypeople are less driven by such utilitarian considerations.

One example is a study by psychologist Kevin Carlsmith and colleagues. In a series of experiments, they found that participants' judgments were highly sensitive to factors associated with the moral severity of the offense, for instance, whether an offender stole money from his employer to help needy coworkers, or to finance his extravagant lifestyle and pay off gambling debts. In the latter case, participants meted out more severe punishments. By contrast, factors associated with deterrence, such as the degree of publicity the sentence would receive, made no difference. Even when participants were instructed to exclusively focus on potential deterrent effects, the moral severity of the crime remained a predictor of their sentencing judgments.

Interestingly, Carlsmith found a discrepancy between what participants *say* and what they *do*. When asked in the abstract participants *say* that they not only consider the moral side of the equation but also take utilitarian principles into account. However, once participants are confronted with concrete examples of wrongdoing, they seem to have forgotten about this. Their sentencing judgments are entirely determined by moral considerations. Carlsmith concludes, "[it seems as if] people do not have a good sense of their own motives for punishment."[40] They endorse utilitarian principles in the abstract, but reject these principles the moment they lead to outcomes that violate retributive intuitions. It is hard to miss the parallel with the free will experiments described in Section 8.3: While people go along with the deterministic denial of moral responsibility in the abstract, they return to their natural tendency to blame wrongdoers the moment things get real. Apparently, when push comes to shove, people are not only "stubborn moralists" but also "pure retributionists."

However, that people are pure retributionists does not mean they simply want offenders to be punished as harshly and severely as possible. The key concept is "proportionality." The sentence must be proportional to the moral wrongness of the transgression. Both real-life examples and preliminary studies demonstrate that people not only react with indignation when wrongdoers are punished too lightly but also when they are punished *too severely*.[41] An oft-mentioned example is the Californian "Three Strikes" law, introduced in the 1990s. In the abstract, this law probably sounded like a good idea, as it was enacted after a 70 percent majority in a statewide referendum voted in its favor. Support plummeted, however, once people witnessed the law in action, and learned about individuals such as Leandro Andrade, who was sentenced to fifty years in prison for stealing a few children's video tapes for a Christmas present.[42]

## Back to Self-Control

What have we learned thus far? First, people are inclined to view others as free agents who may be held responsible for their behavior. People spontaneously react with anger, indignation, or resentment to (alleged) transgressions of rules, norms, or expectations. In other words, the subjective and the objective standpoints tend to pull in diametrically opposed directions. Second, if people suspend their initial reaction and switch to the objective attitude, they do not swing from one extreme to the other, turning into free will skeptics who deny all moral responsibility. They end up somewhere in the middle. They tend to become like judges who carefully attempt to establish *to what extent* wrongdoers may be held responsible for their conduct. The key principle underlying judgments on blameworthiness and punishment is *proportionality*. The severity of blame and punishment should mirror the *degree* of controllability and the *degree* of moral wrongness.

Now let us put these building blocks together. What do they mean for self-control and moral responsibility? Two conclusions can be drawn.

The first is that people tend to assume that, in normal circumstances, others have *sufficient* capacity for exerting self-control. This follows more or less automatically from Peter Strawson's argument on the ubiquity of reactive attitudes and the empirical research supporting his argument. After all, our natural tendency to react with resentment or indignation only makes sense if we believe that the person acted on intention and had the freedom to do otherwise. In other words, we automatically assume she was *unwilling* to do the right thing, not that she was *unable* to do the right thing. If the reverse were true, our natural tendency would be to react with pity and sympathy, not with resentment or indignation. To be sure, once people switch to the objective attitude, they may conclude that in this particular case lack of capacity rather than lack of motivation was the culprit. But they seem to have little talent for this more detached view. According to Strawson, "a sustained objectivity of interpersonal attitude" is beyond our human capabilities, and research has found that even in the objective attitude, people are not immune to the influence of their initial affective responses. Apparently, we are not only stubborn moralists but also stubborn believers in the idea that, absent compelling evidence to the contrary, self-control failure stems from lack of *motivation*.

The second conclusion concerns the importance of proportionality. The hallmark of retributivism is the intuition that people should get what they deserve, *no more and no less*. Hence, if we accept that in some cases poor self-control capacity is a legitimate excuse for (full) responsibility, the principle of proportionality requires that *the extent* to which someone is held responsible for (the consequences) of an instance of self-control failure is attuned to *the level* of self-control that could reasonably be expected from this person, given the specifics of her background and the situation. There has to be some *balance*. Minor impairments of self-control capacity do not justify a complete exoneration of responsibility, whereas the total absence of self-control due to some grave mental defect calls for more than just a slight diminishment of responsibility. This means that if poor self-control is accepted as a potentially valid excuse, rules and regulations must leave sufficient room to tailor the ascription of responsibility to the particulars of the case at hand. The more rigid the rules and regulations, the more often they yield ascriptions of responsibility that feel "out of proportion."

## 8.4 The Instrumental Standpoint

Has Section 8.3 on the subjective standpoint brought us any closer to a solution for the mess the objective standpoint got us in? Again, many free will skeptics will be entirely unconvinced. They will argue that we have not solved anything. All that has been demonstrated is that ordinary people lack philosophical rigor. Ordinary people have a stubborn habit of believing in falsehoods, their moral intuitions are often contradictory, their judgments are affected by irrelevant factors, and they do not seem to really know their own motives. Moreover, when they switch to the objective standpoint, their responses are half-hearted at best. They go one or maybe two steps back in the causal chain, but refuse to go "all the way" and recognize that the ultimate causes of behavior lie in circumstances that were already in place long before they were born. The folk simply refuse to see that moral responsibility cannot exist. Granted, this sobering message may be an inconvenient truth, but we must face up to the facts. Ever since the Enlightenment, the task of science has been to uncover the truth, no matter how inconvenient, because building social practices and institutions on discredited beliefs and ideas is irrational, if not downright delusional.

Or is it? Once we switch to the *instrumental* standpoint, a rather different picture emerges. Viewed from the instrumental standpoint, what counts is not whether beliefs or concepts are objectively true in the sense that they correspond to some reality out there, but whether they are *useful* for achieving our goals. We should adopt those beliefs and concepts that best serve our "all-things-considered practical interests." Whether they are actually true is of secondary importance at best. So even if scientists and philosophers are right that autonomy, agency, and all those other members of the family of freedom concepts are mere illusions, it does not necessarily follow that we should abandon them. We can also decide to simply act "as if" autonomy, agency, and free will are real, and use these concepts as tools for arriving at legitimate judgments on responsibility. What seems irrational from the objective standpoint may well be rational from the instrumental standpoint.

## Useful Fictions

This approach aligns with the view advocated more than a century ago by the German philosopher Hans Vaihinger in his – mostly forgotten – book *The Philosophy of "As If."* According to Vaihinger, we must not judge a thought or proposition on its *verisimilitude* but on its *usefulness*. It is perfectly rational to base our actions on beliefs and ideas we *know* to be false, so long as they help us to achieve our goals and control the world.[43] With his focus on usefulness, Vaihinger joins the ranks of pragmatist thinkers, but there is a crucial difference. Pragmatists often claim that "truth is what works," but Vaihinger emphasizes that "what is true" and "what works" must be kept strictly apart. If certain beliefs help us to navigate the world, we have good reason to treat them *as if* they are true, but we should never deceive ourselves into thinking they really *are* true! They remain fictions – useful perhaps, yet fictions nonetheless.

Useful fictions must be distinguished from hypotheses: thoughts or statements whose truth or falsehood is still undetermined. Hypotheses can become truths if they are verified. Fictions, on the other hand, are thoughts or statements that are deemed untrue because they contradict reality or are even self-contradictory. Take, for example, imaginary numbers, such as the square root of –1. We all know this "quantity" cannot exist, but *assuming* this quantity turns out to be very helpful for making calculations that solve problems in the real world. Another example is the assumption that humans are rational egoists who only care about their wallets. Many economists will readily concede that this assumption is false, but they nonetheless treat it *as if* true, because doing so helps them to make macroeconomic predictions.[44]

According to Vaihinger, the concepts central to this chapter are fictions too. As he notes, human actions "are commonly regarded as free, and therefore as 'responsible' and contrasted with the 'necessary' course of natural events." However, the concept of freedom "not only contradicts observation which shows that everything obeys unalterable laws, but is also self-contradictory, for an absolutely free, chance act, resulting from nothing, is ethically just as valueless as an absolute necessary one."[45] But from this, Vaihinger does not conclude that we should reject these "ideational constructs." Instead, we should simply recognize them for what they are: useful fictions. Even more, they are *necessary* fictions. We cannot live without them. "In the course of their development, men have formed this immanent necessity, because only on this basis is a high degree of culture and morality possible."[46]

As said, useful fictions are tools. They help us to make the step from the perception of facts and events to judgments and decisions on what is to be done. But once this step is made, these tools *have done their duty and can be dropped*, just like imaginary numbers that are helpful for solving certain mathematical problems, but are dropped in the last stages of the calculation. In a criminal case, a judge can use the fiction of freedom to arrive at a sentence, but the premise itself – whether man is *really* free – is not examined by the judge, and once responsibility is established and a verdict is reached, it no longer plays any role. The premise "drops out, as does the middle term in every syllogism."[47] This means we should not become overly attached to these fictions, as if they were the essential thing. We must "refuse to allow ourselves to be enticed and confused by the illusory questions and illusory problems arising out of them."[48]

With Vaihinger's theory, it looks as if we have a way out of the quagmire. The belief in illusory freedom concepts can be reconciled with rationality because these concepts are not just fictions but *useful* fictions. They serve as stepping-stones for getting to the legitimate assignment of praise and blame, reward and punishment. It is not rational to abandon beliefs simply because they are untrue. It is only rational to abandon them when someone comes up with alternative beliefs *that work better*.

## "Building Better Beings"

Vaihinger may be correct, but his solution is rather crude: just do *as if*. It seems a lot to ask from people to run their lives on the basis of beliefs which they *know* to be false, and to unreservedly and wholeheartedly participate in social practices which they *know* to be grounded in illusory concepts. It is dubious whether this can be pulled off.

Prospects seem better for a more recent and subtle strand of philosophical thinking that also fits within the instrumental standpoint. In this strand of thinking, how moral responsibility is to be understood is derived neither from science or metaphysics (the objective standpoint), nor from folk beliefs and intuitions (the subjective standpoint), but from *the work we want this concept to do*. An important representative of this approach is the philosopher Manuel Vargas.[49] In his 2013 book *Building Better Beings*, he distinguishes between two central questions:

- What is the justification for our "responsibility system," that is, the set of attitudes and practices that regulate our assessments of praise and blame?
- Under what conditions should a person be considered a "morally responsible agent," that is, what *makes* agents a proper target of praise and blame?

This distinction runs parallel to the one I made earlier between *holding* and *being* responsible. Now, what Vargas' answers to both questions share is their grounding in the ultimate goal we ought to pursue. Let me explain.

Vargas begins his answer to the first question with the insights from Peter Strawson. As we saw, Strawson holds that our ascriptions of responsibility are rooted in the social practice of praising and blaming. Our moral judgments spring from immediate and affectively charged reactions to other people's conduct, such as anger, resentment, or indignation. Many critics have noted, however, that Strawson provides no *justification* for this social practice. He simply claims that – except for short durations – we cannot escape our natural tendency to react in this emotional manner. And why should we bother to justify what we cannot escape from anyway? But according to Vargas, this deflection does not work. It may be true that we cannot avoid *having* certain emotions, but this does mean we must also *express* them. We can decide to *control* ourselves and *suppress* the reactive attitudes. Given this possibility, "there is no reason to think that the inevitability of our having such attitudes suffices to justify the perpetuation and promulgation of our practices of praising and blaming."[50]

In response, Vargas claims to provide such a justification with an approach he calls the "agency cultivation model." In this model, the decisive criterion is the *effect* of our responsibility practices.

When we hold one another responsible, we participate in a system of practices, attitudes and judgments that support a special kind of self-governance, one whereby we recognize and suitably respond to moral considerations. So roughly, moralized praise and blame are justified by their effects, that is, how they develop and sustain a valuable form of agency, one we ordinarily have reason to care about.[51]

So what we have here is a purely instrumental approach. At the heart of Vargas' account is not what moral responsibility really *is*, but what work this concept is supposed to do – which is to regulate our practices of *holding* responsible, and thus promote a certain kind of agency.[52] The goal is to cultivate agents who, when contemplating what to do, take moral considerations into account. Vargas calls this special kind of self-governance "moral consideration responsive agency."[53]

Vargas is not the first philosopher to embrace the consequentialist perspective. What is new, however, is that he chooses the community *as a whole* as his target, and not the individual. Not every single instance of praising and blaming needs to have a positive effect. The only thing required is "that the system as a whole produces agents that, over time and in a wide range of contexts, are responsive to moral considerations."[54] There will always be instances in which praising or blaming of a specific person will yield the wrong effects but, according to Vargas, this in itself is no reason to reject his overall approach. In fact, such instances may even "indirectly contribute to the general efficacy of the responsibility system over time."[55]

Let us now turn to Vargas' second question. This is the question under what conditions people are proper targets of praise and blame. What are the characteristics a person must possess in order to qualify as a responsible agent who, provided no exempting or excusing circumstances are in place, may be held accountable for his or her conduct? What *makes* a responsible agent?

Once again, Vargas' answer has a strong instrumentalist bent. His point of departure is that one must have the right capacities. What makes an agent "properly subject to norms of moralized praise and blame, is that he or she has the ability to recognize and respond to moral considerations."[56] This is a well-established compatibilist position. However, Vargas then continues with the more innovative claim that circumstances must be taken into account because, in contrast to what many philosophers seem to believe, the relevant capacities are anything but stable and fixed. As we saw in Part I, research clearly shows that human capacities are significantly affected by situational factors. This means that "moral" matters. Vargas introduces this concept to refer to "the circumstances that support and enable exercises of agency in ways that respect and reflect a concern for morality."

Obviously, if the relevant capacities are not fixed but fluctuate with circumstances, it gets much harder to determine who should be considered a responsible agent and who should not. At this point, Vargas makes a similar argument as I did earlier in this chapter: If the relevant capacities are variable, we need to set some threshold, a minimum level that one must surpass to qualify as a responsible agent. What should this threshold be? Vargas' answer is rather technical, but comes down to this: The threshold should be set at the level that, in the eyes of an ideal observer, would best serve the goal of cultivating agents who are responsive to moral considerations. Vargas makes quite an effort to spell out exactly *which* parameters are relevant for determining this optimal threshold level, but delegates judgment on *the proper settings* of these parameters to the – imaginary – ideal observer. He readily concedes that this approach may leave some readers unsatisfied, as this is "more a recipe for a substantive conclusion than a bold, decisive answer."[57] (But later in this book, I will argue that, actually, there is a lot of wisdom in this approach.)

Vargas' approach is an example of the social thesis: "the view that moral responsibility is constituted by our social practices, rather than any metaphysically deep notion antecedent to our social relations."[58] Peter Strawson was the first to adopt this view, and many others have since followed. One of the resulting insights is that social practices not only determine how moral responsibility is understood but also are indispensable for *making* responsible agents. It is through participation in social practices that people learn what moral considerations are potentially relevant, and it is through participation in these practices that people develop and sustain the motivation to adapt their behavior to these considerations. The latter is emphasized by the philosopher Victoria McGeer. She agrees with Vargas on many points but adds a temporal dimension: Mental capacities are not only a function of *space* but also a function of *time*. They can be more or less developed, and improve or diminish over time. This also applies to moral consideration responsive agency. "To keep this fragile capacity from decaying, to maintain or even enhance it, we depend on each other to create the kind of circumstances, or 'moral ecology,' in which we are continually exhorted by one another to exercise that capacity." Having the required capacity "depends on being continuously scaffolded over time through the moralized work of praise and blame."[59]

### What Works Best?

It is time to end the philosophical reflections and shift attention to the empirical question that follows from these reflections: What "moral ecology" works best? What Vaihinger and Vargas effectively do is transform an esoteric philosophical puzzle into a more down-to-earth means-end affair. Both accounts lead to the same question: What beliefs – whether fictional or not – best serve the "all-things-considered practical interest" of our moral community?

Not surprisingly, as we are grappling with big questions here, no simple and empirically tested answers are readily available. But there are scattered bits of relevant research. For instance, psychologists have recently begun to study whether promoting belief in determinism affects social behavior. These studies usually have the following design. First, participants are primed to believe that free will does not exist, for instance by asking them to read statements such as "Science has demonstrated that free will is an illusion" and "All behavior is determined by brain activity, which in turn is determined by a combination of environmental and genetic factors." Then, in an ostensibly unrelated experiment, the dependent variable of interest is measured. In one well-known example, psychologists Jonathan Schooler and Kathleen Vohs asked participants to solve a series of puzzles. They promised participants a financial reward for each puzzle they solved, but deliberately made it easy for them to cheat without anyone noticing, and thus collect a higher financial reward than they were entitled to. It turned out that reading anti-free will statements led to more cheating.[60] Other experiments showed similar results: Undermining the belief in free will led to more small sums of money being stolen from an anonymous stranger, more aggression toward other participants after being made to feel rejected, and less helpful behavior in hypothetical scenarios.[61] What explains these results? Why does promoting the belief in determinism increase antisocial behavior? The most likely explanation is that this belief absolves people of moral responsibility. It provides an excuse for not restraining yourself and legitimizes selfish behavior. After all, you are not to blame, because you could not have done otherwise, could you?

To be sure, research on the effects of anti-free will messages should be interpreted with caution. Not all experiments found significant effects, and several attempts to replicate the Schooler and Vohs study have failed.[62] What these studies make clear, though, is that debates about determinism and free will are not merely of academic interest. They may have real-life consequences. According to the philosopher Saul Smilansky, scientists should therefore be careful about communicating the illusory character of free will beyond the confines of academia. Trumpeting that free will is merely an illusion, as some of them seem to delight in, is "complacent and dangerous."[63] It may undermine the very basis of social cooperation, as it provides an excuse for giving in to selfish impulses and doing whatever you like. Smilansky recommends "free will illusionism" instead. Those who are "in the know" should keep this perilous knowledge to themselves.

Not everyone agrees. Other scholars expect that promoting determinism may have positive effects: It may lead to a better understanding of other people's behavior and less harsh judgments on (alleged) transgressions. In direct opposition to Smilansky, the philosopher Thomas Nadelhoffer defends "free will *dis*illusionism." Philosophers and psychologists "ought to do their part to educate the public – especially when their mistaken beliefs arguably fuel a number of unhealthy emotions and attitudes such as revenge, hatred, intolerance, lack of empathy."[64] Advocates of free will disillusionism have especially focused on punishment for criminal offenses.[65] In a world without free will and moral responsibility, offenders would no longer be punished out of the mistaken belief that they "chose" to break the law and hence "deserve" to suffer. Punishment would be less harsh and more geared toward rehabilitation. These scholars can also point to empirical findings that support their claim. Psychologist Azim Shariff and colleagues, for instance, had participants read a fictional vignette involving an offender who beat a man to death. They found that if participants were primed to believe that free will does not exist, they judged the offender to be less blameworthy and recommended lighter prison sentences. Given the turn toward increasingly harsh punishment discussed in Chapter 7, and given the high incarceration rates in some countries, this might – at least in some circumstances – be a desirable outcome.[66]

In sum, based on the available evidence, there is something to be said for both positions. It all depends on what is deemed most important. If the goal is to promote social cooperation and responsible conduct, we are probably better off promoting *free will illusionism* and maintaining that moral responsibility does indeed exist. If the goal is to avoid individual harm and injustices, however, we may be better off promoting *free will disillusionism* and the implied denial of moral responsibility.

## Moral Credibility

What does all this have to do with self-control? I promise to return to self-control shortly, but first I wish to collect one last building block for answering this chapter's main question. This block concerns the "moral credibility" of our moral ecology – that is, the extent to which the rules and norms of the institutional order track folk intuitions on what is fair and just.[67] What happens if the responsibility system produces judgments of blame and praise that deeply conflict with people's moral intuitions, and metes out punishments and rewards they perceive to be grossly unfair?

These are again big questions, but research on (criminal) law and sentencing provides some indication of what might happen. In a series of experiments, legal scholar Janice Nadler tested how people's perceptions of the fairness of substantive laws (such as criminal statutes) and decisions (such as verdicts and punishment judgments) affect their overall willingness to comply with rules and norms. In one experiment, for instance, participants first read mock newspaper stories describing pieces of legislation that – as confirmed by a pilot study – were generally perceived as either just or unjust. Next, in an ostensibly unrelated experiment, participants were asked about their willingness to engage in unlawful behaviors such as making illegal copies of software, eating a small item without paying in the grocery store, or taking home office supplies for personal use. Nadler found that participants who had been exposed to newspaper stories about legislation perceived as *un*just were more willing to engage in these unlawful behaviors than participants exposed to the stories about legislation perceived as just.[68] In another experiment, she found that legal decisions that are odds with one's moral standards may also affect *actual behavior*. Participants who had just read a news story about a sentencing verdict conflicting with their moral beliefs were *less* likely to return a pen given to them to fill out a questionnaire. In other words, they stole the pen.[69] Nadler's studies are a demonstration of "moral spillover": outcomes violating moral standards in one domain increase deviant behavior in another domain.

Similar results were found by legal scholar Paul Robinson and colleagues. In an internet survey, participants were first asked eight questions to assess their general attitudes and intentions regarding the criminal justice system. For instance, would they pick up a handgun they accidentally found and take it to the police? Would they report someone violating the law to the relevant authorities? Would they believe that if a prisoner is sentenced to life, he probably deserves such a harsh sentence? After participants answered these questions, they were presented with a series of real-world legal cases. For each case, they were told whether the defendant was found guilty, and if so, what sentence was imposed. For half of the participants, this series consisted of cases in which the liability or sentence more or less mirrored what most people consider fair and just. For the other half of the participants, however, the series consisted of cases in which the liability or sentence deviated dramatically from moral intuitions, such as acquittal for a clear case of violent rape, or twenty-five years in prison for having sex with a girl who, unbeknownst to the defendant, was underage. Next, participants were asked to answer the same eight questions again. Robinson found significant differences between the two groups. Participants in the latter group showed less deference to and less willingness to assist or cooperate with the justice system.

Based on this experiment and other studies, Robinson and colleagues conclude that people, after learning about such instances of injustice, may not only be less likely to comply with specific laws they perceive as unjust but *also* less likely to comply with the law in general, less likely to cooperate and assist with the legal system, and less likely to confer moral authority on this system. "The flip side, of course, is that if the criminal justice system reflects ordinary perceptions of justice, it can take advantage of a range of psychological mechanisms that serve to increase assistance, cooperation, compliance, and deference."[70] The upshot is that giving transgressors their "just desert" not only makes sense from the subjective standpoint but also from the instrumental standpoint. "Doing justice may be the most effective means of fighting crime."[71]

## Back to Self-Control

Let me recap the argument thus far. This section began with the radical pragmatism of Hans Vaihinger. In his view, the skeptic position that true freedom cannot exist is entirely irrelevant. We should adopt those beliefs and ideas that are most useful for achieving our goals, regardless of their truth value. I then discussed Manuel Vargas' work and the social thesis. In his view, how we understand moral responsibility should not be derived from metaphysics or folk intuitions, but from the work we want this concept to do, which is to cultivate "moral consideration responsive agency." For people to develop and exercise their capacity for such agency, the social practice of blaming and praising is indispensable. Moral ecology matters! Following these armchair reflections, I turned to empirical research demonstrating that how we talk about free will and determinism can have real-world effects. On the one hand, promoting determinism may undermine social cooperation, but on the other, it may induce a more forgiving attitude. Lastly, I discussed research that suggests that the criminal justice system and its laws work best when they are "morally credible" – that is, when they track people's moral intuitions.

Now let us put these building blocks together. What do they mean for self-control and moral responsibility? I wish to make four points.

The first point is that, viewed from the instrumental standpoint, the whole discussion about how much self-control people "really" have, and to what degree those who fail at self-control are "really" responsible for their conduct, is irrelevant. (And by implication, it is also irrelevant whether there "really" exists some limited energy resource that fuels self-control. In Vaihinger's words, we must not allow ourselves to be confused by "illusory questions and illusory problems"). Instead, we should ask what assumptions are most useful. Which of these two positions works better?

- Position 1: self-control *optimism*. Self-control capacity is virtually unlimited, and therefore we should always hold adults fully responsible for (the consequences of) their self-control failures (except in rare cases such as serious mental illness or insanity).
- Position 2: self-control *pessimism*. Self-control capacity is strictly limited and easily depleted, and therefore we may have to revise our current beliefs and practices with regard to the assigning of responsibility.

The key question is which of these positions will best serve our collective goals or – to put it in philosophical terms – our "all-things-considered practical interests."

This leads to a second point. What are these "all-things-considered practical interests"? What overarching goal or ideal should we pursue? Interestingly, Vargas' answer does not invoke any greater good of a political or ideological nature (freedom, equality, world peace) but stays within the confines of responsibility. We should pursue "a special type of self-governance" that we have reason to value, a type of self-governance he calls "moral consideration responsive agency."[72]

I wish to make a similar move: With regard to self-control, our overall practical interest is to cultivate "perfectly self-controlled agents." This directly follows from Vargas' account, because to the extent that poor self-control impedes us from doing what is morally right, we fail at moral consideration responsive agency. In other words, part of "building better beings" is "building more self-controlled beings." Mortals like us will, of course, never fully *achieve* the ideal of perfect self-control – most of us will not even come close – but we should strive for it anyway. After all, good self-control has become increasingly important. More than ever, society *needs* people who are capable of delaying gratification. If people fail to do so, they may not only harm themselves but also hinder the achievement of wealth, health, and happiness for their fellow citizens. It is in our collective interest that people get as close to the ideal as possible.

Therefore, to continue the parallel with Vargas, we need a "self-control conducive ecology" – a social and symbolic environment that scaffolds the development and exercise of self-control. In McGeer's words: "To keep this fragile capacity from decaying, to maintain or even enhance it, we depend on each other to create the kind of circumstances [...] in which we are continually exhorted by one another to exercise that capacity."[73] We need an environment that fosters the *motivation* for self-control.

This bring me to my third point. Against this background, it may not be a stellar idea to publish a book like this one, arguing that self-control is limited. As discussed, making people believe that according to the latest science *everything is determined* appears to invite undesirable behavior. Making people believe that according to the latest science *self-control is limited* might have a similar effect. People might interpret this as license to take it easy and to give in to selfish impulses, as the message of both claims is the same: You are not to blame. Therefore, to repeat Smilansky, trumpeting the limits of self-control may be "complacent and dangerous." From this point of view, this book does not exactly contribute to a "self-control conducive ecology."

Support for this argument comes from experiments by psychologist Veronika Job and colleagues. In these experiments, participants were first primed to believe that self-control is either strictly limited or unlimited, and were then given two consecutive tasks that called on their self-control capacity.[74] Results showed that *only* participants who were primed to believe that self-control resources are limited performed worse on the second task. In other words, making participants believe that resources are *un*limited seemed to immunize them against ego depletion.[75] Other studies have yielded similar results. Job found that among students who faced high self-control demands, those who believed that self-control resources are unlimited did better than those who believed that resources are strictly limited. They procrastinated less, consumed less unhealthy foods, less often bought things they could not afford, had less trouble controlling their tempers, and earned higher grades.[76] These studies did not include indicators of antisocial behavior, but given these findings, it is not unlikely that loudly proclaiming self-control to be strictly limited will also increase antisocial behavior.

My fourth point, however, stands in direct opposition to the previous one: Too much optimism about self-control capacity is not a good thing either. Readers may be tempted to conclude from the first three points that the most useful of the two competing positions is to assume that self-control is unlimited. After all, if we no longer need to worry about how much self-control people "really" have, if we should strive for the ideal of perfect self-control, and if research shows that believing in unlimited self-control yields the highest utility, *then why spoil things by demonstrating that self-control is actually limited?* What is to be gained by that pessimistic message?

The reason is that there are potential downsides to the belief that self-control capacity is unlimited. So long as this – essentially false – belief remains confined to the private sphere, it will probably do little harm. In most cases, the school of life will correct overblown expectations about one's capacities. But if this belief gains wider currency, and becomes one of the premises underlying formal laws and institutions for assigning responsibility, this may undermine the "moral credibility" of these laws and institutions. This, in turn, may increase the likelihood of transgressive behavior. As discussed, to be perceived as morally credible, rules, and the decisions based on them, should track the community's moral intuitions on what is fair and just. Rules and intuitions, therefore, should allow for the possibility that sometimes people fail to do what is right, *not* for a lack of self-control *motivation* but for a lack of self-control *capacity*. Sometimes it may be fair and just to show some leniency.[77] For instance, suppose that some unlucky person, without realizing it, parked her car in the wrong place but fails to pay the ticket in time, because, after her employer went bankrupt, she got into serious financial trouble and, due to the chronic stress caused by this adversity, did not have enough self-control to keep up her paperwork. Wouldn't it be nice if she were granted a second chance to collect the money and pay the ticket, rather than simply imposing a fine for overdue payment, thereby only making her troubles worse?

Most people would agree that circumstances are sometimes so tough that even the most disciplined person would have trouble mustering the required self-control. However, if those who make or enforce the rules ignore all potentially excusing or mitigating factors, and rigidly stick to the adage that "rules are rules," the resulting judgments and decisions may undermine the moral credibility of these rules and the institutions they represent. This sows the seeds of resistance and subversion. And as the research suggest, this negative effect may spread out like an inkblot, undermining the legitimacy of the system *more generally*. Conversely, if rules and practices for ascribing responsibility acknowledge that people sometimes face challenges that grossly exceed their capacities, and take this into account when making judgments and decisions, this may bolster their moral credibility and thus increase the likelihood of future desirable behavior. To a certain extent, an appropriate amount of compassion for the difficult situation people may find themselves in *today* is an investment in their willingness to behave correctly and responsibly *tomorrow*. The upshot is that there is instrumental value in assuming that self-control capacity has its limits.

## Conclusion

Viewed from the instrumental standpoint, our collective interests are probably best served by a moderately optimistic stance: People usually have more self-control capacity at their disposal than they tend to believe, but this capacity is not unlimited. In other words, what probably works best is a middle ground between the two positions sketched here. This means that, on the one hand, we should not too easily accept poor self-control as an excuse for not living up to rules, norms, or expectations, but, on the other hand, should acknowledge that the demands are sometimes so high and the circumstances so tough that a certain amount of leniency is in order.

## 8.5 Heuristics and Brokenness

Does the instrumental standpoint offer a way out of the mess the objective standpoint got us in? Partly. It somewhat takes the sting out the skeptic threat by showing that adopting fictional or revised beliefs may well be rational, because they may advance our "all-things-considered practical interests." Within this standpoint, a justification can be found for our practice of *holding* responsible that does not depend on shaky metaphysical assumptions about *being* responsible. This opens the door to a viable defense against the unappealing idea that "poor self-control" would automatically excuse people from moral responsibility. The instrumental standpoint is thus the weapon of choice for those eager to push back against lame excuses.

Unfortunately, the instrumental standpoint is plagued by problems of its own. For instance, who is to decide what the "all-things-considered practical interests" of society are? And who is to decide what beliefs are most "useful" for advancing these interests? In earlier times, the belief that some people – say blacks or women – are inferior and do not deserve equal rights, was very useful to those in power. For them, abandoning this belief would cause quite a lot of "disutility." But obviously, this does not make it right, and nowadays we know better. If we focus on self-control, similar problems arise. In today's world, the belief that self-control is *un*limited is very useful to people who are doing well. This "truth" legitimizes a socioeconomic order that works to their advantage, and suggests they need not feel too guilty over others who are doing less well. They simply should have tried harder.[78]

In sum, inherent to the instrumental standpoint is a conservative bias. Those in power have strong incentives to embrace those beliefs that are most useful for protecting their own interests, and to portray these as "objective facts." It is for this reason that we need the objective standpoint. Only this standpoint provides the external basis from which such hegemonic practices can be interrogated. Only from the objective standpoint can we speak "truth to power." Which brings us full circle, right back to where we started.

## Brokenness and Heuristics

So what now? Alas, I have run out of standpoints. There is no fourth standpoint that can subsume and reconcile the other three. Nor does the literature on agency and moral responsibility offer any solutions, to the contrary. According to John Doris, a philosopher well versed in modern psychology, this literature "is mired in a 'dialogical stalemate,' where everybody has damning complaints about everybody else, and nobody has fully satisfying rejoinders."[79] Doris concludes that we better give up on our quest for a single and unified theory of moral responsibility.[80] We should acknowledge the irreducible diverse character of considerations for attributing responsibility, and opt for a more ecumenical approach.

My proposal is along similar lines. In my view, we have no choice but to accept a certain degree of "brokenness" in our beliefs.[81] The objective, subjective, and instrumental standpoint are *all* valid and necessary, and they *all* have their strengths and weaknesses. Given this tripartition (see Figure 8.2), no set of beliefs and ideas about agency, self-control, and moral responsibility can exist that perfectly fits all three standpoints and is perfectly coherent. The best we can hope for is a set of beliefs and ideas that *sufficiently* fits the three standpoints

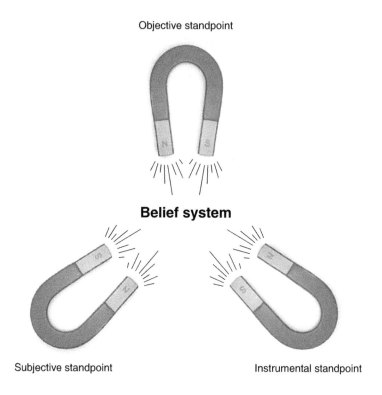

Figure 8.2 Three standpoints.

and is *sufficiently* coherent, a belief system that is not in perfect equilibrium, but which nevertheless comes close enough to that situation to be viable and practically workable. We have to settle for "good enough."

This may seem a poor solution, a sorry substitute for the real thing, but for most everyday purposes, it will do just fine. After all this elaboration on the intricacies of moral responsibility and self-control, one might easily forget that, *in everyday life*, most cases are pretty straightforward. If a healthy teenager of normal intelligence plays video games all day instead of learning for tomorrow's test and, as a result, earns a low grade, few will be plagued by nagging doubts about whether this teenager really *deserved* that grade. It seems rather silly to argue he could not have done otherwise, because no one *forced* him to play video games. Moreover, giving the low grade may be very useful, as it will probably motivate this teenager to study harder next time. Or consider the person who is always late for work because this, she argues, is the inevitable outcome of the biophysical interaction between her warm bed and her tired body. This is a crazy excuse, and if it were tolerated, her company would quickly go out of business. There would be little debate about the proper response: Show some discipline or lose your job. Or think of someone who drank way too much alcohol at the office party, and then, turning down offers from colleagues for a lift, got behind the wheel, raced home at double the speed limit, and caused an accident by running a red light. Everyone would agree that this person deserves punishment. The driver would have a hard time convincing the judge that, like everything in the universe, this accident was completely determined, merely the cosmic unfolding of events, and therefore he does not deserve any blame. Even in the unlikely case that the judge accepts the logic of this argument – maybe she was once a philosophy major – she will almost certainly conclude that this lack of self-control must be punished anyway, to deter future drivers from similar reckless behavior. To sum up, in garden-variety cases, the essentially broken character of our beliefs seems no obstacle for ascriptions of responsibility that are considered both legitimate and effective.

We could go a step further. As our experiences with everyday cases such as these accumulate, we might adopt some general rule to go by, for instance, that *by default* people should be considered autonomous agents who may be held morally responsible for their conduct. This rule is a useful heuristic, because in many circumstances it will yield judgments and decisions that are legitimate and effective. This heuristic is a short and simple summary of everything we have learned over the ages about what is usually deemed fair and what usually works, while it spares us the trouble of every time having to start all over again, and redo the whole debate on free will, moral responsibility, and self-control. In fact, as philosopher Daniel Dennett argues, we have no choice but to rely on heuristics. No decision is ever fully informed, as there is always logical room for more information and more views to be considered. But since time and means are finite, at some point deliberation and reflection must come to a close. So instead of examining, endlessly, whether people really are responsible for their conduct "we simply hold people responsible for their conduct (within limits we take care not to examine too closely). And we are rewarded for adopting this strategy by the higher proportion of 'responsible' behavior we thereby inculcate."[82]

## Instability and Dynamic Equilibrium

This sounds appealing – a quick and easy solution that will often deliver satisfactory results. But this solution is *inherently unstable.* The words between parentheses in Dennett's quote are telling. Once we take a closer look – for example, because we are confronted with an unusual or particularly challenging case – things start falling apart. The fundamental brokenness in our beliefs becomes visible (again), and we are reminded that heuristics – by definition – are imperfect, and sometimes get it wrong. Sure enough, *in everyday life* we may get a long way while ignoring these realities. We may even forget that these cracks and fissures in our epistemological foundation exist, and genuinely believe we have all cases covered. But sooner or later they will resurface, often triggered by a nagging feeling that following the rules in some particular instance would lead to ascriptions of moral responsibility that "just do not feel right" or "simply are not going to work."[83]

So how to proceed? Again, my strategy is to face up to the inevitable. Not only should we accept a certain degree of brokenness, we should also accept its logical corollary: a certain degree of instability. In fact, this is even to be *preferred.* The inherent instability of our beliefs and ideas, and the judgments based on them, is a *blessing in disguise.* A moderate amount of tension between competing beliefs, concepts, and judgments may engender some instability, but is also a precondition for social adaptation, renewal, and justice, as it implies that the process of interrogating of our current beliefs, ideas, and judgments will always keep going. In biology, only *dead* organisms are in perfect equilibrium. Healthy living organisms, however, are in "dynamic equilibrium" – a condition of balance that requires constant work and maintenance to remain sufficiently stable and to adapt to the ever-changing environment. The same goes for belief systems and moral practices. The lack of perfect equilibrium is the fuel that keeps the motor running. When it comes to beliefs about moral responsibility and self-control, the perfect may be the enemy of the good.

## 8.6 Conclusion

Finally, after all these excursions, we can put the pieces together. This chapter asked what the implications are of the psychological findings on self-control for the extent to which people should be considered morally responsible for (the consequences of) their poor self-control. What made this chapter long and complicated is that this question leads us straight to the heart of the obnoxious free will problem. Furthermore, we cannot restrict ourselves to the perspective of science only. We must also include the perspective of the subjects who make up the political community, and the perspective of those who must determine what will probably work best for this community. This means the main question should be approached from three different angles, potentially yielding three different answers. Let me summarize each.

### The Objective Standpoint

Viewed from the objective standpoint, it is hard to draw general conclusions about the appropriate relationship between self-control and moral responsibility. The research presented in Part I shows that self-control is limited and partly a function of circumstance. Empirically speaking, autonomy, agency, and moral responsibility are variable and matters of degree. This conflicts with the assumption of a clear and stable distinction between, on the one side, a very large majority of people who may be considered responsible agents versus, on the other, a small minority who may not. Such a dichotomy is assumed in many public policies and institutional arrangements, but the findings of Part I are a reminder that this dichotomy is a social construction – and not only that, but a social construction that rather poorly fits the facts.

The answer to this chapter's main question also hinges on whether or not determinism is true. Many scientists and philosophers believe that it is, and therefore need to find an answer to what this means for moral responsibility. Broadly speaking, there are two approaches. In the *compatibilist* approach, people are usually considered morally responsible if the behavior is brought about by their *reasons*, such as their desires, intentions, and beliefs. Self-control capacity is not a relevant variable (except perhaps in cases of people suffering severe mental conditions), the only thing that counts is whether you are the "owner" of the behavior. In the *free will skeptic* approach, self-control capacity is not a relevant variable either, but for a different and more radical reason: In this approach, moral responsibility does not exist altogether. Asking how self-control capacity might relate to moral responsibility is as nonsensical as asking how the capacity to stay afloat might relate to witchhood. In sum, both approaches negate the idea that a meaningful relation might exist between moral responsibility and self-control capacity, and that the former should somehow track the latter.

## The Subjective Standpoint

Things look very different from the subjective standpoint. Here, people implicitly assume that all normal adults are autonomous agents who may be held responsible for their behavior, and react with anger, indignation, or resentment toward perceived transgressions of rules and norms. People are "stubborn moralists."

This also means that they implicitly assume that failures of self-control do not derive from a lack of *capacity* but from a lack of *motivation*. Hence, if someone fails at self-control, she is morally responsible for her conduct. Or at least, this is their initial reaction. When people subsequently switch to the more detached view of the objective standpoint, they seek to establish whether the behavior was really under the person's control, and if so, what amount of blame or punishment is *proportionate* to the amount of wrong done. The implication is that the *extent* to which someone is held responsible for (the consequences) of poor self-control, should be attuned to *the level* of self-control that could reasonably be expected from this person, given the specifics of her background and situation.

## Instrumental Standpoint

Viewed from the instrumental standpoint, it does not matter whether people "really" are morally responsible for whatever they say or do, and it does not matter whether self-control capacity is "really" limited or not. The only thing that counts is which beliefs and ideas are most useful for achieving our goals.

Viewed from this standpoint, we are probably best served by a moderately optimistic stance: People usually have more self-control capacity at their disposal than they might believe, but this capacity is not unlimited. Therefore, on the one hand, we should not too readily accept poor self-control as an excuse for not living up to rules, norms, or expectations, but on the other, we should also acknowledge that circumstances are sometimes so tough and stressful that even paragons of discipline will have trouble mustering the required level of self-control. This moderately optimistic stance should be reflected and expressed in institutional arrangements and social practices for the ascription of responsibility.

## Good Enough Solutions

These three standpoints are all valid and none of them can reduced to the others. This means that there is no single and universally applicable answer to the question whether and to what extent some particular behavior is blameworthy. More specifically, there is no single and universally applicable answer to the question whether and to what extent poor self-control is a valid excuse for responsibility. In the epistemic domain, we have to settle for a compromise: a set of beliefs and ideas that does not perfectly cohere with all three perspectives, but nonetheless comes sufficiently close. In the regulatory domain, we have to settle for heuristics: rules that do not pretend to cover all cases but nonetheless are "good enough," as they will regulate most cases sufficiently well. But there will always be exceptions. There will always be hard or unusual cases where following the rules would yield results that are deemed unfair or at odds with our practical interests.

All things considered, therefore, the best answer to this chapter's main question is a partially substantive and partially procedural answer, along the following lines:

- By default, all people should be assumed to be autonomous agents who may be held (fully) responsible for their conduct. By implication, it should be assumed that, by default, all people have enough capacity for exerting self-control. Only certain well-defined categories are exempted, notably children and the insane.
- But in specific instances, there may be good reasons to suspend this rule and (partially) excuse or exempt individuals from moral responsibility. Insufficient self-control capacity may be one of these. Whether such good reasons exist or not, can only be determined on a case-by-case basis. The decision whether individuals should be

(partially) excused or exempted, must be informed by the relevant considerations from all three standpoints: the objective, the subjective, *and* the instrumental standpoint. Put more simply, this decision must be informed by three questions: What are the facts of the case? What intuitively feels fair and just? And what best serves our shared interests?

- The more often excuses or exemptions are in order, the more reason there is to reconsider and revise the above rules. It may be necessary to redefine which categories of people, by default, are considered autonomous agents who may be held (fully) responsible for their conduct. The greater the potential of such a revision to decrease the number of exceptions, the stronger the argument for this revision. And again, decisions on whether the rules should be revised must be informed by the relevant considerations from all three standpoints.

This answer does not once and for all settle the central issue of this chapter, but it furnishes rough guidelines on how to deal with this issue. It explicitly acknowledges that all of our norms and rules are imperfect as they sometimes get it wrong but, at the same time, sets the terms for debate, tells us where the burden of proof lies, and affirms the importance of considering all three standpoints. *Yet others must make the final decision!* In essence, this answer is a plea for adopting the right mindset.

Some readers may find this disappointing. After all these pages, they may want clear answers, not rough guidelines or something as mushy as "the right mindset." I will return to this in Chapter 10. For now, I wish to stress that this partly procedural approach is not an admission of defeat. The lack of closure is not a bug but a feature, because it asserts the inevitably heuristic character of all decision rules, ensures that in individual cases the specifics of the situation are taken into account, and that, as exceptions accumulate, the question is raised whether the rules need revision. As stated, only dead organisms are in perfect equilibrium. It is precisely the lack of closure that keeps the process of interrogation and adaptation in motion, thereby reducing the chances of a widening gap between, on the one hand, the institutional order and the facts of responsibility it creates and, on the other hand, the ever-changing reality of moral intuitions, social conditions, and scientific insight.

# 9 | *Who Should Get What?*

According to Harold Lasswell, one of the pioneers of political science, all politics is about "who gets what, when and how".[1] A great deal of political struggle revolves around the distribution of scarce goods. Often that "good" is money. Of course, people differ widely in their views on what distribution is fair, and the same holds true for philosophers, as they have advanced a wide variety of theories on "distributive justice." The spectrum ranges from, on the one extreme, theories that argue for strict equality of outcomes to, on the other, theories that consider massive inequality no problem at all, so long as people have acquired their fortunes legally. It is not exaggerated to say that philosophy has legitimizing theories on offer for almost every political persuasion.

But despite this variety, over recent decades a consensus has emerged on one key principle: We should distinguish between inequalities that derive from people's *own voluntary choices* and inequalities that derive from circumstances *beyond their control*. The first type of inequality is acceptable, only the second type needs to be redressed. After all, it is only fair that people who act prudently and work hard get more than people who are careless, lazy, and unwilling to work. And it is only fair that people who lose their life savings through no fault of their own – think Enron or Icesave – receive some form of financial relief, whereas people who lose their savings through risky and reckless investments must shoulder the losses themselves. The crucial concept is personal responsibility. Whether inequalities in health, wealth, and happiness should be accepted or not depends on the extent to which people themselves are responsible for those inequalities.

This is a principle that many policymakers, philosophers, and ordinary people seem to embrace. But crucially, the principle hinges on the assumption that we really *are* responsible for the actions that determine our life outcomes. People who work hard and act prudently do so because they have voluntarily *chosen* to do so. And people who are lazy, unwilling to work, and behave carelessly do so because they have voluntarily *chosen* to take it easy and enjoy the good life now. It is precisely this assumption that self-control research casts doubt upon. This research opens up the possibility that differences in behavior and life outcomes do not (only) spring from differences in voluntary choices but (also) from differences in self-control capacity. It may be that people who do not exhibit the discipline required for making their own living, who run from one miserable instance of self-control failure to the next, do not lack the *motivation* to do what is right, but lack the *capacity* to do what is right. And as we saw in Part I, how much self-control capacity one is endowed with is a circumstance beyond our control.

This chapter therefore asks *what the implications are of the psychological findings on self-control for the responsibility approach to distributive justice.* With the term "responsibility approach," I refer to a subset of theories on distributive justice in which the distribution of scarce goods is based on the extent to which people are personally responsible for their life situation. The question is whether – given what we have learned about self-control – this approach can be sustained.

Of course, after Chapter 8, it is clear that concepts such as "voluntary choice" and "responsibility" are deeply problematic. Can these things exist at all? But for reasons I will explain, I will not start the metaphysical debate all over again. Instead, I want to focus on an epistemological puzzle: Can we really *know* to what extent behaviors derive from voluntary choice or from circumstances beyond our control? Can we really *know* what caused what? After all, the responsibility approach rests on the assumption that these two potential causes can be disentangled, that it is possible to tease apart the contributions of voluntary choice on the one hand and circumstances beyond our control on the other. But is this assumption tenable?

## 9.1 The Responsibility Approach: A Happy Marriage ...

Let me begin with a brief overview of some of the answers that have been given to the question "who should get what?" Should everyone get an equal piece of the pie, or should some get a bigger piece than others? And if so, why? In Chapter 8, I distinguished between three standpoints for looking at the world. The same framework is useful here as well.

## Objective Standpoint

The objective standpoint largely corresponds with the branch of philosophy that deals with principles of distributive justice and seeks to identify those principles that are "objective" in the sense that all reasonable people should subscribe to them. In the early 1970s, two famous proposals for such principles were advanced by John Rawls and Robert Nozick. Their respective theories represent opposite sides in the debate on what amounts to a fair distribution of goods.

Rawls is squarely on the egalitarian side of the debate. He argues that "all social values – liberty and opportunity, income and wealth, and the social bases of self-respect – are to be distributed equally *unless* an unequal distribution of any, or all, of these values is to everyone's advantage".[2] Differences in wages, for instance, might compel people to work harder, take risks, and innovate, thus helping the economy to flourish. If this means that everyone, including the poor, will be better off, this wage inequality is acceptable. "Injustice," says Rawls, "is simply inequalities that are not to the benefit of all".[3] Whole libraries have been written on Rawls, but I will confine myself to a single observation: In his distributive principles, personal responsibility is not a criterion. For the question how the pie should be divided, it makes no difference whether one acts prudently and works hard, or behaves irresponsibly and does not pull one's weight. Unfortunately, to many people, this just does not feel right.[4]

Nozick argues for almost the mirror opposite. Unambiguously on the libertarian side, for Nozick, justice is grounded in entitlement: People have an inalienable right to the fruits of their labor. The exchange of goods can only take place on a voluntary basis, for example through inheritance or commercial transactions. So long as people have acquired their holdings lawfully – that is, not through fraud, deceit, or stealing – forced compensation of inequalities is never justified. Redistribution through taxation is nothing other than theft. In contrast to Rawls, Nozick's approach *does* reward prudence and hard work, because people are entitled to keep whatever comes from their labor. But Nozick's approach has problems of its own. It maximizes liberty, but allows for extreme inequality and poverty, perhaps leaving some to starve. To many people, this does not feel right either.

Obviously, these two opposing views cry out for a middle ground. Such a middle ground was developed in the 1980s. It is often called "luck egalitarianism" and mostly associated with the philosophers Ronald Dworkin and Gerald Cohen.[5] According to luck egalitarianism, inequalities that derive from voluntary choices are just, but inequalities that derive from circumstances beyond people's control should be redressed. To give an example, suppose that two young children have equal talent, but the first is blessed with a supportive family and excellent schools right around the corner, whereas the second grows up in a broken home and lives in a bad neighborhood with no decent schools nearby. In this situation, the second child has less chance at academic success, due to circumstances beyond his control. Society therefore has a moral obligation to compensate for this instance of bad luck, perhaps by providing for extra care and education. Both children should have an equal starting position in life.

But now, suppose that after these two children have turned eighteen and have acquired their entrance ticket into society (say a high school diploma), one of them does much better than the other. One now makes a lot of money because he studied hard in college, attended graduate school, found a steady job, works long hours, invests his earnings wisely, and in general acts prudently and responsibly, whereas the other preferred partying to studying, therefore dropped out of college, spends his days slacking off in temporary jobs, and squanders his modest earnings on luxuries. In this situation, the resulting inequality in life outcomes is fair, because they derive from voluntary choices. The second person could have done equally well if only he would have put in the same amount of effort and had acted more responsibly.

### Subjective Standpoint

Now let's move on to the subjective perspective. When it comes to the question "Who should get what?" few people think like philosophers, who carefully deduce their judgments from elaborate theories on equality. Most people base their judgments on intuitions regarding *deservingness*.[6] The importance of desert has long been recognized. John Stuart Mill, for example, wrote that it is "universally considered just that each person should obtain that (whether good or evil) which he *deserves*; and unjust that he should obtain a good, or be made to undergo an evil, which he does not deserve. This is, perhaps, the clearest and most emphatic form in which the idea of justice is conceived by the general mind."[7]

But what exactly is deservingness? That is hard to pin down. It is a highly intuitive yet elusive concept. Nevertheless, in everyday life we appear to have little trouble in making judgments about deservingness. Nearly everyone agrees that people who work hard deserve higher rewards than slackers. This seems so self-evident that many would react with surprise if they were asked to furnish reasons for this judgment. And nearly everyone agrees that someone who has always acted prudently, saved for a rainy day, and tried to do the right thing, is more deserving of financial assistance when bad luck strikes – for instance, during an economic crisis – than someone who spends his days in idleness, doing nothing but watching TV and drinking beer.[8]

The crucial question is *on what grounds* people decide that some individuals are more deserving than others. What is the "desert base"? Several candidates have been proposed, but the most prominent one is – once again – responsibility.[9] Most people hold that a person is "deserving" of some condition – say being rich or poor – to the extent that he him is responsible for this condition, that is, the condition stems from his own choices and actions. Judgments of deservingness thus closely resemble moral judgments (or even *are* moral judgments). But there is one big difference: Judgments of deservingness usually do not concern one *single* behavior that is believed to be right or wrong, but a whole *series* of behaviors that one approves or disapproves of, an overall *pattern* of conduct that tells us something about the person's character. Hence, it is perfectly normal to say that someone whom we admire for his unrelenting effort, exemplary behavior, and good character, does not deserve to live in such poverty or, conversely, that some no-good spoiled brat who never contributed anything to society does not deserve the great wealth he inherited. And hence, in political debate, it is not uncommon to hear talk of the "deserving poor" versus "the underserving poor" (or the "deserving rich" versus the "undeserving rich").[10]

### Instrumental Standpoint

Viewed from the instrumental standpoint, the decisive criterion is what works best for achieving our "all-things-considered practical interests." The relevant question here is what distributive principles and policies best serve our collective goals. Unfortunately, there is no clear-cut answer to this question, as it all depends on what our collective goals are. Is it maximum economic growth? Maximum *sustainable* growth? Maximal happiness and well-being? Maximum social cohesion? Some combination of the above? Moreover, even if there were a consensus on what goals to pursue, it is not always clear what distributive principles and policies are most "useful" for achieving them. The relatively simple question to what extent income differences contribute to economic growth is already a subject of ongoing debate and shifting opinions.

What we do know, however, is what experts *believe* works best for achieving our "all-things-considered practical interests." Assuming that democracy is functioning properly, we can derive this from the actual policies governments pursue, since these are the result of what the political community has defined as its common goals plus the prevailing view among policy experts on how best to achieve them. Going by this heuristic, we can conclude that since the 1970s a gradual shift has occurred in the dominant beliefs about what works best. Before then, many Western states had generous welfare regimes, in which all citizens within the same category received the same benefits, regardless of their individual conduct (see Chapter 7). Also, in many countries, tax rates for the highest incomes were much higher, sometimes reaching levels that people today would consider outrageous (see Figure 9.1). Compared to today, many Western societies came much closer to Rawlsian egalitarianism.

But things have changed. Many entitlements have been made contingent on behavior, while tax rates for the highest incomes have been slashed. The "responsibility crusade" has ushered in "the age of responsibility." Apparently, it is increasingly believed that the doctrines of luck egalitarianism are more "useful" for achieving our "all-things-considered practical interests" than the doctrines of classic egalitarianism.[11]

## Conclusion

So the three standpoints converge to the same answer regarding "who should get what?" Recent decades have witnessed a happy marriage of luck egalitarian philosophy, everyday intuitions, and practical policy considerations. At the heart of this happy marriage is what philosopher Brian Barry calls "the principle of responsibility": unequal outcomes are just *if and only if* they arise from factors for which individuals can

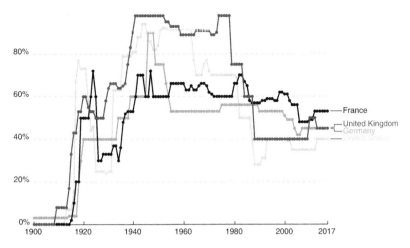

**Figure 9.1** Top marginal income tax rate, 1900–2017. *Source:* Alvaredo et al. (2018), published online at OurWorldInData.org

properly be held responsible.[12] Let us, therefore, call this happy marriage the "responsibility approach" to distributive justice. I am inclined to prefer this term over the philosophical term "luck egalitarianism," because it explicitly mentions the underlying key principle, and is also directly connected to the widespread discourse on "personal responsibility." But essentially both terms mean the same thing.

With the responsibility approach, distributive justice appears to have taken a moralistic turn: The question "who should get what" has morphed into the question "who *deserves* what." How scarce goods are to be distributed is no longer deduced from general principles of justice, such as the ones formulated by Rawls, but from judgments on the merits of personal choices and behavior. Whereas classic strands of egalitarianism *abstract* from individual behavior, the responsibility approach does the exact opposite, and *zooms in* on individual behavior.

## 9.2 ... That Cannot Work

Unfortunately, as soon as we shift the focus toward individual behavior, the metaphysical problems discussed in Chapter 8 reappear with a vengeance. Does there really exist such a thing as "voluntary choice"? Is anyone ever truly responsible for his actions? Gerald Cohen, a prominent advocate of luck egalitarianism, readily concedes that once we make the distinction between choice and circumstance central to distributive justice, "we may indeed be up to our necks in the free will problem".[13]

This is quite annoying. Do we really have to start the discussion of Chapter 8 all over again, now applied to self-control and distributive justice? No, for reasons that I will explain shortly, this is unnecessary. Instead, we better focus on two crucial premises underlying the responsibility approach: The premise that at the starting gate of life, people have (or should have) equal opportunities, and the premise that it is possible to establish *to what extent* behavior derives from voluntary choice rather than circumstances beyond a person's control. These premises were already dubious, but the research on self-control makes them virtually untenable.

### Unequal Opportunities

For the happy marriage to work, all individuals should have an equal starting position in life. According to Rawls, "those who are at the same level of talent and ability, and have the same willingness to use them, should have the same prospects of success regardless of their initial place in the social system".[14] In other words, there must be a level playing field on which people can compete on equal terms. *Only when this is true* can unequal outcomes be attributed to voluntary choice.

Do we live in such a world today? Obviously not. In many societies, factors such as gender, ethnicity, and social background have become less decisive for one's life chances than they once were, but we are still far away from genuinely equal opportunities. Let me give an example. Recall the two children of equal talent from Section 9.1. The first grew up in a stable and wealthy family with good neighborhood schools, whereas the second grew up in a poor and broken home with no decent schools in sight. To guarantee a level playing field, society would have to offset the disadvantage for the second child, perhaps by investing in early childhood education and better schools. But this may not be enough. Wealthy and educated parents are better equipped to invest in their children's academic prospects, for instance by creating a conducive learning environment at home, helping with homework, or hiring a private tutor. Therefore, to guarantee a level playing field, society would have to go further, and match these private investments with similar support for children of less wealthy and educated parents. It is unclear how this could be done.

These concerns are anything but new. That external obstacles can hinder equal opportunities is a staple of the literature on distributive justice. The research on self-control, however, adds a new element: There is another obstacle that must be taken into account – an obstacle that does not reside in people's surroundings but within themselves. Even if two children are of equal talent, ability, and motivation, have similar social backgrounds, live on the same street, attend the same school, have equally helpful parents, get the same tutoring – even if both children are similar in all of these respects, it is still possible that one will do better than the other, *due to differences in self-control capacity.* Perhaps one is endowed with high trait self-control and grows up in a stress-free family environment, and is therefore well equipped with the discipline that learning and studying require, whereas the other is endowed with low trait self-control, grows up amid constant turmoil and stress, and is therefore easily distracted and has trouble delaying gratification. For the latter child, it is much harder to learn and study effectively. He may end up with lower grades or even drop out of school, and thus have poorer future prospects. Can it be sustained that, despite their considerable difference in self-control capacity, both children have equal opportunities? And if not, how can these unequal starting positions be redressed?

The heart of the problem is this: The research on self-control is a stark reminder that genuine equality of opportunities is an ideal that can never be fully attained because no two people are alike. In theory, the principle that people of similar talent and ability ought to have similar prospects of success sounds appealing. But in practice, it poses enormous problems, for it remains entirely unclear what falls under the category of "talent and ability." Should self-control capacity be considered part of talent and ability? This would certainly be logical, because – as Part I made clear – good self-control is an important ingredient for future success, and self-control capacity is largely determined by genes and early upbringing. So perhaps we should add this trait to the category of natural talent and ability. But why stop there? Once we classify self-control as part of talent and ability, why not include other traits that affect life outcomes, such as dispositional optimism?.[15] To be consistent, we should add this one to the list as well. And while we are at it, why not also include extraversion and neuroticism, two other factors known to make a difference?[16] The upshot is that the more characteristics are thrown into the basket of talent and ability, the fewer people will be of equal talent and ability. In the end, we are left with just a collection of individuals, all unique in their idiosyncratic set of qualities. It is no longer possible to attribute unequal outcomes to voluntary choice because there was no equal starting position to begin with.

## *Choice or Circumstance?*

Suppose that, despite these problems, it is somehow possible to create genuine equality of opportunities – that is, a starting moment in life where all individuals of equal talent and ability have equal prospects for success in life. We then encounter the next challenge. For luck egalitarianism aka the responsibility approach to work, we must be able to determine to what extent one's current life situation is the result of voluntary choice, and to what extent the result of circumstances beyond one's control. After all, this approach maintains that if people face hardship or setbacks, they are only entitled to (financial) assistance if these misfortunes stem from circumstances beyond their control. Someone who loses his house due to severe flooding caused by a category 5 hurricane is more deserving of our help and compassion than someone who loses his house due to risky investments. Someone who was always a star employee but is suddenly laid off during an economic crisis and, despite his best efforts, has trouble finding a new job, is more deserving of financial assistance than someone who never had a steady job and appears unwilling to work at all.

But are things really so straightforward? Like the assumption of equal opportunities, the idea that free choice and circumstances beyond our control can easily be disentangled has always been dubious. Suppose the individual above built his house in a low-lying area known to be susceptible to flooding, while not taking out insurance? If he cannot afford to rebuild his home after the category 5 hurricane, is his dire situation really the result of circumstances beyond his control, or the entirely avoidable consequence of his choice not to take out insurance? And what if someone invested his life savings in a fund rated as perfectly safe by reputable financial organizations? If

that fund nonetheless collapses and, as a consequence, he is forced to
sell his house, is his misfortune really the mere result of his own allegedly imprudent investment decisions? Or take the star employee who
is laid off during an economic crisis. Suppose we learn that his company was operating in a rapidly changing market, making products
that, as anyone could foresee, would soon be rendered obsolete by
new technological progress, but that this employee ignored the writing
on the wall, and refused to learn new skills and invest in his employability? If, after being made redundant, he has trouble finding a new
job, is this purely bad luck? Or should he have better prepared for the
changing demands of the labor market? And how about people who
grew up in difficult circumstances and were never taught any basic
job skills, due to absent parents and the lack of decent schools? Who
perhaps also had to care for family members who could not look after
themselves? To what extent do these individuals "choose" not to have
a steady job?

In sum, things are often not so black and white. The facts rarely
speak for themselves, and there is often considerable latitude for con-
structing alternative narratives.

## *Enter Self-Control*

Now, one could simply sweep aside all these ambiguities and com-
plexities by claiming that everything in the universe is determined,
and therefore the whole idea of voluntary choice is illusory. Everything people do is caused by circumstances beyond their control, since
everything people do is the outcome of a long chain of events set in
motion even before they were born. Therefore, no one is ever responsible for anything and no one ever deserves anything – end of story.

However, this metaphysical move is not a solution. In this chapter,
we are faced with an *epistemological* problem: We need to uncover
what happened in *the most recent* steps of the causal chain, *regardless* of what ultimately caused these steps. The responsibility approach
to distributive justice is concerned with *proximate* causes, not with
ultimate causes. And with regard to these proximate causes – so it
is argued – we must distinguish between two types of empirical reality: On the one side, those empirical realities that reside within the
conscious mind and are commonly referred to as "preference," "intention," or "choice" versus, on the other side, those empirical realities

that are deemed beyond our control, such as genetic makeup, social background, economic crises, and natural disasters. For the responsibility approach to work, the challenge is to disentangle these two types of reality and establish their respective contributions. Hence, arguing that ultimately everything is determined misses the point. Even if this is true, we still need to figure out what the proximate causes of one's current life situation are, and to what extent they belong to the category of "voluntary choices" or to the category of "circumstances beyond control."

And that is where the research on self-control spells trouble. First, this research suggests that we should take differences in *trait* self-control into account (that is, one's baseline level of self-control strength). Two individuals may experience similar failures in their attempts to find jobs, stay employed, fulfill workfare requirements, and so forth, but nonetheless differ in how much they "deserve" any resulting hardship, because they differ in the extent to which these failures were attributable to choice or circumstance. One of them may be endowed with excellent self-control, but simply be unwilling to use this capacity for the good, whereas the other may be highly motivated to do whatever it takes, but lack the required self-control capacity. But how do we *know* which of these two possibilities is the case? How can we know *to what extent* the behavior in question can be attributed to poor trait self-control?

Second, we must take fluctuations in *state* self-control into account (that is, one's self-control capacity in a specific situation at a specific moment in time). Maybe the two persons are equal in trait self-control but live in very different circumstances. Perhaps one of them lives in a highly stressful environment and suffers a chronic lack of sleep, compounded by his partner's serious illness, while the other lives a carefree life, never has sleeping problems, and is socially well connected. Due to these different circumstances, they will probably differ in state self-control. It may therefore be much tougher for the first to get a job, stay employed, or fulfill workfare requirements.

But then again, maybe not! It could also be that this specific individual has poor trait self-control and indeed leads a difficult life, but *nonetheless* only has him to blame, because he did not even try in the first place. Sometimes people have poor mental resources *and* poor motivation, so the question becomes which of both was decisive in this particular instance. That may remain unclear. There may not even be a clear ontological distinction between the two. Recent research on self-control suggests that there is a gray area between being unwilling and being unable (see Chapter 4). In this gray area, the boundary between lack of motivation and lack of capacity is fuzzy. It is unclear where the one ends and the other begins – even to the people themselves.

The implication is that we cannot determine "who should get what" by just looking at overt behavior. Life used to be so much simpler. In classical economy, willpower problems did not exist. Barring external obstacles or mental delusions, what one *did* was equal to what one *wanted*. But the research on self-control drives a wedge between the two: What people *do* is not necessarily equivalent to what people *want*. Hence, to assess to what extent a particular behavior is the result of voluntary choice or unchosen circumstance, we have to look beyond overt behavior, into the person's mind. Institutions and officials who have to decide on distributive matters need to obtain detailed information about individuals, not only about their life situation but also about their mental states, and perhaps even their neurobiology – information that, if available at all, many consider deeply private.

## Further Complications

Another problem is that a broad range of behaviors must be taken into account. This is an important departure from the moral responsibility discussed in Chapter 8. There we also faced the difficulty of untangling the contributions of choice and circumstance, but in that chapter, we were concerned with *isolated* behaviors. The problem was restricted to a single act of wrongdoing by a specific individual in a specific situation at a specific moment in time. My proposal there was to adopt the rule that, absent compelling evidence to the contrary, people can be considered morally responsible for the behavior in question. It was not a perfect solution, but probably good enough to settle most cases, and therefore practically workable.

But things are different in the realm of distributive justice, because judgments about "who should get what" do not concern a *single* behavior but *multiple* behaviors. Establishing to what extent someone's situation and life circumstances are the result of his own voluntary choices or circumstances beyond his control, requires considering not just one isolated act or behavior but a whole *series* of behaviors, an (alleged) pattern of conduct. The crucial question is not "could he have done otherwise?" but "could he have done otherwise over *the past three months*? Or over *the past three years*? Could he have *lived his whole life* differently?" For this type of all-things-considered judgment, a default rule that allows for exceptions is no solution. Given the uniqueness of each life story, it will be impossible to furnish a general rule for the respective contributions of choice and circumstance. Every potential rule will immediately be swept away by a flood of exceptions.

For a brief theoretical elaboration, it is instructive to recall the distinction made by Chandra Sripada between "time slice failure" and "cumulative failure" in Chapter 4. Within the context of moral responsibility, it makes sense to take a "time slice" perspective and examine the "point probability" of self-control failure: What are the chances that *this person in this situation at this moment in time* lacked the capacity to inhibit his impulses? We have to make a judgment of what, somewhat awkwardly, might be called "point deservingness." Although sorting out the roles of choice and circumstance in isolated behaviors is no small feat, it is not entirely beyond the realm of possibility. (Moreover, when the stakes are high, for example in serious criminal cases, often sufficient time and resources are available to carefully examine all the details of the case, to hear witness and expert testimony, to reconstruct the situation, and – if necessary – to repeat the whole exercise in higher appeal.)

However, in the realm of distributive justice, it makes more sense to take a broader view, consider a longer stretch of time encompassing multiple behaviors, and examine the "cumulative probability" of self-control failure at critical junctures over this longer stretch of time. We have to make a judgment of what might be called "aggregate deservingness." This is much more difficult because this cumulative perspective adds several layers of complexity. Not only do we have to untangle the roles of choice and circumstance in multiple instances, we also have to decide on how long a time frame to consider, and on what rule for aggregation to apply. These are arbitrary choices, and therefore susceptible to ideological preference.

Which brings me to my final point: We must also take the subjective and instrumental standpoint into account. As said in Chapter 8, in a discussion of what scientific findings imply *for society and policy*, we cannot restrict ourselves to the objective standpoint only. We must also engage the perspective of the *subjects* who make up society, and the perspective of the *policymakers* who have to determine what will probably work best. Unfortunately, this threefold approach only adds to the confusion. The process is now expanded with – some would say corrupted by – moral intuitions and instrumental considerations. The teasing out of choice and circumstance may become an exercise in "motivated reasoning" – a process in which the perception and interpretation of empirical reality is guided by the desire to reach conclusions that "feel right" or which are "useful".[17] The findings of self-control research only increase this risk, as they open up new space for alternative interpretations of the "true" causes of people's behavior – interpretations that might better suit one's personal interests or political goals.

The sum of all these problems and complications is epistemological chaos. The assumption that choices and circumstances can be disentangled was already dubious, but once we bring the psychology of self-control into the equation, the whole enterprise collapses. Determining to what extent one's current life situation is the result of voluntary choice and to what extent of circumstances beyond one's control, turns out to be an impossible task. To quote the philosopher Richard Arneson, "the idea that we might adjust our distributive-justice system based on our estimation of persons' overall deservingness or responsibility seems entirely chimerical. Individuals do not display responsibility scores on their foreheads".[18]

## 9.3  Plan B: Sufficientarianism plus Relational Equality

So the bad news is that, once again, we find ourselves in a mess. But the good news is that there may be an elegant way out. The prospects here are less grim than in Chapter 8. In that chapter, the combination of empirical research and logical reasoning pushed us toward the unappealing conclusion that moral responsibility cannot exist. My strategy to escape the quagmire was to invoke two alternative standpoints, recognize the fundamental brokenness of our beliefs and ideas, and settle for a heuristic that – hopefully – will solve the majority of cases. Granted, this solution is imperfect and ultimately unstable, but it is the best we can do.

In this chapter, however, we do not have to make such a less than ideal move, because there is a perfectly coherent alternative that stays well within the confines of the objective standpoint. This alternative is *to simply give up on (luck) egalitarianism aka the responsibility approach*. We can simply decide to accept that in the great lottery of life some people are just luckier than others, that the resulting material inequalities are a mere fact of life, and not by definition an injustice that must be redressed.[19] If we take this position, we no longer need to ask to what extent people are "personally responsible" for their life outcomes. We no longer need to take on the impossible task of disentangling the roles of choice and circumstance.

At first sight, this may seem an unexpected and radical solution. Is this not an admission of defeat? A textbook example of throwing out the baby with the bathwater? Not necessarily. To see why, it is useful to take a step back. Up to this point in the chapter, the implicit assumption was that justice is about the *equal* distribution of some scarce good – resources, money, happiness, or whatever "equilisandum" one prefers. Everybody should get an equal piece of the pie, and if some people get a bigger piece than others, we need a justification for that inequality. But why should we focus on how much people get *compared to others*? Is the *relative* level of resources really the hallmark of justice? No, according to several philosophers we should focus on the *absolute* level instead. When people are offended by inequality, argues philosopher Harry Frankfurt, it is often not the inequality itself that bothers them, but the fact that some have too little. "If everyone had enough money, it would be of no special concern whether some people had more money than others".[20] What really matters is that each person gets *enough*. Every citizen should have sufficient resources to lead a minimally decent life, and so long as everybody is above this threshold, there is nothing wrong with material inequality as such. This strand of thinking is called "sufficientarianism" (as opposed to "egalitarianism").

Some readers may remain unconvinced. Does the sufficientarian approach not amount to giving up on the ideal of equality? Again, not necessarily. To see this, it is useful to take another step back, and ask what equality is really about. According to philosophers such as Elizabeth Anderson and Samuel Scheffler, the point of equality is *not* to establish some ostensibly fair pattern of distribution, but to *ensure freedom from oppression and establish equal relations*. Equality stands opposed not to luck but to "heritable hierarchies of social status, to ideas of caste, to class privilege and the rigid stratification of classes, and the undemocratic distribution of power".[21] It means that human relations must be based on the assumption that everyone's life is equally important, and all members of society have equal standing. This conception of equality is usually referred to as "relational equality" (or "democratic equality").

To be clear, the ideal of relational equality does not mean that redistribution is always illegitimate and should never happen, as hardcore libertarians would have it. First, redistribution may be necessary to ensure that each citizen has effective access to sufficient resources to avoid being oppressed by others and to be able to interact with fellow citizens on an equal footing. These resources include food, shelter, clothing, medical care, and a basic level of education. "Negatively," says Anderson, "people are entitled to whatever capabilities are necessary to enable them to avoid or escape entanglement in oppressive social relationships. Positively, they are entitled to the capabilities necessary for functioning as an equal citizen in a democratic state".[22] Second, redistribution may be necessary when material inequalities grow so large that relational equality is threatened. Substantial inequalities "can all too easily generate inequalities of power and status that are incompatible with relations among equals," argues Scheffler.[23] The weaker the barriers against commodifying social status, influence, and power, the greater the need for setting limits to material inequality. In both cases – having too little, having too much – redistribution is imperative, *not* because material inequalities are unjust as such, but because they may corrupt relational equality.

The combination of sufficientarianism and relational egalitarianism solves the problem of teasing apart choice and circumstance for the simple reason that "personal responsibility" is no longer part of the equation.[24] If material inequalities are no longer seen as societal wrongs that must be justified or redressed, there is no longer a need to scrutinize to what extent people are personally responsible for their life situation. Only when people fall below the threshold should they be provided with the support needed to bounce back, but here personal responsibility plays no role either. All citizens have a right to the minimum required for functioning as equals *regardless* of their conduct.[25] And it is only when some people accumulate such massive wealth that equal relations are threatened that some sort of intervention may be necessary. But again, personal responsibility is irrelevant. It makes no difference whether this wealth came from hard work or sheer luck. Material inequalities that corrupt relational equality must be offset *regardless* of what brought them about. Relational equality therefore stands in direct contrast to luck egalitarianism aka the responsibility approach in its principled abstraction from individual characteristics and personal conduct. "As a political ideal," writes Scheffler "it highlights the claims that citizens are entitled to make on one another by virtue of their status as citizens, without any need for a moralized accounting of the details of their particular circumstances."[26] We are thus relieved of the impossible task of disentangling the respective contributions of choice and circumstance, and of the equally impossible task of teasing out the disparate roles of self-control capacity and self-control motivation in the behaviors that brought about one's current life situation.

## *How About the Other Standpoints?*

Is this indeed the solution for the mess the responsibility approach got us in? Before we draw this conclusion, we need to check how well this approach fits with the subjective and the instrumental standpoints. After all, the combination of sufficientarianism and relational equality may succeed in putting our self-control worries to rest, but little is gained if this alternative approach is squarely at odds with people's beliefs and intuitions, or would seriously hinder all efforts to promote our collective interests. In that case, this alternative may be philosophically coherent and consistent but nevertheless useless, as it will never work in the real world.

So before celebrating, we need to do a reality check. I will not dwell on this for long, since my aim is fairly modest: I only wish to show that this alternative approach is *not in outright contradiction* with the views from the instrumental and subjective standpoints, and can thus be retained as a viable alternative.

Let me begin with a few words on the instrumental standpoint: What works best? On this question we can be brief: nobody knows. It all depends on the choice of goals. And even if the goals were given, we lack the knowledge to calculate which approach to distributive justice yields the highest utility. Therefore, I will restrict myself to just two remarks. First, if we wish to pursue social cohesion, there is much to be said for relational equality, as this approach, almost by definition, promotes social cohesion. Moreover, several studies have found that greater income inequality is correlated with lower levels of trust, which supports the relational egalitarian position that income differences ought to be kept within bounds.[27] Second, if we wish to pursue economic growth, it is worth noting that economists have begun to abandon the conventional wisdom that greater income differences are *always* correlated with more economic growth. There may be such a thing as too much income inequality after all.[28] Still, I do not want to say too much about these matters, as they are topics of ongoing debate. Let me draw just one careful conclusion: Viewed from the instrumental standpoint, there are no compelling reasons to reject outright the combination of sufficientarianism and relational equality. There is no proof that this alternative could never work.

More can be said about the subjective standpoint: What do ordinary people feel and believe? Things are relatively clear at the extreme ends of the income distribution. For starters, there seems to be broad support for the sufficientarian idea of a threshold, a minimum that no one should fall below. One series of experiments conducted in the United States, Canada, Poland, and South Korea found that nearly all participants preferred distributive schemes that included a guaranteed social minimum. Other studies report similar findings.[29] What happens when people fall below this minimum? According to luck egalitarians, if this happens as a result of their own voluntary choices, then too bad, but they have to shoulder the consequences themselves. But do ordinary people also judge that harshly? Probably not. Suppose that someone without health insurance is struck by a life-threatening lifestyle disease. Many people will agree that this person should be given medical help, even though he did not take out health insurance and, in all likelihood, brought on the disease him through his unhealthy behavior. Or suppose that a San Francisco resident loses her house due to an earthquake. Many people will feel that she deserves some form of financial assistance, even though she could have known of the risks of living above the San Andreas fault. Maybe these individuals do not deserve to be *fully* compensated for *all* of the negative consequences of their choices, but they should at least get the minimal help needed to keep them from ending up in the ditch.

How about the other end of the income distribution? Do people consider it undesirable if some individuals gain such massive wealth that equal relations are corrupted? I am not aware of any studies specifically researching this question,[30] but surveys frequently find that, in Western societies, majorities believe that income inequalities are too large.[31] These findings could be merely a sign of plain envy, but they could also mean that these people sense that large income differences may endanger social and political inequality.

Things are less clear in the area *in between* the extremes of "not enough" and "way too much." As said, many people believe that prudence and hard work should be rewarded. Does the combination of sufficientarianism and relational egalitarianism not run counter to this intuition? Not necessarily. If the folk believe that, for whatever reason, those who are prudent and work hard should get a bigger piece of the pie than those who are careless and lazy, nothing in this alternative approach stands in the way, so long as the resulting inequalities do not undermine relational equality.

The real issue concerns something else, namely the claim that people, as a matter of principle, should be compensated for disadvantages that derive from *bad luck*. This is the claim that Anderson and Scheffler reject. Do ordinary people agree? Is the rejection of this claim compatible with the view from the subjective standpoint? It depends on who you ask. Even a cursory glance at the public debate is enough to see that opinions diverge widely, with people on the political left often more willing to compensate for bad luck than people on the political right. On closer inspection, however, the disagreement is not so much over the principle itself, but about its *reach and scope*. Almost everybody agrees that *in some contexts* it is unfair when people suffer disadvantages due to circumstances beyond their control, and that *in some contexts* it is acceptable (or even desirable) when people suffer disadvantages that derive from their voluntary choices. For instance, few people would dispute that those born with serious physical disabilities should receive some form of (financial) help, and few would dispute that those who have lost their savings through gambling must shoulder the burden themselves. But this does not necessarily mean that they *also* subscribe to the luck egalitarian claim that *in general*, as a matter of principle, it is *always* unfair when people are worse off due to circumstances beyond their control, and that *in general*, as a matter of principle, it is *always* acceptable (or even desirable) when people are worse off as a result of their own voluntary choices. As Scheffler argues, it is "far from clear that, *in its generalized form*, this claim enjoys widespread intuitive support".[32]

In the end, most people are pluralists. They do not rely on just one all-encompassing moral principle.[33] Most people feel that bad luck should be compensated for and that hard work and responsible behavior should be rewarded, but they *also* feel that inequalities should not grow so large that some persons are effectively excluded or detached from the society of equals. Which principle takes priority depends partly on the individual and partly on the situation. Overall, the conclusion is justified that the proposed alternative approach is not squarely at odds with people's beliefs and intuitions – *quod erat demonstrandum*.

## 9.4 Conclusion

This chapter asked what the implications of the psychological findings on self-control are for the "responsibility approach" to distributive justice. Time to wrap up.

A first thing to note is that the responsibility approach to distributive justice is a fairly recent phenomenon. Compare this with Chapter 8 about *moral* responsibility. The belief that praise or blame, reward or punishment for an action should derive from the moral rightness or wrongness of that action is probably as old as humanity itself. In contrast, the belief that the distribution of scarce goods should track "personal responsibility" came to prevail only in the last half-century.[34] During the first decades after the Second World War, both academic and policy thinking on social issues such as poverty was dominated by a "denial of human agency".[35] The focus was almost exclusively on structural obstacles, such as labor market discrimination, educational disadvantages, spatial segregation, class location, and economic restructuring. The last decades of the twentieth century, however, witnessed a strong revival of interest in human agency, and were marked by fierce attacks on the welfare state and its neglect of personal responsibility. Undesirable behavior was no longer seen as the inevitable result of circumstances beyond our control, but as the product of poor character and calculated choice. Governing society became a matter of installing the right (financial) incentives. Tax rates for the highest incomes were cut dramatically, and welfare provision was made conditional on responsible conduct. After decades of dominance, egalitarian philosophers and progressive policymakers found themselves on the defensive.

The rise of luck egalitarianism can be interpreted as an attempt to save egalitarianism from this conservative turning of the tide. Elizabeth Anderson views luck egalitarianism as a hybrid that seeks to reconcile free markets and the welfare state, while Gerald Cohen credits Ronald Dworkin for having performed "for egalitarianism the considerable service of incorporating within it the most powerful idea in the arsenal of the anti-egalitarian right: the idea of choice and responsibility".[36] Unfortunately, today's solutions often sow the seeds of tomorrow's problems. The incorporation of this "most powerful idea of the right" may have rescued egalitarianism from the dustbin of intellectual history, but it also engendered a whole new set of problems. For this latest iteration of egalitarianism to succeed, it is crucial to know the exact causes of people's disadvantage, and to determine the respective contributions of choice and circumstance.

It is against this background that we should evaluate the meaning of self-control research. Apart from the findings of this research, it is already difficult to untangle the contributions of a person's will on the one hand versus his unchosen circumstances on the other. This requires a detailed and rather intrusive assessment of individual situations and histories. But now, the self-control findings deliver another, potentially fatal, blow to the practical feasibility of the luck egalitarian aka responsibility approach, as it turns out we need to dig even deeper. When people's disadvantage stems from (repeated) self-control failures, we need to figure out to what extent these failures were caused by a lack of self-control *motivation* (= voluntary choice) and to what extent by a lack of self-control *capacity* (= circumstance beyond control). In other words, we need to look below the surface, into people's minds and neurobiology. As yet, this remains (mostly) beyond our technological means. And to further complicate matters, even if we were able to look into people's minds and neurobiology, it may not be enough to resolve the issue. What we might find there is a gray zone in which the boundary between being *unable* and being *unwilling* is hopelessly blurred (see Chapter 4). Ultimately, the question to what extent someone's disadvantage was caused by choice or circumstance may be unresolvable, for there is a fundamental opacity at the micro-level of individual motivations and capacities.

In conclusion, the message of self-control research is that the luck egalitarian or responsibility approach to distributive justice is built on quicksand. Given the social and political developments since the Second World War, and given its clear resonance with folk intuitions on deservingness, it is understandable why this approach came to prevail. But in practical terms, it does not work. The findings and insights of self-control research underscore that this approach belongs to the realm of ideal theory: not necessarily wrong, and certainly interesting from an academic point of view, but of little value when it comes to solving concrete problems in the real world. As a response to the conservative attack on egalitarianism, it ultimately fails.

There is an alternative. As argued in Chapter 8, we cannot do without the concept of moral responsibility. That would pose an almost existential threat. But as argued in this chapter, we can certainly do without the responsibility approach to distributive justice. There are good arguments to prefer a combination of sufficientarianism and relational equality instead. In this view, the point of equality is not to compensate for every instance of bad luck, but to ensure freedom from oppression and to establish equal relations. Redistribution may still be necessary, but only to ensure that everyone remains above the threshold of enough and material inequality is kept within bounds. If we adopt this alternative approach, we no longer need to torture ourselves over the hard question to what extent people's fortunes or misfortunes stem from their individual characteristics, including their excellent or miserable self-control. We are relieved of that impossible task.

# 10 | *Conclusion: What Is to Be Done?*

Of all the ills afflicting men
the worst is lack of judgment.

Sophocles

The aim of this book is to explore what the state of the art in the scientific knowledge on self-control implies for society and politics. How well do some key ideas and beliefs underlying the current institutional and social order match with everything psychology has learned about self-control? And if there is mismatch between the two, what is to be done? This last question is the subject of this concluding chapter.

Perhaps I should warn the reader in advance. Books on the implications of new scientific insights for society and policy often exude a spirit of optimism, and conclude with a healthy supply of inspiring new ideas for making the world a better place. This is not one of those books. To be sure, it is absolutely important to explore the potential of interventions and techniques that will hopefully "fix" the problem of poor self-control, or at least shave off some of the rough edges, but at the end of the day, the fact remains that some people simply have less talent for self-control than others. Some people therefore have to overcome bigger obstacles in life than others. We cannot "social engineer" our way out of this reality.

But no need to get depressed! As I will argue, acknowledging this harsh reality may be a first step toward making the world a better place after all. But first, in Section 10.1, I make some general observations about the relationship between (behavioral) science and politics, and then, in Section 10.2, briefly summarize everything we have learned thus far. Along the way, we will meet good old Aristotle who, as it turns out, gave some excellent advice on how to deal with injustices that result from unrealistic assumptions about our capacity for self-control.

238

## 10.1 The Three Standpoints and the Role of Psychology

What is the proper relationship between science and politics? This is not self-evident. Science is about "what is true," whereas politics is about "what is to be done." The answer to the first question is dependent on *external reality*, whereas the answer to the second question is dependent on *internal responses* to that external reality. In other words, the answer to the second question is a matter of *political judgment.*

How to arrive at good political judgments? According to the philosopher Hannah Arendt, judgments are noninferential: They cannot be logically derived from some higher principle or body of knowledge. Judgments are rooted in experiences of like or dislike, pleasure or displeasure – they amount to a kind of mental "tasting" of external reality. And as we all know, whether something tastes good or bad is purely subjective. This poses a problem. On a philosophical level, we may accept that judgments cannot be derived from facts – this is simply a variety of the well-known axiom that "ought" cannot be derived from "is" – but on a practical level, this is unhelpful. After all, we would not want to give philosophical license to our elected leaders to make just any decision and do whatever "feels right." We want them to make *good* decisions grounded in *good* judgment. But how can we tell good from bad if no overarching principles or bodies of knowledge exist for determining judgment?

Arendt's answer is that to arrive at good political judgment, people should look beyond their own particular perspectives. They should try to place themselves in the shoes of their fellow citizens, try to feel and think as they would do with regard to the issue at hand, and incorporate the resulting insights into their own feelings and thoughts. Although the outcome is still the judgment of this particular individual, it is now "enriched" with the views of others, thus making it more intersubjective. The more people's perspectives are included, the better the resulting political judgment.[1]

Now, there is much to be said for this solution, but it goes only halfway, as it does not exclude the possibility that the resulting judgment is still bad in the sense that it will translate into disastrous policies.[2] Even if a judgment is highly intersubjective, when it is based on an entirely false understanding of the workings of the world, we are heading for trouble. This is where science enters the stage: Some political judgments are better than others because they better align with the facts. To arrive at good judgment, one should *also* incorporate what is known about the empirical reality regarding the issue at hand. Again, the resulting judgment remains the judgment of a particular individual – and hence ultimately a matter of taste – but it is now also "enriched" with the state of the art in scientific knowledge, thus making it more resonant with the causal structure of the world. The more empirical facts are included, the better the resulting political judgment.

In sum, science cannot *decide* what is to be done. Sooner or later, there comes a point of "undecidability" – a moment when further inquiry, reasoning, or calculation cannot further reduce uncertainty on what course to pursue. Our cognitive means are exhausted. When this moment arrives, we have no choice but to take a leap of faith and go for "what feels best." However, in the trajectory *leading up to this pivotal moment*, science has a major role to play. Good judgment is the product of the political representation of citizens as subjects *and* the epistemological representation of citizens as objects. Neither can be missed.[3]

## Three Standpoints

So although science cannot decide what it to be done, it is essential for arriving at an *informed judgment* on what is to be done. Few will object to this general conclusion. I want to go further, though, and make two additional claims. The first claim is that in order to arrive at good political judgment, *all three epistemological standpoints* must be taken into account. I have argued that the problems posed by self-control research can only be properly addressed if this threefold approach is followed. But the principle can be generalized. In almost any domain, better policies will result if the objective *and* the subjective *and* the instrumental standpoints are given due consideration.

The underlying reasoning is that, ultimately, the government of society consists in the management of norms.[4] How people interact with one another, how they work and live together, and how they settle their conflicts are not determined by the truths of science but by rules and standards for acceptable and proper conduct. These can be the explicit norms of formal law, the implicit norms underlying financial incentives, norms expressed in the public sphere, and so forth. From the government point of view, therefore, the critical question is not which representations are best for *describing* reality – that is something for science to figure out – but which social norms are best for *governing* reality. These are the norms that meet two criteria:

- They are the most *legitimate* in the sense that they best agree with what citizens deem fair and just.
- They are the most *effective* in the sense that they most help to achieve the intended goals.

In other words, these are the norms that best fit with, respectively, the truths of the subjective and the instrumental standpoints. This is why the objective standpoint alone does not suffice. We need the other two as well.

At the same time, the importance of the objective standpoint cannot be overstated. While it is certainly true that "ought cannot be derived from is," there is another axiom that is equally true: "ought implies can."[5] If norms for proper conduct deviate too far from the realities of the objective standpoint, trouble is in the making. Situations may arise which many people, once they learn of the details, would consider grave injustices, and policies may be implemented that, due to their inadequate empirical grounding, are doomed to fail. The "ought implies can" principle commands inclusion of the objective standpoint. To repeat: All three standpoints must be taken into account.

## A Trias Epistemologica

Unfortunately, this is where things often go wrong. Actors in the policy debate tend to favor the perspective most aligned with their designated role, at the expense of the other two perspectives. For instance, the job of politicians is to represent the people, and hence they must carefully take note of their desires and beliefs. But accidents will happen if politicians rely on the subjective standpoint exclusively, without verifying whether what citizens feel and believe have any resemblance to objective reality. The job of policymakers is to devise policies that realize the administration's goals, for example economic growth. But again, accidents will happen if – in the pursuit of these goals – they reduce people to theoretical constructs, such as the rational egoists who populate many current policies. Such reductionism may lead to the erosion of the very values and norms society is founded on. And scientists should, of course, investigate to what extent the assumptions that underlie public policies are supported by empirical evidence. But if this results in the deconstruction of all policies that assume some level of agency and moral responsibility, they should not be surprised if sooner or later they are kicked out of the policy conversation.

The incentives to consider each standpoint differ in strength. For politicians – the ones who ultimately must decide – the cost of ignoring the subjective standpoint can be high, as it may cost them (re)election. In contrast, the costs of ignoring the other two standpoints are lower, at least in the short run. Although it may lead to policies that do not work as intended, it often takes years before the failure becomes apparent. Politicians or government officials are rarely held personally accountable when, after all those years, their policies turn out to be a fiasco – if they are still around at all. The resulting imbalance in attention to each standpoint is, I believe, one of the major weak spots of our current democracies. Several centuries ago, Montesquieu introduced the *trias politica*, the separation of the legislature, the executive, and the judiciary. This tripartition has become one of the pillars of constitutional democracy. Maybe we should also introduce a *trias epistemologica*, a distinction between the objective, the subjective, and the instrumental standpoint – perhaps not in the formal institutional sense, but as a framework for judgment and policymaking. In a well-ordered state *all three standpoints* are adequately covered and given due consideration before the policy die is cast.

## The Role of Psychological Knowledge

My second claim is that in order to arrive at good judgment, politics should pay more heed to psychology. This book is a case study of what more attention to psychology might yield. I have chosen to focus on self-control, but similar books could be written about other personality traits, for example extraversion, emotional stability, or dispositional optimism. Some people have an open, outgoing, and optimistic character, deal with problems head-on, and can handle stress well, whereas others are shy, anxious, and uncertain, and tend to avoid problems. Like self-control, these traits predict all kinds of life outcomes, and like self-control, these traits are largely determined by genetic inheritance and early upbringing. These other books would probably arrive at the same conclusion: Many current policies are based on an idealized image of citizens and their capacities, an image that does not accord with reality. Real humans are neither

---

**Box 10.1 Behavioral Science and COVID-19**

What role did behavioral science play in the fight against COVID-19? As the virus spread around the world, authorities realized that dramatic behavioral changes were needed – social distancing, working from the home, self-quarantine in case of symptoms – and that for many people this was going to pose enormous demands on their coping skills and resilience. Psychologists recognized the challenge and quickly began producing papers synthesizing the state of the art in knowledge on how to meet these behavioral and psychological challenges.[6] Some papers focused on practical tips and tricks, for example with regard to hand-disinfecting or dealing with loneliness, others addressed general strategy and conditions for compliance, such as emphasizing the "we're all in this together" character of the pandemic.

However, despite the critical importance of sustained behavior change, behavioral experts seemed mostly absent from major government COVID-19 taskforces and advisory boards. These consisted almost exclusively of virologists and other medical experts. That may have been understandable in the first stage of the pandemic, but after it became clear that the crisis was going to last many months or perhaps even years, the situation hardly changed. In a 2020 survey among behavioral experts of Organisation for Economic Co-operation and Development (OECD) member states, some grumblings were heard: "There are concerns that the skills of [behavioral insights] practitioners and policymakers are being underutilised." The behavioral insights community "strongly supports a broader use of their skills and to ensure that they are not relegated to 'quality assurance' or 'advisory' roles".[7] And in late 2020, after president-elect Biden had presented the members of his Transition COVID-19 Advisory Board, the Association for Psychological Science (APS) wrote an open letter to the chairs of the board, stating that it was "disheartened to see no psychologists on the Board." The APS urged them to consider adding a psychological scientist: "Psychological science expertise will prove indispensable to devise community-level strategies and interventions to contain the virus."[8] Apparently to no avail, because a few weeks later another letter followed: "Please act now to add additional needed expertise in the psychological sciences."[9]

For the record, these lines were written in the summer of 2021. By the time this book has reached the reader, the situation may have changed. Still, during the first year of the pandemic, the situation closely resembled the prepandemic state of affairs, in which behavioral science does not enjoy a prominent place at the tables where the principal decisions are made, and only enters the stage during the implementation phase.[10]

perfectly rational nor perfectly self-controlled nor emotionally perfectly balanced nor always full of optimism, and so forth.

Fortunately, government interest in behavioral science is on the rise. This development was primarily triggered by the financial crisis of 2008, which clearly indicated that people are not so rational after all, and by the publication of several high-profile books on behavioral insights, notably by Richard Thaler, Cass Sunstein, and Daniel Kahneman. Since then, so-called Behavioral Insight Teams (BITs) have mushroomed around the world, new peer-reviewed journals on behavioral insights and public administration have seen the light of day, and conferences on the topic have been organized almost everywhere, from London to Bahrein, and from Sydney to New York.

But despite all the hype surrounding this development, its impact should not be overstated. First, many initiatives that go under the umbrella of "applying behavioral insights" are basically just attempts to improve communication, for example by making labels on energy efficiency less confusing, or by implementing a traffic light system indicating the nutritional value of foods. Of course, it is highly desirable that consumers can easily detect whether some food item is healthy or not, but little is gained if they lack the self-control to subsequently act on this information. Second, most efforts have focused on the implementation phase and not on the policymaking phase.[11] The typical behavioral insights project concerns goals such as increasing tax compliance, improving financial decision-making, promoting healthy behavior, or enhancing the effectiveness of welfare programs. The policy goals themselves, however, are taken as a given. Behavioral experts only enter the scene after the relevant political decisions have been made and the course is set. This is too late. They should be consulted much earlier, way more upstream in the policymaking process.

## 10.2 Limited Self-Control and the "Correction" of the Law

The remainder of this chapter will focus on self-control. What are the implications of everything we have learned about self-control for judgments on "what is to be done"? Let me begin by briefly summarizing the findings so far.

As discussed in Chapter 2, the evidence for the beneficial effects of good self-control is overwhelming. Self-control is a significant predictor of school and work achievement, socioeconomic status, financial struggle and planfulness, psychological adjustment, and so on. Self-control is clearly distinct from intelligence, since there is only a weak correlation between the two. Self-control is indeed the *other* important quality.

Three individual characteristics determine the likelihood of exerting self-control:

- *Working memory capacity*. This capacity determines one's ability to mentally simulate future rewards and goals, keep attention focused on these rewards and goals, monitor progress, and inhibit irrelevant or distracting thoughts and feelings.
- *Available resources*. This is the "energy" that self-control runs on. How long self-control can be sustained partly depends on one's level of available resources. Although it is unclear what exactly this limited resource might be and whether it really is some form of energy, the case for its existence is fairly strong.
- *Future orientation*. This is the general tendency to be moved and motivated by future rewards rather than immediate rewards. The stronger one's future orientation, the higher the subjective value assigned to delayed rewards, and thus the greater the motivation to exert self-control.

People's average or baseline positions on these dimensions are mostly determined by genetic inheritance, early upbringing, and child-hood environment. Together these three dimensions constitute one's basic propensity to exercise self-control. But situational factors also play a role. Five conditions were identified that can undermine the capacity or motivation for self-control: negative affect, cognitive load, prior top-down mental effort, acute stress, and lack of sleep. Last but not least, a crucial factor is the perceived likelihood that self-control will pay off. If a person does not believe that exercising self-control will deliver the goods, she will not be inclined to invest precious resources in that course of action in the first place.

To illustrate the power of these findings, I discussed the relationship between poverty and self-control. Several studies suggest that, on aver-age, poor people are less inclined to control their impulses and delay gratification than people higher up on the socioeconomic ladder. Why is this? Some observers have postulated the existence of a "culture of poverty" – a distinct set of values and beliefs characteristic of the poor, in which a strong present orientation is a defining feature. But the "culture of poverty" thesis is highly controversial, and now that we have mapped out the scientific findings on self-control and its determinants, an alternative explanation comes into view. There may or may not be such a thing as a *culture* of poverty, but there certainly is such a thing as a *psychology* of poverty. The causality runs in both directions. First, poverty may be a *consequence* of low self-control. This is quite obvious. Getting a good education, finding and keeping a decent job, and staying out of financial trouble all require a certain amount of self-control. If you are unwilling or unable to muster this amount of self-control, chances are you end up poor. But, second, more and more research suggests that poverty may also be a *cause* of low self-control. Children who grow up in poor families are more likely to experience harsh and unresponsive parenting and chronic stress, which may hinder the development of adequate trait self-control. They are also more likely to live in a harsh and unpredictable environment, which increases the chances of developing an overall disposition toward short-term reward. Furthermore, adults with financial problems are more likely to experience conditions such as cognitive load, negative affect, and severe stress – conditions that undermine self-control and induce a stronger focus on the present. And again, last but not least, people who live in unstable and unpredictable environments have less reason to believe that exerting self-control will actually pay off, which reduces the motivation to exert self-control.

In sum, poor people's relative lack of self-control may – *at least partly* – be caused by financial hardship. If this is true, incentives such as heavy fines or cuts in benefits are not necessarily the most effective way to bring about the more disciplined and future-oriented behavior that could lift them out of poverty. In fact, such incentives may even further undermine their self-control, thus only making matters worse.

## Responsible Conduct

Do these findings form psychological research mean that people who land in trouble due to failures of self-control are the innocent victims of forces beyond their power? Can someone rightfully claim that her bad genes kept her from making a living and getting ahead? That his harsh and unresponsive parents are responsible for his inability to meet his social duties and obligations? That she should not be blamed for taking the items without paying because she was suffering a severe case of ego depletion? Questions such as these come up every time a new potential cause of undesirable behavior is discovered. Poor self-control capacity is only the latest addition to an ever-growing list of potentially excusing or exempting conditions that have been proposed over the ages, ranging from "rotten social background" to "post-traumatic stress disorder."

How should we respond to this proliferation of excusing or exempting conditions? If we only reason from the objective standpoint, we seem to have no choice but to bite the bullet and accept that, indeed, moral responsibility cannot exist, since everything people do is determined, the inevitable result of a long chain of cause and effect set in motion even before we were born. We simply could not have done otherwise.

As I argued in Chapter 8, however, this is not my position. In any discussion of the implications of scientific findings *for society and policy* we must also engage the subjective and the instrumental standpoints. Once these enter the equation, we can start pushing back against the complete dissolution of moral responsibility. I will not repeat the whole argument here, but restrict myself to the main conclusions:

- By default, all adult persons must be assumed to be autonomous agents who may be held (fully) responsible for their conduct. By implication, it must be assumed that, by default, all adult persons have sufficient capacity for exerting self-control, and therefore cannot claim to be merely the "innocent victims" of their circumstances.
- In specific instances, though, there may be good reasons to suspend this rule and (partially) excuse or exempt individuals from responsibility. Insufficient self-control capacity may be one of these. Whether such good reasons exist or not can only be determined on a case-by-case basis. The decision whether individuals should be (partially) excused or exempted must be informed by the relevant considerations from all three standpoints: the objective, the subjective, *and* the instrumental standpoints.
- The more often excuses or exemptions are in order, the more reason there is to reconsider and revise the above rules. It may be necessary to redefine which categories of people are, by default, considered autonomous agents who may be held (fully) responsible for their conduct. Again, the decision whether the rules should be revised must be informed by the relevant considerations from all three standpoints.

These three rules provide guidance on all matters of moral responsibility. They set the terms of debate, tell us where the burden of proof lies, and affirm the importance of considering all three standpoints. But importantly, these rules do not provide closure. They do not purport to settle all potential cases, but acknowledge their own limitations, and offer a criterion for their own revision. This lack of closure is inevitable, as it logically follows from the fundamentally broken character of the ideas and beliefs that underlie all rules for assessing (moral) responsibility. Given this brokenness, all rules have the character of heuristics: They – hopefully – work in most cases, but no matter how fine-grained or sophisticated, inevitably they sometimes get it wrong or simply fall silent.

Some observers may lament this less-than-perfect "regulatory condition." I have argued, however, that this condition is to be preferred. It is precisely this lack of closure that prompts us to stay alert. It more or less guarantees that in individual cases the specifics of the situation are taken into account, and that, as exceptions accumulate, the question will be raised whether the rules are in need of revision. As so often is the case, the perfect is the enemy of the good. We do not want "perfect equilibrium," because that would entail the end of all responsiveness to changes in outside reality, such as new or unforeseen circumstances, new scientific developments and insights, or shifts in moral beliefs and intuitions. Only dead organisms are in perfect equilibrium. We are better off with a situation of "dynamic equilibrium."

This set of rules does not only offer guidance on all things moral but also speaks to issues that fall under the heading of distributive justice. To be sure, it is impossible to accurately assess to what extent people are "responsible" for their overall life situation. Any attempt to establish a pattern of distribution that accurately reflects differences in "aggregate deservingness" is doomed to run aground in the epistemological impossibility of unraveling the complicated patchwork of choices and circumstances that brought about one's life situation. Therefore, all proposals to distinguish between the "deserving" and "the undeserving poor" (or rich) remain dubious.[12] Nevertheless, this set of rules may be useful for the more mundane practice of benefits provision. Since the 1970s, this practice has gradually been "moralized." Whether one is entitled to financial support – say unemployment benefits or welfare – has been made contingent on responsible behavior. It no longer suffices to meet general criteria, for example regarding citizenship status or employment history. One must also meet certain behavioral requirements. In these administrative matters, it seems logical to adopt the rule that, as with judgments on moral responsibility, by default, recipients may be held responsible for the extent to which they meet these behavioral requirements, but that in specific instances there may be good reasons to suspend this rule. Sometimes people truly are the innocent victims of circumstances beyond their control.

## Epieikeia

The crucial question then becomes what exactly the "specific instances" are that should prompt us to suspend the default position. In what situations or circumstances is a (partial) excuse or exemption of responsibility in order?

Ultimately, this is matter of good judgment – that elusive mental activity Arendt likened to a "tasting" of external reality. But whose good judgment? Who is to make the call? With regard to the *making* of laws and regulations, it is politicians at the top who have to judge and decide. That is their job. With regard to the *carrying out* of laws and regulations, however, it is the people on the ground who have to judge and decide, because the question whether an excuse or exemption is in order can only be determined on a case-by-case basis. That is the job of public officials such as judges, social security employees, and other "street level bureaucrats".[13] When laws and regulations are well crafted, this task should not be too difficult. Then the majority of cases can be decided by simple application of the rules.[14] In essence, this could be left to a computer. But not all cases can be settled in this way. As I argued in Chapter 8, the world is always more complex and varied than even the best decision rules can encompass. All laws and regulations thus have the character of heuristics, rules that will – hopefully – yield satisfactory results in the bulk of cases, but sometimes get it wrong. There will always be cases where simply following the rules "just does not feel right," and deviating from the rules may be in order. In such cases, we have no choice but to rely on the good judgment of street-level officials.

I suspect this answer will not satisfy everyone, as it leaves part of reality unregulated – and not just any part, but precisely the part where the "hard cases" are and clear guidelines are most in need. It is precisely here that we are faced with a hole in the regulatory fabric, to

be filled by whomever happens to be in charge. Is this really the best
we can do?

Well, actually the answer is yes. According to none other than
Aristotle, this is indeed the best we can do. In a famous passage on
"equity" (*epieikeia*), he wrote that

all law is general, but concerning some matters it is not possible to speak
correctly in a general way. In those cases, then, in which it is necessary to
speak generally, but it is not possible to do so correctly, the law takes what
is for the most part the case, but without being ignorant of the error in so
doing. And the law is no less correct for all that: the error resides not in the
law or in the lawgiver but in the nature of the matter at hand. For such is
simply the stuff of which actions are made. Whenever the law speaks generally, then, but what happens in a given case constitutes an exception to
the general rule, then it is correct, where the lawgiver omits something and
erred by speaking unqualifiedly, to rectify that omission with what the lawgiver himself would have said if he had been present and, if he had known
of this case, what he would have legislated.[15]

Aristotle considered this form of "equity" – the prudential correction
of the law in specific cases – as the highest form of justice.[16] This
implies that the occasional need to switch from default to exception is
not merely the regrettable consequence of our limited understanding
of the world and the inevitably heuristic character of all positive law,
but an expression of our deepest intuitions on what is fair and right.

If we wish to create sufficient scope for this form of justice in our
present time, a twofold strategy is needed. First, public officials must
be given sufficient discretionary powers to follow their own judgment
on what is fair and just. Within limits, they must have the leeway to
decide "hard cases" on their merits. Of course, this does not mean that
anything goes. The risk of flimsy or biased decisions must be mini-
mized. This highest form of justice calls for *good* judgment on whether
to follow the default or to grant an exception, based on sound reasons.
Aristotle gave clear guidelines: Those who have to make the final call
should decide as "the lawgiver" himself would have done, had he been
present and known the case. One might say that street-level officials
must engage in "reverse political representation" – in their handling of
the case, they must act as the representatives of the lawgiver. Second,
it is important to invest in the "conditions of possibility" for good
judgment by public officials, for instance by developing their "feel"
for the moral intuitions and considerations underlying the laws and

regulations they have to carry out, by providing them with sufficient time and resources to gather all relevant data on specific cases, and by rewarding them for demonstrations of good judgment. It may also be advisable to set professional standards, and to facilitate and encourage reflection and intervision, thereby fostering the development of so-called professional learning communities.[17]

In conclusion, it may be argued that in times of strict budget constraints and ever-increasing computing power, all decisions that can be left to algorithms should be left to algorithms. For standard cases, that seems a viable option. But *epieikeia* cannot be outsourced to a machine. We will always need humans to make the final call, and to decide whether *in this particular case* the conclusion is justified that the person in question, due to circumstances beyond her control, lacked the necessary self-control capacity, and therefore was not so much *unwilling* as *unable* to do the right thing.

## 10.3 Five Potential Strategies for Closing Self-Control Gaps

Chapter 7 discussed Max Weber's famous essay on the Protestant ethic and the spirit of capitalism. On the last pages of his essay, Weber argued that with the advent of modern society, the Protestant foundations for the ethos of self-control, discipline, and hard work gradually died out. Yet the ethos itself remained very much alive. It became self-sustaining, anchored in the structures and institutions of the capitalist society that had come into being. The powerful cosmos of the modern economic order had become an "iron cage."[18] With this haunting metaphor, Weber was among the first to draw attention to the tendency of man-made structures and institutions to develop into autonomous and self-perpetuating systems that force people into their molds.

Are such "iron cages" a bad thing? Not by definition. No society can exist without structures and institutions that create social order, and inevitably these will set certain limits to individual freedom. To some degree, for rights and liberties to be guaranteed and for society to thrive, we *need* an iron cage. The real issue, I would argue, concerns the *living conditions* within the cage. How well do these conditions enable people to pursue their life projects? And how well do they match human psychology? Problems arise when the imperatives and demands of the cage are no longer commensurate with the personality traits and mental capacities of its inhabitants.

Unfortunately, this is exactly what appears to have happened. More than ever, society is confronted with "self-control gaps": discrepancies between, on the one side, the capacity for self-control that is *presupposed* by institutional arrangements, public policies, and social practices and, on the other side, the capacity for self-control people *actually have*.[19] Of course, for some people the gap is wider than for others, but even true self-control aristocrats may experience periods in life when their willpower falls short. This is not only bad for these individuals themselves but also for society as a whole. More than ever, the world *needs* people who are able to delay gratification. The main question of this section is therefore how we can reduce or even close these self-control gaps. In the following, I discuss five potential strategies.

## Strategy 1: Training and Education

For starters, an obvious strategy seems to be education. If a substantial part of the population has trouble meeting the demands of modern life, then teach them the qualities or skills they need to do better, for instance at school or through adult education. An example of this strategy is the approach advocated by economist James Heckman and the OECD. They emphasize the importance of "non-cognitive skills" – a broad category that, in their definition, includes not only self-control but also conscientiousness, attentiveness, empathy, self-efficacy, resilience, perseverance, and so on.[20] According to Heckman and the OECD, early childhood education and schools could play a prominent role in helping children master these skills. Importantly, the OECD authors insist on speaking of noncognitive *skills* rather than *personality traits*. They wish to avoid the term "trait" because, so they argue, this word suggests a sense of permanence and possibly also heritability, whereas the term "skill" suggests that these attributes can be learned. "The distinction between skills and traits is not just a matter of semantics. It suggests new and productive avenues for public policy".[21]

What are the chances of this first strategy succeeding? The research discussed in Chapter 4 suggests that we should not raise our hopes too high. Exercising our self-control "muscles" seems to have modest effects at best, whereas teaching self-control techniques will probably work only for those who already have a modicum of self-control. Moreover, there is always the problem of Matthew effects. Programs open to all often turn out to be most beneficial for those who were already doing well, thus only increasing the gap between the bottom and the top. In sum, maybe someday in the future science will discover a successful treatment or simple drug to "cure" poor self-control. But until that day has come, improving trait self-control will remain difficult.

In this respect, it should be noted that the terminology in the OECD report is somewhat misleading. It may be true that framing the desired qualities as "skills" rather than "traits" opens up more space for public policies, but the suggestion of permanence and heritability the OECD seeks to avoid is more than just a suggestion. For many personality traits – including trait self-control – it is an *empirical fact*.[22] Although these traits are relatively malleable during the first years of life, and although in later years they are not set in stone either but keep slowly evolving, the suggestion that these are "skills" that can be easily shaped or changed is simply false – and may be a recipe for frustration and disappointment.[23] For those already poor in talent, this may become yet another area in which they fail. And to add insult to injury, framing self-control as a "skill" may fuel the belief that these individuals only have themselves to blame for their failure. They just should have tried harder.

## Strategy 2: Nudging

A second strategy is nudging, the novel technique we met in Chapter 4. Nudging seeks to counteract problems that stem from limited rationality or limited willpower by altering the choice architecture. One of the best-known examples is enrollment in 401(k) pension plans. In the United States, switching the default from "opt in" to "opt out" has vastly increased the number of employees participating in these schemes. Other nudges have targeted unhealthy lifestyle behaviors, for instance by making portions smaller or by placing fatty snacks at the back of the school cafeteria.

Nudging has been welcomed with lots of enthusiasm but has also met fierce criticism.[24] Objections have been raised against, inter alia, the paternalistic character of nudges, their (allegedly) manipulative nature, and their (allegedly) negative influence on people's choice-making abilities. Other criticisms do not concern the technique itself, but its role and function within the broader context. Both nudging and the strategy of education mentioned aim to fix problems associated with the current institutional and social order *while leaving its foundations intact*. The geographer Mark Whitehead and colleagues have coined the term "neuroliberalism" to describe this approach. Neuroliberalism refers to "the use of behavioral, psychological and neurological insights to deliberately shape and govern human conduct within free societies"[25] and thus "support the market-based orthodoxies of neoliberal government".[26]

What should we make of this? A lot can (and has) been said about these normative issues, but I wish to focus on a practical issue instead: Nudging will only solve a *fraction* of the problems that stem from poor self-control. First, certainly not all nudges have been proven effective. At the time of writing, only a few reviews and meta-analyses of the effectiveness of nudges have been published, but these suggest that nudging is not the miracle cure that some believed or hoped it to be. In general, prospects seem fairly good for nudges that go *with* the grain of one's habitual beliefs, feelings, or behaviors, but less good for nudges that go *against* the grain, especially when it concerns frequent behaviors. Second, many choice situations in which people with poor self-control could surely use a helping hand are not embedded in a tangible choice architecture amenable to manipulation. Life is an endless string of self-control challenges that simply spring from the ongoing flow of events. People must get up from the couch, do their best at school or work, behave correctly toward significant others, ranging from superiors to customers to their spouses, and so on and on. It is hard to see how nudging could be of any help here.

### Strategy 3: Make People Try Harder

So neither training and education nor nudging will do the trick. What other approaches are there? Perhaps we should start at the other end of the gap and see if we can change society for the better. Perhaps we could modify institutional arrangements, social practices, and public policies in such a way that the distance is reduced between the level of self-control people are willing and able to muster, and the level of self-control demanded by these arrangements, practices, and policies.

This leads to a third potential strategy. People could be encouraged to invest a greater share of their limited mental resources in meeting the various self-control challenges that cross their paths. As discussed in Chapter 3, experiments have found that if the rewards are increased, participants are both willing and able to maintain self-control for a longer time. Apparently, the limits to self-control are not that strict. When needed, people have an "energy reserve" they can call upon. So perhaps the solution is to tap into these reserves – to unleash these dormant energies, as it were – and direct them to the exertion of self-control. The most logical way to achieve this would be to make successful self-control more rewarding and poor self-control more costly, for example through financial incentives, or through naming and shaming of those who make a mess of things. In short, we can narrow self-control gaps by motivating people to try harder.

However, there are two reasons to be skeptical about this strategy. First, it might work well for those who have plenty of mental reserves left, but it will only make matters worse for those who have already used up their reserves. The larger the second group is, the greater the risk that the aggregate outcome of this strategy will be negative, and the greater the risk that well-meaning people who are already trying as hard as they can will get punished too. Second, lack of "energy" is not the only potential cause of self-control failure. Other potential causes are negative affect, cognitive load, sleep deprivation, and too much stress. It is unclear how raising the stakes would help to counter failures that stem from these other causes. In fact, to the extent that this strategy induces stress, it could make keeping self-control only harder. Basically, this strategy is a doubling down on the policies that were introduced since the 1970s, and which have, at least for part of the population, only widened self-control gaps.

## Strategy 4: A Less Exhausting and More Needs-Oriented Society

A fourth strategy is, in a sense, the mirror image of the third one, as it seeks to *enlarge* the reservoir of mental resources people have for exerting self-control, rather than forcing them to eat into their precious reserves. If sleep deprivation, stress, and the frequent exertion of self-control reduce self-control capacity, we could attempt to change society in such a way that the likelihood of experiencing these harmful conditions is decreased. People would be better able to exercise self-control in a world that does not force them to cut back on their sleep and take two jobs, is not full of stress-generating conditions such as income insecurity, and is not saturated with self-control challenges, such as fast-food outlets on every street corner. And if satisfying basic psychological needs produces mental "energy," we could attempt to modify society in such a way that the likelihood of need satisfaction is increased. This would mean more jobs that are interesting and challenging, and that match people's talents and skills, while leaving them enough time for family, friends, and leisure.

This strategy sounds more appealing than the previous one. Rather than further tightening the screws, the idea is to increase the chances for successful self-control by making life less exhausting and more psychologically rewarding. What would this mean for public policy? Should governments actively promote such social changes? In societies where pressures are high and opportunities for satisfying needs are few, this argument could well be made. After all, it is standard policy to stimulate the *motivation* for self-control by installing the right incentives. Then why not also try to enhance the *capacity* for self-control? Many governments promote population health by improving the *physical* environment, for example by reducing air pollution and securing clean water. Creating more easygoing and needs-satisfying social circumstances could be considered a form of fighting toxic *mental* environments.

But granted, given the current state of affairs, this strategy also sounds rather utopian. This more easygoing and needs-satisfying society is not going to arrive anytime soon. It is better to regard this vision not as a concrete objective that actually can and must be realized, but as a regulatory ideal, a benchmark that can guide policymaking by showing which direction to go. For example, given the harmful effects of sleep deprivation and given the favorable effects of social relatedness, it is undesirable if wages are so low that people are forced to work multiple jobs. Given the depleting effects of exercising self-control for extended periods of time, it may be desirable to set certain limits to the freedom of businesses to lure people into behaviors that pose serious risks to their health or finances. Given the detrimental effects of stress and the vitalizing power of experiencing autonomy and competence, it might be wise to combat the proliferation of temporary and mind-numbing jobs, and to invest in "decent jobs" that are psychologically rewarding. But as said, this vision remains a regulatory ideal. It is improbable that it will be realized in the foreseeable future.

## Strategy 5: Making Life Less Demanding

Which brings me to the final strategy: Change society in such a way that having good self-control becomes less critical for navigating life. This approach is well accepted for many other abilities. Most citizens are incapable of understanding official government documents, but rather than insisting that these people overcome their "poor" reading and comprehension skills, government agencies typically provide clear and simple versions of these documents. Some people are in wheelchairs. But rather than setting up "interventions" to enhance their "walking capacity," it is common to adjust the physical environment, for example by removing doorsteps and adding wheelchair ramps and elevators in public buildings. In short, it is anything but unusual to attune regulations, institutions, and social practices to people's limited capabilities.

How could life be made easier for people with less than stellar self-control? The most logical solution would be to reduce the number of choices they have to confront, and minimize the presence of harmful temptations and distractions in their surroundings. In the realm of consumption this could translate into reduced availability of unhealthy foods and risky financial products, a curb on advertising for harmful products, a restriction on buying on credit, required cooling-off periods, and so forth. Maybe some products should be banned altogether. In the realm of education and work, this approach could translate into educational tracks and jobs that require less self-regulation. That would entail clear tasks, goals, and schedules, intensive coaching and supervision, plenty of short-term rewards, and a big stick to keep everyone on course. For labor and income in general, it could mean government regulations to strengthen job security, income protection for those who have paid work, and less conditionality in welfare provisions and other forms of social support.

But again, we are mostly talking about theoretical possibilities. Restrictions on the consumer market may be acceptable for some products such as tobacco and alcohol, but these comprise only a fraction of the choices, temptations, and distractions people have to deal with every day. If we truly wish to protect people from the risks of self-control failure, much further-reaching restrictions are needed, restrictions that would seriously limit opportunities for businesses, the food industry, the financial services industry – in short, all those actors who present people with choices that may impact their fortunes. Free enterprise would become virtually impossible. In the domain of education and work, things are hardly less complicated. While governments may have some leverage in how education is organized, workplaces are generally beyond their reach. The state cannot command employers to organize work in accordance with the latest insights from behavioral science. Governments have more leeway with regard to labor conditions and income protection, and they also have the formal authority to end conditionality in entitlements. It is unclear, however, whether doing so would be wise in the highly competitive global economy of the twenty-first century.

Essentially, this fifth strategy is an attempt to offset the effects of history. As I argued in Chapter 7, the ever-growing importance of self-control is ultimately driven by long-term social, economic, cultural, and technological developments. It is difficult to see how in a free society the consequences of these trends can be undone. Moreover, there is a fundamental issue at stake. Making life less demanding through strict regulations and severe restrictions may benefit people with poor self-control, but the price for this would be paid by their fellow citizens who are better capable of dealing with the many self-control challenges of modern life, who may even relish all the wonderful choices and freedoms today's world has on offer. They will be robbed of opportunities for choice *as well*. This fifth strategy is a form of leveling down. Life is made simpler by reducing choice and freedom to a level that even the least self-controlled can handle. For many people, this is not a utopian but an utterly *dystopian* vision, reminiscent of some of the worst excesses in human history.

Once again, the conclusion is that expectations should be tempered. Maybe we could smooth off some of the rougher edges in the handful of cases where the protection of people's enlightened self-interest is deemed more important than freedom of choice and unfettered markets. Drug use or predatory lending might be examples. But exceptions are few. The bulk of self-control challenges are intrinsic to life in general and advanced liberalism in particular. Any serious effort to make life easier for people with poor self-control may harm the interests of people with better self-control.

## 10.4 Getting Real?!

So what now? I have discussed five potential strategies for narrowing self-control gaps, but none of them qualifies as the proverbial silver bullet. To be clear, this is not an excuse for doing nothing. It is important to further explore the potential of each strategy, and where quick and easy fixes are available for remedying or neutralizing the consequences of poor self-control, we should not hesitate to use them. But the upshot is that we should not raise our hopes too high. The prospects for eliminating self-control gaps are just not very bright.

This leads to an alternative and rather different response to the problem of self-control gaps. It could be argued that we simply have to accept the inevitable: *There is no real solution*. After all is said and done, the fact remains that self-control is limited, and after all is said and done, the fact remains that some people have more self-control than others. Nothing will ever change this state of affairs. Therefore, some people will have better chances at realizing their hopes and dreams than others but – so the argument goes – that is something we must accept. It is the same as with that other important quality: intelligence. Some of us are smarter than others, and therefore have better life chances than others, but that is just the way things are. Or take physical attractiveness. Some people are better looking than others, and research unambiguously shows that attractive people have better prospects for health, wealth, and happiness than less attractive people, but – again – that is just the way things are. So it is with self-control. Whether we like it or not, the undeniable fact is that some are endowed with more talent for self-control than others, and therefore have better life chances than others. But hey, nobody ever said that life was fair!

Not everyone will feel comfortable with this "realistic turn" (and to be honest, I am one of those people). This line of reasoning seems rather harsh on the less fortunate. Basically, the message to them is that they simply lost in the natural lottery and should accept their sorry fate. Too bad, but we cannot return to the simpler world of bygone days. That would require a drastic curtailment of choice and freedoms that – if at all possible – is a price we are just not willing to pay. And it seems, conversely, rather lenient on the fortunate. Basically, the message to them is that they should not lose too much sleep over the inequalities and misfortunes that stem from some of their fellow citizens' poor self-control, since there is nothing they can do about it anyway. Science confirms that you cannot change deeply ingrained personality traits.

But there is an upside to this "realistic turn" that might soften the pain. If people wish to adopt this realistic stance, they must be consistent and be realistic across the board. More to the point: If they agree that differences in and limits to self-control are an inevitable fact of life that cannot easily be fixed through intervention, they must also agree that people who are struggling in life not do necessarily only have themselves to blame. You cannot have it both ways. You cannot maintain that with regard to the distribution of *resources* some people are just luckier than others, and at the same time maintain that with regard to the distribution of *outcomes* life is fair and everyone gets exactly what they deserve. In other words, insisting that differences in self-control are an inevitable fact of life, and therefore some people have more luck than others, ought to have consequences for moral judgment.

## A Plea for Paradigm Relaxation

This brings me to my own view on the question "what is to be done." As I said at the outset of this chapter, this book lacks the optimistic "can do" spirit that animates so many other books on new behavioral scientific insights, and is sparse on practical solutions to make the world a better place. This book ends more in a "can't do" spirit.

Why this emphasis on what can*not* be achieved? What is to be gained with such a gloomy message? My reason for emphasizing what can*not* be achieved is that too much optimism about the viability and effectiveness of strategies or interventions to close self-control gaps may keep us from facing up to some deeper issues. So long we believe that interventions such as nudging or self-control training will work, we can comfort ourselves in the reassuring thought that problems emanating from poor self-control can be fixed. All we need to do is figure out the right mechanisms and techniques, and then we can simply "social engineer" our way out. Once again, to avoid any misunderstanding, it is definitively important to further explore the potential of these interventions, and to see under what conditions and to what extent they are effective. But we should acknowledge that, given everything psychology has learned about the limited nature of self-control, these interventions are not going to solve all problems. They will *mitigate* them at best. We must face up to the very real possibility that society has simply become too difficult and demanding for substantial parts of the population. And if that state of affairs is deemed unacceptable, a few nudges here and a couple of regulatory tweaks there are not going to be enough. A more fundamental change of direction is needed.

I think the time is ripe for the somewhat sobering message of this book. As discussed in Chapter 7, the increasing importance of good self-control is partly the result of autonomous developments. The past centuries have witnessed an enormous population growth, and due to economic and technological transformations, people have become ever more interdependent in ever-denser networks. It is hard to see how those developments could be reversed. But the increasing importance of good self-control is also the result of deliberate policies. Before the 1970s, much of what went wrong in people's lives was interpreted as the result of factors beyond their control, which was reflected in public policies. By today's standards, expectations regarding people's capacities and obligations were rather low – perhaps too low – thus inviting irresponsible behavior and moral hazard. Since then, the pendulum has swung the other way. In our present time, much of what goes wrong in people's life is interpreted as the result of imprudent behavior or lack of effort, and policies have been adjusted accordingly. In today's advanced liberal democracies, all citizens are expected to adopt the attitude of the responsibilized, competitive entrepreneur, actively calculating their future and providing for their own (financial) security and that of their families.

But perhaps we have gone too far in the other direction. Many people, at least part of the time, lack the capacities required to meet the ever-rising standards. Simply pushing them to try harder may have little effect or even be counterproductive, as they have already hit the limits of their capabilities. Perhaps the time has come to reconsider some current policies. We do not need a complete paradigm *shift* – this is no plea for a return to the situation as it existed before the 1970s – but there is certainly a case to be made for a paradigm *relaxation*. Would it not be a good idea to set certain limits to the freedom of businesses to exploit people's less-than-perfect self-control and lure them into behaviors that pose serious risks to their future health or finances? Should we not strive toward a little more income security and a little less conditionality in benefits and entitlements? Policy measures like these would be a blessing to people who have the bad fortune of being endowed with little talent for self-control.

Of course, mistakes will be made. If demands are lowered and regulations are relaxed, people will sometimes be wrongly let off the hook. But mistakes are inevitable. Every rule and regulation is merely a heuristic that will – hopefully – work in the bulk of cases, but sometimes gets it wrong. The crucial question is *which* mistake you would rather make. Would you, as a citizen or a policymaker, rather run the risk that every now and then someone who is able but unwilling to exert self-control gets away with irresponsible behavior and gets more than she deserves? Or would you rather run the risk that every now and then someone who is willing but unable to exert self-control is punished for her incapacity to do what is right and gets less than she deserves? It would be naïve to assume that everyone who ever fails at self-control is the innocent victim of circumstances beyond their control. That is not a useful fiction. But it would be cynical to assume the opposite, and believe that everyone who seems to fail at self-control actually fails at nothing and is simply revealing her true preferences. That is not a useful fiction either. At the end of the day, both extreme positions will undermine the social contract that lies at the heart of the political community.

### Toward a Better World After All

A society that displays a reasonable degree of moral and institutional tolerance toward the self-control failures to which all of us can fall prey may well be a more pleasant place to live than the overly demanding society that has developed in many corners of the world. No one is perfectly self-controlled, and many people do not even come close to this ideal. We should therefore be careful in blaming or stigmatizing everyone who does not always measure up to the self-control demands of modern life. We all have an obligation to take responsibility for our lives and do our very best, but we are also entitled to recognition for who we really are, including our all too human imperfections.

In fact, the argument can be taken further. A society that somewhat loosens the reins may not only be more pleasant to live in but also more productive. The relationship between self-control demands on the one hand, and desirable outcomes such as health and productivity on the other, will often have the shape of an inverted U. This pattern is very common in stress research, and has also been observed in other domains of life, such as sports and education.[27] Therefore, the optimum level of self-control demands will not be at the extremes, but closer to the middle – at a level ambitious enough to challenge people to try hard, maybe to exceed their own and others' expectations, but not so overly ambitious that, except for the minority of true self-control aristocrats, failure is almost guaranteed. In other words, *less may be more*. Less pressure may yield more health, happiness, and productivity. Accepting the reality of the limits to self-control may, perhaps unexpectedly, prove to be a next logical step in the journey toward a better world.

# Notes

## 1 Introduction

1 Ronson (2015).
2 Hofmann et al. (2012).
3 De Ridder et al. (2012: 77). There are, of course, other definitions. Fujita notes that "[a] common notion shared by many psychological conceptualizations of self-control is that self-control entails the *effortful inhibition of temptation impulses*" (Fujita 2011: 32, emphasis added). Recently, Fujita and several other social psychologists proposed to define self-control more broadly. Milyavskaya et al. (2019: 80), for instance, define self-control as "the process or behavior of overcoming a temptation or prepotent response in favor of a competing goal (either concurrent or longer-term)." In this broader conceptualization, effortful inhibition ("Just say no!") is not the defining core of self-control, but only one of many possible strategies for exercising self-control. Another strategy might be to avoid temptation in the first place, say, by not going to the store when hungry or by blocking one's phone for a predetermined period. In this book, however, I stick to the "narrow" definition given in the main text, as this is more in line with the tradition in self-control research over the past decades. See also note 8 of Chapter 4.
4 The latter distinction comes from Arneson (1997). In the psychological literature, this gap is often called the intention–behavior gap. While poor self-control is one of the factors behind this gap, the literature identifies other potentially relevant factors, for example beliefs about self-efficacy and goal difficulty (for a concise review see Sheeran and Webb [2016]).
5 Cited in Mele (1995: 4).
6 Here I roughly follow Holton (2009), Mele (2010), and May and Holton (2012) – recent contributions to the age-old debate on *akrasia* and weakness of will (see also Section 4 in Chapter 3). Their main question is whether "weakness of will" should be understood as acting contrary to one's best *judgment* (and thereby synonymous with *akrasia*) or as overreadily revising one's *intentions or resolutions* (and thus something else). As I write these lines, a consensus seems to have emerged – at least in the eyes of ordinary people – that weakness of will can refer

264

to both: violating one's better judgment and violating one's intentions. Also, we should not overstate the difference between these two. What both mental states have in common is that they entail (the violation of) a practical commitment to some future course of action.

7  Mele (1995: 121–122) talks of an "ideally self-controlled person" rather than a "perfectly self-controlled person." I prefer the latter due to the parallel with the more familiar "perfectly rational person."

8  See http://induecourse.ca/what-do-libertarians-and-pedophiles-have-in-common/, retrieved June 22, 2021.

9  Rank (2004).

10  Some behavioral scientists have added to the confusion by treating the preference for delayed reward as an indicator for self-control. Others have suggested conceptualizing self-control not so much as a capacity but as a set of behavioral strategies for goal achievement (Fujita 2011, see also note 3 of this chapter). Last but not least, philosophers have their own take on things. Beginning with Aristotle, they seem to have a broader understanding of self-control, one more grounded in overall conduct and character and thus – implicitly or explicitly – encompassing both capacity and motivation. Alfred Mele, for instance, defines "self-controlled individuals [as] agents possessed both of significant motivation to conduct themselves as they judge best and a robust capacity to do what it takes so to conduct themselves in the face of (actual or anticipated) competing motivation" (Mele 1995: 5).

11  Smart (1961/1973).

12  Several reputable scholars have argued that such a thing is very well possible, or even preferable. I discuss their position in Chapter 8.

13  Block (1995).

14  A concept that has gained some popularity in recent years is "grit." Although there is certainly conceptual and empirical overlap between self-control and grit, in the latter the emphasis lies on perseverance in the pursuit of long-term goals. "Grit is the tendency to pursue a singular, challenging goal over extremely long stretches of time, doing so despite inevitable obstacles, setbacks, and long plateaus during which progress may not be obvious" (Eskries-Winkler et al. 2016: 389).

15  But see also note 3 of this chapter and note 8 of Chapter 4.

16  Henrich (2020).

## 2  A Gift for Life

1  Mischel et al. (1988); Shoda et al. (1990). In a recent study, Watts et al. (2018) sought to (conceptually) replicate the findings of the classic marshmallow studies. Their sample consisted of 918 children, including

552 children of mothers who had not completed college – a sample about 10 times as large as the sample of the original Mischel and Shoda study, and much more diverse. Watts and colleagues analyzed to what extent a marshmallow test administered at age four predicted socioemotional behaviors and academic achievement at age fifteen. In contrast to Mischel and Shoda, they found no correlation between waiting time at age four and later behavior. They *did* find a correlation between waiting time at age four and academic achievement at age fifteen, but the correlations were much smaller, and even shrunk to nonsignificant levels after controlling for cognitive abilities and mothers' reports of internalizing and externalizing behaviors at age four.

Is this an example of yet another classic psychological finding proving to be a fluke, the latest victim in the replication crisis haunting social psychology? That was indeed the story in some news media (see, for example, *The Guardian*, "Famed impulse control 'marshmallow test' fails in new research," June 1, 2018). But this sobering conclusion is wrong, as critics of the Watts et al. study have convincingly argued (Doebel et al. 2020; Falk et al. 2020). On the one hand, it is true that Watts found no significant correlation between waiting time at age four and socioemotional behaviors at age fifteen. However, this may be explained by their use of different indicators for behavior at age fifteen than were used in the original study. Therefore, the absence of this correlation "does not necessarily contradict Shoda et al.'s findings" (Falk et al. 2020: 102). On the other hand – and perhaps more importantly – Watts *did* find significant correlations between waiting time at age four and academic achievement at age fifteen, *even after controlling* for sociodemographic variables such as socioeconomic status, and for aspects of the home environment known to affect cognitive, emotional, and behavioral functioning. Granted, these correlations were considerably smaller than those in the original study, but this is not unusual when larger samples are used. Moreover, as Falk and colleagues argue, these correlations may be downward biased, as the maximum waiting time in the Watts study was seven rather than fifteen minutes.

It was only after adding *a second set of control variables*, indexing cognitive ability and potential problem behaviors at age four, that waiting time was no longer significantly correlated with later academic outcomes. However, as both Doebel and Falk point out, adding this second set of control variables is questionable given the potential overlap between delay of gratification and the behavioral aspects that were controlled for, and given the possibility that the ability to resist the marshmallow is partly dependent on cognitive ability. These variables, they argue, should not have been included as confounds. When Falk and colleagues reanalyzed Watts' data and *only* controlled for exogenous and predetermined variables such as race and socioeconomic status, they found significant correlations that were much closer to the ones in the Mischel and Shoda study.

Last but not least, there is another point that is highly relevant for our purposes, but only briefly mentioned in the Watts paper: the study found that an indicator for self-control at age four *based on parent and teacher reports* actually *did* predict academic achievement *and* socioemotional behavior at age fifteen (see Watts et al. 2018: table S4). This is fully in line with the findings from other longitudinal studies, notably Moffitt et al. (2011).

All in all, the most likely conclusion is that: 1) childhood self-control is indeed a significant predictor of later life outcomes, but 2) the marshmallow test is probably not the best instrument currently on the market for measuring this capacity, as it also seems to tap into cognitive abilities (see also Duckworth et al. 2013).

2  Tangney et al. (2004: 315).

3  From Tangney et al. (2004). Items 2, 3, 4, 5, 7, 9, 10, 12, 13 are reverse coded.

4  School achievement was measured in various ways. Duckworth and Seligman included report card grades, a standardized achievement test, school attendance, and selection for a competitive high school program. Duckworth and Seligman studied two cohorts of eighth graders. The second cohort also took an intelligence test and answered questions about their study and lifestyle habits (e.g. "What time do you usually start with your homework?").

5  In the first cohort, this was a hypothetical delayed gratification test, assessed through a questionnaire. In the second cohort, a real-life delayed gratification test was also included.

6  Duckworth and Seligman (2005: 944).

7  In a later round of the same long-running study, Richmond-Rakerd et al. (2021) found that better childhood self-control also predicted the pace of aging at midlife (as measured by nineteen biomarkers) and preparedness for old age (for example in terms of financial security and strong social bonds, as measured through questionnaires and open-ended interviews).

8  Such behavior may even be interpreted as an instance of self-control failure. According to Tangney and colleagues, overcontrolled people "may be said to lack the ability to control their self-control" (Tangney et al. 2004: 314).

9  See also Baumeister and Alquist (2009: 126), who conclude that a high level of trait self-control "seems an unmixed blessing." Studies also consistently find that better self-control is correlated with higher subjective well-being, thus refuting the idea that people with strong self-control

may perhaps succeed in achieving their long-term goals but lead joyless lives devoid of fun and pleasure in the here and now (see Hofmann et al. 2014; Cheung et al. 2014; Wiese et al. 2018).

To be clear, we are talking here about the benefits of self-control for the individual, not for society at large. If people who do harm to others or society – say, criminals or crooked politicians – suffer poor self-control and fail at enacting their heinous plans, that is to our benefit. When talking about such malignant actors, there may indeed be such a thing as "too much self-control." These cases are sometimes referred to as "Huckleberry Finn cases." Huckleberry Finn intended to turn in Jim, a fugitive slave, but in the end failed to act on this intention. Through this self-control failure, he brought about what – by today's moral standards – is considered the better outcome.

10 The psychological literature sometimes refers to this pattern of behavior as "John Henryism," after the legend of John Henry, a nineteenth-century black railroad worker who was said to have defeated a steam-powered drill in a steel-driving contest, only to die of exhaustion afterwards. "John Henryism" refers to a prolonged high-effort coping style, a strong and unwavering determination to succeed accompanied by an uncompromising work ethic, even in the face of great adversity. To some extent, "John Henryism" can be viewed as an extreme form of self-control. Several studies among lower socioeconomic status African Americans, have found that "John Henryism" can have serious health consequences, such as hypertension and heightened risk of developing chronic disease (Bennett et al. 2004; Brody et al. 2018). See also Chapter 3, page xx.

11 See also Caspi et al. (2016), who found that children with low self-control were more likely to become adults posing an (above average) economic burden on society, for example in terms of the number of months they received welfare benefits and the number of night they occupied hospital beds.

12 Devine (1989).

13 Payne (2005: 500).

14 See Payne (2005); Muraven (2008). Both speak of executive functioning rather than self-control.

15 T. D. Evans et al. (1997). These findings are not confined to the United States. Alexander Vazsonyi and colleagues surveyed 8,000 adolescents in Hungary, Switzerland, the Netherlands, and the United States. In each country, they found a clear and consistent correlation between self-control and deviant behavior, such as vandalism, school misconduct, theft, and assault (Vazsonyi et al. 2001).

16  Wolff et al. (2020); Keinan et al. (2021); Kukowski et al. (2021); Tu et al. (2021); Xu and Cheng (2021).

17  Only one factor proved to be an even stronger predictor: COVID-19 moral disengagement, that is, the extent to which one feels morally obligated to adhere to the rules. However, this was a concurrent factor assessed during the interview.

18  Martarelli et al. (2021).

19  Kokkoris and Stavrova (2020).

20  Li et al. (2020); Schnell and Krampe (2020).

21  Pratt and Cullen (2000: 951/952). A more recent meta-analysis by Vazsonyi and colleagues confirms this finding. Based on nearly 100 new studies published since the Pratt and Cullen review, it finds "a strong link between low self-control and deviance or crime" (Vazsonyi et al. 2017: 59). See also Wright et al. (1999).

22  Polderman et al. (2015) conducted an extensive meta-analysis of twins research. Based on 2,748 studies from the period 1958 to 2012 that report a total of 17,804 characteristics for a total of 14,558,903 twin pairs, they conclude that "all human traits are heritable." (This is a not a new insight, though. Three decades ago, Turkheimer and Gottesman (1991) called this the "First Law of Behavioral Genetics"). The average contribution of heredity and environment was found to be almost the same: 49 percent and 51 percent, respectively.

23  Willems et al. (2019).

24  That genetic and environmental factors are *analytically* separated in heritability research, does not mean they are also *empirically* separate. There is substantial interplay between genetic and environmental factors. This is commonly described as gene–environment correlation: people select, modify, or create experiences and situations that fit with their genetic propensities. Someone with a genetic propensity for high self-control, for instance, will probably seek out or evoke different situations and experiences than someone with low self-control – which may then affect the (further) development of their self-control. Quantifying gene–environmental interplay, however, is complex as it entails longitudinal datasets that include both genetic and environmental measures. For a recent attempt regarding self-control, see Willems et al. (2020).

25  Bouchard (2013); Polderman et al. (2015); Vukasovic and Bratko (2015); Knopik et al. (2017); Maranges and Reynolds (2020). Almost all studies in the Willems and colleagues' meta-analysis are among children and adolescents. As yet, little is known about the heritability of self-control among (older) adults. However, it may be that, just as with intelligence, heritability of self-control among (older) adults is even higher than for children or

adolescents. As people get older, they usually become more independent, and their behavior will usually be less affected by the contingencies of their (childhood or adolescent) environment, and hence more reflective of their "true self" in terms of genetic endowment.

26  This section is based on Blair (2010); Shonkoff et al. (2012); Hamoudi et al. (2015); Murray et al. (2015); and McEwen and McEwen (2017).

27  Duckworth et al. (2013) found that the number of reported negative life events in children or young adolescents was correlated with lower rank order self-control about a year later. Meldrum et al. (2020) found that Michigan adolescents who reported more adverse childhood experiences, scored lower on the Grasmick Low Self-Control Scale. Li et al. (2019: 974) found in a meta-analysis a correlation between parenting and self-control among ten- to twenty-two-year-old adolescents (although they use a somewhat broader definition of self-control, including studies that measure "self-regulation, effortful control, or domain specific forms of control such as impulse regulation.") Both a positive parenting style and a good parent–child relationship were significantly correlated with better adolescent self-control, but only if both were assessed at the same moment in time. Studies with a time lag between the measurement of both variables (varying from one month to many years) found no significant correlation. See also Willems et al. (2018).

28  Shonkoff et al. (2012: 6).

29  Hamoudi et al. (2015).

30  Rothbart (2011: 57).

31  See Rothbart (2011).

32  Roberts et al. (2006).

33  Roberts et al. (2014); Saunders et al. (2018).

34  Somerville et al. (2010). Several studies have also found what might be called a blip in conscientiousness or discipline in early adolescence, for example Soto et al. (2011).

35  Caspi et al. (2003).

36  All people will follow more or less the same trajectory. Therefore, people who had relatively poor self-control as children will probably still have relatively poor self-control when they are grown up because, even though they may have become better at self-control, so have their peers. This is called rank order stability or consistency. Based on a meta-analysis, Roberts and DelVecchio (2000: 20) conclude that "traits are quite consistent over the life course."

37  Readers may object that correlation does not equal causation, and that the correlation between self-control and these individual and social outcomes could be spurious. Regarding the first objection, however, it should be noted that in several of the above studies self-control was

assessed months or even years before the predicted outcomes, so reverse causality can be ruled out. Regarding the second objection, it remains unclear what the hidden underlying third variable causing the spurious correlation might be. It cannot be intelligence as several of the studies discussed controlled for intelligence but nonetheless found significant correlations between self-control and the outcomes of interest. For the same reason, it cannot be socioeconomic status.

The best candidate I can think of would be working memory capacity. As I explain in the coming chapters, working memory capacity is (at least in some definitions of the concept) correlated to intelligence *and* self-control capacity *and* self-control motivation. So is working memory capacity the critical variable? In my view, partly at best. There is certainly a correlation between intelligence, self-control capacity, and self-control motivation, and the connecting element between the three may be working memory capacity, but these three mental realities cannot be entirely reduced to each other. Although they partly overlap, they remain disparate mental realities.

## 3 How Situation Undermines Self-Control

1 Wagner and Heatherton (2014: 623).
2 This paragraph is based on reviews by Baumeister et al. (2007) and Wagner and Heatherton (2015). A logical question would be whether the reverse is also true. Does positive affect increase self-control? This is less clear. Only a few studies have examined the impact of positive mood, with ambiguous results. For instance, one study found that people who feel happy are more inclined to exercise self-control when they are made to think of self-improvement, but not when they are made to think of maintaining a positive mood (Fishbach and Labroo 2007). Another study found that positive mood facilitates resistance to tempting sweets, but the effect is diminished when positive mood is accompanied by elevated arousal (Fedorikhin and Patrick 2010). The effects of positive emotions on food indulgence are also inconsistent. Some studies find an increase in food intake, whereas others find the reverse, and yet others find no effect at all (Evers et al. 2013). In conclusion, only the effects of negative mood are unequivocal.
3 Tice et al. (2001).
4 Baumeister et al. (1994: 244). Baumeister and colleagues mostly use the term self-regulation but consider it as more or less synonymous to self-control.
5 Other studies have found that cognitive load leads to stronger preference for chocolate over fruit (Friese et al. 2008).

6 Ward and Mann (2000). The latter point is noteworthy. Studies have found that cognitive load can sometimes *reduce* the impact of tempting stimuli, namely when the cognitive task is so all-absorbing that people do not have enough cognitive capacity left to recognize and process the hedonic qualities of these stimuli in the first place. Therefore, high cognitive load "may actually diminish the captivating power of temptation" (Van Dillen et al. 2013: 427; see also Volz et al. 2021). This suggests a nonlinear relationship in which moderate levels of cognitive load may be the most detrimental to self-control.

7 Friese et al. (2008). See also Shiv and Fedorikhin (1999).

8 These two systems are today often referred to as system 2 and system 1, respectively.

9 See Hofmann et al. (2011); Hofmann et al. (2012).

10 Diamond (2013).

11 Miller (1956); Cowan (2001).

12 Notably Baddeley and Hitch (1974), Kane and Engle (2002).

13 Engle (2002, 2018).

14 See Ackerman et al. (2005); Kane et al. (2005).

15 See Chapter 1, page xx.

16 That self-control and intelligence are somehow related aligns with theories on executive functions, now popular in developmental psychology. Executive functions are top-down mental processes that regulate thought and action, the building blocks of the part of working memory that is responsible for attention control. Unsurprisingly, research has found a substantial correlation between executive functions and intelligence. According to psychologist Akıra Miyake (Miyake et al. 2000), executive functions can be grouped into three "core" executive functions: updating (constant monitoring and rapid addition/deletion of working memory contents), inhibition (deliberate overriding of dominant or prepotent responses), and shifting (switching flexibly between tasks or mental sets). The correlations among these three "core" executive functions are substantial, which suggests some shared underlying mental ability. But they are far from perfect, which suggests separability. In the words of Miyake and colleagues, executive functions show both unity and diversity. Obviously, the second of these three core executive functions is closely related (if not equivalent) to self-control. The research on executive function thus leads to the same conclusion: Self-control and intelligence, while distinct constructs, are linked together somewhere in the mind.

17 Ward and Mann (2007).

18 Baumeister et al. (1994).

19 Baumeister and colleagues are certainly not the first to come up with this idea of limited mental energy. Freud, for example, already postulated the existence of "psychic energy" and Hans Selye the existence of "adaptation energy."

20 See Richter and Stanek (2015) for a critical discussion of the muscle metaphor.

21 Baumeister et al. (1998).

22 A meta-analysis by Hagger et al. (2010) found an average effect size of d = 0.61.

23 It is interesting to compare one of these ego depletion experiments with Mann and Ward's experiment, discussed in Section 3.1. The Mann and Ward study found that cognitive load had diverging effects on chronic dieters and nondieters. It only made the chronic dieters eat more. In the same year that Mann and Ward published their results, Kathleen Vohs and Todd Heatherton (2000) found essentially the same effect, but now due to ego depletion. When chronic dieters were confronted with tempting high-calorie foods within easy reach in a first task, they ate more ice cream in a subsequent "tasting" task. Again, this effect was only found with dieters, not with nondieters. The first task had apparently depleted the dieters (who by definition try to inhibit their eating urges) but not the nondieters, who feel no inhibitory pressure. In conclusion, cognitive load and earlier attempts at resisting urges have the same result – they make self-control harder – although the responsible psychological mechanisms differ: limited working memory in the former and limited energy in the latter.

24 Hagger et al. (2016)

25 Dang et al. (2021) and Vohs et al. (2021). Dang et al. (2021) found an average effect size of d = 0.10. After excluding participants who might have responded randomly, the effect size increased to d = 0.16. See also Garrison et al. (2019), who found an effect size of d = 0.20.

26 Carter et al. (2015); Baumeister and Vohs (2016); Blazquez et al. (2017); Cunningham and Baumeister (2016); Dang (2016a, 2018); Friese et al. (2019); Baumeister et al. (2020). For a recent history of the ego depletion saga see Inzlicht and Friese (2019).

27 Another way of putting this, is that stronger experimental manipulations are needed to bring about the effect than was initially believed. In the typical dual-task experiment, the first task (depletion manipulation) usually takes about five to ten minutes. Such a short duration may yield only a very weak effect, meaning that very large samples are needed to detect them. Recent experiments using stronger manipulations taking half an hour or longer, have found larger effects (see, for example, Sjåstad and Baumeister 2018). In studies on mental fatigue, participants usually have

to engage in tasks that require executive control for at least two hours before the dependent variables are measured (see Van der Linden et al. 2003; Boksem et al. 2005, 2006; Van der Linden and Eling 2006).

Baumeister (2020) poses the fundamental question whether the size of effects found in laboratory settings are relevant at all. What matters is whether an effect is found or not, not its exact size. "A laboratory effect may be artificially inflated or deflated in comparison with the same causal process outside the laboratory." In many cases the very notion of a true effect size simply makes no sense "[I]s it even meaningful to talk about the size of ego depletion laboratory effects? Ego depletion is a form of psychological fatigue, so by analogy one might as well ask, how big is the effect of being tired? Put that way, the question seems absurd [...] Would anyone think that a statement such as 'a tired person will do 0.12 standard deviations worse than a non-tired one, across all tasks' is meaningful?" (Baumeister 2020: 807).

28 Friese et al. (2019: 119) examined the merits and shortcomings of both the critiques suggesting that ego depletion does not exist and arguments that might be used to defend ego depletion research against these critiques. They arrive at the following conclusion: "First, the doubts and criticisms against ego depletion are substantial and challenging. At the same time, none of these critical issues provides conclusive evidence that ego depletion does not exist. Hence, it appears premature to dismiss the phenomenon. Second, none of the arguments provides conclusive evidence for the existence of ego depletion effects beyond reasonable doubt either. This is frustrating to realize. If this is a central conclusion of a review article after two decades of research and several hundred published studies, something must have gone seriously wrong."

29 See also Muraven et al. (2005), Sonnentag and Jelden (2009), and Allan et al. (2019).

30 Hofmann et al. (2012: 587).

31 Dai et al. (2015).

32 Vohs et al. (2008).

33 Schmeichel et al. (2003).

34 Sjåstad and Baumeister (2018).

35 In fact, researchers of working memory have suggested that the part of working memory responsible for attentional control uses the same depletable resource (Schmeichel 2007; Ilkowska and Engle 2010; Hofmann et al. 2011). This implies that fluctuations in working memory capacity may result either from simultaneous task load or from prior self-control, and that sustained exertion of self-control may undermine attentional control. So there is a common depletable resource fueling mental top-down processes, of which self-control is one.

36 It was initially suspected to be glucose, as the intake of glucose seems to enhance self-control (Gailliot and Baumeister 2007), but later research has cast doubt on this idea (see Dang 2016b for a meta-analysis). But if not glucose, then what? There must be *some* source of energy. The laws of physics state that no work can be done without energy, and this applies to human bodies and brains as well. Ampel et al. (2018), in their discussion of these doubts, agree that "the direct cause of reduced self-control depletion may not be a transient decrease in brain glucose." The initial hypothesis may have been too simple. But this does not mean that glucose plays no role at all in the exertion of self-control. According to the authors, "[t]he brain's reliance on glucose as a primary fuel source is well established" (Ampel et al. 2018: 1). Arguing that the human brain "is not highly sensitive to glucose depletion would be […] an overreaction, and one that would be overlooking a century of research on brain metabolism" (Ampel et al. 2018: 3). Unfortunately, since there is (as yet) no way to directly measure the level of glucose in the relevant brain areas during the exertion of self-control, "we can conclude only that a limitation on such processes by glucose supply is plausible; we cannot and do not conclude that it is a fact" (Ampel et al. 2018: 8).

37 Muraven and Slessareva (2003); Boksem et al. (2006).

38 Inzlicht and Berkman (2015: 520).

39 Other behavioral scientists have proposed alternative models that similarly explain self-control failure through shifts in motivation. See also the appendix. Here I focus on the Inzlicht and Schmeichel model as it is perhaps the most explicit in the rejection of the existence of some depletable resource.

40 This is to say, leaving aside the effects of other potentially self-control undermining factors such as situational influences. I do not mention them here as Inzlicht and Schmeichel (and other like-minded critics) focus entirely on the role of scarce resources, as proposed by the resource model. I suspect they would immediately agree that working memory capacity is a potential limit that must be taken into account.

41 Hockey (1997, 2013) makes a similar point. If we want to properly understand the effects of mental effort, he argues, we need to look not only at the effects on performing the task at hand, but also the effects on other bodily or mental states. These "secondary effects" are usually not registered as most researchers are only interested in performance decrements in the task at hand. But keeping task performance at the required level may draw resources away from other bodily or mental functions, leading to "secondary task decrements." In other words, keeping task performance at the required level may have hidden costs. "One of the most reliable costs of the use of increased effort to protect performance

is the observation of increased levels of activation [...] The most common changes involve the physiological systems that are activated by the SAM and HPA stress responses (sympathetic dominance in the ANS, neuroendocrine hormonal responses, and musculoskeletal activity)" (Hockey 2013: 118).

42  See Roberts et al. (2014); Saunders et al. (2018).

43  Brody et al. (2013).

44  Miller et al. (2015).

45  Miller et al. (2016).

46  Brody et al. (2020).

47  The studies mentioned do not answer the question of what causes the detrimental health effects of relentless self-control. The epigenetic aging study explored whether obesity or general life stress might be a mediating variable but found no evidence for this. The inoculation study explored whether sleep duration, unhealthy behaviors, and daily cortisol secretion might be meditating variables but found no evidence for these either. Miller and colleagues speculate that navigating the challenges that disadvantaged youth face "requires intense and persistent self-control, which is metabolically and behaviorally demanding to sustain. Acutely, exerting self-control triggers the release of stress hormones and erodes the ability to resist tempting stimuli, like high-fat food. These effects subside when people can suspend willpower and indulge in restorative activities. However, for lower-SES youth, opportunities for respite are likely to be infrequent" (Miller et al. 2015: 10328).

48  See also Chapter 2, note 9, on John Henryism.

49  Ryan and Deci (2017: 256).

50  Ryan and Deci (2017: 259).

51  Ryan and Deci (2017: 263).

52  See also Muraven et al. (2006).

53  In addition, it cannot be ruled out that if one day we have this knowledge and technology, research will find that *within this gray zone* capacity and motivation are not ontologically distinct realities, but two articulations or framings of the same underlying prelinguistic reality – a distinction rooted in language and not in empirical reality.

54  Schwabe and Wolf (2011: 327); see also Schwabe and Wolf (2009). A similar picture emerges from studies on the impact of acute stress on decision-making. Although the results of these studies vary, they all suggest that acute stress leads to a decrease in controlled processes and an increase in lower-level responses (Starcke and Brand 2012). Other studies suggesting a relationship between stress and reduced self-control are experience sampling studies by Park et al. (2016) and Hisler et al. (2019).

55 See Baumeister et al. (1999). Indeed, Klein and Boals found an association between the number of stressful life events people had experienced over the last six months and their performance on a working memory task. The more stressful events they reported, the poorer their performance (Klein and Boals 2001). A study by Schoofs and her colleagues found that acute stress induced in the lab reduced working memory capacity (Schoofs et al. 2009).
56 Wagner and Heatherton (2011: 137). This paragraph is based on their work.
57 Perhaps unsurprisingly, the PFC is also the prime locus of working memory and executive functioning. Although mental functions often implicate a larger circuitry of interconnected brain areas, there is general agreement that the PFC is critical for both (see Kane and Engle 2002).
58 It is not uncommon today to refer to the separate brain circuits as system 1 versus 2. I prefer not to use these terms as they are imprecise and in all likelihood an oversimplification. See Evans (2008).
59 Arnsten (2009: 4).
60 Harrison and Horne (2000); Lim and Dinges (2010); Lowe et al. (2017); Krause et al. (2017).
61 Lowe et al. (2017: 596).
62 Hamidovic and De Wit (2009); Heath et al. (2012). There is also a well-established association between sleep deprivation and obesity. See Smith et al. (2019); Khatib et al. (2017).
63 See also Baumeister et al. (2019: 520), whose data suggest that "good sleep improves self-control and good self-control improves sleep, with quality being more strongly linked than quantity," and Hisler et al. (2019), who found that reduced sleep was correlated with more self-control difficulties the next day, and that this relationship was partly mediated by increased stress due to this lack of sleep. Christian and Ellis (2011) found that participants who had not slept for at least twenty-four hours were less persistent in performing simple but tedious arithmetic problems, a classic self-control measure.
64 Krizan and Hisler (2016: 189). See also Pilcher and Huffcutt (1996).
65 Yoo et al. (2007).
66 Goldstein and Walker (2014: 683).
67 Barber et al. (2013) found a significant correlation between self-control (assessed with the Brief Self-Control Scale) and sleep hygiene (assessed with the Sleep Hygiene Index).
68 Kroese et al. (2016: 859–860).
69 See Kalis (2011); Stroud (2014).
70 Holton (1999, 2009); Sripada (2014). Sripada explicitly acknowledges the overlap between his and Holton's proposals.

71 Intentions are "conduct-controlling pro-attitudes, ones which we are disposed to retain without reconsideration, and which play a significant role as inputs to [means-end] reasoning" (Bratman 1987: 20).

72 Kotabe and Hofmann (2015: 619), writing on the role of desire in the context of self-control, describe "desire" as "a driving force that begins as a subcortically mediated visceral state of 'wanting' [...] usually followed by cognitive elaboration, that directs a person toward immediate reward-related stimuli." In opposition to desires, they place "higher order goals." "A higher order goal is a more cortically mediated and largely cognitive construct associated with an *endorsed* end state that motivates instrumental psychological (cognitive, affective, and behavioral) activity. Unlike desires, higher order goals are often pursued *intentionally* and associated with declarative expectations of long-term benefits" (Hofmann and Kotabe 2015: 619, emphasis added).

73 Sripada is not the first to suggest "mind portioning." The idea goes back to Plato and his famous metaphor of the soul as a charioteer controlling two horses, and, more recently, to Davidson's account of the divided mind.

74 See also Kalis (2011).

75 The argument in this paragraph is inspired by Sripada (2018).

76 Sripada (2018: 586).

77 Inzlicht and Schmeichel (2016: 176).

78 Kurzban et al. (2013); Molden et al. (2016).

79 Inzlicht and Berkman (2015: 520).

80 Kool et al. (2010).

81 This idea forms the basis of "the opportunity cost model of self-control" in Kurzban et al. (2013).

82 Inzlicht and Schmeichel (2016: 173).

83 For example, Schmeichel et al. (2010).

84 See Inzlicht and Schmeichel (2016: 175); Milyavskaya and Inzlicht (2017: 17).

85 Hockey (2013: 111).

86 See also Kurzban (2016) and Shenhav et al. (2017).

## 4 Building Self-Control?

1 These fifteen tips are based on McGonigal (2011) and the following webpages (all retrieved on April 4, 2018):
- www.wikihow.com/Build-Self%E2%80%90Control
- www.americanexpress.com/us/small-business/openforum/articles/8-easy-ways-to-increase-your-self-control/
- www.psychologytoday.com/us/blog/science-choice/201703/10-strategies-developing-self-control

- www.quickanddirtytips.com/health-fitness/mental-health/
  8-tips-to-improve-your-self-control
- www.willpowered.co/learn/strengthen-your-willpower
- www.inc.com/jeff-haden/the-science-of-self-control-6-ways-to-develop-
  grea.html
- www.forbes.com/sites/travisbradberry/2012/09/17/the-six-secrets-of-
  self-control/#1326d87942d4
- www.psychologytoday.com/us/blog/good-thinking/201306/how-boost-
  your-willpower
- www.fabhow.com/how-to-boost-your-self-control.html
- https://smallbiztrends.com/2014/07/how-to-improve-your-self-
  control.html
- http://dailyburn.com/life/lifestyle/willpower-how-to-achieve-goals/
2 McGonigal (2013: 42).
3 Muraven (2010).
4 Oaten and Cheng (2006a, 2006b, 2007).
5 Four meta-analyses have been conducted:
- Hagger et al. (2010): d = 1.07 (based on only nine studies, including
  three questionable studies by Oaten and Cheng; no correction for
  publication bias);
- Inzlicht and Berkman (2015): after exclusion of studies by Oaten
  and Cheng, and after correction for bias, depending on correction
  method: d = 0.62 (with a wide confidence interval) or d = 0.17
  (not significantly different from zero);
- Friese et al. (2017): g = 0.30; after correction for publication bias:
  depending on correction method: g = 0.24 or g = 0.13 (not significantly different from zero);
- Beames et al. (2018): g = 0.36; after correction for publication
  bias: g = 0.28.
6 The worldwide prevalence of ADHD is estimated at a little over 5 percent for children, and roughly half of that for adults (Polanczyk et al.
  2014; Fayyad et al. 2017).
7 Barkley (2013: 47).
8 In recent years, several psychologists have proposed to conceptualize
  self-control more broadly, not as effortful inhibition per se, but "as
  the process of advancing distal rather than proximal motivations when
  the two compete" (Fujita 2011: 352) or "the process or behavior of
  overcoming a temptation or prepotent response in favor of a competing goal" (Milyavskaya et al. 2019: 80). In this broader conceptualization, effortful inhibition is no longer the defining core of self-control but
  merely one of the potential strategies to achieve one's goals in the face
  of temptation. An alternative strategy might be, for example, to avoid

temptation in the first place, say by not going to the grocery store when hungry, or by studying in the library where distractions are minimal (see Milyavskaya et al. 2021 for first empirical findings on the effectiveness of various strategies). For those proficient in self-control, effortful inhibition may be "a strategy of last resort" (Fujita 2011: 359) only deployed in unforeseen events or when other strategies are not feasible or nothing else works.

This portrayal of how people deal with potential temptations in everyday life may be correct, but I disagree with the suggestion that "effortful inhibition" is just one potential strategy for overcoming temptations, on an equal footing with other strategies such as cognitive reframing or developing beneficial habits. There is a fundamental ontological difference: The capacity for effortful inhibition is already there at birth (at least in rudimentary form). It is grounded in our neurophysiological makeup. In contrast, strategies for self-control are the product of social learning. They only develop (or not) as one grows up, perhaps only after many, many years of hard learned lessons. Effortful inhibition is hence not only the strategy of *last* resort but also the strategy of *first* resort.

All things considered, my view is that it is better to (conceptually) distinguish between limited capacity for effortful inhibition (self-control *strength*) on the one hand, and strategies to get the maximum mileage out of this limited capacity (self-control *technique*) on the other.

9  Not all distracting thoughts seem to be effective. Suggesting to children they think sad thoughts, such as falling down and getting a bloody knee, or crying when there is no one to help, was ineffective.

10  Mischel and Ebbesen (1970: 335, emphasis in original).

11  There were in fact four variants, but describing two suffices to make the point.

12  See Metcalfe and Mischel (1999).

13  See Hofmann et al. (2010) for similar results.

14  De Ridder et al. (2012); Galla and Duckworth (2015); Gillebaart and De Ridder (2015). In an experience sampling study, De Ridder et al. (2020) found that participants who practiced a personally important behavior requiring self-control over a four-month period, gradually increased their (self-reported) level of self-control (as measured with the Brief Self-Control Scale). It is difficult to say what exact mechanism was responsible for the improvement, but "[I]t may well be that due to long-term practice, self-control behavior became more routinized over time" (2019: 318). This interpretation is supported by the fact that when, after the four-month period, De Ridder tested participants' susceptibility to ego depletion, they found no significant effect of behavioral practice. Apparently, over these four months, participants had improved their self-control *technique* but not their self-control *strength*.

15 Oettingen (2000, 2016).
16 Gollwitzer (1999).
17 Oettingen and Cachia (2015: 564).
18 See Wood (2016) and Galla and Duckworth (2015: study 5), but also Van der Weiden et al. (2020).
19 See Diamond and Lee (2011); Heckman et al. (2014); Murray et al. (2016); Pandaj et al. (2018).
20 Piquero et al. (2010, 2016).
21 Diamond and Lee (2011: 963).
22 Giné et al. (2010).
23 Bryan et al. (2010); Rogers et al. (2014); Duckworth et al. (2018).
24 The nudging literature contains many examples of attempts to influence behavior through new and better ways to provide information, for example a traffic light system indicating the (un)healthiness of food items, or labels indicating the energy efficiency of household appliances. However, I would not consider these "nudges" as meant by Thaler and Sunstein (2008) but as "provision of information" or "communication." These forms of influencing people do not exploit people's bounded rationality or willpower.
25 Thaler and Sunstein (2008: 8).
26 Thaler and Benartzi (2004). One interesting feature of nudges such as these is that they are "asymmetrical" in their effect. They increase the probability that employees who remain passive end up with a decent pension, but have no discernable effect on employees who make an active and well-considered choice. After all, the latter are free to select the option they prefer. If their preference is not the same as the default option, all they have to do is tick the box for their preferred alternative.
27 My favorite example is Van der Steeg and Waterreus (2015). For a review of the effectiveness of various types of nudges, see Hummel and Maedche (2019).
28 This leaves aside the potential ethical issues with nudging, which should certainly be taken seriously. See, for example, Bovens (2008), White (2013), Sunstein (2014), and Schmidt and Engelen (2020).
29 For reviews and meta-analyses on nudging and diet and food-related behavior, see Arno and Thomas (2016), Broers et al. (2017), Bauer and Reisch (2019), and Vecchio and Cavallo (2019).
30 This widening of the gap is an instance of the so-called Matthew effect, after the verse in the New Testament which reads "to everyone who has will more be given, and he will have abundance; but from him who has not, even what he has will be taken away" (Matthew 25:29, RSV, see Merton 1968).
31 Rimke (2000, 2017).

32 Duckworth et al (2018). To be sure, recent years witnessed a veritable avalanche of studies on food-related nudges, which by definition are interventions in the environment. The Duckworth et al. (2018) review also mentions several nudges, but in my view, these interventions do not count as interventions in the environment that *improve* self-control capacity or motivation, either temporarily or structurally. Nudges are merely techniques to influence behavior that leave individuals' capacities or motivations unaffected. Paradoxically, if nudges really were to improve people's choice-making or choice-following capacities, they would – over the course of time – render themselves ineffective because people would be cured of their limited rationality and willpower.

Some critics go further, and argue that nudges may even negatively affect people's choice-making and choice-following capabilities by inviting them to just go with the flow. As a result, people may *unlearn* how to make well-considered choices and to stick to their resolutions. According to these critics, nudging leads to infantilization (Bovens 2008). Partly in response to these shortcomings of the nudging paradigm, some social scientists advocate an alternative paradigm they have dubbed "boost," which explicitly seeks to enhance people's choice-relevant competencies (Hertwig and Grüne-Yanoff 2017).

## 5 The Value of the Future

1 Strathman et al. (1994).
2 Zimbardo and Boyd (1999).
3 A handful of exploratory studies have directly correlated the CFC or ZPTI to trait self-control:
  • CFC: Joireman et al. (2008) found that the CFC items that refer to immediate rewards (CFC-I) are negatively correlated to self-control, while CFC items that refer to future rewards (CFC-F) are positively related to self-control. See Wang et al. (2017) for similar results.
  • ZPTI: Barber et al. (2009) found that the future subscale of the ZPTI was positively correlated with self-control. Kim et al. (2017) found that the present subscales of the ZPTI were negatively related to self-control, and the future subscale of the ZPTI was positively correlated to self-control. See Germano and Brenlla (2021) for similar results.
4 Nor is the Brief Self-Control Scale – the most used scale to assess self-control (see Chapter 2) – immune to this problem. Compared to the scales mentioned in this chapter, its statements are more unambiguously about capacities, but it cannot be ruled out that some (also) tap into motivation. For example, what does it mean when someone endorses

the statement that "pleasure and fun sometimes keep me from getting work done." Does this mean that she is sometimes incapable of resisting the temptation of pleasure and fun? Or that she sometimes simply prefers having a good time now over getting work done?

5 For example, Shamosh and Gray (2008), in their meta-analysis, more or less equate delay discounting with self-control. In their review of studies on the impact of affect and stress on time discounting, Haushofer and Fehr (2014, additional material) also include studies in which some indicator of self-control was the dependent variable. Some papers explicitly address whether impulsivity and delay discounting are distinct concepts or not, for example Reimers et al. (2009).

6 Levitt et al. (2020).

7 If these two constructs are not the same thing, one would expect at best moderate correlations between measures of delay discounting and behavioral measures of self-control capacity, such as the marshmallow test. Surprisingly, despite the vast amount of research on self-control and other related concepts, no studies directly tested this relationship. The literature offers only indirect evidence.

First, a meta-analysis investigated the convergence between the numerous tasks, scales, and questionnaires that aim to measure to what extent people prefer or pursue long-term benefits at the expense of short-term gratification. The analysis found only moderate correlations (Duckworth and Kern 2011). It would thus be surprising if research on the relation between delay discounting and self-control capacity would yield something totally different, to wit, a near perfect correlation between the two.

Second, the development of delay discounting seems to follow a different trajectory than the development of self-control capacity. As we saw, four-year-olds are already able to delay gratification in a way that predicts a broad range of future outcomes. In contrast, the ability to make choices that involve differing delay lengths seems to develop later, between the ages seven and eleven (Reynolds and Schiffbauer 2005). The period between thirteen and sixteen is especially important for the development of specific capacities that underlie discounting behavior (Steinberg et al. 2009). All this supports the claim that self-control capacity and delay discounting are not only conceptually but also empirically separate.

8 Some studies have explored the correlation between delay discounting and time perspective. They show that steeper discounting rates are associated with a stronger present (rather than future) orientation as measured with the CFC or ZTPI (Daugherty and Brase 2010; Basile and Toplak 2015; Cosenza and Nigro 2015; Guo et al. 2017; Macaskill et al. 2019).

9 From Kirby et al. (1999).

10 Odum and Baumann (2010); Odum (2011); Odum et al. (2020).
11 Odum (2011); Anokhin et al. (2015); Urminsky and Zauberman (2015).
12 Lerner et al. (2013: 76).
13 Ifcher and Zarghamee (2011).
14 Fields et al. (2014). See also Haushofer and Fehr (2014).
15 Reimers et al. (2009). Previous lab testing had shown that this single question correlated well with longer and more traditional measures for delay discounting.
16 Odum and Baumann (2010); Urminsky and Zauberman (2015); Keidel et al. (2021). Another important variable is age. Children and adolescents under sixteen have steeper discount rates than adolescents over sixteen and adults (Steinberg et al. 2009).
17 This is in line with the results of a meta-analysis by Shamosh and Gray (2008), which found a moderate correlation ($r = -0,23$) between intelligence and discounting. Not all twenty-four studies included in this meta-analysis were "pure" discounting tasks because, in six studies, the delay discounting measure was a sustained choice task. However, no significant differences were found between the effect size in these studies and the other eighteen studies. Since then, there have been many more studies on the relation between intelligence and discounting. These later studies "generally confirm the significant association of temporal discounting and intelligence found by Shamosh and Gray (2008) with similar effect sizes" (Keidel et al. 2021: 8).
18 For a theoretical model that accounts for delay discounting, see Kurth-Nelson et al. (2012). This model posits that the subjective value assigned to an outcome is proportional to how easy it is to find/construct this outcome in memory, and that less delayed outcomes are typically easier to find/construct.
19 Diamond (2013: 142).
20 Hinson et al. (2003). See also Deck and Jahedi (2015) and Israel et al. (2021) for comparable results. There is some debate over how to interpret Hinson's findings. Do they indicate that participants get less patient under cognitive load, or do they indicate that participants choose more randomly under cognitive load, because they lack sufficient processing resources for evaluating the responses (see Franco-Watkins et al. 2010)? The results of Deck and Jahedi suggest that the former is the case, and that the results are not driven by randomness. Further evidence comes from Wesley and Bickel (2014), who found a strong overlap in the brain between delay discounting and working memory processes, and from Bickel et al. (2011), who conducted an experiment among substance abusers. Participants in the experimental condition received a memory training program consisting of four to fifteen sessions, depending on

their progress. Delay discounting was measured both before and after training. Discount rates in the experimental group decreased significantly more than in the control group; the more training sessions, the greater the change in discount rate.

21 This model may also explain why delay discounting and self-control capacity are often mixed up. What ties them together is their connection to working memory capacity. It is thus unsurprising that, viewed from a distance, it is hard to keep them apart.

22 Or "episodic foresight" or "episodic future thinking" or "prospection."

23 Bulley et al. (2016). The term "mental time travel" also encompasses travels to the past (i.e. remembering things), but I use the term here only in the prospective meaning.

24 Some scholars claim that the capacity for mental time travel is the crucial difference between humans and animals (Suddendorf and Corballis 2007). Our favorite pets can travel a temporal distance of several minutes, maybe half an hour, but no more. There are hardly any limits, however, to the temporal distances human beings can cover. Human behavior is often guided by goals that will only materialize after many years of hard work, such as attaining a college degree, being a successful businessman or woman, or winning an Olympic gold medal.

25 Bulley et al. (2016).

26 By definition, mental time travel requires working memory as it involves holding something that is perceptually not present in mind. However, it remains unclear how exactly working memory and mental time travel are related. Lin and Epstein (2014) found that primes of future events led to stronger reductions in delay discounting in subjects who scored higher on a working memory task that measured short-term retention of information. They speculate that "persons with limited cognitive resources may be less capable of delaying gratification because they have difficulty vividly visualizing future outcomes" (Lin and Epstein 2014: 18). Hill and Emery (2013) found that the executive/attentional control component of working memory may be implicated in mental time travel. Although probably not relevant to the elaboration of event details, it may contribute to the construction of a single, coherent depiction of a future event.

27 Boyer (2008: 219).

28 Gilbert and Wilson (2007: 1354).

29 Bulley et al. (2016: 2).

30 Boyer (2008: 219).

31 For more empirical support, see Bromberg et al. (2015). They found that participants who gave more details about events they might experience in the coming (half) year were more inclined to favor larger delayed future rewards over immediate smaller rewards.

32 For similar results, see Van Gelder et al. (2013, 2015). For the effect of feeling connected to your future self, see Hershfield (2011), Bartels and Urminsky (2011), and Adelman et al. (2017).

33 Bulley and Gullo (2017).

34 Peters and Büchel (2010); Daniel et al. (2013a, 2013b); Lin and Epstein (2014); Bromberg et al. (2015); Daniel and Epstein (2015); Dassen et al. (2016); O'Neill et al. (2016); Snider et al. (2016); Stein et al. (2016), for reviews, see Rung and Madden (2018) and Scholten et al. (2019).

35 Peters and Büchel (2010); Benoit et al. (2011: 6774).

36 O'Donnel et al. (2017).

37 Liu et al. (2013).

38 Bulley et al. (2016: 7). The object of mental time travel does not need to be the consumption of the delayed reward itself. As the study by Bulley and Gullo (2017) and similar studies show, envisioning other future events that will take place at about the same time also leads to increased preference for the delayed reward. What is more, simply imagining future events in general seems to work as well. Cheng et al. (2012) found lower discount rates when participants were first asked to imagine what their everyday life circumstances and a typical day might be like four years into the future. Priming participants to think about the future induces a future-oriented mindset, which increases preferences for delayed rewards.

39 Kidd et al. (2013: appendix A).

40 Ellis et al. (2009: 217) define environmental harshness as "the rates at which external factors causes disability and death at each age in a population" and environmental unpredictability as "the rates at which environmental harshness varies over time and space" (Ellis et al. 2009: 207).

41 Some scholars argue that a general factor of personality (GFP) can indeed be identified that correlates with slow life history and high planning effort (see Figueredo et al. 2007; Rushton et al. 2008). The ontological status of this GFP remains unclear.

42 For reviews, see Ellis et al. (2009), Belsky (2012), and Del Giudice (2014). For a meta-analysis see Wu et al. (2020). The latter found that "early-life stress in various forms relates to greater risk taking, greater present orientation, and less prosociality in adulthood" (Wu et al. 2020: 567).

43 Ellis et al. (2009: 247). See also Belsky (2012).

44 This was a fictitious article made to look like a *New York Times* article.

45 Griskevicius et al. (2011).

46 Griskevicius et al. (2013). There is one caveat. As Griskevicius notes, it remains unclear which features of low childhood SES are driving these diverging response patterns. Low SES is associated with a wide range of life history experiences, including lack of resources, harsh or neglectful

parenting, household instability, exposure to violence, and so forth. It is unclear to what extent these possible aspects of low SES drive the diverging life history strategies.
47 Deck and Jahedi (2015).

## 6 The Self-Control Effects of Poverty

1 Banfield (1968: 53).
2 Guy Standing, for instance, asserts that "the precariat" – a newly emerging social class comprised of groups on the lowest rungs of the social ladder – "is defined by short-termism" (Standing 2011: 18).
3 Similar differences were found in a survey among a largely representative sample of the Dutch population (Tiemeijer 2016).
4 Baumeister at al. (2019). Studies using other methodologies than the standard delay discounting task also found this group to be more present-oriented. See Fieulaine and Apostolidis (2015).
5 G. Evans (2004: 88).
6 Conger and Donnellan (2007).
7 See also Grant et al. (2003). Evans published his review in 2004. To my knowledge, no new data have been published since then that are fundamentally at odds with his assessment.
8 In the last wave, the mothers were not included.
9 Evans and English (2002).
10 Evans and Kim (2012); Evans (2016).
11 The correlation between income and delay of gratification was 0.24. An almost similar correlation was obtained in an analysis of a larger sample of 4.5-year-old children in a marshmallow-like test (Evans and Rosenbaum 2008). See also Watts et al. (2018).
12 Evans (2016); Evans and De France (2021). For the record, Evans does not mention self-control in this paper. He presents this test as a means to measure "helplessness."
13 An extensive literature addresses the relationship between income and happiness, but since (un)happiness is not the same as negative or positive affect, it is not discussed here. Another study that warrants mention is Haushofer and Fehr's review of (natural) experimental studies on the effect of changes in income on affect and stress. They found that "the large majority of the findings suggests that increases in poverty often lead to negative affect and stress, and decreases in poverty have the opposite effect" (Haushofer and Fehr 2014: 864). But the studies underlying their review are a mixed bag, using very disparate independent and dependent variables, including outcomes such as (changes in) "self-esteem", "depression," and "general mental health."

14 This was about the median US income in the period in which this study was conducted.
15 Shah et al. (2012: 682).
16 Mani et al. (2013).
17 Similar results were obtained by Ong et al. (2019), who tested low-income debtors in Singapore both before and after they received a relief worth up to 5,000 Singapore dollars (the equivalent of three months' household income). As part of the test, delay discounting rate was also measured. "Comparing the poor before and after debt relief, those with more debt accounts paid off experienced greater improvements in cognitive functioning, reported less anxiety, and became less present-biased" (Ong et al. 2019: 7244). It should be noted, however, that some studies failed to replicate the Mani et al. (2013) findings. See De Bruijn and Antonides (2021) for a narrative review.
18 Spears (2011).
19 Another of Spears' studies, set in a shopping mall in the United States, examined secondary eating (eating while doing other activities such as driving or watching TV) among a representative sample of American shoppers. Secondary eating is a form of "mindless eating" and is considered an indication of lack of self-control. Spears found that poor people are significantly more likely to be engaged in secondary eating while shopping than rich people. Apparently, people who have to contemplate every spending decision they make are left with fewer resources for exerting self-control. It is not entirely clear, however, to what extent the reduced self-control in this study is a result of reduced working memory (as in the Mani experiments) or reduced resources (as in Spears' handgrip experiments).

Additional support for the hypothesis that poverty may deplete resources comes from a study by Chou et al. (2016). In one of their experiments, participants were first primed to feel economically insecure, and then asked to keep their hand in a bucket of ice-cold water as long as they could. It is known that people with greater self-control tend to keep their hand in the water longer than people with less self-control. Chou and colleagues found that, compared to a control group, participants who were primed to feel insecure withdrew their hand sooner.
20 Cohen and Janicki-Deverts (2012); Cohen et al. (2006).
21 Haushofer and Shapiro (2013).
22 Chemin et al. (2013).
23 In 2016, the Gallup Organization found that of the 140 countries it surveyed for its Global Emotions project, Greece was the country with the most people reporting stress. In that period, Greeks were suffering draconic austerity programs to pay off the country's debt. Between 2002 and 2017, minimum wages dropped by 22 percent, while unemployment in 2017 remained at over 20 percent (Gallup 2017).

24 Grandner et al. (2016); Grandner et al. (2010).

25 Stamatakis et al. (2007).

26 This accords with other studies that suggest that sleep duration in the United States has been declining, albeit very slowly (Bin et al. 2010; Knutson et al. 2010).

27 Grandner (2017: 10).

28 Grandner (2017: 10); Grandner et al. (2016). Sleep quality is also related to race/ethnicity. Several studies have found that African Americans sleep both objectively and subjectively worse than Caucasian Americans (Ruiter et al. 2010). Stamatakis and colleagues also found this pattern. It is not fully clear what causes these differences. The relationship is partly explained by the lower socioeconomic position of African Americans, but that may not be the whole story, as one study found that the relationship was robust after controlling for a host of demographic and socioeconomic indicators (Whinnery et al. 2014). Two other factors that might contribute to this link are occupation and perceived discrimination. Ethnic minorities are more likely to work long hours and later shifts and to have multiple jobs, which may all hinder sufficient and consistent sleep. Perceived discrimination and racism also appear to play a role. Grandner and his colleagues found, for instance, that exposure to racial discrimination was associated with sleep disturbance, even when race, sociodemographic, and depressed mood were partialled out (Grandner et al. 2012). See also Slopen and Williams (2014). Apparently, discrimination is a unique stressor that undermines sleep quality.

29 Pepper and Nettle (2017).

30 Adler et al. (2008: 6).

31 Chetty et al. (2016).

32 Mackenbach et al. (2008). The strength of the association varied from country to country.

33 Stringhini et al. (2017).

34 Adler et al. (1994).

35 Marmot (2015).

36 Sampson and Lauristen (1994: 63), cited in Pridemore (2011: 752).

37 See Pridemore (2002, 2008); Messner et al. (2010); Pare and Felson (2014).

38 US Department of Justice, *Criminal Victimization 2019*.

39 These facts are not contested. The scientific debate revolves around the question of what explains these associations. What, for instance, is the role of health behavior? And what is the impact of neighborhoods? For our purposes, this debate is irrelevant. On these pages, what matters is the bare fact that low-SES environments are associated with higher risks of early death and disease.

40 Western et al. (2012). Economic *insecurity* is not the same as economic *inequality*. The latter refers to differences in financial situation between individuals, whereas the former refers to *changes* within the same individual's financial situation.

41 See Ranci et al. (2017) for an exception.

42 Moffitt (2020). Most studies have examined men's earnings. The longitudinal picture for women's earnings is (even) less clear.

43 Gottschalk and Moffitt (2009); for brief reviews see Dynan et al. (2012) and Western et al. (2012).

44 Gottschalk and Moffitt (2009: 14).

45 Gottschalk and Moffitt (2009). See also Bania and Leete (2009), Dynan et al. (2012), and Morris et al. (2015).

46 Carr and Wiemers (2016: 1). Western et al. (2016), analyzing data for households with children, found that from 1984 to 2010 income instability increased significantly for low-income families but remained relatively unchanged for middle- and high-income families.

47 Western et al. (2012: 355, emphasis added).

48 The idea of a "culture of poverty" was introduced by the anthropologist Oscar Lewis in his ethnographic study of Mexicans and Puerto Ricans. Among the key features of this culture is a specific configuration of personality traits, including "a lack of impulse control, a strong present-time orientation with relatively little ability to defer gratification and to plan for the future …" (Lewis, quoted in Katz 2013: 15). The culture of poverty thesis derives much of its infamy from the so-called Moynihan Report, published in 1965. Although not explicitly mentioning the culture of poverty, it was clearly based on its main ideas. It became one the most controversial documents in the history of American social science.

According to Katz (2013), one of the main problems with the "culture of poverty" thesis is its assumption that the mechanism primarily responsible for perpetuation of this culture is socialization: families are believed to pass on this particular set of values and beliefs to their children. But an alternative, situational explanation is also possible: each new generation readopts these values and beliefs, not because they are passed on by their parents, but because they must adapt to similar constraints. The behaviors typically associated with this culture are the "contextually appropriate responses" to their social isolation and precarious situation. If this is true, the mechanism responsible for perpetuation of this culture is not socialization, but the lack of improvement in living conditions. The culture of poverty would be the effect rather than the cause of their life situation. In any case, Katz notes that most representations of the culture of poverty lack clearly specified independent and dependent variables and, therefore, "leave cause and effect hopelessly tangled" (Katz 2013: 33).

49 See, for example, Banerjee and Duflo (2011), Mullainathan and Shafir (2013), Haushofer and Fehr (2014), Sheehy-Skeffington and Haushofer (2014), and Pepper and Nettle (2017).

## 7 The Ever-Growing Importance of Self-Control

1 Elias' portrayal of the Middle Ages is based on Johan Huizinga's *The Waning of the Middle Ages*.
2 Elias (2000: 370).
3 Figure 7.1 only gives the broader trend. A closer look would reveal fluctuations, hiccups, and holes in the trend line. Most nations started collecting systematic statistical information on homicide about 200 years ago. For older data, criminologists must rely on scattered data points from historical documents, such as police or hospital records. These need to be handled with care, and comparability can be a problem.
    According to criminologist Manuel Eisner (2014: 17), the main reason behind the downward trend was a sharp decline in intermale violence in public spaces (as opposed to domestic spaces). This supports Elias' claim that, over time, pacified public spaces emerged. Since the late Middle Ages, therefore, the chances that one would actually live to see the benefits of exerting self-control have increased significantly.
4 Elias (2000: 318).
5 Ricard (1781: 463) (translation from Hirschman 1982: 1465). The idea that the market fosters virtue has become known as the *doux commerce* thesis (see Hirschman 1982). It stands in opposition to the self-destruction thesis, which holds that markets crowd out virtues such as trustfulness and mutual respect. Unfortunately, little empirical research has been done on the *doux commerce* thesis. Graafland (2009: 13), reviewing the literature, concludes that the overall picture is "highly uncertain [...] the impact of market operation on virtues is too diverse for taking sides in the debate about the doux commerce or self-destruction thesis." It may be that both theses hold at the same time. Hirschman (1982: 1483) considers this "overwhelmingly likely."
6 Elias (2000: 370).
7 Elias (2000: 367–378).
8 Elias (2000: 374).
9 W. Miller (1998: 171).
10 Elias (2000: 381).
11 Elias (2000: 383, emphasis added).
12 Van Krieken (1989).
13 Van Krieken (1989: 209).
14 Van Krieken (1990: 362, emphasis in original).

15  Mennell (2007: 295).
16  Spierenburg (2006: 113).
17  In 2019, the rates in Louisiana and Mississippi, the two states with the highest incidence of homicide, were nearly ten times as high as in Idaho and Maine, the two states with the lowest incidence of homicide. www .cdc.gov/nchs/pressroom/sosmap/homicide_mortality/homicide.htm, retrieved June 22, 2021.
18  Haskell (1985: 550).
19  Weber (2001: 70–71, emphasis in original).
20  Weber (2001: 72).
21  Haskell (1985: 561).
22  Mennell (2007: 111).
23  The United States, England, Germany, and the Netherlands.
24  Wouters (2011a).
25  Wouters (2011b: 151).
26  Mennell (2007: 76).
27  Wouters (2007: 4).
28  Elias (2000: 368).
29  Wouters (2011b: 148).
30  Elias used this expression in a lecture in Amsterdam in 1970, but only in the narrower context of sports and leisure. One of the attendees was Cas Wouters, who picked up the expression and then extended its use to much wider social and psychological processes (Wouters and Dunning 2019: 11).
31  Elias (2000: 157).
32  *The Civilizing Process* was published in 1939. As Figures 7.2 and 7.3 show, the population explosion was by then well underway.
33  The trend is largely similar for nearly all other major countries in the world.
34  Elias (2000: 376–338).
35  Some readers will have missed a reference to Stephen Pinker's (2011) *The Better Angels of Our Nature*. In this book, Pinker argues that violence has decreased over the centuries, largely due to growing self-control. I tend to agree with this part of Pinker's analysis – unsurprising as he also builds his argument on Elias, whom he calls the "the most important thinker you have never heard of" (Pinker 2011: 59).
    In one respect, however, I disagree with Pinker. He seems to suggest that, over the ages, people's self-control *strength* has increased. As self-control became more important for life chances, people were encouraged to actively use and train their "self-control muscles," thus making them stronger. "The exogenous first domino [in the chain of explanation that makes up the theory of the civilizing process] is a change in law

enforcement and opportunities for economic cooperation that objectively tilt the payoffs so that a deferral of gratification, in particular, an avoidance of impulsive violence, pays off in the long run. The knock-on effect is a strengthening of people's self-control muscles that allow them (among other things) to inhibit their violent impulses, above and beyond what is strictly necessary to avoid being caught and punished" (Pinker 2011: 609). Since Pinker's book was published, however, new research gives reason to be more pessimistic about the prospects for training self-control strength (see Chapter 4). The effects are modest at best, and it is unclear how long they last. It is simply not that easy to enhance raw willpower.

To the extent that self-control strength has increased over the ages, I think this is better explained by other factors. For instance, early childhood, over time, may have become characterized by, on average, less poverty, instability, stress, and other factors that hamper the development of good self-regulation, and, as birth rates declined, by more warm and responsive parental investment. Moreover, as self-control became more important for negotiating life, parents may also have given more attention to teaching their children techniques to control their impulses, and may have set better examples. It is also likely that the overall motivation to exert self-control has increased, thus encouraging people to invest a greater share of their mental resources toward this end. In fact, the change in external incentives lies at the heart of Elias' argument.

In sum, my hypothesis would be that, over the centuries, people's *nature* with regard to self-control capacity – that is, their hardwired potential for developing good self-control – has essentially remained the same, and that the increase in self-control is to be explained by changes in *nurture* and *culture*.

36 As this book went to press, the latest US data showed a remarkable surge in homicides for the year 2020. At the time of writing, it was unclear whether this was the beginning of an upward trend, or just a temporary spike due to – for example – the stresses of COVID-19 pandemic. The numbers for many other crimes continued their downward trend, see www.theguardian.com/us-news/2021/jun/30/us-crime-rate-homcides-explained, retrieved July 1, 2021.

37 The idea is that this resulted in less unwanted babies who, so the theory goes, have an above average chance of growing up to be criminal.

38 Pinker (2011); Michael Tonry (2014). According to Baumer and Wolff (2014: 18), "[t]he list of possible explanations for the crime drop is long and impressive. Provocative arguments have been made for the primacy of the following: objective and perceptual economic shifts, changes in the quantity and quality of policing and punishment practices, public

and personal security efforts, the stabilization of drug markets, increases in immigration, changes in abortion laws, regulations of and changes in lead gas exposure, increased video gaming, rising civility and self-control, transformations of family arrangements, reduced alcohol consumption, and increased use of psychiatric pharmaceutical therapies."

39 Garland (2001: 15).
40 Garland (2001: 117).
41 Garland (2001: 15, emphasis added).
42 See www.upi.com/Archives/1994/09/09/British-PM-lashes-out-against-crime/2813779083200/, retrieved June 22, 2021.
43 Garland (2001: 156).
44 Pratt et al. (2013).
45 Garland (2001: 204).
46 Brown (2009).
47 Mounk (2017).
48 Hacker (2008).
49 Murray (1984).
50 Mead (1986: 1).
51 Deacon and Mann (1999).
52 Mead (1986: 18, emphasis added).
53 Mead (1986: 82).
54 Mead's proposals did not mean a retrenchment of the state. To the contrary, with regard to welfare, Mead advocated a more authoritative government, especially vis-à-vis those who viewed unemployment as some kind of rebellious political act. "Many young people today, especially at the bottom of society, simply are not as well socialized by adults as they used to be. They cannot be integrated unless they become something closer to the disciplined workers the economy demands. In some form government must take over the socializing role" (Mead 1986: 87).
55 Reflecting the specific US understanding of welfare, one of the stated goals of TANF is to reduce the incidence of out-of-wedlock pregnancies and to encourage marriage.
56 Slater (2012: 2), quoted in Fletcher and Wright (2018: 333).
57 Fletcher and Wright (2018: 333).
58 Watts et al. (2014: 12); Watts and Fitzpatrick (2018).
59 Hemerijck (2017: 19, emphasis added).
60 Anthony Giddens and the Danish sociologist Gøsta Esping-Andersen are often mentioned as the intellectual fathers of this new perspective.
61 The qualifier "of those days" is crucial here, as were the words "seemed to abandon" some paragraphs earlier. Quite a few social critics would vehemently disagree that "the third way" should in any way be understood as an alternative to neoliberalism, to the contrary. Although

*presented* as an alternative to neoliberal policies, it fell entirely within the neoliberal paradigm, given its insistence on competition, markets, and personal responsibility as the foundation of the social and economic order. See, for example, Dardot and Laval (2014: 182ff.). In this view, the best that can be said about "third way politics" and the "social investment state" is that these amount to "neoliberalism with a human face."

62 Since the Hemerijck volume was published, the world has been hit by the COVID-19 pandemic, which has prompted governments everywhere to spend massively on (financial) support for people who suddenly found themselves without a job or income. The situation today may hence be quite different from what it was only a few years ago.

63 Unfortunately, this strong intertemporal orientation introduces new problems. First, the main obstacle to the diffusion of social investment policies is, according to Hemerijck, the time it takes before investments pay off. It takes almost two decades before investments in early child-hood translate into higher productivity. In the short term, such policies only cost money and offer few electoral rewards. Second, inherent to the investment perspective is a focus on those citizens who will yield the highest return on investment. This may invite a new dichotomy between the deserving and undeserving. The first group comprises chil-dren, youth, and, more generally, those with potential to successfully develop their capabilities and contribute to future productivity. The sec-ond group comprises the elderly, the severely disabled, and all those "inactivable individuals" in whom investing scarce resources would be "a waste of money".

64 Rose (2000: 323–324).

65 Rose and Miller (1991/2010: 272, emphasis added). What does it mean to say that personal autonomy has become "a key term in its exercise"? This seemingly paradoxical formulation is a direct reference to Michel Foucault's (2010) seminal 1978–1979 lectures on neoliberalism (and to the work of scholars following in his footsteps, including Rose). Let me briefly explain the argument.

According to Foucault and like-minded scholars, one of the hallmarks of neoliberalism is an inversion of the locus of power and government. In classic models, the (often implicit) assumption is that society is best served by a top-down approach, in which democratic bodies decide what substantive goals to pursue – say, workplace safety, a fair distribution of resources, universal healthcare – and then government does whatever is necessary to bring about these goals. In the neoliberal model, however, the (usually explicit) assumption is that society is best served if govern-ment refrains from the ever-present temptation to intervene in society, and places its trust in the bottom-up dynamic of market competition. The role of government is to create markets and ensure that everybody plays by the rules, but it should stay out of the game itself. This approach will yield superior results. First, due to the fundamental opaqueness of social reality, all top-down interventions to achieve some collective goal are doomed to fail. Second, the "invisible hand of the market" ensures that if all market actors pursue their self-interest, overall utility will be maximized, and the common good is thus best served.

Many of these ideas had been gestating for decades, but it was from the 1970s onward that they came to dominate. Governments curbed their own powers and responsibilities, tying themselves to the mast, so to speak, in order to protect themselves from any temptation to relapse into the old tendency to interfere in society.

Crucially, however, for the system to work, ordinary people must play their designate roles. They must become entrepreneurs who skillfully and effectively develop their human capital to achieve their personal goals, and they must also become responsible citizens who refrain from acting on their self-interest if doing so would harm others or future generations. Now, what if people fail to do so? In the classic top-down model, government simply coerced them into the desired behavior – end of story. In the neoliberal model, however, government has cut off that possibility, leaving itself empty-handed. The only remaining strategy is to act on people's preferences and capabilities, and hope that people behave in the desired manner of their own accord, because they are both willing and able to do so. This means that individual choice-making and choice-following have become the axes of governance. In the words of Foucault scholar Thomas Lemke, if "the neo-liberal strategy does indeed consist of replacing (or at least supplementing) outdated rigid regulatory mechanisms by developing techniques of self-regulation, then political analysis *must start to study the 'autonomous' individuals' capacity for self-control ...*" (Lemke 2001: 203, emphasis added).

66 Abarca-Gómez et al. (2017).
67 WHO (World Health Organization), Global Health Observatory, https://apps.who.int/gho/data/view.main.BMI30CREGv?lang=en, retrieved June 11, 2021.
68 Brownell et al. (2010). In fact, in most countries smoking is on the decline (Bilano et al. 2015).
69 Puhl and Heuer (2009: 7). The results on avoidance or delaying preventive healthcare apply only to the United States, no data are available for other countries.
70 Puhl and Heuer (2009: 950).
71 Pearl and Puhl (2018).

72 Watson et al. (2018).
73 Elias (2000: 398).
74 Castells (1996).
75 Ronson (2015).
76 Zuboff (2019).

## 8 Self-Control and Moral Responsibility

1 Bonnie (1983: 196).
2 Hollander-Blumoff (2012: 511).
3 Eshleman (2014).
4 Mele (1995), quote taken from abstract on https://oxford.university-pressscholarship.com/view/10.1093/0195150430.001.0001/acprof-9780195150438, retrieved on June 10, 2021.
5 Christman (2018).
6 Schlosser (2015). This suggests a broader understanding of the concept of intention than was used in Chapter 3. If one willingly acts in accordance with one's desires, this would also qualify as an instance of agency.
7 Generally speaking, it looks as if the term "autonomy" is more often used in relation to *determining* your preferences, and "agency" more often in relation to *enacting* your preferences.
8 Wallace (1994: 1).
9 Much has been written on the threats that modern psychological research poses to the reflective prong. This research clearly shows that the relevant capacities are not fixed and stable, but a function of circumstantial features. The power to grasp and apply moral reasons may be impaired by, for example, psychologically threatening situations or stress. This emphasis on situational effects and circumstantial features is sometimes referred to as "situationism" or "circumstantialism" (Flanagan 1991; Doris 2002, 2015; Vargas 2013). We are often unaware of such situational influences. Even worse, some neuroscientific research suggests that the reasons we provide for our actions are mere confabulations – that is, after-the-fact rationalizations. These findings have prompted quite some philosophical handwringing, as it is generally held that for moral responsibility to obtain, behavior must be ordered by self-conscious reflection on what to do. Considerable effort and ingenuity have therefore been invested in attempts to rescue moral responsibility from these troublesome findings.

In contrast, much less has been written about the consequences of modern psychological research for the control prong of moral responsibility. It seems as if philosophers assume that once proper reflection has taken place, the heavy lifting is done. Barring external obstacles, normal and healthy adults will have no trouble translating the results of their reflective work into the corresponding behavior, and to sustain this behavior for as long as necessary. *Quod non.*

10 In the philosophical literature, it is common to distinguish between exempting circumstances and excusing circumstances. In the legal literature, it is more common to take both categories together and talk of excusing conditions.

11 Those in the know may object that I have lumped together two different versions of determinism in this paragraph, and they would be right. In this paragraph, I have mixed the leeway argument (given the state of the universe, the agent could not have done other than x) and the sourcehood argument (the agent is not the ultimate source of the decision to do x). The latter version of determinism is more powerful, as it implies that free will cannot exist "either way" – that is, regardless of the question whether determinism or *in*determinism is true. Since these nuances are not relevant to my argument, I prefer the – simplified – representation in the main text.

12 I am well aware that contemporary free will skeptics maintain that if *in*determinism is true, free will and moral responsibility cannot exist either. For the purposes of my argument, however, this nuance is unnecessary.

13 To be more precise, moral responsibility makes no sense if understood in the "basic desert" sense. According to Derk Pereboom, for an agent "to be morally responsible for an action [in the basic desert sense] is for it to belong to her in such a way that she would deserve blame if she understood that it was morally wrong, and she would deserve credit or perhaps praise if she understood that it was morally exemplary. The desert at issue here is basic in the sense that the agent, to be morally responsible, would deserve the blame or credit just because she has performed the action (given that she understands its moral status) and not by virtue of consequentialist or contractualist considerations" (Pereboom 2014: 86). If moral responsibility is defined in such a way that "basic desert" is not a necessary ingredient for moral responsibility, determinism is not necessarily at odds with moral responsibility.

14 Smart (1973: 54).

15 Until recently, this school of thought was referred to as "hard determinism." This term is no longer deemed correct because, so it is argued, if determinism is false, free will cannot exist either. If *in*determinism is true (for instance, due to quantum indeterminacies), our choices would be purely random, which poses just as much a threat to free will as determinism.

16 Or at least, not in itself. It can become a valid excuse, though, when adverse circumstances, character, or poor self-control leads to one of the excusing circumstances that are commonly recognized, such as insanity.
17 Morse (2011: 163).
18 Strawson and Watson (1998).
19 See, for example, Delgado (1985) on "rotten social background."
20 "The sense of agency [...] refers to the experience or judgment that one initiates and that [one] controls an action, particularly an intentional, goal-directed action, regardless of whether one objectively initiated, or is responsible for, that action" (Haggard and Eitam 2015: xi).
21 Having a sense of agency is unconditionally positive. The belief that one has the ability, resources, and opportunities to get positive outcomes and avoid negative outcomes through one's own actions is correlated with better results in almost all domains of life (Thompson 2009). In fact, a persistent lack of sense of agency is often a sign of serious mental or neurological disorders. Who could live with the terrifying idea that he is merely a body governed by outside forces? That is the stuff of horror movies (or philosophical thought experiments) in which malignant actors have secretly implanted chips in your body that control all of your thoughts and actions. The severe discomfort this idea causes has aptly been called "agency panic" (Melley 2000).
22 G. Strawson (2004: 380).
23 G. Strawson (1994: 10).
24 Dennett (1989). We frequently use the language of free will and intention even for non-human objects (Heider and Simmel 1944). These phenomena become mental reality from a very early age. One of the first "illusions" infants learn (and delight in!) is that they can make things happen, thus experiencing "the joy of being a cause" (Groos 1901 cited in White 1959: 316) and developing a sense of agency. Children also quickly learn that praise or blame are only justified when the behavior is intentional. Within two years, toddlers have mastered the basic ideas of intention and responsibility. As every parent knows, "I don't want to" and "I didn't mean to" become all too common phrases.
25 P. F. Strawson (1962/2008: 344).
26 P. F. Strawson (1962/2008: 345).
27 Haidt (2007: 998).
28 Nichols and Knobe (2007: 669, emphasis in original).
29 Nichols and Knobe (2007: 670).
30 Nichols and Knobe (2007: 781, emphasis in original).
31 Pizarro and Helzer (2010: 103).

32  See, for more empirical evidence, Clark et al. (2014, 2019).
33  Clark et al. (2019).
34  Schuman and Presser (1981); Zaller (1992).
35  Weiner (1995: 12). See also Weiner (2006).
36  See, for example, Alicke (2000) and Malle et al. (2014).
37  Zajonc (1980); Kunda (1990).
38  For example, Alicke (2000).
39  For reviews, see Carlsmith and Darley (2008) and Wenzel and Okimoto (2016).
40  Carlsmith and Darley (2008: 207).
41  See also Finkel et al. (1996) and Finkel (2001) on commonsense unfairness. Finkel analyzed about 5,000 descriptions of events that made ordinary folk cry out "Not fair!" Many were instances of disproportionate punishment, say, for someone who, through no fault of her own, shows up to work late just once and is fired on the spot.
42  Carlsmith (2008).
43  Or as the evolutionary biologist David Sloan Wilson wrote many years later: "Even massively fictitious beliefs can be adaptive, as long as they motivate behaviors that are adaptive in the real world" (Wilson 2002, quoted in Boyd 2009: 205). Vaihinger would certainly have agreed, as his book is explicitly inspired by evolutionary theory, which was still young when he began developing his ideas. Thought, Vaihinger (2015: 5) contended, is a "serviceable tool" for "the preservation and enrichment of the life of organisms" (Vaihinger 2015: 11). This focus on usefulness makes perfect evolutionary sense. "Given a choice between a useful fiction and a useless fact, natural selection will choose the useful fiction every time" (Austin 2010: 137).
44  Friedman (1953: 15): "[T]he relevant question to ask about the 'assumptions' of a theory is not whether they are descriptively 'realistic,' for they never are, but whether they are sufficiently good approximations for the purpose in hand. And this question can be answered only by seeing whether the theory works, which means whether it yields sufficiently accurate predictions."
45  Vaihinger (1915/2015: 32).
46  Vaihinger (1915/2015: 32).
47  Vaihinger (1915/2015: 83).
48  Vaihinger (1915/2015: 68).
49  Vargas' approach is sometimes referred to as revisionism, as it maintains that moral responsibility is not a fiction but does indeed exist, and that we only need to revise our ideas about what the concept actually entails. We must jettison some of our ingrained beliefs about what moral responsibility is, because they turn out to be wrong, but the concept itself can and should be preserved. Consider, for example, the concept

of "whale." As science learned more about these creatures, we had to abandon the belief that whales are fish but it clearly does not follow that whales are mere illusions. So it is with moral responsibility.

Still, it is a matter of debate to what extent such a revisionist account of moral responsibility is helpful and permissible. A standard objection against revisionist proposals is that they amount to "changing the subject." Although the term itself is maintained, that to which it refers is changed so substantially that we are no longer talking about the same thing (see McCormick 2013).

50 Vargas (2013: 164). This is a summary of Vargas' position. It remains a matter of debate to what extent not expressing one's emotions is a genuine possibility. The message of this book, of course, is that self-control is – ultimately – limited, and that there are many circumstances in which it is more or less impossible to inhibit one's emotional reactions. This would potentially support Strawson's argument. For a debate about the "inevitability" of (the feeling of) anger, see Flanagan (2017).

51 Vargas (2013: 2).

52 Vargas explicitly positions his work within the recent "renaissance" of instrumentalist theories of moral responsibility (Vargas 2022). The overarching goal of the moral responsibility system is to cultivate agents who, when contemplating what to do, take moral considerations into account. As the name makes clear, the model has a strong developmental hue. "Internalization of norms or praise and blame is the key" (Vargas 2013: 2). Blame and praise initially work by providing external motivation to track moral considerations and to regulate behavior in their light. But over time, the norms expressed through blaming and praising may be internalized. When this happens, individuals will go on to both perpetuate and enforce those norms without external encouragement.

53 Vargas (2013: 175).

54 Vargas (2013: 177).

55 Vargas (2013: 203).

56 Vargas (2013: 203).

57 Vargas (2013: 222).

58 Holroyd (2018: 137).

59 McGeer (2015: 2647). McGeer (2019) dubs her approach the "Scaffolding View" of agency and moral responsibility. Philosopher Maureen Sie (2018) similarly emphasizes the importance of expressing and communicating norms and expectations. It is through interactions with others that norms of moral responsibility arise, are developed, maintained, and adapted. The ideal is a certain kind of agency, and the key for cultivating this type of agency is social practices in which the relevant norms and expectations are expressed and discussed.

60 Vohs and Schooler (2008).

61 Baumeister and Monroe (2014: 25) conclude that "when people's belief in free will is reduced, they are more likely to engage in cheating, stealing, aggressing, neglecting to help, and so forth." See also Protzko et al. (2016).

62 See, for example, Embley et al. (2015), Monroe et al. (2017), Buttrick et al. (2020), and Nadelhoffer et al. (2020). Part of the problem is that it appears rather difficult to alter people's belief in free will. Experiments show that, unlike in the Vohs and Schooler study, the reading of a text or set of statements is often not enough to change people's apparently very stubborn belief in free will, not even for the duration of the experiment. Nadelhoffer et al. (2020), for instance, had to use a "sledgehammer" approach (very large sample, one-tailed significance test) to find only a small effect on belief in free will.

63 See www.theatlantic.com/magazine/archive/2016/06/theres-no-such-thing-as-free-will/480750/, retrieved June 22, 2021.

64 Nadelhoffer (2011: 184).

65 See, for example, Greene and Cohen (2004).

66 Shariff et al. (2014). Krueger et al. (2013) also found that perceptions of reduced free will correlate with less harsh punishment, but only for transgressions that are not emotionally arousing. Martin et al. (2017) analyzed World Value Survey data from forty-six countries, and found that stronger belief in free will is correlated with a stronger desire to see criminals severely punished.

It is an open question how these findings should be judged. A less harsh and punitive climate is not desirable by definition. It may be more desirable in the United States, with its exceptionally high incarceration rate and harsh prison climate, than in other countries. Both on retributive and utilitarian grounds, one could also view a less punitive climate as a negative outcome.

67 Robinson and Holcomb (2021).

68 Nadler (2005).

69 Mullen and Nadler (2008).

70 Robinson et al. (2010: 2016).

71 Bowers and Robinson (2012: 216).

72 Vargas (2013: 175).

73 McGeer (2015: 2647).

74 Specifically, they completed a biased questionnaire that either contained items supporting a limited resource theory (e.g. "Working on a strenuous mental task can make you feel tired such that you need a break before accomplishing a new task") or items supporting a nonlimited resource theory ("Sometimes, working on a strenuous mental task can make you feel energized for further challenging activities").

75 Job et al. (2010).

76 Job et al. (2015). To be clear, these studies do not contradict the findings presented in Chapter 3. They do not refute that self-control capacity is ultimately limited, nor do they refute that situational factors such as cognitive load or stress may impair self-control. These studies only focus on the *idea* of a strictly limited energy resource, and show that if people believe in this idea, they tend to exert less self-control.

77 But perhaps not for so-called "core wrongdoings" (i.e. physical aggression, taking property, and deception in exchanges).

78 We could, of course, shave off some rough edges here, as I did in Section 8.4, and argue that the most useful belief is some middle position between boundless self-control optimism and disillusioned self-control realism, thus obliging ourselves to have a fair level of compassion for those in tough life circumstances. But this does not make the problem go away.

First, self-control in itself is neither good nor bad. It all depends on what this capacity is used for. In a world of aspiring cheaters, crooks, and criminals, you would not want to promote perfectly self-controlled agency, rather the opposite. In such a world, our all-things-considered practical interest would probably be to promote "categorically failing agency." The wider the gap between intention and behavior, the better. Second, why should our all-things-considered practical interest revolve around self-control? Why shouldn't we, instead, aspire to maximum authenticity, or to maximum spontaneity, or to maximum altruism, or to maximize whatever human characteristic is the defining feature of one's preferred ideal world?

The upshot of both arguments is that the choice of type of agency we want to optimize is ultimately contingent on circumstances, and cannot be derived from some higher principle antecedent to social and institutional practices.

79 Doris (2015: 10).

80 Nichols (2015) is another example.

81 This brokenness does not halt at the boundaries of concepts but extends to their very core. In other words, there seems to be a deep indeterminacy and ambiguity in the terms and concept that are central to the debate on free will and moral responsibility. Chapter 1 of Galen Strawson's book opens with the sentence: "Are we free agents? It depends on what you mean by 'free'" (Strawson 1986). Anyone who has ever participated in a debate on the issue will recognize the lament. Furthermore, an important point of early twenty-first-century scholarly debate on the question whether moral responsibility exists or not, is what exactly the term refers to – more specifically, to what extent "basic desert" is an essential and constitutive part of moral responsibility (see, for example, the debate in Dennett and Caruso 2021). McCormick (2013) calls this the "reference-anchoring problem."

82  Dennett (1984: 164).
83  This is also the point where we hit on the limits of Vargas' approach.
    To recall, in his account, it is not required that every single instance of
    praising and blaming yields a positive effect, as long as the responsibility
    system *as a whole* is successful in producing the type of agents we have
    reason to value it. But what happens when this system produces a judg-
    ment of praise or blame that is squarely at odds with our beliefs and intu-
    itions on when someone is *genuinely* responsible for her conduct? Vargas
    is, of course, fully aware of this possibility. His first line of defense is that,
    in his account, such mismatches will be quite rare, exactly because the
    norms of moral responsibility "are given in part by their general efficacy"
    (Vargas 2013: 182). Most cases will fall unproblematically under their
    scope. But having said that, Vargas acknowledges that this leaves some
    nonstandard cases uncovered. More specifically, we need a solution for
    "cases with agents in new, unusual, or particularly challenging contexts
    of action" (Vargas 2013: 183). His solution is, basically, to bracket these
    cases. These are exceptions that should be judged on their own merits.
    After all, there is more to life than moral responsibility! Other concerns –
    say, considerations of justice or prudence – may *trump* judgments of
    responsibility. If your favored theory of ethics holds, for instance, that it
    is unfair to hold people accountable for what they did not do, or that it is
    unfair to hold people accountable for what was not under their control,
    "then that principle and its independent standing can constitute a fixed
    normative point around which the responsibility norms must conform"
    (Vargas 2013: 193). (He only mentions the first of these two possible
    principles, I added the second principle here.)
        While it sounds like a sensible solution, once we zoom in on self-control,
    this line of reasoning becomes highly problematic. If poor self-control
    capacity were indeed such a rare phenomenon, something restricted to the
    small subgroup of the mentally ill or other clinical cases, we could safely
    follow Vargas' lead. Then we could set aside these unusual cases and
    judge them on their own merits. But as I have argued *ad nauseam*, poor
    self-control is quite common, something that can happen to all of us, and
    that may become even more common in the future, as there are no indica-
    tions that the historical trend toward ever-higher self-control demands
    will reverse anytime soon. Should all these instances of self-control failure
    be exempted from the standing rules and procedures and judged on their
    own merits? Is that practically feasible? And if so, how do we stave off the
    skeptic threat? How can we forestall the seemingly inevitable conclusion
    that, since everything is determined, none of these "unusual cases" can be
    judged morally responsible? At the end of the day, Vargas' account proves
    to be unstable too – or at least, when applied to self-control.

## 9  Who Should Get What?

1  Lasswell (1936/2018).
2  Rawls (1999: 54).
3  Rawls (1999: 54).
4  Actually, there is debate over the extent to which Rawls' theory takes the role of personal responsibility into account. Kymlicka (2002), for instance, argues that Rawls acknowledged the crucial role of responsibility, but fails to fully think through and work out the logical consequences of his own assumptions on this matter. Scheffler (2003), however, maintains that this is based on an incorrect reading of Rawls.
5  Although Dworkin does not seem to approve of this label. See Arneson (2018: 44).
6  Research shows that in the subjective standpoint, not equality but deservingness takes first place within the economic domain. With regard to nondistributive issues such as political and legal rights, or access to education and healthcare, equality is favored over deservingness (Miller 1999; Sachweh 2016).
7  John Stuart Mill, *Utilitarianism*, ch 5, para 7 (emphasis added).
8  Van Oorschot (2006: 23) found that "Europeans share a common and fundamental deservingness culture: across countries and social categories there is a consistent pattern that elderly people are seen as most deserving, closely followed by sick and disabled people; unemployed people are seen as less deserving still, and immigrants as least deserving of all."
9  Van Oorschot (2000).
10  The close link between desert and responsibility is illustrated by a psychological phenomenon called "belief in a just world" (Lerner 1980). People tend to believe that the world is basically just and people generally get what they deserve. This belief helps people cope with the inequalities and atrocities that are so ubiquitous in our world. But although belief in a just world may alleviate psychological discomfort, it also induces people to assume responsibility where none may exist. If something bad happens to someone, there must be a reason. This person must have done something wrong or stupid, and brought about the misfortune herself, thereby making it more or less deserved. The textbook example is the tendency to blame victims of rape for their tragedy ("By wearing that short skirt she was asking for it"), but the mechanism is also visible with respect to distributional issues. Many people are convinced that opportunities abound for anyone who is willing to work hard. People who are able-bodied but remain poor must therefore have done something wrong or irresponsible. Or they are simply lazy. In any case, they deserve to be poor.

11 And apparently, given the fact that those who behave responsibly are still entitled to welfare and given the fact that not all income redistribution has been eliminated, people also believe that the doctrines of luck egalitarianism are more "useful" than the doctrines of libertarianism.

12 Barry (2003), cited in Scheffler (2005).

13 Cohen (1989: 934).

14 Rawls (1971/1999: 63).

15 Carver and Scheier (2014).

16 See, for example, Roberts et al. (2007), Poropat (2009), and Kotov et al. (2010).

17 Kunda (1990).

18 Arneson (2000: 97).

19 To avoid any misunderstanding: This is definitively not the same as claiming that material inequalities that stem from differences in self-control are by definition *justified*. This social Darwinist position does not logically follow and is an example of the "naturalistic fallacy." What distribution of scarce goods is fair and just is, ultimately, a matter of good judgment: 1) that cannot be derived from an empirical state of affairs, but only informed by it, and 2) for which the relevant empirical state of affairs is not necessarily restricted to data on (differences in) individual talent only, but may also comprise other empirical data, for example about the effects of alternative patterns of distribution on, say, social cohesion or economic productivity.

20 Frankfurt (2015: 7).

21 Scheffler (2003: 22).

22 Anderson (1999: 316).

23 Scheffler (2003: 23).

24 These two approaches overlap but they are not the same. Sufficientarianism pertains to a certain pattern of distribution, whereas relational equality pertains to a certain relationship between people. While the two often go together, this does not necessarily have to be the case. For instance, one could maintain that relations of equality require more than just "everyone having enough," and can only obtain when all material inequality is completely eliminated.

25 At least, in Anderson's rendering (she only makes an exception for convicted criminals). Not all "relational egalitarians" would agree with this. One could argue that if people repeatedly refuse to act prudently, they should at some point lose their entitlement to "enough" resources.

26 Scheffler (2005: 21).

27 LaPorta et al. (1997); Alesina and Ferarra (2000); Uslaner (2002); Knack and Zak (2003); Delhey and Newton (2005); Bjørnskov (2007); Wilkinson and Pickett (2009). There is some discussion about causality, though, as it might run both ways.

28 See Ostry et al. (2019).

29 Frohlich and Oppenheimer (1993). See also Miller (1999), Chan (2005), and Sachweh (2012). In line with this intuition, many governments and organizations such as the United Nations have defined a social minimum that all citizens are entitled to, including a minimal income, basic education, and access to essential services (see Article 25 of the Universal Declaration of Human Rights). While people may differ in their opinions on what is "enough," the idea of a social minimum itself hardly seems controversial.

30 Except perhaps for Sachweh (2012). Based on twenty in-depth interviews with privileged and disadvantaged men and women, Sachweh found that, although his respondents generally accepted income inequality based on merit, "specific instances of inequality – poverty and excessive wealth – are criticized. The backdrop of this critique is an implicit collective understanding of a common way of life in which everybody should, at least in principle, be able to participate, and from which deviations – upwards and downwards – are seen as objectionable [...] Inequality thus seems to be acceptable as long as people have the feeling of belonging to the same 'social world' and, in turn, is objectionable when ways of living diverge to such an extent that they lead to a segregation of life-worlds, thereby threatening the social bond" (Sachweh 2012: 436–437). However, it is unclear how representative these findings are as they are based on interviews with twenty German adults only.

31 Osberg and Bechert (2017).

32 Scheffler (2003: 32, emphasis added). A somewhat related point is made by Olsaretti (2013), who notes that Cohen, in his defense of luck egalitarianism, remains silent on the question what the *stakes* of people's choices should be – that is, the subset of consequences that people ought to carry themselves after imprudent behavior. The question of stakes asks: "Just what costs (or benefits) should be attached to whatever features constitute the justifiable grounds of responsibility" (Olsaretti 2013: 56). The intuition that those who behave imprudently ought to bear *some* of the consequences themselves does not necessarily mean they have to bear *all* of the consequences themselves, including whatever may result from that behavior in the near or distant future.

For example, if someone decides to go skiing and ends up in hospital with two broken legs, many people will agree he has to cover the medical costs him. But if this accident consigns him to a wheelchair for the rest of his life, few people would argue that he also must shoulder all further consequences of this unfortunate episode in perpetuity. True, it was his choice to go skiing, but this does not automatically mean that his employer is free to fire him for his handicap, or that he is not entitled to any help in making physical adjustments at work or in his home. In sum, luck egalitarianism and the responsibility approach tend to raise the stakes higher than what many people consider fair.

33 In this respect, Kluegel and Mateju (1995) note that people seem to have a "split-consciousness" vis-à-vis redistributive issues. They hold both egalitarian and inegalitarian attitudes at the same time, without fully realizing – or without being bothered by – their potentially conflicting nature.

34 Of course, this idea was not entirely new. There have been earlier periods in history in which "help for the poor" was made dependent on responsible conduct, and in which a distinction was made between the deserving and the undeserving poor. It can be maintained, however, that only since the 1970s, moral responsibility became the foundation of a formal theory of distributive justice and of a set of public policies covering the whole of society.

35 Deacon and Mann (1999).

36 Cohen (1989: 933).

## 10 Conclusion

1 "The more people's standpoints I have present in my mind while I am pondering a given issue and the better I can imagine how I would feel and think if I were in their place, the stronger will be my capacity for representative thinking and the more valid my final conclusions, my opinion" (Arendt 1968: 241).

2 Did Arendt not see this? She remains vague on the matter. On the one hand, she adamantly insists that truth and political judgment be kept strictly apart. Politics is a sphere of human experience and an activity *sui generis* that neither can nor should be reduced to the application of the "how to" knowledge so characteristic of science, technology, and craftsmanship. On the other hand, she also writes that not just any unreflective comment one might drop in the conversation deserves to be treated as a sound opinion. "Facts inform opinions, and opinions, inspired by different interests and passions, can differ widely and still be legitimate *as long as they respect factual truth. Freedom of opinion is a farce unless* factual information is guaranteed and the facts themselves are not in dispute" (Arendt 1968: 238, emphasis added).

3 Similar ideas have been proposed by Latour (2004), one of the inspirations for this paragraph.

4 The government of "nonhumans" such as nature and physical infrastructure is obviously another matter. Here I only discuss the government of humans.

5 In the words of Immanuel Kant in his *Critique of Pure Reason*: "The action to which the 'ought' applies must indeed be possible under natural conditions" (A548/B576).

6 For example, Lunn et al. (2020), OECD (2020), Van Bavel et al. (2020), and West et al. (2020).

7 OECD (2020: 20).

8 Letter from the APS to President-elect Biden's Transition COVID-19 Advisory Board, November 19, 2020.

9 Letter from the APS to President-elect Biden's Transition COVID-19 Advisory Board, December 4, 2020.

10 That behavioral expertise can literally make a difference between life and death is illustrated by the role of "behavioral fatigue" in the United Kingdom's relatively late (first) national lockdown. In a government press conference on March 9, 2020, when the virus was spreading rapidly around the globe, the authorities said they feared that if the country would go into lockdown too soon, people might perhaps comply during the first couple of weeks, but then "behavioral fatigue" would set in – people would tire of the limitations and revert to their prior behavior – and this would happen *just* at the point when the pandemic was expected to reach its peak and compliance was most required. In the words of Chief Medical Officer Chris Whitty: "There is a risk that if we go too early, people will understandably get fatigued and it will be difficult to sustain this over time" (quoted in Harvey 2020: 1).

But is "behavioral fatigue" really a thing? Does the phenomenon actually exist? Behavioral scientists were quick to distance themselves from the concept. On March 16, 2000, a week after the press conference, no less than 681 UK behavioral scientists published an open letter to the government, stating there is no evidence for the reality of behavioral fatigue or its relevance to the behavioral challenges at hand. "If 'behavioural fatigue' truly represents a key factor in the government's decision to delay high-visibility interventions, we urge the government to share an adequate evidence base in support of that decision. If one is lacking, we urge the government to reconsider these decisions" (https://sites.google.com/view/covidopenletter/home, retrieved June 21, 2021).

Of course, one may doubt whether all 681 signatories were experts on fatigue – usually only a handful of specialists are really knowledgeable about the state of the art on any given subject. Moreover, open letters never mention the "nonresponse" – the number of experts who were also invited to sign but declined. Still, the fact remains that the UK government never came forward with the evidence. In a later review of the relevant literature, psychologist Nigel Harvey (one of the signatories) concludes that "[b]ehavioral fatigue is not a real phenomenon" (Harvey 2020: 5).

So where did this concept of "behavioral fatigue" come from? Nobody really knows. Suddenly it was there and it caught on, as it seemed to make intuitive sense and may have been politically expedient. The belief in this psychological phenomenon was one of the (alleged) reasons why the UK went into national lockdown only on March 23, later than many countries on the continent. This delay may have been quite costly. "Had we introduced lockdown a week earlier we'd have reduced the final death toll by at least half," said former scientific advisor Neil Ferguson to the House of Commons Science Committee. That would amount to about 20,000 lives saved (*The Guardian*, June 11, 2020).

11 OECD (2017: 37/8).

12 Sociologist Michael Katz (2013), rather unsurprisingly, finds that in the history of the United States, no one has ever succeeded in drawing the boundary between the deserving and the underserving poor with any precision.

13 Lipsky (1980/2010).

14 This is also a form of judgment, more specifically what Kant called determinant judgment. This is the type of judgment that is made when particulars need to be subsumed under overarching or universal rules or principles. The type of judgment I discuss here, however, is what Kant called reflective judgment. Here such overarching rules or principles are unavailable.

15 Aristotle's *Nicomachean Ethics*, 1137a31–1138a1.

16 Thiele (2006: 24).

17 Fullan (2001).

18 This has become known as the "iron cage" metaphor because Talcott Parsons, the first translator of Weber's essay in English, translated the original German term ("Stahlhartes Gehäuse") as "iron cage." Although less speaking to the imagination, a later translation by Stephen Kalberg used the more accurate "steel-hard casing."

19 This is a variation on the concept of "autonomy gaps," which was advanced by the philosopher Joel Anderson (2009), and refers to a discrepancy between the capacities for choice presupposed by institutional arrangements, public policies and social practices, and the capacities for choice people actually have. I find this a very useful concept, but for my purposes, I prefer to speak of "self control gaps." After all, my argument

is not that people sometimes find it difficult to determine their authentic wants and desires, but that they sometimes lack the necessary self-control to translate these authentic wants and desires into corresponding actions.

20 Kautz et al. (2014: 9).

21 Kautz et al. (2014: 10).

22 Equating personality traits and skills is also conceptually problematic. In psychology, personality traits can be defined as "enduring patterns of thoughts, feelings, and behaviors that reflect the tendency to respond in certain ways under certain circumstances" (Roberts 2009: 140). Given this definition, equating personality traits with skills would mean that the latter not only refer to behaviors, but also to thoughts or feelings. This is quite different from the standard dictionary meaning. Dictionaries usually describe skills as an *ability* to do something well (often as a result of practice or training), and not in terms of (patterns of) thoughts or feelings.

23 Heckman and like-minded others often invoke the Perry Preschool Program as a success story for improving later social outcomes through early intervention. This two-year program targeted three- and four-year-olds from low SES families with an IQ between 70 and 85. These children were trained in, among other things, self-regulating skills such as planning, self-control, and social skills. Every school day devoted 2.5 hours to the program, and the children's mothers were visited every week for 1.5 hours to involve them in the social-emotional development of their children. In 2020 dollars, the cost of the program is estimated at about $22,800 per child (Heckman et al. 2010, adjusted for inflation). In sum, it was a *very intensive* program targeting a population that is hardly representative of all three- and four-year-olds.

Reviewing the literature on personality interventions, Jackson et al. (2021: 795) conclude that "childhood programs appear to be effective in later life [but] there is limited evidence that their effectiveness is due to changes in personality." More generally, the – thus far limited – literature on interventions to change personality is quite sobering, as it suggests no clear way to change one's personality. "If a person is unhappy with his or her personality, it is currently not possible to provide a solution with a well-validated intervention" (Jackson et al. 2021: 801).

24 See, for example, Bovens (2008) and White (2013) for criticism, and Sunstein (2014) for a defense.

25 Whitehead (2018: 1).

26 Whitehead (2018: 3).

27 Yerkes and Dodson (1908).

# Bibliography

Abarca-Gómez, L., Abdeen, Z. A., Hamid, Z. A., Abu-Rmeileh, N. M., Acosta-Cazares, B., Acuin, C., ... & Agyemang, C. (2017). Worldwide trends in body-mass index, underweight, overweight, and obesity from 1975 to 2016: A pooled analysis of 2416 population-based measurement studies in 128.9 million children, adolescents, and adults. *The Lancet, 390*(10113), 2627–2642.

Ackerman, P. L., Beier, M. E., & Boyle, M. O. (2005). Working memory and intelligence: The same or different constructs? *Psychological Bulletin, 131*(1), 30–60.

Adelman, R. M., Herrmann, S. D., Bodford, J. E., Barbour, J. E., Graudejus, O., Okun, M. A., & Kwan, V. S. (2017). Feeling closer to the future self and doing better: Temporal psychological mechanisms underlying academic performance. *Journal of Personality, 85*(3), 398–408.

Adler, N. E., & Stewart, J. (with Cohen, S., Cullen, M., Diez Roux, A., Dow, W., et al.). (2007). *Reaching for a healthier life: Facts on socioeconomic status and health in the U.S.* John D. and Catherine T. MacArthur Foundation Research Network on Socioeconomic Status and Health.

Adler, N. E., Boyce, T., Chesney, M. A., Cohen, S., Folkman, S., Kahn, R. L., & Syme, S. L. (1994). Socioeconomic status and health: The challenge of the gradient. *American Psychologist, 49*(1), 15–24.

Adler, N. E., & Stewart, J. (2010). Health disparities across the lifespan: Meaning, methods, and mechanisms. *Annals of the New York Academy of Sciences, 1186*(1), 5–23.

Alesina, A., & Ferrara, E. L. (2000). *The determinants of trust* (no. w7621). National Bureau of Economic Research.

Alicke, M. D. (2000). Culpable control and the psychology of blame. *Psychological Bulletin, 126*(4), 556–574.

Allan, J. L., Johnston, D. W., Powell, D. J., Farquharson, B., Jones, M. C., Leckie, G., & Johnston, M. (2019). Clinical decisions and time since rest break: An analysis of decision fatigue in nurses. *Health Psychology, 38*(4), 318–324.

Alvaredo, F., Chancel, L., Piketty, T., Saez, E., & Zucman, G. (Eds.). (2018). *World inequality report 2018.* Belknap Press.

Ampel, B. C., Muraven, M., & McNay, E. C. (2018). Mental work requires physical energy: Self-control is neither exception nor exceptional. *Frontiers in Psychology*, *9*, 1005.

Anderson, E. S. (1999). What is the point of equality? *Ethics*, *109*(2), 287–337.

Anderson, J. H. (2009). Autonomy gaps as a social pathology: Ideologiekritik beyond paternalism. In R. Forst, M. Hartmann, R. Jaeggi, & M. Saar (Eds.), *Sozialphilosophie und Kritik*. Suhrkamp Verlag.

Anokhin, A. P., Grant, J. D., Mulligan, R. C., & Heath, A. C. (2015). The genetics of impulsivity: Evidence for the heritability of delay discounting. *Biological Psychiatry*, *77*(10), 887–894.

Arendt, H. (1968). *Between past and future*. Viking Press.

Aristotle. (2011). *Nicomachean ethics*. Translation Robert C. Bartlett and Susan D. Collins. University of Chicago Press.

Arneson, R. J. (1997). Egalitarianism and the undeserving poor. *Journal of Political Philosophy*, *5*(4), 327–350.

Arneson, R. J. (2000). Egalitarian justice versus the right to privacy. *Social Philosophy and Policy*, *17*(2), 91–119.

Arneson, R. J. (2018). Dworkin and luck egalitarianism. In S. Olsaretti (Ed.), *The Oxford handbook of distributive justice*. Oxford University Press, 41–64.

Arno, A., & Thomas, S. (2016). The efficacy of nudge theory strategies in influencing adult dietary behaviour: A systematic review and meta-analysis. *BMC Public Health*, *16*(1), 1–11.

Arnsten, A. F. (2009). Stress signaling pathways that impair prefrontal cortex structure and function. *Nature Reviews Neuroscience*, *10*(6), 410–422.

Arnsten, A. F. (2015). Stress weakens prefrontal networks: Molecular insults to higher cognition. *Nature Neuroscience*, *18*(10), 1376–1385.

Austin, M. (2010). *Useful fictions: Evolution, anxiety, and the origins of literature*. University of Nebraska Press.

Baddeley, A. D., & Hitch, G. (1974). Working memory. In G. A. Bower (Ed.), *Psychology of learning and motivation* (Vol. 8, pp. 47–89). Academic Press.

Banerjee, A., & Duflo, E. (2011). *Poor economics: A radical rethinking of the way to fight global poverty*. Public Affairs.

Banfield, E. C. (1968). *The unheavenly city*. Little, Brown and Company.

Bania, N., & Leete, L. (2009). Monthly household income volatility in the US, 1991/92 vs. 2002/03. *Economics Bulletin*, *29*(3), 2100–2112.

Barber, L. K., Grawitch, M. J., & Munz, D. C. (2013). Are better sleepers more engaged workers? A self-regulatory approach to sleep hygiene and work engagement. *Stress and Health*, *29*(4), 307–316.

Barber, L. K., Munz, D. C., Bagsby, P. G., & Grawitch, M. J. (2009). When does time perspective matter? Self-control as a moderator between time perspective and academic achievement. *Personality and Individual Differences*, 46(2), 250–253.

Barkley, R. A. (2013). *Taking charge of ADHD: The complete, authoritative guide for parents* (3rd ed.). Guilford Press.

Bartels, D. M., & Urminsky, O. (2011). On intertemporal selfishness: How the perceived instability of identity underlies impatient consumption. *Journal of Consumer Research*, 38(1), 182–198.

Basile, A. G., & Toplak, M. E. (2015). Four converging measures of temporal discounting and their relationships with intelligence, executive functions, thinking dispositions, and behavioral outcomes. *Frontiers in Psychology*, 6, 728.

Bauer, J. M., & Reisch, L. A. (2019). Behavioural insights and (un)healthy dietary choices: A review of current evidence. *Journal of Consumer Policy*, 42(1), 3–45.

Baumeister, R. F. (2020). Do effect sizes in psychology laboratory experiments mean anything in reality? *Psychology: Journal of the Higher School of Economics*, 17(4), 803–811.

Baumeister, R. F., & Alquist, J. L. (2009). Is there a downside to good self-control? *Self and Identity*, 8(2–3), 115–130.

Baumeister, R. F., Bratslavsky, E., Muraven, M., & Tice, D. M. (1998). Ego depletion: Is the active self a limited resource? *Journal of Personality and Social Psychology*, 74(5), 1252–1265.

Baumeister, R. F., Faber, J. E., & Wallace, H. M. (1999). Coping and ego depletion: Recovery after the coping process. In C. R. Snyder (Ed.), *Coping: The psychology of what works* (pp. 50–69). Oxford University Press.

Baumeister, R. F., Heatherton, T. F., & Tice, D. M. (1994). *Losing control: How and why people fail at self-regulation*. Academic Press.

Baumeister, R. F., & Monroe, A. E. (2014). Recent research on free will: Conceptualizations, beliefs, and processes. In *Advances in experimental social psychology* (Vol. 50, pp. 1–52). Academic Press.

Baumeister, R. F., & Vohs, K. D. (2016). Misguided effort with elusive implications. *Perspectives on Psychological Science*, 11(4), 574–575.

Baumeister, R. F., Vonasch, A. J., & Sjåstad, H. (2020). The long reach of self-control. In A. R. Mele (Ed.), *Surrounding self-control* (17–46). Oxford University Press.

Baumeister, R. F., Wright, B. R., & Carreon, D. (2019). Self-control "in the wild": Experience sampling study of trait and state self-regulation. *Self and Identity*, 18(5), 494–528.

Baumeister, R. F., Zell, A. L., & Tice, D. M. (2007). How emotions facilitate and impair self-regulation. In J. J. Gross (Ed.), *Handbook of emotion regulation* (pp. 408–426). Guilford Press.

Baumer, E. P., & Wolff, K. T. (2014). Evaluating contemporary crime drop(s) in America, New York City, and many other places. *Justice Quarterly, 31*(1), 5–38.

Beames, J., Schofield, T. P., & Denson, T. F. (2018). A meta-analysis of improving self-control with practice. In D. De Ridder, M. Adriaanse, & K. Fujita (Eds.), *Routledge international handbook of self-control in health and well-being* (pp. 405–417). Routledge.

Belsky, J. (2012). The development of human reproductive strategies: Progress and prospects. *Current Directions in Psychological Science, 21*(5), 310–316.

Bennett, G. G., Merritt, M. M., Sollers III, J. J., Edwards, C. L., Whitfield, K. E., Brandon, D. T., & Tucker, R. D. (2004). Stress, coping, and health outcomes among African-Americans: A review of the John Henryism hypothesis. *Psychology & Health, 19*(3), 369–383.

Benoit, R. G., Gilbert, S. J., & Burgess, P. W. (2011). A neural mechanism mediating the impact of episodic prospection on farsighted decisions. *Journal of Neuroscience, 31*(18), 6771–6779.

Bickel, W. K., Yi, R., Landes, R. D., Hill, P. F., & Baxter, C. (2011). Remember the future: Working memory training decreases delay discounting among stimulant addicts. *Biological Psychiatry, 69*(3), 260–265.

Bilano, V., Gilmour, S., Moffiet, T., d'Espaignet, E. T., Stevens, G. A., Commar, A., … & Shibuya, K. (2015). Global trends and projections for tobacco use, 1990–2025: An analysis of smoking indicators from the WHO Comprehensive Information Systems for Tobacco Control. *The Lancet, 385*(9972), 966–976.

Bin, Y. S., Marshall, N. S., & Glozier, N. (2010). Secular trends in adult sleep duration: A systematic review. *Sleep Medicine Reviews, 16*(3), 223–230.

Bjørnskov, C. (2007). Determinants of generalized trust: A cross-country comparison. *Public Choice, 130*(1–2), 1–21.

Blair, C. (2010). Stress and the development of self-regulation in context. *Child Development Perspectives, 4*(3), 181–188.

Blázquez, D., Botella, J., & Suero, M. (2017). The debate on the ego-depletion effect: Evidence from meta-analysis with the p-uniform method. *Frontiers in Psychology, 8,* 197.

Block, J. (1995). A contrarian view of the five-factor approach to personality description. *Psychological Bulletin, 117*(2), 187–215.

Boksem, M. A., Meijman, T. F., & Lorist, M. M. (2005). Effects of mental fatigue on attention: An ERP study. *Cognitive Brain Research, 25*(1), 107–116.

Boksem, M. A., Meijman, T. F., & Lorist, M. M. (2006). Mental fatigue, motivation and action monitoring. *Biological Psychology, 72*(2), 123–132.

Bonnie, R. J. (1983). The moral basis of the insanity defense. *American Bar Association Journal, 69*(2), 194–197.

Bouchard Jr., T. J. (2004). Genetic influence on human psychological traits: A survey. *Current Directions in Psychological Science, 13*(4), 148–151.

Bovens, L. (2008). The ethics of nudge. In T. Grune-Yanoff and S. O. Hansson (Eds.), *Preference change: Approaches from philosophy, economics and psychology* (pp. 207–219). Springer.

Bowers, J., & Robinson, P. H. (2012). Perceptions of fairness and justice: The shared arms and occasional conflicts of legitimacy and moral credibility. *Wake Forest Law Review, 47,* 211–284.

Boyd, B. (2009). *On the origin of stories.* Harvard University Press.

Boyer, P. (2008). Evolutionary economics of mental time travel? *Trends in Cognitive Sciences, 12*(6), 219–224.

Bratman, M. (1987). *Intention, plans, and practical reason.* Harvard University Press.

Brody, G. H., Yu, T., Chen, E., & Miller, G. E. (2020). Persistence of skin-deep resilience in African American adults. *Health Psychology, 39*(10), 921–926.

Brody, G. H., Yu, T., Chen, E., Miller, G. E., Kogan, S. M., & Beach, S. R. (2013). Is resilience only skin deep? Rural African Americans' socio-economic status-related risk and competence in preadolescence and psychological adjustment and allostatic load at age 19. *Psychological Science, 24*(7), 1285–1293.

Brody, G. H., Yu, T., Miller, G. E., Ehrlich, K. B., & Chen, E. (2018). John Henryism coping and metabolic syndrome among young Black adults. *Psychosomatic Medicine, 80*(2), 216–221.

Broers, V. J., De Breucker, C., Van den Broucke, S., & Luminet, O. (2017). A systematic review and meta-analysis of the effectiveness of nudging to increase fruit and vegetable choice. *European Journal of Public Health, 27*(5), 912–920.

Bromberg, U., Wiehler, A., & Peters, J. (2015). Episodic future thinking is related to impulsive decision making in healthy adolescents. *Child Development, 86*(5), 1458–1468.

Brown, A. (2009). *Personal responsibility: Why it matters.* Bloomsbury Publishing.

Brownell, K. D., Kersh, R., Ludwig, D. S., Post, R. C., Puhl, R. M., Schwartz, M. B., & Willett, W. C. (2010). Personal responsibility and obesity: A constructive approach to a controversial issue. *Health Affairs, 29*(3), 379–387.

Bryan, G., Karlan, D., & Nelson, S. (2010). Commitment devices. *Annual Review of Economics*, 2(1), 671–698.

Bulley, A., & Gullo, M. J. (2017). The influence of episodic foresight on delay discounting and demand for alcohol. *Addictive Behaviors*, 66, 1–6.

Bulley, A., Henry, J., & Suddendorf, T. (2016). Prospection and the present moment: The role of episodic foresight in intertemporal choices between immediate and delayed rewards. *Review of General Psychology*, 20(1), 29–47.

Buttrick, N. R., Aczel, B., Aeschbach, L. F., Bakos, B. E., Brühlmann, F., Claypool, H. M., … & Wood, M. J. (2020). Many Labs 5: Registered replication of Vohs and Schooler (2008), experiment 1. *Advances in Methods and Practices in Psychological Science*, 3(3), 429–438.

Carlsmith, K. M. (2008). On justifying punishment: The discrepancy between words and actions. *Social Justice Research*, 21(2), 119–137.

Carlsmith, K. M., & Darley, J. M. (2008). Psychological aspects of retributive justice. In M. P. Zanna (Ed.), *Advances in experimental social psychology* (Vol. 40, pp. 193–236). Elsevier.

Carr, M. D., & Wiemers, E. E. (2016). *The increasingly unstable earnings of less-educated workers*.

Carter, E. C., Kofler, L. M., Forster, D. E., & McCullough, M. E. (2015). A series of meta-analytic tests of the depletion effect: Self-control does not seem to rely on a limited resource. *Journal of Experimental Psychology: General*, 144(4), 796–815.

Carver, C. S., & Scheier, M. F. (2014). Dispositional optimism. *Trends in Cognitive Sciences*, 18(6), 293–299.

Caspi, A., Harrington, H., Milne, B., Amell, J. W., Theodore, R. F., & Moffitt, T. E. (2003). Children's behavioral styles at age 3 are linked to their adult personality traits at age 26. *Journal of Personality*, 71(4), 495–514.

Caspi, A., Houts, R. M., Belsky, D. W., Harrington, H., Hogan, S., Ramrakha, S., … & Moffitt, T. E. (2016). Childhood forecasting of a small segment of the population with large economic burden. *Nature Human Behaviour*, 1(1), 1–10.

Castells, M. (1996). *The rise of the network society*. Vol. I of *The information age: Economy, society and culture*. Blackwell.

Chan, H. M. (2005). Rawls' theory of justice: A naturalistic evaluation. *Journal of Medicine and Philosophy*, 30(5), 449–465.

Chemin, M., De Laat, J., & Haushofer, J. (2013). Negative rainfall shocks increase levels of the stress hormone cortisol among poor farmers in Kenya. Available at SSRN 2294171.

Cheng, Y. Y., Shein, P. P., & Chiou, W. B. (2012). Escaping the impulse to immediate gratification: The prospect concept promotes a future-oriented mindset, prompting an inclination towards delayed gratification. *British Journal of Psychology*, *103*(1), 129–141.

Chetty, R., Stepner, M., Abraham, S., Lin, S., Scuderi, B., Turner, N., ... & Cutler, D. (2016). The association between income and life expectancy in the United States, 2001–2014. *JAMA*, *315*(16), 1750–1766.

Cheung, T. T., Gillebaart, M., Kroese, F., & De Ridder, D. (2014). Why are people with high self-control happier? The effect of trait self-control on happiness as mediated by regulatory focus. *Frontiers in Psychology*, *5*, 722.

Chou, E. Y., Parmar, B. L., & Galinsky, A. D. (2016). Economic insecurity increases physical pain. *Psychological Science*, *27*(4), 443–454.

Christian, M. S., & Ellis, A. P. (2011). Examining the effects of sleep deprivation on workplace deviance: A self-regulatory perspective. *Academy of Management Journal*, *54*(5), 913–934.

Christman, J. (2018). Autonomy in moral and political philosophy. In E. N. Zalta (Ed.), *Stanford encyclopedia of philosophy*. Stanford University Press.

Clark, C. J., Luguri, J. B., Ditto, P. H., Knobe, J., Shariff, A. F., & Baumeister, R. F. (2014). Free to punish: a motivated account of free will belief. *Journal of personality and social psychology*, *106*(4), 501.

Clark, C. J., Winegard, B. M., & Baumeister, R. F. (2019). Forget the folk: Moral responsibility preservation motives and other conditions for compatibilism. *Frontiers in Psychology*, *10*, 215.

Clark, C. J., Winegard, B. M., & Shariff, A. F. (2021). Motivated free will belief: The theory, new (preregistered) studies, and three meta-analyses. *Journal of Experimental Psychology: General*, *150*(7), e22–e47.

Cohen, G. A. (1989). On the currency of egalitarian justice. *Ethics*, *99*(4), 906–944.

Cohen, S., Doyle, W. J., & Baum, A. (2006). Socioeconomic status is associated with stress hormones. *Psychosomatic Medicine*, *68*(3), 414–420.

Cohen, S., & Janicki-Deverts, D. (2012). Who's stressed? Distributions of psychological stress in the United States in probability samples from 1983, 2006, and 2009. *Journal of Applied Social Psychology*, *42*(6), 1320–1334.

Conger, R. D., & Donnellan, M. B. (2007). An interactionist perspective on the socioeconomic context of human development. *Annual Review of Psychology*, *58*, 175–199.

Cosenza, M., & Nigro, G. (2015). Wagering the future: Cognitive distortions, impulsivity, delay discounting, and time perspective in adolescent gambling. *Journal of Adolescence*, *45*, 56–66.

Cowan, N. (2001). The magical number 4 in short-term memory: A reconsideration of mental storage capacity. *Behavioral and Brain Sciences*, 24(1), 87–114.

Cunningham, M. R., & Baumeister, R. F. (2016). How to make nothing out of something: Analyses of the impact of study sampling and statistical interpretation in misleading meta-analytic conclusions. *Frontiers in Psychology: Personality and Social Psychology*, 7, 1639.

Dai, H., Milkman, K. L., Hofmann, D. A., & Staats, B. R. (2015). The impact of time at work and time off from work on rule compliance: The case of hand hygiene in health care. *Journal of Applied Psychology*, 100(3), 846–862.

Dang, J. (2016a). Commentary: A multilab preregistered replication of the ego-depletion effect. *Frontiers in Psychology*, 7, 1155.

Dang, J. (2016b). Testing the role of glucose in self-control: A meta-analysis. *Appetite*, 107, 222–230.

Dang, J. (2018). An updated meta-analysis of the ego depletion effect. *Psychological Research*, 82(4), 645–651.

Dang, J., Barker, P., Baumert, A., Bentvelzen, M., Berkman, E., Buchholz, N., ... & Zinkernagel, A. (2021). A multilab replication of the ego depletion effect. *Social Psychological and Personality Science*, 12(1), 14–24.

Daniel, T. O., Stanton, C. M., & Epstein, L. H. (2013a). The future is now: Reducing impulsivity and energy intake using episodic future thinking. *Psychological Science*, 24(11), 2339–2342.

Daniel, T. O., Stanton, C. M., & Epstein, L. H. (2013b). The future is now: Comparing the effect of episodic future thinking on impulsivity in lean and obese individuals. *Appetite*, 71, 120–125.

Daniel, T. O., Said, M., Stanton, C. M., & Epstein, L. H. (2015). Episodic future thinking reduces delay discounting and energy intake in children. *Eating Behaviors*, 18, 20–24.

Dardot, P., & Laval, C. (2014). *The new way of the world: On neoliberal society*. Verso Trade.

Dassen, F. C., Jansen, A., Nederkoorn, C., & Houben, K. (2016). Focus on the future: Episodic future thinking reduces discount rate and snacking. *Appetite*, 96, 327–332.

Daugherty, J. R., & Brase, G. L. (2010). Taking time to be healthy: Predicting health behaviors with delay discounting and time perspective. *Personality and Individual Differences*, 48(2), 202–207.

De Bruijn, E. J., & Antonides, G. (2021). Poverty and economic decision making: A review of scarcity theory. *Theory and Decision*, 1–33.

De Ridder, D. T., Lensvelt-Mulders, G., Finkenauer, C., Stok, F. M., & Baumeister, R. F. (2012). Taking stock of self-control: A meta-analysis of how trait self-control relates to a wide range of behaviors. *Personality and Social Psychology Review*, 16(1), 76–99.

De Ridder, D.T., Van der Weiden, A., Gillebaart, M., Benjamins, J., & Ybema, J. F. (2020). Just do it: Engaging in self-control on a daily basis improves the capacity for self-control. *Motivation Science*, 6(4), 309–320.

Deacon, A., & Mann, K. (1999). Agency, modernity and social policy. *Journal of Social Policy*, 28(3), 413–435.

Deck, C., & Jahedi, S. (2015). The effect of cognitive load on economic decision making: A survey and new experiments. *European Economic Review*, 78, 97–119.

Del Giudice, M. (2014). An evolutionary life history framework for psychopathology. *Psychological Inquiry*, 25(3–4), 261–300.

Delgado, R. (1985). Rotten social background: Should the criminal law recognize a defense of severe environmental deprivation. *Minnesota Journal of Law & Inequality*, 3, 9–90.

Delhey, J., & Newton, K. (2005). Predicting cross-national levels of social trust: Global pattern or Nordic exceptionalism? *European Sociological Review*, 21(4), 311–327.

Dennett, D. C. (2015). *Elbow room: The varieties of free will worth wanting*. MIT Press.

Dennett, D. C. (1989). *The intentional stance*. MIT Press.

Dennett, D. C., & Caruso, G. D. (2021). *Just deserts: Debating free will*. Polity Books.

Devine, P. G. (1989). Stereotypes and prejudice: Their automatic and controlled components. *Journal of Personality and Social Psychology*, 56(1), 5–18.

Diamond, A. (2013). Executive functions. *Annual Review of Psychology*, 64, 135–168.

Diamond, A., & Lee, K. (2011). Interventions shown to aid executive function development in children 4 to 12 years old. *Science*, 333(6045), 959–964.

Doebel, S., Michaelson, L. E., & Munakata, Y. (2020). Good things come to those who wait: Delaying gratification likely does matter for later achievement (a commentary on Watts, Duncan, & Quan, 2018). *Psychological Science*, 31(1), 97–99.

Doris, J. M. (2002). *Lack of character: Personality and moral behavior*. Cambridge University Press.

Doris, J. M. (2015). *Talking to our selves: Reflection, ignorance, and agency*. Oxford University Press.

Duckworth, A. L., & Kern, M. L. (2011). A meta-analysis of the convergent validity of self-control measures. *Journal of Research in Personality*, 45(3), 259–268.

Duckworth, A. L., Kim, B., & Tsukayama, E. (2013). Life stress impairs self-control in early adolescence. *Frontiers in Psychology, 3*, 608.

Duckworth, A. L., Milkman, K. L., & Laibson, D. (2018). Beyond willpower: Strategies for reducing failures of self-control. *Psychological Science in the Public Interest, 19*(3), 102–129.

Duckworth, A. L., & Seligman, M. E. (2005). Self-discipline outdoes IQ in predicting academic performance of adolescents. *Psychological Science, 16*(12), 939–944.

Duckworth, A. L., Tsukayama, E., & Kirby, T. A. (2013). Is it really self-control? Examining the predictive power of the delay of gratification task. *Personality and Social Psychology Bulletin, 39*(7), 843–855.

Dynan, K., Elmendorf, D., & Sichel, D. (2012). The evolution of household income volatility. *BE Journal of Economic Analysis & Policy, 12*(2), 1–42.

Eisner, M. (2003). Long-term historical trends in violent crime. *Crime and Justice, 30*, 83–142.

Eisner, M. (2014). From swords to words: Does macro-level change in self-control predict long-term variation in levels of homicide? *Crime and Justice, 43*(1), 65–134.

Elias, N. (2000). *The civilizing process: Sociogenetic and psychogenetic investigations.* Wiley-Blackwell.

Ellis, B. J., Figueredo, A. J., Brumbach, B. H., & Schlomer, G. L. (2009). Fundamental dimensions of environmental risk. *Human Nature, 20*(2), 204–268.

Embley, J., Johnson, L. G., & Giner-Sorolla, R. (2015). Reproducibility project: Replication report – Replication of study 1 by Vohs & Schooler (2008). *OSF*, February 3, 2022. https://osf.io/uwt5f/.

Engle, R. W. (2002). Working memory capacity as executive attention. *Current Directions in Psychological Science, 11*(1), 19–23.

Engle, R. W. (2018). Working memory and executive attention: A revisit. *Perspectives on Psychological Science, 13*(2), 190–193.

Eshleman, A. (2014). Moral responsibility. In E. N. Zalta (Ed.), *The Stanford encyclopedia of philosophy.* Palo Alto, CA: Stanford University.

Eskreis-Winkler, L., Gross, J. J., & Duckworth, A. L. (2016). Grit: Sustained self-regulation in the service of superordinate goals. In K. D. Vohs & R. F. Baumeister (Eds.), *Handbook of self-regulation: Research, theory and applications* (3rd ed., pp. 380–395). New York: Guilford Press.

Evans, G. W. (2004). The environment of childhood poverty. *American Psychologist, 59*(2), 77–92.

Evans, G. W. (2016). Childhood poverty and adult psychological well-being. *Proceedings of the National Academy of Sciences, 113*(52), 14949–14952.

Evans, G. W., & De France, K. (2021). Childhood poverty and psychological well-being: The mediating role of cumulative risk exposure. *Development and Psychopathology*, 1–11. doi:10.1017/S0954579420001947

Evans, G. W., & English, K. (2002). The environment of poverty: Multiple stressor exposure, psychophysiological stress, and socioemotional adjustment. *Child Development*, 73(4), 1238–1248.

Evans, G. W., & Kim, P. (2012). Childhood poverty and young adults' allostatic load: The mediating role of childhood cumulative risk exposure. *Psychological Science*, 23(9), 979–983.

Evans, G. W., & Rosenbaum, J. (2008). Self-regulation and the income-achievement gap. *Early Childhood Research Quarterly*, 23(4), 504–514.

Evans, J. S. B. (2008). Dual-processing accounts of reasoning, judgment, and social cognition. *Annual Review of Psychology*, 59, 255–278.

Evans, T. D., Cullen, F. T., Burton Jr., V. S., Dunaway, R. G., & Benson, M. L. (1997). The social consequences of self-control: Testing the general theory of crime. *Criminology*, 35(3), 475–504.

Evers, C., Adriaanse, M., de Ridder, D. T., & de Witt Huberts, J. C. (2013). Good mood food: Positive emotion as a neglected trigger for food intake. *Appetite*, 68, 1–7.

Falk, A., Kosse, F., & Pinger, P. (2020). Re-revisiting the marshmallow test: A direct comparison of studies by Shoda, Mischel, and Peake (1990) and Watts, Duncan, and Quan (2018). *Psychological Science*, 31(1), 100–104.

Fayyad, J., Sampson, N. A., Hwang, I., Adamowski, T., Aguilar-Gaxiola, S., Al-Hamzawi, A., ... & WHO World Mental Health Survey Collaborators. (2017). The descriptive epidemiology of DSM-IV adult ADHD in the World Health Organization world mental health surveys. *Attention Deficit and Hyperactivity Disorders*, 9(1), 47–65.

Fedorikhin, A., & Patrick, V. M. (2010). Positive mood and resistance to temptation: The interfering influence of elevated arousal. *Journal of Consumer Research*, 37(4), 698–711.

Fields, S. A., Lange, K., Ramos, A., Thamotharan, S., & Rassu, F. (2014). The relationship between stress and delay discounting: A meta-analytic review. *Behavioural Pharmacology*, 25(5–6), 434–444.

Fieulaine, N., & Apostolidis, T. (2015). Precariousness as a time horizon: How poverty and social insecurity shape individuals' time perspectives. In M. Stolarski, N. Fieulaine, & W. van Beek (Eds.), *Time perspective theory: Review, research and application* (pp. 213–228). Springer International.

Figueredo, A. J., Vásquez, G., Brumbach, B. H., & Schneider, S. M. (2007). The K-factor, covitality, and personality. *Human Nature*, 18(1), 47–73.

Finkel, N. J. (2001). *Not fair! The typology of commonsense unfairness.* American Psychological Association.

Finkel, N. J., Maloney, S. T., Valbuena, M. Z., & Groscup, J. (1996). Recidivism, proportionalism, and individualized punishment. *American Behavioral Scientist, 39*(4), 474–487.

Fishbach, A., & Labroo, A. A. (2007). Be better or be merry: How mood affects self-control. *Journal of Personality and Social Psychology, 93*(2), 158–173.

Flanagan, O. (1991). *Varieties of moral personality: Ethics and psychological realism.* Harvard University Press.

Flanagan, O. (2017). *The geography of morals: Varieties of moral possibility.* Oxford University Press.

Fletcher, D. R., & Wright, S. (2018). A hand up or a slap down? Criminalising benefit claimants in Britain via strategies of surveillance, sanctions and deterrence. *Critical Social Policy, 38*(2), 323–344.

Foucault, M. (2010). *The birth of biopolitics: Lectures at the Collège de France, 1978–1979.* Palgrave Macmillan.

Franco-Watkins, A. M., Rickard, T. C., & Pashler, H. (2010). Taxing executive processes does not necessarily increase impulsive decision making. *Experimental Psychology, 57*(3), 193–201.

Frankfurt, H. (2015). *On equality.* Princeton University Press.

Friedman, M. (1953). The methodology of positive economics. In *Essays in positive economics.* University of Chicago Press.

Friedman, N. P., Miyake, A., Young, S. E., DeFries, J. C., Corley, R. P., & Hewitt, J. K. (2008). Individual differences in executive functions are almost entirely genetic in origin. *Journal of Experimental Psychology: General, 137*(2), 201–225.

Friese, M., Frankenbach, J., Job, V., & Loschelder, D. D. (2017). Does self-control training improve self-control? A meta-analysis. *Perspectives on Psychological Science, 12*(6), 1077–1099.

Friese, M., Hofmann, W., & Wänke, M. (2008). When impulses take over: Moderated predictive validity of explicit and implicit attitude measures in predicting food choice and consumption behaviour. *British Journal of Social Psychology, 47*(3), 397–419.

Friese, M., Loschelder, D. D., Gieseler, K., Frankenbach, J., & Inzlicht, M. (2019). Is ego depletion real? An analysis of arguments. *Personality and Social Psychology Review, 23*(2), 107–131.

Frohlich, N., & Oppenheimer, J. A. (1993). *Choosing justice: An experimental approach to ethical theory.* University of California Press.

Fujita, K. (2011). On conceptualizing self-control as more than the effortful inhibition of impulses. *Personality and Social Psychology Review, 15*(4), 352–366.

Fullan, M. (2001). *The new meaning of educational change*. Routledge.

Gailliot, M. T., & Baumeister, R. F. (2007). The physiology of willpower: Linking blood glucose to self-control. *Personality and Social Psychology Review*, *11*(4), 303–327.

Galla, B. M., & Duckworth, A. L. (2015). More than resisting temptation: Beneficial habits mediate the relationship between self-control and positive life outcomes. *Journal of Personality and Social Psychology*, *109*(3), 508.

Gallup (2017). *Gallup 2017 global emotions report*, February 7, 2022. https://news.gallup.com/reports/212648/gallup-global-emotions-report-2017.aspx.

Garland, D. (2001) *The culture of control: Crime and social order in contemporary society*. Oxford University Press.

Garrison, K. E., Finley, A. J., & Schmeichel, B. J. (2019). Ego depletion reduces attention control: Evidence from two high-powered preregistered experiments. *Personality and Social Psychology Bulletin*, *45*(5), 728–739.

Germano, G., & Brenlla, M. E. (2021). Effects of time perspective and self-control on psychological distress: A cross-sectional study in an Argentinian sample. *Personality and Individual Differences*, *171*, 110512.

Gilbert, D. T., & Wilson, T. D. (2007). Prospection: Experiencing the future. *Science*, *317*(5843), 1351–1354.

Gillebaart, M., & de Ridder, D. T. (2015). Effortless self-control: A novel perspective on response conflict strategies in trait self-control. *Social and Personality Psychology Compass*, *9*(2), 88–99.

Giné, X., Karlan, D., & Zinman, J. (2010). Put your money where your butt is: A commitment contract for smoking cessation. *American Economic Journal: Applied Economics*, *2*(4), 213–235.

Goldstein, A. N., & Walker, M. P. (2014). The role of sleep in emotional brain function. *Annual Review of Clinical Psychology*, *10*, 679–708.

Gollwitzer, P. M. (1999). Implementation intentions: Strong effects of simple plans. *American Psychologist*, *54*(7), 493.

Gottfredson, M. R., & Hirsch, T. (1990). *A general theory of crime*. Stanford University Press.

Gottschalk, P., & Moffitt, R. (2009). The rising instability of US earnings. *Journal of Economic Perspectives*, *23*(4), 3–24.

Graafland, J. J. (2009). *Doux commerce and self-destruction in a curvilinear relation between competition and virtues*. Tilburg University, Conference paper.

Grandner, M. A. (2017). Sleep, health, and society. *Sleep Medicine Clinics*, *12*(1), 1–22.

Grandner, M. A., Hale, L., Jackson, N., Patel, N. P., Gooneratne, N. S., & Troxel, W. M. (2012). Perceived racial discrimination as an independent predictor of sleep disturbance and daytime fatigue. *Behavioral Sleep Medicine*, 10(4), 235–249.

Grandner, M. A., Patel, N. P., Gehrman, P. R., Xie, D., Sha, D., Weaver, T., & Gooneratne, N. (2010). Who gets the best sleep? Ethnic and socioeconomic factors related to sleep complaints. *Sleep Medicine*, 11(5), 470–478.

Grandner, M. A., Williams, N. J., Knutson, K. L., Roberts, D., & Jean-Louis, G. (2016). Sleep disparity, race/ethnicity, and socioeconomic position. *Sleep Medicine*, 18, 7–18.

Grant, K. E., Compas, B. E., Stuhlmacher, A. F., Thurm, A. E., McMahon, S. D., & Halpert, J. A. (2003). Stressors and child and adolescent psychopathology: Moving from markers to mechanisms of risk. *Psychological Bulletin*, 129(3), 447–466.

Greene, J. D., & Cohen, J. D. (2004). For the law, neuroscience changes nothing and everything. *Philosophical Transactions of the Royal Society B: Biological Sciences*, 359, 1775–1785.

Griskevicius, V., Ackerman, J. M., Cantú, S. M., Delton, A. W., Robertson, T. E., Simpson, J. A., ... & Tybur, J. M. (2013). When the economy falters, do people spend or save? Responses to resource scarcity depend on childhood environments. *Psychological Science*, 24(2), 197–205.

Griskevicius, V., Tybur, J. M., Delton, A. W., & Robertson, T. E. (2011). The influence of mortality and socioeconomic status on risk and delayed rewards: A life history theory approach. *Journal of Personality and Social Psychology*, 100(6), 1015–1026.

Groos, K. (1901). *The play of man*. Appleton and Company.

Guo, Y., Chen, Z., & Feng, T. (2017). The effect of future time perspective on delay discounting is mediated by the gray matter volume of vmPFC. *Neuropsychologia*, 102, 229–236.

Hacker, J. S. (2008). *The great risk shift* (rev. and exp. ed.). Oxford University Press.

Haggard, P., & Eitam, B. (Eds.). (2015). *The sense of agency. Social cognition and social neuroscience*. Oxford University Press.

Hagger, M. S., Chatzisarantis, N. L., Alberts, H., Anggono, C. O., Batailler, C., Birt, A. R., ... & Calvillo, D. P. (2016). A multilab preregistered replication of the ego-depletion effect. *Perspectives on Psychological Science*, 11(4), 546–573.

Hagger, M. S., Wood, C., Stiff, C., & Chatzisarantis, N. L. (2010). Ego depletion and the strength model of self-control: A meta-analysis. *Psychological Bulletin*, 136(4), 495–525.

Haidt, J. (2007). The new synthesis in moral psychology. *Science, 316*(5827), 998–1002.

Hamidovic, A., & de Wit, H. (2009). Sleep deprivation increases cigarette smoking. *Pharmacology Biochemistry and Behavior, 93*(3), 263–269.

Hamoudi, A., Murray, D. W., Sorensen, L., & Fontaine, A. (2015). *Self-regulation and toxic stress: A review of ecological, biological, and developmental studies of self-regulation and stress* (OPRE report 2015-30). Office of Planning, Research and Evaluation, Administration for Children and Families, US Department of Health and Human Services.

Harrison, Y., & Horne, J. A. (2000). The impact of sleep deprivation on decision making: A review. *Journal of Experimental Psychology: Applied, 6*(3), 236.

Harvey, N. (2020). Behavioral fatigue: Real phenomenon, naïve construct, or policy contrivance? *Frontiers in Psychology, 11*, 2960.

Haskell, T. L. (1985). Capitalism and the origins of the humanitarian sensibility, Part 2. *American Historical Review, 90*(3), 547–566.

Haushofer, J., & Fehr, E. (2014). On the psychology of poverty. *Science, 344*(6186), 862–867.

Haushofer, J., & Shapiro, J. (2016). The short-term impact of unconditional cash transfers to the poor: Experimental evidence from Kenya. *Quarterly Journal of Economics, 131*(4), 1973–2042.

Heath, G., Roach, G. D., Dorrian, J., Ferguson, S. A., Darwent, D., & Sargent, C. (2012). The effect of sleep restriction on snacking behaviour during a week of simulated shiftwork. *Accident Analysis & Prevention, 45*, 62–67.

Heatherton, T. F., & Wagner, D. D. (2011). Cognitive neuroscience of self-regulation failure. *Trends in Cognitive Sciences, 15*(3), 132–139.

Heckman, J. J., Moon, S. H., Pinto, R., Savelyev, P. A., & Yavitz, A. (2010). The rate of return to the High/Scope Perry Preschool Program. *Journal of Public Economics, 94*(1–2), 114–128.

Heider, F., & Simmel, M. (1944). An experimental study of apparent behavior. *American Journal of Psychology, 57*(2), 243–259.

Hemerijck, A. (Ed.). (2017). *The uses of social investment.* Oxford University Press.

Henrich, J. (2020). *The weirdest people in the world: How the West became psychologically peculiar and particularly prosperous.* Farrar, Straus and Giroux.

Hershfield, H. E., Goldstein, D. G., Sharpe, W. F., Fox, J., Yeykelis, L., Carstensen, L. L., & Bailenson, J. N. (2011). Increasing saving behavior through age-progressed renderings of the future self. *Journal of Marketing Research, 48*(SPL), S23–S37.

Hertwig, R., & Grüne-Yanoff, T. (2017). Nudging and boosting: Steering or empowering good decisions. *Perspectives on Psychological Science*, 12(6), 973–986.

Hill, P. F., & Emery, L. J. (2013). Episodic future thought: Contributions from working memory. *Consciousness and Cognition, 22*(3), 677–683.

Hinson, J. M., Jameson, T. L., & Whitney, P. (2003). Impulsive decision making and working memory. *Journal of Experimental Psychology: Learning, Memory, and Cognition, 29*(2), 298–306.

Hirschman, A. O. (1982). Rival interpretations of market society: Civilizing, destructive, or feeble? *Journal of Economic Literature, 20*(4), 1463–1484.

Hisler, G. C., Krizan, Z., & DeHart, T. (2019). Does stress explain the effect of sleep on self-control difficulties? A month-long daily diary study. *Personality and Social Psychology Bulletin, 45*(6), 864–877.

Hockey, G. R. J. (1997). Compensatory control in the regulation of human performance under stress and high workload: A cognitive-energetical framework. *Biological Psychology, 45*(1–3), 73–93.

Hockey, R. (2013). *The psychology of fatigue: Work, effort and control.* Cambridge University Press.

Hofmann, W., Baumeister, R. F., Förster, G., & Vohs, K. D. (2012). Everyday temptations: An experience sampling study of desire, conflict, and self-control. *Journal of Personality and Social Psychology, 102*(6), 1318.

Hofmann, W., Deutsch, R., Lancaster, K., & Banaji, M. R. (2010). Cooling the heat of temptation: Mental self-control and the automatic evaluation of tempting stimuli. *European Journal of Social Psychology, 40*(1), 17–25.

Hofmann, W., Friese, M., Schmeichel, B. J., & Baddeley, A. D. (2011). Working memory and self-regulation. *Handbook of Self-Regulation: Research, Theory, and Applications, 2*, 204–225.

Hofmann, W., Luhmann, M., Fisher, R. R., Vohs, K. D., & Baumeister, R. F. (2014). Yes, but are they happy? Effects of trait self-control on affective well-being and life satisfaction. *Journal of Personality, 82*(4), 265–277.

Hofmann, W., Schmeichel, B. J., & Baddeley, A. D. (2012). Executive functions and self-regulation. *Trends in Cognitive Sciences, 16*(3), 174–180.

Hollander-Blumoff, R. (2012). Crime, punishment, and the psychology of self-control. *Emory Law Journal, 61*, 501–553.

Holroyd, J. (2018). Two ways of socializing responsibility: Circumstantialism versus scaffolded-responsiveness. In K. Hutchison, C. Mackenzie, & M. Oshana (Eds.), *Social dimensions of moral responsibility* (pp. 137–162). Oxford University Press.

Holton, R. (1999). Intention and weakness of will. *Journal of philosophy*, 96(5), 241–262.

Holton, R. (2009). *Willing, wanting, waiting*. Oxford University Press.

Hummel, D., & Maedche, A. (2019). How effective is nudging? A quantitative review on the effect sizes and limits of empirical nudging studies. *Journal of Behavioral and Experimental Economics*, 80, 47–58.

Ifcher, J., & Zarghamee, H. (2011). Happiness and time preference: The effect of positive affect in a random-assignment experiment. *American Economic Review*, 101(7), 3109–3129.

Ilkowska, M., & Engle, R. W. (2010). Working memory capacity and self-regulation. In R. H. Hoyle (Ed.), *Handbook of personality and self-regulation* (pp. 265–290). Wiley-Blackwell.

Inzlicht, M., & Berkman, E. (2015). Six questions for the resource model of control (and some answers). *Social and Personality Psychology Compass*, 9(10), 511–524.

Inzlicht, M., & Friese, M. (2019). The past, present, and future of ego depletion. *Social Psychology*, 50(5–6), 370–378.

Inzlicht, M., & Schmeichel, B. J. (2016). Beyond limited resources: Self-control failure as the product of shifting priorities. In K. D. Vohs, & R. F. Baumeister (Eds.), *Handbook of self-regulation: Research, theory, and applications* (pp. 165–181). Guilford Press.

Israel, A., Rosenboim, M., & Shavit, T. (2021). Time preference under cognitive load: An experimental study. *Journal of Behavioral and Experimental Economics*, 90, 101633.

Jackson, J. J., Beck, E. D., & Mike, A. (2021). Personality interventions. In O. P. John, & R. W. Robins (Eds.), *Handbook of personality theory and research* (4th ed., pp. 793–805). Guilford Press.

Jenson, J., & Saint-Martin, D. (2003). New routes to social cohesion? Citizenship and the social investment state. *Canadian Journal of Sociology*, 28(1), 77–99.

Job, V., Dweck, C. S., & Walton, G. M. (2010). Ego depletion—Is it all in your head? Implicit theories about willpower affect self-regulation. *Psychological Science*, 21(11), 1686–1693.

Job, V., Walton, G. M., Bernecker, K., & Dweck, C. S. (2015). Implicit theories about willpower predict self-regulation and grades in everyday life. *Journal of Personality and Social Psychology*, 108(4), 637–647.

Joireman, J., Balliet, D., Sprott, D., Spangenberg, E., & Schultz, J. (2008). Consideration of future consequences, ego-depletion, and self-control: Support for distinguishing between CFC-Immediate and CFC-Future sub-scales. *Personality and Individual Differences*, 45(1), 15–21.

Kahneman, D., & Deaton, A. (2010). High income improves evaluation of life but not emotional well-being. *Proceedings of the National Academy of Sciences*, *107*(38), 16489–16493.

Kalis, A. (2011). *Failures of agency: Irrational behavior and self-understanding*. Lexington Books.

Kane, M. J., & Engle, R. W. (2002). The role of prefrontal cortex in working-memory capacity, executive attention, and general fluid intelligence: An individual-differences perspective. *Psychonomic Bulletin & Review*, *9*(4), 637–671.

Kane, M. J., Hambrick, D. Z., & Conway, A. R. (2005). Working memory capacity and fluid intelligence are strongly related constructs: Comment on Ackerman, Beier, and Boyle. *Psychological Bulletin*, *131*(1), 66–71.

Katz, M. B. (2013). *The undeserving poor: America's enduring confrontation with poverty: Fully updated and revised*. Oxford University Press.

Kautz, T., Heckman, J. J., Diris, R., Ter Weel, B., & Borghans, L. (2014). *Fostering and measuring skills: Improving cognitive and non-cognitive skills to promote lifetime success*. OECD Education Working Paper, *110*.

Keidel, K., Rramani, Q., Weber, B., Murawski, C., & Ettinger, U. (2021). Individual differences in intertemporal choice. *Frontiers in Psychology*, *12*, 991.

Keinan, R., Idan, T., & Bereby-Meyer, Y. (2021). Compliance with COVID-19 prevention guidelines: Active vs. passive risk takers. *Judgment and Decision Making*, *16*(1), 20.

Khatib, H. K. Al., Harding, S. V., Darzi, J., & Pot, G. K. (2017). The effects of partial sleep deprivation on energy balance: A systematic review and meta-analysis. *European Journal of Clinical Nutrition*, *71*(5), 614–662.

Kidd, C., Palmeri, H., & Aslin, R. N. (2013). Rational snacking: Young children's decision-making on the marshmallow task is moderated by beliefs about environmental reliability. *Cognition*, *126*(1), 109–114.

Kim, J., Hong, H., Lee, J., & Hyun, M. H. (2017). Effects of time perspective and self-control on procrastination and Internet addiction. *Journal of Behavioral Addictions*, *6*(2), 229–236.

Kirby, K. N., Petry, N. M., & Bickel, W. K. (1999). Heroin addicts have higher discount rates for delayed rewards than non-drug-using controls. *Journal of Experimental Psychology General*, *128*(1), 78–87.

Klein, K., & Boals, A. (2001). The relationship of life event stress and working memory capacity. *Applied Cognitive Psychology: The Official Journal of the Society for Applied Research in Memory and Cognition*, *15*(5), 565–579.

Kluegel, J. R., & Mateju, P. (1995). Egalitarian vs. inegalitarian principles of distributive justice. In J. R. Kluegel, D. S. Mason, & B. Wegener

(Eds.), *Social justice and political change: Public opinion in capitalist and post-communist states* (pp. 209–238). Walter de Gruyter.

Knack, S., & Zak, P. J. (2003). Building trust: Public policy, interpersonal trust, and economic development. *Supreme Court Economic Review, 10,* 91–107.

Knopik, V. S., Neiderhiser, J. M., DeFries, J. C., & Plomin, R. (2017). *Behavioral genetics.* Worth Publishers, Macmillan Learning.

Knutson, K. L., Van Cauter, E., Rathouz, P. J., DeLeire, T., & Lauderdale, D. S. (2010). Trends in the prevalence of short sleepers in the USA: 1975–2006. *Sleep, 33*(1), 37–45.

Kokkoris, M. D., & Stavrova, O. (2021). Staying on track in turbulent times: Trait self-control and goal pursuit during self-quarantine. *Personality and Individual Differences, 170,* 110454.

Kool, W., McGuire, J. T., Rosen, Z. B., & Botvinick, M. M. (2010). Decision making and the avoidance of cognitive demand. *Journal of Experimental Psychology: General, 139*(4), 665–682.

Kotabe, H. P., & Hofmann, W. (2015). On integrating the components of self-control. *Perspectives on Psychological Science, 10*(5), 618–638.

Kotov, R., Gamez, W., Schmidt, F., & Watson, D. (2010). Linking "big" personality traits to anxiety, depressive, and substance use disorders: A meta-analysis. *Psychological Bulletin, 136*(5), 768–821.

Krause, A. J., Simon, E. B., Mander, B. A., Greer, S. M., Saletin, J. M., Goldstein-Piekarski, A. N., & Walker, M. P. (2017). The sleep-deprived human brain. *Nature Reviews Neuroscience, 18*(7), 404–418.

Krizan, Z., & Hisler, G. (2016). The essential role of sleep in self-regulation. In K. D. Vohs, & R. F. Baumeister (Eds.), *Handbook of self-regulation: Research, theory, and applications* (pp. 182–197). Guilford Press.

Kroese, F. M., Evers, C., Adriaanse, M. A., & de Ridder, D. T. (2016). Bedtime procrastination: A self-regulation perspective on sleep insufficiency in the general population. *Journal of Health Psychology, 21*(5), 853–862.

Krueger, R. F., Hoffman, M., Walter, H., & Grafman, J. (2013). An fMRI investigation of the effects of belief in free will on third-party punishment. *Social Cognitive and Affective Neuroscience, 9*(8), 1143–1149.

Kukowski, C., Bernecker, K., & Brandstätter, V. (2021). Self-control and beliefs surrounding others' cooperation predict own health-protective behaviors and support for COVID-19 government regulations: Evidence from two European countries. *Social Psychological Bulletin, 16*(1), 1–28.

Kunda, Z. (1990). The case for motivated reasoning. *Psychological Bulletin, 108*(3), 480–498.

Kurth-Nelson, Z., Bickel, W., & Redish, A. D. (2012). A theoretical account of cognitive effects in delay discounting. *European Journal of Neuroscience, 35*(7), 1052–1064.

Kurzban, R. (2016). The sense of effort. *Current Opinion in Psychology, 7*, 67–70.

Kurzban, R., Duckworth, A., Kable, J. W., & Myers, J. (2013). An opportunity cost model of subjective effort and task performance. *Behavioral and Brain Sciences, 36*(6), 661–679.

Kymlicka, W. (2002). *Contemporary political philosophy: An introduction.* Oxford University Press.

LaPorta, R., Lopez-Silanes, F., Schleifer, A., & Vishney, R. W. (1997). Trust in large organizations. *American Economic Review Papers and Proceedings, 87*, 333–338.

Lasswell, H. D. (2018). *Politics: Who gets what, when, how.* Pickle Partners.

Latour, B. (2004). *Politics of nature.* Harvard University Press.

Lemke, T. (2001). "The birth of bio-politics": Michel Foucault's lecture at the Collège de France on neo-liberal governmentality. *Economy and society, 30*(2), 190–207.

Lerner, J. S., Li, Y., & Weber, E. U. (2013). The financial costs of sadness. *Psychological Science, 24*(1), 72–79.

Lerner, M. J. (1980). *The belief in a just world: A fundamental delusion.* New York: Plenum Press.

Levitt, E., Sanchez-Roige, S., Palmer, A. A., & MacKillop, J. (2020). Steep discounting of future rewards as an impulsivity phenotype: A concise review. *Current Topics in Behavioral Neurosciences, 47*, 113–138.

Li, J. B., Willems, Y. E., Stok, F. M., Deković, M., Bartels, M., & Finkenauer, C. (2019). Parenting and self-control across early to late adolescence: A three-level meta-analysis. *Perspectives on Psychological Science, 14*(6), 967–1005.

Li, J. B., Yang, A., Dou, K., & Cheung, R. Y. (2020). Self-control moderates the association between perceived severity of coronavirus disease 2019 (COVID-19) and mental health problems among the Chinese public. *International Journal of Environmental Research and Public Health, 17*(13), 4820.

Lim, J., & Dinges, D. F. (2010). A meta-analysis of the impact of short-term sleep deprivation on cognitive variables. *Psychological Bulletin, 136*(3), 375–389.

Lin, H., & Epstein, L. H. (2014). Living in the moment: Effects of time perspective and emotional valence of episodic thinking on delay discounting. *Behavioral Neuroscience, 128*(1), 12–19.

Lipsky, M. (1980/2010). *Street-level bureaucracy: Dilemmas of the individual in public service.* Russell Sage Foundation.

Liu, L., Feng, T., Chen, J., & Li, H. (2013). The value of emotion: How does episodic prospection modulate delay discounting? *PLoS One*, *8*(11), e81717.

Lowe, C. J., Safati, A., & Hall, P. A. (2017). The neurocognitive consequences of sleep restriction: A meta-analytic review. *Neuroscience & Biobehavioral Reviews*, *80*, 586–604.

Lunn, P. D., Belton, C. A., Lavin, C., McGowan, F. P., Timmons, S., & Robertson, D. A. (2020). Using behavioral science to help fight the coronavirus. *Journal of Behavioral Public Administration*, *3*(1), 1–15.

Macaskill, A. C., Hunt, M. J., & Milfont, T. L. (2019). On the associations between delay discounting and temporal thinking. *Personality and Individual Differences*, *141*, 166–172.

Mackenbach, J. P., Stirbu, I., Roskam, A. J. R., Schaap, M. M., Menvielle, G., Leinsalu, M., & Kunst, A. E. (2008). Socioeconomic inequalities in health in 22 European countries. *New England Journal of Medicine*, *358*(23), 2468–2481.

Malle, B. F., Guglielmo, S., & Monroe, A. E. (2014). A theory of blame. *Psychological Inquiry*, *25*(2), 147–186.

Mani, A., Mullainathan, S., Shafir, E., & Zhao, J. (2013). Poverty impedes cognitive function. *Science*, *341*(6149), 976–980.

Mann, T., & Ward, A. (2007). Attention, self-control, and health behaviors. *Current Directions in Psychological Science*, *16*(5), 280–283.

Maranges, H. M., & Reynolds, T. A. (2020). Heritability. *The Wiley Encyclopedia of Personality and Individual Differences: Models and Theories*, 243–247.

Martarelli, C. S., Pacozzi, S. G., Bieleke, M., & Wolff, W. (2021). High trait self-control and low boredom proneness help COVID-19 homeschoolers. *Frontiers in Psychology*, *12*, 331.

Martin, N. D., Rigoni, D., & Vohs, K. D. (2017). Free will beliefs predict attitudes toward unethical behavior and criminal punishment. *Proceedings of the National Academy of Sciences*, *114*(28), 7325–7330.

May, J., & Holton, R. (2012). What in the world is weakness of will? *Philosophical Studies*, *157*(3), 341–360.

McCormick, K. A. (2013). Anchoring a revisionist account of moral responsibility. *Journal of Ethics and Social Philosophy*, *7*(3), 1–20.

McEwen, C. A., & McEwen, B. S. (2017). Social structure, adversity, toxic stress, and intergenerational poverty: An early childhood model. *Annual Review of Sociology*, *43*, 445–472.

McGeer, V. (2015). Building a better theory of responsibility. *Philosophical Studies*, *172*(10), 2635–2649.

McGeer, V. (2019). Scaffolding agency: A proleptic account of the reactive attitudes. *European Journal of Philosophy*, *27*(2), 301–323.

McGonigal, K. (2011). *The willpower instinct: How self-control works, why it matters, and what you can do to get more of it.* Penguin.

Mead, L. (1986). *Beyond entitlement: The limits of benevolence.* Free Press.

Meldrum, R. C., Campion Young, B., Soor, S., Hay, C., Copp, J. E., Trace, M., ... & Kernsmith, P. D. (2020). Are adverse childhood experiences associated with deficits in self-control? A test among two independent samples of youth. *Criminal Justice and Behavior, 47*(2), 166–186.

Mele, A. R. (2010). Weakness of will and akrasia. *Philosophical Studies, 150*(3), 391–404.

Mele, A. R. (1995). *Autonomous agents: From self-control to autonomy.* Oxford University Press.

Melley, T. (2000). *Empire of conspiracy: The culture of paranoia in post-war America.* Cornell University Press.

Mennell, S. (2007). *The American civilizing process.* Polity Books.

Merton, R. K. (1968). The Matthew effect in science: The reward and communication systems of science are considered. *Science, 159*(3810), 56–63.

Messner, S. F., Raffalovich, L. E., & Sutton, G. M. (2010). Poverty, infant mortality, and homicide rates in cross-national perspective: Assessments of criterion and construct validity. *Criminology, 48*(2), 509–537.

Metcalfe, J., & Mischel, W. (1999). A hot/cool-system analysis of delay of gratification: Dynamics of willpower. *Psychological Review, 106*(1), 3–19.

Miller, D. (1999). *Principles of social justice.* Harvard University Press.

Miller, G. A. (1994). The magical number seven, plus or minus two: Some limits on our capacity for processing information. *Psychological Review, 63*(2), 81–97.

Miller, G. E., Cohen, S., Janicki-Deverts, D., Brody, G. H., & Chen, E. (2016). Viral challenge reveals further evidence of skin-deep resilience in African Americans from disadvantaged backgrounds. *Health Psychology, 35*(11), 1225–1234.

Miller, G. E., Yu, T., Chen, E., & Brody, G. H. (2015). Self-control forecasts better psychosocial outcomes but faster epigenetic aging in low-SES youth. *Proceedings of the National Academy of Sciences, 112*(33), 10325–10330.

Miller, W. I. (1998). *The anatomy of disgust.* Harvard University Press.

Milyavskaya, M., Berkman, E. T., & De Ridder, D. T. (2019). The many faces of self-control: Tacit assumptions and recommendations to deal with them. *Motivation Science, 5*(1), 79–85.

Milyavskaya, M., & Inzlicht, M. (2017). Attentional and motivational mechanisms of self-control. In D. De Ridder, M. Adriaanse, & K. Fujita (Eds.), *Routledge international handbook of self-control in health and well-being* (pp. 11–23). Routledge.

Milyavskaya, M., Saunders, B., & Inzlicht, M. (2021). Self-control in daily life: Prevalence and effectiveness of diverse self-control strategies. *Journal of Personality, 89*(4),634–651.

Mischel, W., & Ebbesen, E. B. (1970). Attention in delay of gratification. *Journal of Personality and Social Psychology, 16*(2), 329–337.

Mischel, W., & Baker, N. (1975). Cognitive appraisals and transformations in delay behavior. *Journal of personality and social psychology, 31*(2), 254–261.

Mischel, W., Shoda, Y., & Peake, P. K. (1988). The nature of adolescent competencies predicted by preschool delay of gratification. *Journal of Personality and Social Psychology, 54*(4), 687–696.

Miyake, A., Friedman, N. P., Emerson, M. J., Witzki, A. H., Howerter, A., & Wager, T. D. (2000). The unity and diversity of executive functions and their contributions to complex "frontal lobe" tasks: A latent variable analysis. *Cognitive Psychology, 41*(1), 49–100.

Moffitt, R. A. (2020). *Reconciling trends in US male earnings volatility: Results from a four data set project* (no. w27664). National Bureau of Economic Research.

Moffitt, T. E., Arseneault, L., Belsky, D., Dickson, N., Hancox, R. J., Harrington, H., ... & Sears, M. R. (2011). A gradient of childhood self-control predicts health, wealth, and public safety. *Proceedings of the National Academy of Sciences, 108*(7), 2693–2698.

Molden, D. C., Hui, C. M., & Scholer, A. A. (2016). Understanding self-regulation failure: A motivated effort-allocation account. In E. R. Hirt, J. J. Clarkson, & L. Jia (Eds.), *Self-regulation and ego control* (pp. 425–459). Academic Press.

Monroe, A. E., Brady, G. L., & Malle, B. F. (2017). This isn't the free will worth looking for: General free will beliefs do not influence moral judgments, agent-specific choice ascriptions do. *Social Psychological and Personality Science, 8*(2), 191–199.

Morris, P. A., Hill, H. D., Gennetian, L. A., Rodrigues, C., & Wolf, S. (2015). Income volatility in US households with children: Another growing disparity between the rich and the poor? IRP Discussion Paper Series No. 1429-15. Institute for Research on Poverty, University of Wisconsin Institute for Research on Poverty.

Morse, S. J. (2011). Severe environmental deprivation (aka RSB): A tragedy, not a defense. *Alabama Civil Rights & Civil Liberties Law Review, 2*, 147–173.

Mounk, Y. (2017). *The age of responsibility*. Harvard University Press.

Mullainathan, S., & Shafir, E. (2013). *Scarcity: Why having too little means so much*. Times Books.

Mullen, F., & Nadler, J. (2008). Moral spillovers: The effect of moral violations on deviant behavior. *Journal of Experimental Social Psychology, 44*(5), 1239–1245.

Muraven, M. (2008). Prejudice as self-control failure. *Journal of Applied Social Psychology, 38*(2), 314–333.

Muraven, M. (2010). Building self-control strength: Practicing self-control leads to improved self-control performance. *Journal of Experimental Social Psychology, 46*(2), 465–468.

Muraven, M., Collins, R. L., Shiffman, S., & Paty, J. A. (2005). Daily fluctuations in self-control demands and alcohol intake. *Psychology of Addictive Behaviors, 19*(2), 140 147.

Muraven, M., Shmueli, D., & Burkley, E. (2006). Conserving self control strength. *Journal of personality and social psychology, 91*(3), 524.

Muraven, M., & Slessareva, E. (2003). Mechanisms of self-control failure: Motivation and limited resources. *Personality and Social Psychology Bulletin, 29*(7), 894–906.

Murray, C. (1984). *Losing ground*. Basic Books.

Murray, D. W., Rosanbalm, K., & Christopoulos, C. (2016). *Self-regulation and toxic stress report 3: A comprehensive review of self-regulation interventions from birth through young adulthood*. Administration for Children and Families, US Department of Health and Human Services.

Murray, D. W., Rosanbalm, K., Christopoulos, C., & Hamoudi, A. (2015). *Self-regulation and toxic stress: Foundations for understanding self-regulation from an applied developmental perspective* (OPRE report 2015-21). Administration for Children and Families, US Department of Health and Human Services.

Nadelhoffer, T. (2011). The threat of shrinking agency and free will disillusionism. In W. Sinnott-Armstrong & L. Nadel (Eds.), *Conscious will and responsibility: A tribute to Benjamin Libet* (pp. 173–188). Oxford University Press.

Nadelhoffer, T., Shepard, J., Crone, D. L., Everett, J. A., Earp, B. D., & Levy, N. (2020). Does encouraging a belief in determinism increase cheating? Reconsidering the value of believing in free will. *Cognition, 203*, 104342.

Nadler, J. (2005). Flouting the law. *Texas Law Review, 83*, 1399–1441.

Nichols, S. (2015). *Bound: Essays on free will and responsibility*. Oxford University Press.

Nichols, S., & Knobe, J. (2007). Moral responsibility and determinism: The cognitive science of folk intuitions. *Nous, 41*(4), 663–685.

Nivette, A., Ribeaud, D., Murray, A., Steinhoff, A., Bechtiger, L., Hepp, U., ... & Eisner, M. (2021). Non-compliance with COVID-19-related public health measures among young adults in Switzerland: Insights from a longitudinal cohort study. *Social Science & Medicine, 268,* 113370.

Nozick, R. (1974). *Anarchy, state, and utopia.* Basic Books.

Oaten, M., & Cheng, K. (2006a). Improved self-control: The benefits of a regular program of academic study. *Basic and Applied Social Psychology, 28*(1), 1–16.

Oaten, M., & Cheng, K. (2006b). Longitudinal gains in self-regulation from regular physical exercise. *British Journal of Health Psychology, 11*(4), 717–733.

Oaten, M., & Cheng, K. (2007). Improvements in self-control from financial monitoring. *Journal of Economic Psychology, 28*(4), 487–501.

O'Donnell, S., Daniel, T. O., & Epstein, L. H. (2017). Does goal relevant episodic future thinking amplify the effect on delay discounting? *Consciousness and Cognition, 51,* 10–16.

Odum, A. L. (2011). Delay discounting: Trait variable? *Behavioural Processes, 87*(1), 1–9.

Odum, A. L., & Baumann, A. A. (2010). Delay discounting: State and trait variable. In G. J. Madden & W. K. Bickel (Eds.), *Impulsivity: The behavioral and neurological science of discounting* (pp. 39–65). American Psychological Association.

Odum, A. L., Becker, R. J., Haynes, J. M., Galizio, A., Frye, C. C., Downey, H., ... & Perez, D. M. (2020). Delay discounting of different outcomes: Review and theory. *Journal of the Experimental Analysis of Behavior, 113*(3), 657–679.

OECD (Organisation for Economic Co-operation and Development) (2017). *Behavioural insights and public policy: Lessons from around the world.* OECD.

OECD (Organisation for Economic Co-operation and Development) (2020). *Regulatory policy and COVID-19: Behavioural insights for fast-paced decision making.* OECD.

Oettingen, G. (2000). Expectancy effects on behavior depend on self-regulatory thought. *Social Cognition, 18*(2), 101–129.

Oettingen, G., & Cachia, J. Y. (2016). The problems with positive thinking and how to regulate them. In K. D. Vohs & R. F. Baumeister (Eds.), *Handbook of self-regulation: Research, theory, and application* (pp. 547–570). Guilford Press.

Olsaretti, S. (2013). Rescuing justice and equality from libertarianism. *Economics & Philosophy, 29*(1), 43–63.

O'Neill, J., Daniel, T. O., & Epstein, L. H. (2016). Episodic future thinking reduces eating in a food court. *Eating Behaviors, 20,* 9–13.

Ong, Q., Theseira, W., & Ng, I. Y. (2019). Reducing debt improves psychological functioning and changes decision-making in the poor. *Proceedings of the National Academy of Sciences*, *116*(15), 7244–7249.

Oorschot, W. V. (2000). Who should get what, and why? On deservingness criteria and the conditionality of solidarity among the public. *Policy & Politics*, *28*(1), 33–48.

Osberg, L., & Bechert, I. (2016). Social values for equality and preferences for state in-*tervention: Is the USA Exceptional?*, Working Paper 2016-04, Department of Economics, Dalhouse University.

Ostry, J. D., Loungani, P., & Berg, A. (2019). *Confronting inequality*. Columbia University Press.

Pandey, A., Hale, D., Das, S., Goddings, Λ. L., Blakemore, S. J., & Viner, R. M. (2018). Effectiveness of universal self-regulation-based interventions in children and adolescents: A systematic review and meta-analysis. *JAMA Pediatrics*, *172*(6), 566–575.

Pare, P. P., & Felson, R. (2014). Income inequality, poverty and crime across nations. *British Journal of Sociology*, *65*(3), 434–458.

Park, C. L., Wright, B. R., Pais, J., & Ray, D. M. (2016). Daily stress and self-control. *Journal of Social and Clinical Psychology*, *35*(9), 738–753.

Payne, B. K. (2005). Conceptualizing control in social cognition: How executive functioning modulates the expression of automatic stereotyping. *Journal of Personality and Social Psychology*, *89*(4), 488–503.

Pearl, R. L., & Puhl, R. M. (2018). Weight bias internalization and health: A systematic review. *Obesity Reviews*, *19*(8), 1141–1163.

Pepper, G. V., & Nettle, D. (2017). The behavioural constellation of deprivation: Causes and consequences. *Behavioral & Brain Sciences*, *40*, e31.

Pereboom, D. (2014). *Free will, agency, and meaning in life*. Oxford University Press.

Peters, J., & Büchel, C. (2010). Episodic future thinking reduces reward delay discounting through an enhancement of prefrontal-mediotemporal interactions. *Neuron*, *66*(1), 138–148.

Pilcher, J. J., & Huffcutt, A. I. (1996). Effects of sleep deprivation on performance: A meta-analysis. *Sleep*, *19*(4), 318–326.

Pinker, S. (2011). *The better angels of our nature: The decline of violence in history and its causes*. Penguin UK.

Piquero, A. R., Jennings, W. G., Diamond, B., Farrington, D. P., Tremblay, R. E., Welsh, B. C., & Gonzalez, J. M. R. (2016). A meta-analysis update on the effects of early family/parent training programs on anti-social behavior and delinquency. *Journal of Experimental Criminology*, *12*(2), 229–248.

Piquero, A. R., Jennings, W. G., & Farrington, D. P. (2010). On the malleability of self-control: Theoretical and policy implications regarding a general theory of crime. *Justice Quarterly*, *27*(6), 803–834.

Pizarro, D. A., & Helzer, E. G. (2010). Stubborn moralism and freedom of the will. In R. F. Baumeister, A. R. Mele, & K. D. Vohs (Eds.), *Free will and consciousness: How might they work* (pp. 102–120). Oxford University Press.

Polanczyk, G. V., Willcutt, E. G., Salum, G. A., Kieling, C., & Rohde, L. A. (2014). ADHD prevalence estimates across three decades: An updated systematic review and meta-regression analysis. *International Journal of Epidemiology*, *43*(2), 434–442.

Polderman, T. J., Benyamin, B., De Leeuw, C. A., Sullivan, P. F., Van Bochoven, A., Visscher, P. M., & Posthuma, D. (2015). Meta-analysis of the heritability of human traits based on fifty years of twin studies. *Nature Genetics*, *47*(7), 702–709.

Poropat, A. E. (2009). A meta-analysis of the five-factor model of personality and academic performance. *Psychological Bulletin*, *135*(2), 322–338.

Pratt, J., Brown, D., Brown, M., Hallsworth, S., & Morrison, W. (Eds.). (2013). *The new punitiveness*. Routledge.

Pratt, T. C., & Cullen, F. T. (2000). The empirical status of Gottfredson and Hirschi's general theory of crime: A meta-analysis. *Criminology*, *38*(3), 931–964.

Pridemore, W. A. (2002). What we know about social structure and homicide: A review of the theoretical and empirical literature. *Violence and Victims*, *17*(2), 127–156.

Pridemore, W. A. (2008). A methodological addition to the cross-national empirical literature on social structure and homicide: A first test of the poverty-homicide thesis. *Criminology*, *46*(1), 133–154.

Pridemore, W. A. (2011). Poverty matters: A reassessment of the inequality–homicide relationship in cross-national studies. *British Journal of Criminology*, *51*(5), 739–772.

Protzko, J., Ouimette, B., & Schooler, J. (2016). Believing there is no free will corrupts intuitive cooperation. *Cognition*, *151*, 6–9.

Puhl, R. M., & Heuer, C. A. (2009). The stigma of obesity: A review and update. *Obesity*, *17*(5), 941–964.

Ranci, C., Parma, A., Bernard, & Beckfeild, J. (2017). *The rise of economic insecurity in the EU: Concepts and measures*. Lives Working Paper, *62*.

Rank, M. R. (2004). *One nation, underprivileged: Why American poverty affects us all*. Oxford University Press.

Rawls, J. (1999). *A theory of justice* (rev. ed.). Harvard University Press.

Reimers, S, Maylor, E. A., Stewart, N., & Chater, N. (2009). Associations between a one-shot delay discounting measure and age, income, education and real world impulsive behavior. *Personality and Individual Differences*, 47(8), 973–978.

Reynolds, B., & Schiffbauer, R. (2005). Delay of gratification and delay discounting: A unifying feedback model of delay-related impulsive behavior. *Psychological Record*, 55(3), 439–460.

Richmond-Rakerd, L. S., Caspi, A., Ambler, A., d'Arbeloff, T., de Bruine, M., Elliott, M., ... & Moffitt, T. E. (2021). Childhood self-control forecasts the pace of midlife aging and preparedness for old age. *Proceedings of the National Academy of Sciences*, 118(3).

Richter, M., & Stanek, J. (2015). The muscle metaphor in self-regulation in the light of current theorizing on muscle physiology. In G. H. E. Gendolla, M. Tops, & S. L. Koole (Eds.), *Handbook of biobehavioral approaches to self-regulation* (pp. 55–67). Springer.

Rimke, H. (2000). Governing citizens through self-help literature. *Cultural Studies*, 14(1), 61–78.

Rimke, H. (2017). Self-help ideology. In F. M. Moghaddam (Ed.), *SAGE encyclopedia of political behavior* (pp. 734–737). SAGE.

Roberts, B. W. (2009). Back to the future: Personality and assessment and personality development. *Journal of Research in Personality*, 43(2), 137–145.

Roberts, B. W., & DelVecchio, W. F. (2000). The rank-order consistency of personality traits from childhood to old age: A quantitative review of longitudinal studies. *Psychological Bulletin*, 126(1), 3–25.

Roberts, B. W., Kuncel, N. R., Shiner, R., Caspi, A., & Goldberg, L. R. (2007). The power of personality: The comparative validity of personality traits, socioeconomic status, and cognitive ability for predicting important life outcomes. *Perspectives on Psychological Science*, 2(4), 313–345.

Roberts, B. W., Walton, K. E., & Viechtbauer, W. (2006). Patterns of mean-level change in personality traits across the life course: A meta-analysis of longitudinal studies. *Psychological Bulletin*, 132(1), 1–25.

Robinson, P. H., Goodwin, G. P., & Reisig, M. D. (2010). The disutility of injustice. *NYU Law Review*, 85, 1940–2033.

Robinson, P. H., & Holcomb, L. (2021). *In defense of moral credibility*. University of Pennsylvania Law School, Public Law Research Paper 21-07.

Rogers, T., Milkman, K. L., & Volpp, K. G. (2014). Commitment devices: Using initiatives to change behavior. *JAMA*, 311(20), 2065–2066.

Ronson, J. (2015). *So you've been publicly shamed*. Riverhead Books.

Rose, N. (2000). Government and control. *British Journal of Criminology*, 40(2), 321–339.

Rose, N., & Miller, P. (2010). Political power beyond the state: Problematics of government. *British Journal of Sociology*, 61, 271–303.

Rothbart, M. K. (2011). *Becoming who we are: Temperament and personality in development.* Guilford Press.

Ruiter, M. E., DeCoster, J., Jacobs, L., & Lichstein, K. L. (2010). Sleep disorders in African Americans and Caucasian Americans: A meta-analysis. *Behavioral Sleep Medicine, 8*(4), 246–259.

Rung, J. M., & Madden, G. J. (2018). Experimental reductions of delay discounting and impulsive choice: A systematic review and meta-analysis. *Journal of Experimental Psychology: General, 147*(9), 1349–1381.

Rushton, J. P., Bons, T. A., & Hur, Y. M. (2008). The genetics and evolution of the general factor of personality. *Journal of Research in Personality, 42*(5), 1173–1185.

Ryan, R. M., & Deci, E. L. (2017). *Self-determination theory: Basic psychological needs in motivation, development, and wellness.* Guilford Press.

Sachweh, P. (2012). The moral economy of inequality: Popular views on income differentiation, poverty and wealth. *Socio-Economic Review, 10*(3), 419–445.

Sachweh, P. (2016). Social justice and the welfare state: Institutions, outcomes, and attitudes in comparative perspective. In C. Sabbagh & M. Schmitt (Eds.), *Handbook of social justice theory and research* (pp. 293–313). Springer.

Sampson, R. J., & Lauritsen, J. L. (1994). Violent victimization and offending: Individual-, situational-, and community-level risk factors. In A. J. Reiss, Jr., J. A. Roth, & National Research Council (Eds.), *Social influences. Vol. III of Understanding and preventing violence* (pp. 1–114). National Academy Press.

Saunders, B., Milyavskaya, M., Etz, A., Randles, D., Inzlicht, M., & Vazire, S. (2018). Reported self-control is not meaningfully associated with inhibition-related executive function: A Bayesian analysis. *Collabra: Psychology, 4*(1), 39.

Scheffler, S. (2003). What is egalitarianism? *Philosophy & Public Affairs, 31*(1), 5–39.

Scheffler, S. (2005). Choice, circumstance, and the value of equality. *Politics, Philosophy & Economics, 4*(1), 5–28.

Schlosser, M. (2015). Agency. In E. N. Zalta (Ed.), *Stanford encyclopedia of philosophy.* Stanford University Press.

Schmeichel, B. J. (2007). Attention control, memory updating, and emotion regulation temporarily reduce the capacity for executive control. *Journal of Experimental Psychology: General, 136*(2), 241–255.

Schmeichel, B. J., Harmon-Jones, C., & Harmon-Jones, E. (2010). Exercising self-control increases approach motivation. *Journal of Personality and Social Psychology, 99*(1), 162–173.

Schmeichel, B. J., Vohs, K. D., & Baumeister, R. F. (2003). Intellectual performance and ego depletion: Role of the self in logical reasoning and other information processing. *Journal of Personality and Social Psychology, 85,* 33–46.

Schmidt, A. T., & Engelen, B. (2020). The ethics of nudging: An overview. *Philosophy Compass, 15*(4), e12658.

Schnell, T., & Krampe, H. (2020). Meaning in life and self-control buffer stress in times of COVID-19: Moderating and mediating effects with regard to mental distress. *Frontiers in Psychiatry, 11,* 983.

Scholten, H., Scheres, A., De Water, E., Graf, U., Granic, I., & Luijten, M. (2019). Behavioral trainings and manipulations to reduce delay discounting: A systematic review. *Psychonomic Bulletin & Review, 26*(6), 1803–1849.

Schoofs, D., Wolf, O. T., & Smeets, T. (2009). Cold pressor stress impairs performance on working memory tasks requiring executive functions in healthy young men. *Behavioral Neuroscience, 123*(5), 1066–1075.

Schuman, H., & Presser, S. (1981). *Questions and answers: Experiments on question form, wording, and context in attitude surveys.* Academic Press.

Schwabe, L., & Wolf, O. T. (2009). Stress prompts habit behavior in humans. *Journal of Neuroscience, 29*(22), 7191–7198.

Schwabe, L., & Wolf, O. T. (2011). Stress-induced modulation of instrumental behavior: From goal-directed to habitual control of action. *Behavioural Brain Research, 219*(2), 321–328.

Segerstrom, S., Boggero, I. and Evans, D. (2016). Pause and plan. In K. Vohs, & R. Baumeister (Eds.), *Handbook of Self-Regulation: Research, Theory, and Applications* (pp. 131–145). Guilford Press.

Shah, A. K., Mullainathan, S., & Shafir, E. (2012). Some consequences of having too little. *Science, 338*(6107), 682–685.

Shamosh, N. A., & Gray, J. R. (2008). Delay discounting and intelligence: A meta-analysis. *Intelligence, 36*(4), 289–305.

Shariff, A. F., Greene, J. D., Karremans, J. C., Luguri, J. B., Clark, C. J., Schooler, J. W., ... & Vohs, K. D. (2014). Free will and punishment: A mechanistic view of human nature reduces retribution. *Psychological Science, 25*(8), 1563–1570.

Sheehy-Skeffington, J., & Haushofer, J. (2014). The behavioural economics of poverty. In D. P. Bhawuk, S. C. Carr, A. E. Gloss, & L. F. Thompson (Eds.), *Barriers to and opportunities for poverty reduction, poverty reduction* (pp. 96–112). United Nations Development Programme.

Sheeran, P., & Webb, T. L. (2016). The intention–behavior gap. *Social and Personality Psychology Compass, 10*(9), 503–518.

Shenhav, A., Musslick, S., Lieder, F., Kool, W., Griffiths, T. L., Cohen, J. D., & Botvinick, M. M. (2017). Toward a rational and mechanistic account of mental effort. *Annual Review of Neuroscience, 40,* 99–124.

Shiv, B., & Fedorikhin, A. (1999). Heart and mind in conflict: The interplay of affect and cognition in consumer decision making. *Journal of Consumer Research, 26*(3), 278–292.

Shoda, Y., Mischel, W., & Peake, P. K. (1990). Predicting adolescent cognitive and self-regulatory competencies from preschool delay of gratification: Identifying diagnostic conditions. *Developmental Psychology, 26*(6), 978–986.

Shonkoff, J. P., Garner, A. S., Siegel, B. S., Dobbins, M. I., Earls, M. F., McGuinn, L., ... & Committee on Early Childhood, Adoption, and Dependent Care. (2012). The lifelong effects of early childhood adversity and toxic stress. *Pediatrics, 129*(1), e232–e246.

Sie, M. (2018). Sharing responsibility: The importance of tokens of appraisals to our moral practices. In K. Hutchison, C. Mackenzie, & M. Oshana (Eds.), *Social dimensions of moral responsibility* (pp. 300–323). Oxford University Press.

Sjåstad, H., & Baumeister, R. F. (2018). The future and the will: Planning requires self-control, and ego depletion leads to planning aversion. *Journal of Experimental Social Psychology, 76,* 127–141.

Slater, T. (2012). The myth of "Broken Britain": Welfare reform and the production of ignorance. *Antipode, 45*(4), 1–22.

Slopen, N., & Williams, D. R. (2014). Discrimination, other psychosocial stressors, and self-reported sleep duration and difficulties. *Sleep, 37*(1), 147–156.

Smart, J. J. C. (1961/1973). An outline of a system of utilitarian ethics. In J. J. C. Smart & B. Williams (Eds.), *Utilitarianism: For and against.* Cambridge University Press.

Smith, I., Saed, K., & St-Onge, M. P. (2019). Sleep and food intake. In M. A. Grandner (Ed.), *Sleep and health* (pp. 243–255). Academic Press.

Snider, S. E., LaConte, S. M., & Bickel, W. K. (2016). Episodic future thinking: Expansion of the temporal window in individuals with alcohol dependence. *Alcoholism: Clinical and Experimental Research, 40*(7), 1558–1566.

Somerville, L. H., Jones, R. M., & Casey, B. J. (2010). A time of change: Behavioral and neural correlates of adolescent sensitivity to appetitive and aversive environmental cues. *Brain and Cognition, 72*(1), 124–133.

Sonnentag, S., & Jelden, S. (2009). Job stressors and the pursuit of sport activities: A day level perspective. *Journal of Occupational Health Psychology, 14*(2), 165–181.

Soto, C. J., John, O. P., Gosling, S. D., & Potter, J. (2011). Age differences in personality traits from 10 to 65: Big Five domains and facets in a large cross-sectional sample. *Journal of Personality and Social Psychology, 100*(2), 330–348.

Spears, D. (2011). Economic decision-making in poverty depletes behavioral control. *The BE Journal of Economic Analysis & Policy, 11*(1), 1–44.

Spierenburg, P. (2006). Democracy came too early: A tentative explanation for the problem of American homicide. *American Historical Review, 111*(1), 104–114.

Sripada, C. (2014). How is willpower possible? The puzzle of synchronic self-control and the divided mind. *Noûs, 48*(1), 41–74.

Sripada, C. (2018). Addiction and fallibility. *Journal of Philosophy, 115*(11), 569–587.

Stamatakis, K. A., Kaplan, G. A., & Roberts, R. E. (2007). Short sleep duration across income, education, and race/ethnic groups: Population prevalence and growing disparities during 34 years of follow-up. *Annals of Epidemiology, 17*(12), 948–955.

Standing, G. (2011). *The precariat: The new dangerous class.* Bloomsbury Academic.

Starcke, K., & Brand, M. (2012). Decision making under stress: A selective review. *Neuroscience & Biobehavioral Reviews, 36*(4), 1228–1248.

Stein, J. S., Wilson, A. G., Koffarnus, M. N., Daniel, T. O., Epstein, L. H., & Bickel, W. K. (2016). Unstuck in time: Episodic future thinking reduces delay discounting and cigarette smoking. *Psychopharmacology, 233*(21–22), 3771–3778.

Steinberg, L., Graham, S., O'Brien, L., Woolard, J., Cauffman, E., & Banich, M. (2009). Age differences in future orientation and delay discounting. *Child Development, 80*(1), 28–44.

Strathman, A., Gleicher, F., Boninger, D. S., & Edwards, S. (1994). The consideration of future consequences: Weighing immediate and distant outcomes of behavior. *Journal of Personality and Social Psychology, 66*(4), 742–752.

Strawson, G. (1994). The impossibility of moral responsibility. *Philosophical Studies: An International Journal for Philosophy in the Analytic Tradition, 75*(1–2), 5–24.

Strawson, G. (1986). *Freedom and Belief.* Clarendon Press.

Strawson, G. (2004). Free agents. *Philosophical Topics, 32*(1/2), 371–402.

Strawson, G., & Watson, G. (1998). Free will. In E. Craig (Ed.), *Routledge encyclopedia of philosophy.* Routledge.

Strawson, P. F. (2008). *Freedom and resentment and other essays.* Routledge.

Stringhini, S., Carmeli, C., Jokela, M., Avendaño, M., Muennig, P., Guida, F., … & Chadeau-Hyam, M. (2017). Socioeconomic status and the

25×25 risk factors as determinants of premature mortality: A multi-cohort study and meta-analysis of 1.7 million men and women. *The Lancet, 389*(10075), 1229–1237.

Stroud, S. (2008). Weakness of will. In E. N. Zalta (Ed.), *The Stanford encyclopedia of philosophy*. Stanford University Press.

Suddendorf, T., & Corballis, M. C. (2007). The evolution of foresight: What is mental time travel, and is it unique to humans? *Behavioral and Brain Sciences, 30*(3), 299–313.

Sunstein, C. R. (2014). *Why nudge? The politics of libertarian paternalism.* Yale University Press.

Tangney, J. P., Baumeister, R. F., & Boone, A. L. (2004). High self-control predicts good adjustment, less pathology, better grades, and interpersonal success. *Journal of Personality, 72*(2), 271–324.

Thaler, R. H., & Benartzi, S. (2004). Save More Tomorrow™: Using behavioral economics to increase employee saving. *Journal of Political Economy, 112*(S1), S164–S187.

Thaler, R. J., & Sunstein, C. R. (2008). *Nudge: Improving decisions about health, wealth, and happiness.* Yale University Press.

Thiele, L. P. (2006). *The heart of judgment: Practical wisdom, neuroscience, and narrative.* Cambridge University Press.

Thompson, S. C. (2009). The role of personal control in adaptive functioning. In C. R. Snyder, & S. J. Lopez (Eds.), *Handbook of positive psychology* (pp. 202–213). Oxford University Press.

Tice, D. M., Bratslavsky, E., & Baumeister, R. F. (2001). Emotional distress regulation takes precedence over impulse control: If you feel bad, do it! *Journal of Personality and Social Psychology, 80*(1), 53–67.

Tiemeijer, W. L. (2016). *Eigen schuld? Een gedragswetenschappelijk perspectief op problematische schulden.* Amsterdam University Press.

Tonry, M. (2014). Why crime rates are falling throughout the Western world. *Crime and Justice, 43*(1), 1–63.

Tu, K. C., Chen, S. S., & Mesler, R. M. (2021). Trait self-construal, inclusion of others in the self and self-control predict stay-at-home adherence during COVID-19. *Personality and Individual Differences, 175*, 110687.

Turkheimer, E., & Gottesman, I. I. (1991). Is H2 = 0 a null hypothesis anymore? *Behavioral and Brain Sciences, 14*(3), 410–411.

Urminsky, O., & Zauberman, G. (2015). The psychology of intertemporal preferences. In G. Keren, & G. W. (Eds.), *Wiley-Blackwell handbook of judgment and decision making* (Vol. 2, pp. 141–181). Wiley-Blackwell.

Uslaner, E. M. (2002). *The moral foundations of trust.* Cambridge University Press.

Vaihinger, H. (1925/2015). *The philosophy of "as-if": A system of the theoretical, practical, and religious fictions of mankind.* CreateSpace Independent Publishing Platform.

Van Bavel, J. J., Baicker, K., Boggio, P. S., Capraro, V., Cichocka, A., Cikara, M., ... & Willer, R. (2020). Using social and behavioural science to support COVID-19 pandemic response. *Nature Human Behaviour*, 4(5), 460–471.

Van der Linden, D., & Eling, P. (2006). Mental fatigue disturbs local processing more than global processing. *Psychological research*, 70(5), 395–402.

Van der Linden, D., Frese, M., & Meijman, T. F. (2003). Mental fatigue and the control of cognitive processes: Effects on perseveration and planning. *Acta psychologica*, 113(1), 45–65.

Van der Steeg, M., & Waterreus, I. (2015). Gedragsinzichten benutten voor beter onderwijsbeleid. *Economisch Statistische Berichten*, 100(4707), 219–221.

Van der Weiden, A., Benjamins, J., Gillebaart, M., Ybema, J. F., & de Ridder, D. (2020). How to form good habits? A longitudinal field study on the role of self-control in habit formation. *Frontiers in Psychology*, 11, 560.

Van Dillen, L. F., Papies, E. K., & Hofmann, W. (2013). Turning a blind eye to temptation: How cognitive load can facilitate self-regulation. *Journal of Personality and Social Psychology*, 104(3), 427–443.

Van Gelder, J. L., Hershfield, H. E., & Nordgren, L. F. (2013). Vividness of the future self predicts delinquency. *Psychological Science*, 24(6), 974–980.

Van Gelder, J. L., Luciano, E. C., Weulen Kranenbarg, M., & Hershfield, H. E. (2015). Friends with my future self: Longitudinal vividness intervention reduces delinquency. *Criminology*, 53(2), 158–179.

Van Krieken, R. (1989). Violence, self-discipline and modernity: Beyond the "civilizing process." *The Sociological Review*, 37(2), 193–218.

Van Krieken, R. (1990). The organization of the soul: Elias and Foucault on discipline and the self. *European Journal of Sociology*, 31(2), 353–371.

Van Oorschot, W. (2006). Making the difference in social Europe: Deservingness perceptions among citizens of European welfare states. *Journal of European Social Policy*, 16(1), 23–42.

Vargas, M. (2013). *Building better beings: A theory of moral responsibility*. Oxford University Press.

Vargas, M. (2022). Instrumentalist theories of moral responsibility. In D. Nelkin and D. Pereboom (Eds.), *The Oxford handbook of moral responsibility* (pp. 3–26). Oxford University Press.

Vazsonyi, A. T., Mikuška, J., & Kelley, E. L. (2017). It's time: A meta-analysis on the self-control-deviance link. *Journal of Criminal Justice*, 48, 48–63.

Vazsonyi, A. T., Pickering, L. E., Junger, M., & Hessing, D. (2001). An empirical test of a general theory of crime: A four-nation comparative study of self-control and the prediction of deviance. *Journal of Research in Crime and Delinquency, 38*(2), 91–131.

Vecchio, R., & Cavallo, C. (2019). Increasing healthy food choices through nudges: A systematic review. *Food Quality and Preference, 78*, 103714.

Vohs, K. D., Baumeister, R. F., Schmeichel, B. J., Twenge, J. M., Nelson, N. M., & Tice, D. M. (2008). Making choices impairs subsequent self-control: A limited-resource account of decision making, selfregulation, and active initiative. *Journal of Personality and Social Psychology, 94*, 883–898.

Vohs, K. D., & Heatherton, T. F. (2000). Self-regulatory failure: A resource-depletion approach. *Psychological science, 11*(3), 249–254.

Vohs, K. D., Schmeichel, B. J., Lohmann, S., Gronau, Q. F., Finley, A. J., Ainsworth, S. E., ... & Albarracín, D. (2021). A multisite preregistered paradigmatic test of the ego-depletion effect. Psychological Science, 32(10), 1566–1581.

Vohs, K. D., & Schooler, J. W. (2008). The value of believing in free will: Encouraging a belief in determinism increases cheating. *Psychological Science, 19*(1), 49–54.

Volz, S., Ward, A., & Mann, T. (2021). Eating up cognitive resources: Does attentional consumption lead to food consumption? *Appetite, 162*, 105165.

Vukasović, T., & Bratko, D. (2015). Heritability of personality: A meta-analysis of behavior genetic studies. *Psychological Bulletin, 141*(4), 769–785.

Wagner, D. D., & Heatherton, T. F. (2014). Emotion and self-regulation failure. In J. J. Gross (Ed.), *Handbook of emotion regulation* (pp. 613–628). Guilford Press.

Wagner, D. D., & Heatherton, T. F. (2015). Self-regulation and its failure: The seven deadly threats to self-regulation. In M. E. Mikulincer, P. R. Shaver, E. E. Borgida, & J. A. Bargh (Eds.), *APA handbook of personality and social psychology* (Vol. 1, pp. 805–842). American Psychological Association.

Wallace, R. J. (1994). *Responsibility and the moral sentiments*. Harvard University Press.

Wang, Y. J., Dou, K., & Tang, Z. W. (2017). The relationship between trait self-control, consideration for future consequence and organizational citizenship behavior among Chinese employees. *Work, 58*(3), 341–347.

Ward, A., & Mann, T. (2000). Don't mind if I do: Disinhibited eating under cognitive load. *Journal of personality and social psychology, 78*(4), 753.

Watson, L., Levit, T., & Lavack, A. (2018). Obesity and stigmatization at work. In S. B. Thomson, & G. Grandy (Eds.), *Stigmas, work and organizations* (pp. 11–34). Palgrave Macmillan.

Watts, B., & Fitzpatrick, S. (2018). *Welfare conditionality*. Routledge.

Watts, B., Fitzpatrick, S., Bramley, G., & Watkins, D. (2014) *Welfare sanctions and conditionality in the UK*. Joseph Rowntree Foundation.

Watts, T. W., Duncan, G. J., & Quan, H. (2018). Revisiting the marshmallow test: A conceptual replication investigating links between early delay of gratification and later outcomes. *Psychological Science*, 29(7), 1159–1177.

Weber, M. (2001). *The Protestant and the spirit of capitalism*. Routledge.

Weiner, B. (1995). *Judgments of responsibility: A foundation for a theory of social conduct*. Guilford Press.

Weiner, B. (2006). *Social motivation, justice, and the moral emotions: An attributional approach*. Psychology Press.

Wenzel, M., & Okimoto, T. G. (2016). Retributive justice. In C. Sabbagh, & M. Schmitt (Eds.), *Handbook of social justice theory and research* (pp. 237–256). Springer.

Wesley, M. J., & Bickel, W. K. (2014). Remember the future II: Meta-analyses and functional overlap of working memory and delay discounting. *Biological Psychiatry*, 75(6), 435–448.

West, R., Michie, S., Rubin, G. J., & Amlôt, R. (2020). Applying principles of behaviour change to reduce SARS-CoV-2 transmission. *Nature Human Behaviour*, 4(5), 451–459.

Western, B., Bloome, D., Sosnaud, B., & Tach, L. (2012). Economic insecurity and social stratification. *Annual Review of Sociology*, 38, 341–359.

Western, B., Bloome, D., Sosnaud, B., & Tach, L. M. (2016). Trends in income insecurity among US children, 1984–2010. *Demography*, 53(2), 419–447.

Whinnery, J., Jackson, N., Rattanaumpawan, P., & Grandner, M. A. (2014). Short and long sleep duration associated with race/ethnicity, sociodemographics, and socioeconomic position. *Sleep*, 37(3), 601–611.

White, M. (2013). *The manipulation of choice: Ethics and libertarian paternalism*. Springer.

White, R. W. (1959). Motivation reconsidered: The concept of competence. *Psychological Review*, 66(5), 297–333.

Whitehead, M., Jones, R., Lilley, R., Pykett, J., & Howell, R. (2017). *Neuroliberalism: Behavioural government in the twenty-first century*. Routledge.

Wiese, C. W., Tay, L., Duckworth, A. L., D'Mello, S., Kuykendall, L., Hofmann, W., ... & Vohs, K. D. (2018). Too much of a good thing? Exploring the inverted-U relationship between self-control and happiness. *Journal of Personality*, 86(3), 380–396.

Wilkinson, R., & Pickett, K. (2009). *The spirit level: Why more equal societies almost always do better*. Penguin.

Willems, Y. E., Boesen, N., Li, J., Finkenauer, C., & Bartels, M. (2019). The heritability of self-control: A meta-analysis. *Neuroscience & Biobehavioral Reviews*, *100*, 324–334.

Willems, Y. E., Li, J. B., Hendriks, A. M., Bartels, M., & Finkenauer, C. (2018). The relationship between family violence and self-control in adolescence: A multi-level meta-analysis. *International Journal of Environmental Research and Public Health*, *15*(11), 2468.

Willems, Y. E., de Zeeuw, E. L., van Beijsterveldt, C. E., Boomsma, D. I., Bartels, M., & Finkenauer, C. (2020). Out of control: Examining the association between family conflict and self-control in adolescence in a genetically sensitive design. *Journal of the American Academy of Child & Adolescent Psychiatry*, *59*(2), 254–262.

Wilson, D. (2002). *Darwin's cathedral: Evolution, religion, and the nature of society*. University of Chicago Press.

Wolff, W., Martarelli, C. S., Schüler, J., & Bieleke, M. (2020). High boredom proneness and low trait self-control impair adherence to social distancing guidelines during the COVID-19 pandemic. *International Journal of Environmental Research and Public Health*, *17*(15), 5420.

Wood, W. (2016). The role of habits in self-control. In K. D. Vohs & R. F. Baumeister (Eds.), *Handbook of self-regulation: Research, theory, and applications* (pp. 95–108). The Guilford Press.

Wouters, C. (2007). *Informalization: Manners and emotions since 1890*. SAGE.

Wouters, C. (2011a). How civilizing processes continued: Towards an informalization of manners and a third nature personality. *Sociological Review*, *59*, 140–159.

Wouters, C. (2011b). Informalization. In D. Southerton (Ed.), *Encyclopedia of consumer culture* (Vol. 1, pp. 780–782). SAGE.

Wouters, E. B. C., & Dunning, M. (2019). *Civilisation and informalisation*. Springer.

Wright, B. R. E., Caspi, A., Moffitt, T. E., & Silva, P. A. (1999). Low self-control, social bonds, and crime: Social causation, social selection, or both? *Criminology*, *37*(3), 479–514.

Wu, J., Guo, Z., Gao, X., & Kou, Y. (2020). The relations between early-life stress and risk, time, and prosocial preferences in adulthood: A meta-analytic review. *Evolution and Human Behavior*, *41*(6), 557–572.

Xu, P., & Cheng, J. (2021). Individual differences in social distancing and mask-wearing in the pandemic of COVID-19: The role of need for cognition, self-control and risk attitude. *Personality and Individual Differences*, *175*, 110706.

Yerkes, R. M., & Dodson, J. D. (1908). The relation of strength of stimulus to rapidity of habit-formation. *Journal of Comparative Neurology and Psychology, 18*(5), 459–482.

Yoo, S. S., Gujar, N., Hu, P., Jolesz, F. A., & Walker, M. P. (2007). The human emotional brain without sleep: A prefrontal amygdala disconnect. *Current Biology, 17*(20), R877–R878.

Zajonc, R. B. (1980). Feeling and thinking: Preferences need no inferences. *American Psychologist, 35*(2), 151–175.

Zaller, J. R. (1992). *The nature and origins of mass opinion.* Cambridge University Press.

Zimbardo, P. G., & Boyd, J. N. (1999). Putting time in perspective: A valid, reliable individual difference metric. *Journal of Personality and Social Psychology, 77*, 1271–1288.

Zuboff, S. (2019). *The age of surveillance capitalism: The fight for a human future at the new frontier of power.* Profile Books.

# Index